Toward a Theory of Spacepower: Selected Essays

For sale by the Superintendent of Documents, U.S. Government Printing Office
Internet: bookstore.gpo.gov   Phone: toll free (866) 512-1800;   DC area (202) 512-1800
Fax: (202) 512-2104 Mail: Stop IDCC, Washington, DC 20402-0001

ISBN   978-1-78039-385-8

Toward a Theory of Spacepower

Selected Essays

Edited by Charles D. Lutes
and Peter L. Hays with
Vincent A. Manzo, Lisa M. Yambrick,
and M. Elaine Bunn

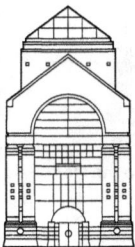

National Defense University Press
Washington, D.C.
2011

First Printing, February 2011

NDU Press publications are sold by the U.S. Government Printing Office. For ordering information, call (202) 512-1800 or write to the Superintendent of Documents, U.S. Government Printing Office, Washington, DC 20402.

For the U.S. Government On-Line Bookstore, go to: http://bookstore.gpo.gov

For current publications of the Institute for National Strategic Studies, please go to the National Defense University Web site at: http://www.ndu.edu/inss

Contents

List of Illustrations. ix

Acknowledgments xi

Introduction xiii

Part I: The Building Blocks of Spacepower Theory

Chapter 1
Theory Ascendant? Spacepower and the Challenge of
Strategic Theory
John B. Sheldon and Colin S. Gray 1

Chapter 2
On the Nature of Military Theory
Harold R. Winton 19

Chapter 3
International Relations Theory and Spacepower
Robert L. Pfaltzgraff, Jr. 37

Chapter 4
Real Constraints on Spacepower
Martin E.B. France and Jerry Jon Sellers. 57

Part II: Space and National Security

Chapter 5

Increasing the Military Uses of Space
Everett C. Dolman and Henry F. Cooper, Jr. 97

Chapter 6

Preserving Freedom of Action in Space: Realizing the
Potential and Limits of U.S. Spacepower
Michael Krepon, Theresa Hitchens, and
Michael Katz-Hyman 119

Chapter 7

Balancing U.S. Security Interests in Space
Michael E. O'Hanlon 137

Chapter 8

Airpower, Spacepower, and Cyberpower
Benjamin S. Lambeth 155

Part III: Civil, Commercial, and Economic Space Perspectives

Chapter 9

History of Civil Space Activity and Spacepower
Roger D. Launius. 179

Chapter 10

Commercial Space and Spacepower
Henry R. Hertzfeld 215

Chapter 11

Merchant and Guardian Challenges in the
Exercise of Spacepower
Scott Pace 241

Part IV: The Future of Spacepower

Chapter 12

Emerging Domestic Structures: Organizing the Presidency for
Spacepower
John M. Logsdon 277

Chapter 13

Space Law and the Advancement of Spacepower
Peter L. Hays 299

Chapter 14

Future Strategy and Professional Development: A Roadmap
Simon P. Worden 319

About the Contributors. 341

Illustrations

Figures

Figure 4–1. Mission Architecture. 60
Figure 4–2. Elliptical Orbit Parameters. 63
Figure 4–3. Classical Orbital Elements for Earth Orbits. 64
Figure 4–4. Satellite Field of View 65
Figure 4–5. Types of Orbits and their Inclinations 66
Figure 4–6. Satellite Ground Tracks 67
Figure 4–7. Orbital Ground Tracks with Different Periods 68
Figure 4–8. Orbital Ground Tracks with Different Inclinations. . 68
Figure 4–9. Orbital Ground Tracks with Different
    Perigee Locations 69
Figure 4–10. Hohmann Transfer 70
Figure 4–11. Coplanar Rendezvous. 71
Figure 4–12. Co-orbital Rendezvous. 72
Figure 4–13. Simple Inclination Plane Change 73
Figure 4–14. Simple Ω Plane Change 73
Figure 4–15. Effects of Drag on Eccentric Low Earth Orbit. 74
Figure 4–16. Perigee Rotation Rate 75
Figure 4–17. Nodal Regression Rate 76
Figure 4–18. Launch Windows. 77
Figure 4–19. Phases of Launch Vehicle Ascent. 78
Figure 4–20. Interaction between Solar Wind and Earth's
    Magnetic Field 85
Figure 4–21. Electromagnetic Spectrum. 88
Figure 4–22. Atmospheric Windows 88
Figure 4–23. Satellite Coverage Strategies. 91

Figure 5–1. Triangulating the Space Exploitation Debate...... 100
Figure 5–2. Gravitational Terrain of Earth-Moon Space....... 105
Figure 9–1. NASA Budget as a Percentage of Federal Budget... 187
Figure 9–2. Public Attitudes about Government Funding for
     Space Trips.. 188
Figure 9–3. Launch Vehicles, 1953–2000................... 190
Figure 9–4. Is the Soviet Union Ahead of the
     United States in Space?................................ 197
Figure 10–1. Degrees of Globalization 218
Figure 10–2. Commercial Space in
     Presidential Space Policy 224
Figure 14–1. Timetable: High Resolution and
     Synthetic Aperture Radar Satellites..................... 324

Tables

Table 4–1. Space Mission and Constraints 61
Table 4–2. Satellite Missions and Orbits 66
Table 4–3. Rocket Propulsion Types and
     Performance Comparison 79
Table 11–1. Viability of Space Settlement................... 264

Acknowledgments

The editors thank all of the authors who contributed their time, insights, and energy to completing the papers that form this volume.

The editors also express their deep appreciation to their fellow members of the Spacepower Theory Project—Colonel Michael S. Bell, USA; Colonel M.V. Smith, USAF; Lieutenant Colonel Robert Klingseisen, USA; and Mr. Will Lahneman, formerly of the Institute for National Strategic Studies (INSS) at the National Defense University (NDU)—for their dedicated work in conducting this multifaceted effort. The spacepower team did an exceptionally fine job in reaching out to diverse communities of experts in all aspects of space activity.

The editors also thank key offices in the Department of Defense for their steadfast support and insights. We are particularly grateful to Mr. Thomas G. Behling, former Deputy Undersecretary of Defense for Intelligence (Preparation and Warning); Mr. Ryan Henry, former Principal Deputy Undersecretary of Defense for Policy; Major General James B. Armor, USAF (Ret.), former Director of the National Security Space Office; Mr. Joseph Rouge, current Director of the National Security Space Office; and all their staffs. We benefited greatly from our close collaboration with the Eisenhower Center for Space and Defense Studies at the U.S. Air Force Academy and its director, Ambassador Roger Harrison. Indeed, a multitude of individuals, too numerous to mention here, contributed essays, presentations, dialogue, and intellectual insights in support of this effort, and we are most grateful for their assistance.

At NDU, special thanks are due to former NDU President, Lieutenant General Frances C. Wilson, USMC (Ret.), and current President, Vice Admiral Ann E. Rondeau, USN, for their unstinting support. We thank current and former INSS colleagues Dr. Phillip C. Saunders, Colonel Michael P. Hughes, USAF, Mr. Joseph McMillan, Dr. Eugene B. Rumer, Captain Mark E. Redden, USN, and Dr. James A. Schear. We also thank former INSS directors Dr. Stephen J. Flanagan and Dr. Patrick M. Cronin, former interim director Dr. Christopher J. Lamb, and current director Dr. Hans Binnendijk. We are indebted to the INSS

Center for Strategic Conferencing, specifically Mr. Gerald Faber and Mr. Edwin Roman, for hosting a number of workshops and conferences. NDU Press has provided invaluable support in editing and publishing our products. We specifically thank its former director, Colonel David H. Gurney, USMC (Ret.), and its current acting director, Dr. Thomas F. Lynch III, and his staff, including Mr. George Maerz. Finally, our work was ably assisted by a number of interns, especially Bradley Miller, Jennifer Roark, and Melissa Latham.

Introduction

The concept and rationale for a study of spacepower theory originated in conversations among Department of Defense (DOD) officials during the latter phases of the George W. Bush administration's final Quadrennial Defense Review.[1] After several discussions with researchers in the Institute for National Strategic Studies (INSS) at National Defense University (NDU), the Deputy Undersecretary of Defense for Intelligence (Preparation and Warning) requested that NDU "craft a spacepower theory similar to that of other domains, for example, sea power."[2] The terms of reference for this project specifically asked INSS to:

> develop a theoretical framework for examining the fundamental aspects of spacepower and its relation to the pursuit of national security, economic, informational, and scientific objectives. The theory should document the views and perspectives of the principal users of space and should focus on the underlying assumptions regarding why and how we as a society, nation, or military might use space—either alone or, more likely, in tandem with other means—to accomplish specific ends.[3]

The task for the INSS Spacepower Theory Project team has been to consider the space domain in a broad and holistic way, incorporating a wide range of perspectives from U.S. and international space actors engaged in scientific, commercial, intelligence, and military enterprises. Through a series of 20 seminars, 2 workshops, and 2 major conferences, experts in the global space community provided and exchanged a rich set of viewpoints, ideas, and theories in an ongoing dialogue. Additionally, members of the Spacepower Theory Project team traveled to Japan, China, India, and Europe to capture viewpoints in regions witnessing increasingly diverse and burgeoning space activity.

Defining Spacepower

What exactly is spacepower? The concept of power in the social and physical sciences invariably triggers a wide range of perspectives. The starting point for this study was Joseph Nye's simple definition of *power* as "the ability to achieve one's purposes or goals."[4] It is therefore a natural, although perhaps simplistic, extrapolation to define *spacepower* as "the ability to use space to achieve one's purposes or goals." In a further expansion of the definition of power, Nye suggests that it is the ability to influence others that creates power. While that is true for spacepower, space capabilities may also be able to influence natural events as well as human behavior. An expanded definition of spacepower could then be "the ability to use space to influence others, events, or the environment to achieve one's purposes or goals."

The INSS Spacepower Theory Project developed a holistic view of power as it is applied to space over the course of this study. Space is relevant to all forms of power (including both "hard" and "soft" power), and spacepower manifests itself in various ways as sociocultural, economic, information, and security power.

About this Volume

Although examples of spacepower abound, the body of evidence from which aspiring spacepower theorists can draw is small. This proved to be one of the principal challenges that the Spacepower Theory Project team encountered. As John Sheldon and Colin Gray argue, compared to land, sea, and even airpower, spacepower is a new phenomenon; aspiring spacepower theorists have little empirical evidence to examine.[5] For example, Alfred Thayer Mahan's theory of spacepower was rooted in a long history of naval practice, which provided empirical evidence for the concepts that Mahan articulated.

Despite a dedicated and disciplined effort by the INSS Spacepower Theory team, it ultimately proved impossible to find a "Mahan on demand" who could develop a fully formed theory of spacepower. The team produced a series of drafts that contained some useful insights but that did not add up to a coherent theoretical framework that could fulfill all the project's objectives. The Spacepower Theory Project team ultimately concluded that it could not develop a spacepower theory worthy of the name within the specified timeframe.

Nevertheless, our efforts generated a rich dialogue about the issues and challenges surrounding human activity in space. The papers commissioned by the project, as well as discussions at the series of seminars, workshops, and conferences that comprised the spacepower project, go a long way toward meeting the charge to "document the views and perspectives of the principal users of space" and to highlight assumptions and perspectives about how the United States and other actors might use space for a range of civil, social, economic, and military ends.

This volume of commissioned papers serves as a starting point for continued discourse on ways to extend, modify, refine, and integrate a broad range of viewpoints about human-initiated space activity, its relationship to our globalized society, and its economic, political, and security interactions. Even though this volume does not provide the foundational precepts of a theory of spacepower, it will equip practitioners, scholars, students, and citizens with the historical background and conceptual framework to navigate through and assess the challenges and opportunities of an increasingly complex space environment. We hope that it will serve as a foundation for future work in developing a comprehensive theory of spacepower.

Part I: The Building Blocks of Spacepower Theory

The first section establishes the building blocks for a theoretical study of spacepower, defining theory, explaining the possible goals of a theory and its role in the formulation of strategy and policy, examining the relationship between international relations theory and social interactions in outer space, and identifying the physical constraints and technological obstacles facing spacefaring actors.

John Sheldon and Colin Gray argue that creating a theory of spacepower is exceedingly difficult. Compared to land, sea, and even airpower, spacepower is a new phenomenon; aspiring spacepower theorists have little empirical evidence to examine. And the nations that exercise spacepower prefer to keep many of their activities cloaked in secrecy, shrinking the already small body of material from which theorists can draw. They argue that James Oberg, Everett Dolman, and John Klein's efforts at theory building are valuable and laudable but ultimately fall short of a comprehensive theory of spacepower. Sheldon and Gray conclude with their own thoughts on what a theory of spacepower should and should not do, reminding that a successful theory will "provide a common framework from which all can refer and a conceptual means by which spacepower is exploited to its full potential to attain policy objectives."

Harold Winton posits that the function of a theory is fivefold: it defines its field of study, divides it into subcategories, explains the phenomenon, connects the field of study to other fields, and anticipates what comes next. Winton explains why the military profession is difficult to theorize about, briefly summarizes the theories of Clausewitz and Jomini to demonstrate the difference between descriptive and prescriptive military theories, and argues that the connection between military theory and practice lies in the development of doctrine. Winton concludes that a theory of spacepower should assist the self-education of space force commanders and policymakers by explaining the interrelationships between subcategories of the space domain and the relationship between spacepower and other dimensions of the military-political universe.

Robert Pfaltzgraff's essay discusses spacepower from the perspective of international relations (IR) theory. Pfaltzgraff demonstrates that there is a symbiotic relationship between the two through his analysis of the interplay between spacepower and geopolitical theory, realist theory, liberal theory, and constructivism; these theories must grapple with the impact of spacepower on international relations if they are to remain relevant, while they also form the prism through which we will theorize and speculate about sociopolitical interactions in space.

Martin E.B. France and Jerry Jon Sellers explain the physical characteristics and constraints of space, the technological challenges of overcoming these constraints, and the components and operations of common space systems. France and Sellers distill these complicated issues into a text that the layman can understand even as they demonstrate how difficult it is to design, develop, and operate space systems. France and Sellers argue that making strategic decisions about spacepower without a basic understanding of space technology is "akin to formulating a maritime strategy using a team of 'experts' who had never seen the ocean or experienced the tides, had no concept of buoyancy, or seen sail or shore."

Part II: Space and National Security

The second section highlights the connection between space and national security with a focus on the unique contribution of space capabilities to U.S. national security. It provides three perspectives on the difficult issues of space weapons, arms control, and U.S. national security strategy, and examines the relationship between spacepower, airpower, and cyberpower.

Everett Dolman and Henry Cooper argue that the United States can and should deploy weapons in space to seize control of low Earth orbit. U.S. military predominance in space would ensure that all peaceful nations can utilize space for economic and scientific development, while also enabling the United States to further exploit space assets for strategic purposes, such as the ability to employ space-based missile defense against enemy missile launches anywhere in the world. If the United States does not use its military, economic, and diplomatic influence to create a global space regime, they argue, other nations will. Dolman and Cooper's assessment and policy prescriptions stem from their application of geopolitical and realist theories to space politics.

Michael Krepon, Theresa Hitchens, and Michael Katz-Hyman observe that orbiting satellites are involved with a wide range of major power military and economic activities yet are inherently vulnerable. Whereas Dolman and Cooper argue that this vulnerability and the strategic value of space assets make the weaponization of space inescapable, these authors see the indiscriminate and unpredictable consequences of a military conflict in space as creating strong incentives for states to avoid testing and deploying antisatellite and space-to-Earth weapons. The final section of the chapter articulates the key elements of a multilateral code of conduct to guide the behavior of responsible space actors and preserve the U.S. ability to exercise all elements of spacepower.

Michael O'Hanlon argues that the U.S. national security strategy in space is a balance between competing trends and interests. On the one hand, the United States might face contingencies and threats where antisatellite weapons and space-based missile defense systems would prove useful; other countries are researching and developing capabilities that could threaten U.S. space assets. On the other hand, the United States currently enjoys nearly unfettered access to space, and multilateral confidence-building measures and unilateral U.S. restraint in space may preserve this status quo, or at least prolong it. O'Hanlon concludes that the United States should hedge by developing better situational awareness in space, hardening its satellites, and preserving its ability to deploy military space capabilities while stopping short of actually testing and deploying them. At the same time, the United States should pursue multilateral agreements that codify acceptable behavior in space.

Benjamin Lambeth discusses airpower, spacepower, and cyberpower. Lambeth surveys U.S. capabilities in each domain, highlights the parallels and overlaps between space and cyberspace, and suggests that a unified theory of air, space, and cyberpower in joint operations is preferable to standalone theories for each.

Part III: Civil, Commercial, and Economic Space Perspectives

The third section discusses the economic, civil, and commercial dimensions of spacepower, examining the relationship between U.S. civil and national security space programs, commercial space, technological innovation, and globalization from both a historical and a contemporary perspective.

Roger Launius provides a comprehensive history of U.S. civil space efforts. He argues that the prestige and soft power that the U.S. civil space program generated were important elements of national power during the Cold War. Looking to the future, Launius concludes that decisions about spaceflight must take into account the potential effects on soft power and that policymakers should maintain as much distance as possible between civil and military spaceflight programs, even though the technology that drives both will inevitably overlap.

Henry Hertzfeld offers an overview of commercial space issues. He details the relationship between commercial space and globalization: the global connectivity that satellite communications provide has contributed to globalization, while globalization has created a larger market for the commercial space sector. Hertzfeld also highlights key U.S. policies for regulating commercial space, arguing that attempts to cement U.S. dominance of the commercial sector "encouraged other nations to invest in competitive systems so as to develop and maintain their own independent capabilities in space." Isolating U.S. companies from the international commercial space market will not prevent foreign companies from providing space services, Hertzfeld concludes, so the United States should instead find ways to help U.S. providers become more competitive.

Scott Pace further explores the relationship between the public and private sector in U.S. space activities. The public sector (the Guardians) enforces the law and protects against foreign and domestic threats to maintain a stable environment in which the private sector (the Merchants) can provide goods and services for profit. The contrasting roles of the Merchants and the Guardians breed different worldviews and professional cultures. Pace explains that the ubiquity of space services and the overlap between military, civil, and commercial space systems create difficult questions about how much Merchants and Guardians should rely on each other: "To what extent should the government rely on commercial space services, such as communications satellites or expendable launch vehicles? To what extent should the government provide space-based navigation and environmental monitoring services, which have commercial applications?" The challenge, Pace concludes, is for the U.S. Government to partner with the private sector to advance U.S. interests in space and shape the global space industry.

Part IV: The Future of Spacepower

The final section contemplates the future of spacepower, examining how the President has and should organize the U.S. Government to exercise spacepower, offering suggestions for refining the international space law regime to facilitate sustainable security and economic opportunities in space, and exploring potential visions for U.S. space strategy.

John Logsdon explores what organizational structure will best enable the President to marshal civil, military, intelligence, and commercial space programs to advance U.S. national interests. Logsdon reviews the approaches that previous administrations adopted to unify U.S. space strategy, from the Eisenhower White House to the second Bush administration, and concludes that "only the National Security Council within the White House structure brings to bear the requisite perspectives and institutional position to have a reasonable chance to be effective in advancing U.S. spacepower and linking it to U.S. scientific, economic, and national security interests." But Logsdon cautions that this is not a panacea. For the National Security Council to effectively formulate and coordinate U.S. space strategy, it must also draw from an interagency body and have a staff with expertise in all sectors of U.S. space activity.

Peter Hays argues that space law can facilitate a stable, predictable space environment in which state and nonstate actors responsibly harvest wealth from space. He explains that the existing body of space law, the Outer Space Treaty (OST), provides a useful legal foundation, but it must evolve as human activity in space evolves. The OST could facilitate international and public-private sector cooperation on issues ranging from sharing space situational awareness, clarifying the different standards of conduct by which to judge military, civil, and commercial space activities, and spurring economic development by adopting laws governing liability and wealth creation in space. Hays concludes with a discussion of the challenges of protecting civilization from environmental degradation and dangerous near Earth objects, suggesting that the evolution of space law will help the international community utilize space to combat these hazards.

Simon Worden's chapter concludes the volume with a discussion of the future of U.S. space strategy. Worden argues that the United States should capitalize on the spread of information technology to enhance collective security. Space-enabled capabilities would contribute to this goal. According to Worden, the United States should join with other nations to produce global utilities similar to the U.S. Global Positioning System. As an example, a "responsive space surveillance system might be launched by the

United States or another nation to guarantee an agreement between two potentially hostile neighbors." To fulfill this vision, the United States needs to embrace the development of small, less costly space systems, such as microsatellites, to achieve a more agile and responsive presence in space. It also needs to replenish its aging space workforce and reinvigorate the public's opinions of space by emphasizing the value of space assets for crisis management and war prevention.

Notes

[1] *Quadrennial Defense Review Report* (Washington, DC: Department of Defense, February 6, 2006). Although little was written in the 2006 report about space or spacepower theory, these conversations took place among the members of the Strategic Enablers Integrated Product Team (IPT).

[2] Thomas G. Behling, Deputy Under Secretary of Defense (Preparation and Warning), Memorandum to the President, National Defense University, Subject: Space Power Theory, February 16, 2006.

[3] Ibid.

[4] Joseph S. Nye, Jr., *Understanding International Conflicts: An Introduction to Theory and History* (New York: Pearson-Longman, 2005), 59.

[5] John Sheldon and Colin Gray, "Theory Ascendant? Spacepower and the Challenge of Strategic Theory," in *Toward a Theory of Spacepower: Selected Essays,* ed. Charles D. Lutes and Peter L. Hays (Washington, DC: National Defense University Press, 2011, 1–17).

Part I: The Building Blocks of Spacepower Theory

Theory Ascendant? Spacepower and the Challenge of Strategic Theory

John B. Sheldon and Colin S. Gray

Some time ago, one of us asked, "Where is the theory of spacepower? Where is the Mahan for the final frontier?"[1] Over 10 years later, such an exhortation still has resonance as the realm of spacepower still lacks a "space focused strategic theory" and a "binding concept" that can "aid understanding of what it is all about."[2] This chapter seeks to provide an explanation, or at least plausible reasons, as to why such a theory of spacepower has yet to transpire. First, we shall discuss the difficulties involved in creating a theory of spacepower that is able to endure the test of time and that has universal applicability. The chapter then examines recent attempts at theorizing on spacepower by James Oberg, Everett Dolman, and John Klein. Lastly, the chapter outlines what a theory of spacepower should look like, and just as importantly, what it should not look like, as a guide for future theorists.

It should be noted that an exhortation of an "Alfred Thayer Mahan for the final frontier" is not to be confused with an endorsement of a Mahanian style of theory. Such a style of strategic theory may yet suffice (for the present, at least) for the purposes of guidance for spacepower, but we do encourage all plausible methods of elucidating a theory of spacepower, be it directly influenced by the thought and style of either Mahan or of any other strategic theorist. Instead, the call for a Mahan for spacepower is in fact a call for a theory that can match the *stature* of Mahan's collected thoughts on seapower.

This chapter uses the word *strategy* in an unashamedly Clausewitzian sense, and for clarity of meaning we offer up a definition of strategy as well as spacepower. *Strategy* is defined here as the use that is made of force and

1

the threat of force for the ends of policy.[3] This definition is preferred because it takes into account the instrumental character of strategy that uses a variety of means as well as its ubiquitous applicability in both peace and war. This definition is distinctly military in scope, but we do not dismiss the notion of spacepower serving diplomatic, economic, and cultural aspects of a state's wider grand strategy. B.H. Liddell Hart defined *grand strategy* as the process and ability "to co-ordinate and direct all the resources of a nation, or band of nations, towards the attainment of the political object of the war."[4] Most satellite systems are dual-use; military systems such as the U.S. global positioning system (GPS) navigation satellites have myriad civil and commercial applications, and commercial systems, such as high-resolution imaging satellites, have myriad military applications. *Spacepower* is defined here as "the ability in peace, crisis, and war to exert prompt and sustained influence in or from space."[5] This influence can be exerted by commercial, civil, or military satellites as appropriate, though it should be noted that a theory of spacepower should have little to say about the purely commercial and civil exploitation of space, just as air- and seapower theories have little to say about the purely commercial and civil exploitation of the sea and air. A theory of spacepower should not try to overreach its mandate and be all things to all agendas. Instead, a theory of spacepower is about the ability to exert prompt and sustained influence in or from space for the purposes and furtherance of *policy* in peace and war.

Impediments to a Theory of Spacepower

Why spacepower theory has yet to produce a notable theorist is the subject of speculation on numerous plausible and seemingly implausible factors. There is much to impede the creation and development of a sound theory for spacepower. Some of these impediments are unintentional and random incidents, phenomena and events that are the stuff of everyday defense planning and strategic decisionmaking. Other impediments are more insidious, the product of institutional prejudices and failings, or flaws in military and strategic culture. Spacepower theorists must try to remove themselves from these day-to-day impediments and institutional and cultural prejudices and failings in order to produce theory that is enduring and universally applicable.

Among the many impediments to the creation and development of spacepower theory, the following seem most pertinent for the purposes of our discussion.

Limited Spacepower History

At present, spacepower cannot draw upon any informative historical experience that can provide valuable lessons, as compared to the experience of land, air-, or seapower. Even the nuclear realm can draw upon historical experience, albeit a mercifully brief and limited one. Some might plausibly argue that spacepower has plenty of historical experience to draw upon from the Cold War and from military operations since Operation *Desert Storm* in 1991. The problem with the Cold War is that it was a unique moment in the history of international politics. Spacepower is a child of the Cold War but has also survived its erstwhile parent, which imposed a unique political context that dictated how spacepower was used. As the international system shifts from a unipolar to an eventual multipolar complexion, the political context in which spacepower operates shall also change and will likely resemble, in broad terms, previous multipolar experiences. This is not to say that the Cold War holds no lessons whatsoever for spacepower, but it does mean that it cannot be our sole data point.

Similarly, the exploitation of spacepower in the several wars of choice since the end of the Cold War from *Desert Storm* through to the present war on terror can be illustrative only to the extent that the largely unchallenged use of spacepower ever can be. In its numerous wars of choice since the early 1990s, the United States and its allies have become increasingly reliant upon spacepower for the threat and application of military force, yet real and potential adversaries have been relatively slow to counteract the strategic leverage derived from U.S. spacepower. This initially tardy response from those who have the most to fear from overwhelming U.S. military dominance, derived in large part from spacepower, is beginning to take greater urgency as more polities exploit space for their own security objectives as well as develop and obtain their own counterspace capabilities.[6]

Of course, it might be argued that adversaries of the United States and its allies have countered the overwhelming advantages that are derived from spacepower by fighting in a manner that renders space-derived combat power irrelevant, such as terrorism and other asymmetric tactics. This argument is plausible to a point but is rendered moot when one discovers that even these adversaries are the beneficiaries of spacepower in their own unique ways. For example, al Qaeda is known to have used satellite telephones for tactical command and control, and Hizballah uses its own satellite television station, Al-Manar TV, to disseminate its virulent propaganda. These examples aside, as the offense-defense competition of fielded space capability versus counterspace capability is liable to continue, so the theorist is likely to glean meaningful lessons as the U.S. and allied reliance upon spacepower is increasingly challenged.

Among the calls for a theory of spacepower, it is often forgotten that the use and practice of spacepower is quite young in comparison to land, air-, and seapower. Land power has been in existence for thousands of years and yet it was not until the 16ᵗʰ century that a concerted effort at theorymaking truly began,[7] and it was not until the 19ᵗʰ century that we saw the greatest exponents of land power, and strategic theory in general, in Jomini and Clausewitz.[8] The naval and maritime theories of Mahan, Julian Corbett, Raoul Castex, and Charles Edward Callwell only appeared after sea and maritime power had been practiced for several thousand years.[9] It is only with the arrival of airpower in the early 20ᵗʰ century that we have seen attempts to theorize about its exploitation in parallel with its continuing evolution. It cannot be denied, however, that airpower theory is the subject of considerable debate and even controversy. For some, the body of work created by the likes of Giulio Douhet, William Mitchell, J.C. Slessor, and John Warden[10] is far from conclusive, and in many cases should perhaps be regarded more as vision than as theory. As David MacIsaac points out, "Air power . . . has nonetheless yet to find a clearly defined or unchallenged place in the history of military or strategic theory. There has been no lack of theorists, but they have had only limited influence in a field where the effects of technology and the deeds of practitioners have from the beginning played greater roles than have ideas."[11] Harold R. Winton is even more explicit on this point when he writes that "there simply does not exist any body of codified, systematic thought that can purport to be called a comprehensive theory of air power."[12] Winton goes on to assert that one of the reasons why this is so is because airpower has a very thin historical base upon which to draw for the purposes of creating a comprehensive and universal theory.[13]

Attempts to craft a plausible theory of spacepower at this early juncture in spacepower history are indeed unique in the history of military thought, especially if the aim is (as it indeed should be) to develop a theory that avoids the worst excesses of airpower theory. We are far from convinced that it is too early in the history of spacepower to begin crafting a theory that can guide its action and relate it to all other forms of military and national power, but such a possibility cannot be entirely discounted.

Confusion over Definitions

This chapter is emphatic in what it means by *spacepower*, *strategy*, and a *theory of spacepower*. Unfortunately, many misunderstand, misconstrue, or are ignorant of such terms. Much of this confusion is innocent enough in intent but has and continues to cause much damage to the quest for a theory of spacepower. For example, at a symposium associated with the project resulting in this book, several delegates seemed to think that a theory of spacepower was essentially a theory for the unilateral domination of space by the United States. Such an interpretation is mistaken, though it should be noted that a plausible theory of spacepower should be able to lend itself to imperialist space ambitions *as well as* efforts to create a multilateral regime in space. For what purposes spacepower is used is entirely up to the policymakers of the day. All that a theory of spacepower should do is assist the policymaker in achieving those purposes, regardless of what they are. Nor is spacepower alone in this matter. Airpower too has had problems in pinning down a consensus on key and fundamental definitions.[14]

The exploitation and capabilities of spacepower in the United States and other states are, and have been, highly classified, thus preventing many would-be theorists from accessing any lessons learned from previous applications of spacepower and publicly promulgating any theory based on such access. There are many good reasons to keep certain aspects of spacepower classified, especially as it relates to intelligence gathering and the technical details of satellite capabilities, yet there is also a culture of secrecy that has evolved over the decades that has kept not only adversaries, but for a long while much of the U.S. military and government, in the dark about U.S. space capability. The classification of spacepower is not a uniquely American phenomenon, as the space powers of Russia, China, Israel, and several European countries attest, but the dissemination of space capabilities to developing countries may see, from a theorist's perspective, greater transparency in how spacepower is used as space increasingly becomes an arena for greater and more intense competition.

Tales of Derring-do

Over the decades, civil space programs, such as the first Soviet and U.S. manned space missions, the Apollo moon landings, and the International Space Station, have helped divert public and media attention away from military and intelligence space programs. In the United States, a high-profile civil space program, in the form of the National Aeronautics and Space Administration (NASA), was set up deliberately to distract attention from the overhead reconnaissance satellite capability as well as other military space programs in order to lend credence to the principle of peaceful uses of outer space in the longstanding U.S. national space policy. This is not to argue that the U.S. civil space program does not have any intrinsic value beyond that of providing useful political cover for more sensitive programs, but rather to point out that the focus on the scientific and civil aspects of spacepower has done little to encourage the development of a theory of spacepower.

Portrayal of Space in Popular Culture

The influence of popular science fiction programs and films, such as *Star Trek* and *Star Wars*, has helped generate a public perception and expectation of space that are far removed from reality. Among the media, science fiction has had a deleterious effect, creating a view of it as a place of grandiose yet broken dreams, little green men, and alien abductions. As a result, space, and therefore spacepower, is not taken as seriously as it should be.

Complexity

A theory of spacepower has to explain and translate action in space into strategic effect on Earth, and *vice versa*. It must take into account not only spacepower itself, but also the effect and influence of land, air-, and seapower, nuclear and information operations, as well as special operations upon each other and upon spacepower. A theory of spacepower also has to consider the roles and influence of science, technology, politics, law, diplomacy, society, and economics, among others. It is a daunting subject.[15]

Policy Distractions

Debates on nuclear deterrence and stability theory, ballistic missile defense, revolutions in military affairs, and, more recently, global insurgencies have all impeded the quest for a theory of spacepower. Elements of information-enabled warfare, such as precision strike and persistent battlespace surveillance, are all, to varying degrees, enabled by space systems. At present, spacepower is often thought about in these terms, yet there is a danger that a theory for spacepower is conflated with information-led warfare when, in fact, spacepower has the potential to be much more than an enabler. Space systems play a vital role in maintaining nuclear postures, any proposed missile defense system, and information-enabled operations. More recently, spacepower has been playing a critical but quiet role in the war on terror. Yet spacepower is not just the maintenance of nuclear postures, missile defense, precision strike, or supporting counterinsurgencies; it is all of these things and more.[16]

Perils of Linear Thinking

To say that spacepower is dependent on science, engineering, and technology risks insulting even the most theoretically challenged person. However, such a dependency may encourage spacepower practitioners and commanders to think of spacepower in a mechanistic and linear fashion. A theory of spacepower, or at least one worthy of the name, should respect the nonlinear, interactive, and paradoxical nature of strategy and its dimensions, which defy mechanistic analysis or mathematical equation.[17]

Technological Determinism

Similarly, because spacepower is so obviously dependent upon technology for strategic performance, there is a danger that theory is either blinded or sidelined by a culture that is technocentric. A theory of spacepower simply cannot afford to ignore the role of technology, but it would not be a theory at all if this were the sole focus at the expense of the other dimensions of strategy.[18]

Understanding Orbitology

On a related issue, perhaps because spacepower *is* so dependent on science, engineering, and technology, strategic theorists (who normally have an educational background in the social sciences or history) have tended to avoid it. Any individual attempting to contribute to a theory of spacepower must have, at the very least, a working knowledge of orbitology and other principles of spaceflight.

Out of Sight, Out of Mind

Lastly, in many ways spacepower is discrete (even allowing for classification issues) and does not attract much attention in the way that armies, navies, and air forces do. Apart from the awesome sights and sounds of a space launch, one does not *see* spacepower. One does, however, *feel* spacepower, as its presence in the battlespace is ubiquitous. Indeed, spacepower can be likened to intelligence operations: one only hears of it when something goes wrong.

Small Steps: Building on Previous Spacepower Theory

Despite the importance the Department of Defense attaches to a theory of spacepower, there have been surprisingly few works on the subject within the body of spacepower literature that exists. The reasons for this may be ascribed to some of the impediments listed above, but perhaps the biggest reason is that developing and creating strategic theory, much like its practice, are very difficult to do. As Clausewitz pointed out, "Everything in war is very simple, but the simplest thing is difficult."[19] David Lonsdale is even more blunt: "Strategy is difficult; very difficult."[20] Discerning enduring and universal theory from scant (and often contradictory where it exists) evidence is "very difficult," despite the fact that many will not argue with the relatively simple proposition that a theory of spacepower is needed. Yet a number of thinkers have risen to the challenge in recent years and have attempted to fill the theoretical void. Among these are James Oberg (*Space Power Theory*), Everett Dolman (*Astropolitik*), and John Klein (*Space Warfare*).[21] Each deserves credit for placing himself above the parapet, and each in his own way has made unique contributions to the nascent body of theory. Can any of these authors lay claim to the mantle of being the Mahan of the space age? Alas, the answer must be a reluctant "no." Each has furthered our understanding of spacepower considerably, but none has offered a comprehensive theory of spacepower.

James Oberg

Oberg provides us with a comprehensive account of spacepower's role in everyday activities on Earth[22] but falls short in his effort to outline its nature, though his distillation of spacepower into Mahanian elements is a useful starting point for any analysis.[23] Oberg's writing is excellent for a description, in laymen's terms, of the physical workings and constraints of spacepower.[24] Oberg is also to be thanked for many of his axioms—or "Truths and Beliefs"[25]—that attempt to distill something enduring about spacepower. These axioms include the following:

- "The primary attribute of current space systems lies in their extensive view of the Earth."[26] Spacepower is able to provide global coverage with relatively few assets.

- "A corollary to this attribute is that a space vehicle is in sight of vast areas of Earth's surface."[27] Spacepower can be vulnerable due to a lack of natural cover in space, though sheer distance can afford some protection.

- "Space exists as a distinct medium."[28] At the tactical and operational levels of war, space is most certainly a distinct medium, though it should be noted that there is nothing about space that places it beyond strategy. The nature of spacepower is the use, or threatened use, of space systems for political purposes.

- "Space power, alone, is insufficient to control the outcome of terrestrial conflict or ensure the attainment of terrestrial political objectives."[29] The same is true of air- and seapower. The seat of political power for all polities resides on the land, where people live. Control of such power can only be ultimately won or lost by controlling land. Spacepower, along with air- and seapower, can help leverage—even critically—land power to achieve victory on land, but can never do so by itself. An exception to this may come about should human beings colonize other celestial bodies, such as the Moon or Mars. In that event, one might see spacepower take the lead role in delivering sovereign effects, with other forms of military power (especially land and airpower delivered by a preponderant spacepower) providing support.

- "Space power has developed, for the most part, without human presence in space, making it unique among other forms of national power."[30] Spacepower is unique in that, for the time being at least, it is the only form of military power that generates strategic effect through robotic proxies. Whether this situation will change in the future with manned platforms performing the spacepower mission remains to be seen, and will be subject to myriad factors. However, the trend in the air and sea environments among the assorted militaries of the industrialized world is toward unmanned platforms.

- "Technological competence is required to become a space power, and conversely, technological benefits are derived from being a space power."[31] As space technologies disseminate throughout the world at a rapid pace, Oberg reminds us that true spacepower is that which can be organically sustained rather than purchased on the open market. It may prove critical to be able to develop, manufacture, launch, and operate one's own spacepower without having to rely upon a third party for technological expertise. Technological competence in this area undoubtedly will have strategic benefits as well as economic ones.

- "As with the earth-bound media [land, sea, and air], the weaponization of space is inevitable, though the manner and timing are not at all predictable."[32] Because spacepower is not beyond strategy, so it is not beyond the fate that has befallen every other environment that humankind has exploited. We may debate the desirability of space weaponization as a policy option in the near and mid-term, and, indeed, what that may or may not look like, but weaponization in one form or another will happen.

- "Situational awareness in space is a key to successful application of space power."[33] Space situational awareness at present is sketchy at best, and yet it is required in order to carry out many of the simplest and most mundane spacepower functions, as well as to be able to distinguish between natural hazards and intentional threats or interference.

- "Control of space is the linchpin upon which a nation's space power depends."[34] In fact, Oberg does not reach far enough here. Because terrestrially based armed forces have become so space-dependent, the control of space will become critically important for a nation's land, air-, and seapower, not just spacepower.

Oberg's *Space Power Theory* should be viewed as an initial foray into theory-making. It does not meet our Mahanian criteria in that it lacks a comprehensiveness that links spacepower to national power in a manner that elucidates the nature of spacepower, and perhaps overly focuses on the technological dimension at the expense of others. Given that Oberg courageously stepped into the breach at the last minute of a troubled project sponsored by the then–Unified U.S. Space Command, *Space Power Theory* has aged not too badly, and provides sturdy shoulders upon which others may climb.

Everett Dolman

Everett Dolman's *Astropolitik* has been the most controversial book to appear on spacepower in recent years and yet, in many respects, is perhaps the most rigorous intellectually. Dolman posits spacepower within a classical geopolitical model based on the works of geopolitical theorists such as Mahan, Halford Mackinder, and Nicholas Spykman, among others.[35] His analysis finds that certain points in space may prove strategically advantageous to those powers that would control them. These points include low Earth orbit (LEO), geostationary orbit, Hohmann orbital transfers, and the Libration points L4 and L5 between the Earth and the Moon.[36] Others, such as Dandridge Cole and Simon "Pete" Worden,[37] have made similar arguments in the past, but not with the intellectual power that Dolman has mustered.

Dolman's signal contribution to the field is his outstanding explanation of the geographical and geopolitical relationships between spacepower and land, air-, and seapower. The assertion made by Dolman that the United States should seize LEO (unilaterally if necessary) in order to preserve a liberal global order is questionable in intent and implausible,[38] although a U.S.-led alliance might feasibly have a more legitimate claim to controlling LEO for more attainable and realistic goals. Similarly, Dolman may yet be proven right in his claim that the current outer space legal regime has stifled healthy competition in space that may have brought about more robust military and civil space capabilities, although blaming the failure of the space age to materialize solely on the space regime can come across as reductionism.[39]

Dolman has done the field a great service with *Astropolitik*. He fearlessly questions spacepower's sacred cows and throws down an intellectual gauntlet in the process. This said, Dolman's work cannot lay claim to be a comprehensive theory of spacepower, as its argument only resonates in the United States and lacks the universalism that marks all great works of strategic theory. Furthermore, *Astropolitik*'s durability may arise from its controversial assertions rather than from any overt attempt by Dolman to speak to the ages. Many of the policy concerns rightly raised by Dolman are unlikely to be of any broad interest to an audience seeking strategic guidance in the future.

John Klein

In Klein's *Space Warfare*, we see the first comprehensive attempt to apply a strategic analogy to spacepower. Klein takes Sir Julian Corbett's *Some Principles of Maritime Strategy* and applies it to spacepower, with mixed success. Corbett advocated a maritime approach to strategy that emphasized the interaction between land and seapower. Klein takes this a step further and advocates a spacepower version of maritime strategy that emphasizes the strategic interaction of spacepower with land, air-, and seapower.[40] The application, in broad terms, of Corbettian concepts of limited liability in war and the temporary nature of control to spacepower is useful, but when Klein seeks to apply the same framework to concepts such as offense, defense, concentration, and dispersal, the real limitations of the Corbettian strategic analogy are revealed.

The term *strategic analogy* is new, yet its theoretical roots can be found in the scholarship on historical analogies in statecraft and policymaking. An analogy "signifies an inference that if two or more things agree in one respect, then they might also agree in another."[41] Based on this definition, among others, a definition for the strategic analogy can be extrapolated. If two or more strategic environments separated, among other things, by time (though this is not a necessary criterion; strategic analogies may be used contemporaneously), geographical characteristics, doctrine, technology, culture, and political context agree in one respect, then they may also agree in another. Scholars, policymakers, military planners, and commanders use strategic analogies to provide a rational means for the comprehension and planning of novel strategic environments by retrieving information, principles, and past experiences from other, more established strategic environments and applying them to the new, unfamiliar strategic environment. In short, strategic analogies may provide a "shortcut to rationality"[42] in new and poorly understood strategic environments where there is little or no known strategic experience or established principles for effective operations. Strategic analogies are similar to historical analogies, except that the former use the strategic experiences and theories of other environments—such as the sea and the air—rather than the specific and particular historical events used in the latter. A strategic analogy may state that nascent spacepower is similar to seapower in several key respects, and then may infer that because of this it must be similar in other respects. A strategic analogy uses the body of theory and principles that has developed over the years, as well as the strategic history of the environment (land, sea, air) in question.

Klein's *Space Warfare* is an exercise in making strategic analogies and as a result reveals the limitations of this process. To be fair, Klein does state that "space is a unique environment, and any historically based strategic framework—whether naval, air, or maritime—cannot realistically be taken verbatim in its application to space strategy. Only the most fundamental concepts of maritime strategy, therefore, will and should be used to derive the strategic principles of space warfare."[43] Yet despite this acknowledgment, Klein at times seems to make the reality fit the theory, or at the very least, let the theory gloss over awkward facts. For example, Klein overreaches in his discussion of spacepower dispersal and concentration, where it is far from clear whether he is speaking about the dispersal and concentration of actual satellites (impossible, given the constraints of orbital dynamics) or the dispersal and concentration of effects generated by spacepower (which is plausible).[44]

The use of strategic analogies is a necessary step on the road to creating and developing an enduring and universal theory of spacepower. Problems arise, however, when we become overreliant on strategic analogies at the expense of critical thinking. Strategic analogies should be nothing more than a cognitive crutch that allows us to ask the right questions of spacepower. We shall make progress in theorymaking when we kick away these crutches and engage our critical faculties to start the process of inductive reasoning.

Guide for the Future

The authors discussed above have all made valuable contributions to a theory of spacepower. Even their mistakes and omissions are useful, as they allow those of us who follow to climb on their shoulders and adjust the theoretical framework accordingly. We are forced to address and correct their mistakes and omissions, and future theorists will have to rectify ours. Truly, a Mahan for the space age may yet appear, but in lieu of such a person, it is perhaps prudent to assume that the continued development of a theory of spacepower will be a team effort that will build on the labors of others that have gone before. It may seem churlish to critique these works, but criticism is made with gratitude to those who have intellectually dared, and the theory of spacepower ultimately will be best served by constantly striving through honest debate.

With these sentiments in mind, we offer our own thoughts on a theory of spacepower for others to ruminate upon, critique, and, ultimately and hopefully, improve in their own turn. Many of the thoughts offered here have been asserted before by us but are worth repeating for their strategic value.

Space is a Place

The idea that space can redeem human sin still persists in many quarters. The reason for this persistence is as much about the perception of space as a place, and what that place purports to represent, as it is about the technologies required for its manned and unmanned exploration and use. This particular way of framing space can be described as *astrofuturism*, which "posits the space frontier as a site of renewal, a place where we can resolve the domestic and global battles that have paralyzed our progress on earth."[45] We believe that space as a place is no different from the land, sea, and air, and we reject the astrofuturist credo as a fallacy. Human beings and their robotic proxies operate and (in the case of the land) live every day in these environments, carrying out myriad functions from the spiritual and artistic to the martial (and these are by no means mutually exclusive).

Our entry into space must respect the human condition in its entirety, good and bad, and attempts to redeem human nature through the wonders of technology or hopes that the infinite expanse of space will offer the opportunity to unite humankind where our existence on Earth has failed are bound to disappoint. It is tragic but true that "short of a revolution in the heart of man and the nature of states, by what miracle could interplanetary space be preserved from military use?"[46]

Strategy, Eternal and Universal

In the quest for a theory of spacepower, it is perhaps wise to first state categorically what such a theory should *not* be. In particular, a theory of spacepower should not be at odds with the universal and eternal logic of strategy. Instead, it should be a theory of its use in the service of strategy. Edward N. Luttwak points out that to postulate such a thing as "nuclear strategy," "naval strategy," or, in this case, "space strategy" is to argue that each of these kinds of strategy is somehow fundamentally different from the strategy that governs them all. Luttwak writes, "If there were such a thing as naval strategy or air strategy or nuclear strategy in any sense other than a conflation of the technical, tactical, or operational levels of the same universal strategy, then each should have its own peculiar logic."[47] A theory of spacepower should not claim such a "peculiar logic," and the foundations for this theory should be cognizant and respectful of a superior and overarching logic of strategy.

Sir Julian Corbett wrote of the purpose of theory in strategy:

> It is a process by which we co-ordinate our ideas, define the meaning of the words we use, grasp the difference between essential and unessential factors, and fix and expose the fundamental data on which every one is agreed. In this way we prepare the apparatus of practical discussion; we secure the means of arranging the factors in manageable shape, and of deducing from them with precision and rapidity a practical course of action. Without such an apparatus no two men can even think on the same line; much less can they ever hope to detach the real point of difference that divides them and isolate it for quiet solution.[48]

Given the relative infancy of spacepower, it is important that sensible theoretical foundations be established. Spacepower has made itself ubiquitous in modern war and statecraft, yet discerning a strategic experience of spacepower has proved to be notoriously difficult. Over time, strategic experience will doubtless accumulate, and so eventually a comprehensive theory of spacepower will develop and evolve synergistically with its actual practice. Although spacepower is relatively new, the need for theory is not. As Corbett's thoughts suggest, a theory of spacepower should provide a common framework from which all can refer and a conceptual means by which spacepower is exploited to its full potential in order to attain policy objectives.

Pragmatism

That said, a theory of spacepower must guard against a creeping inflexibility and orthodoxy that stifle innovative thinking or constructive criticism. It will evolve along with its actual use, and it may be found that some tenets of spacepower thought are in fact wrong. A theory of spacepower must also guard against flights of fancy and overactive imaginations that make theory useless as a guide to practice. Spacepower could be especially susceptible to such problems given that it is, conceptually, a blank canvas and is bound up for many people with science fiction. Spacepower is not science fiction, and its intellectual guardians, the theorists, much like the protagonists in the "widening gyre" of W.B. Yeats's "The Second Coming" who are either "lacking all conviction" or are "full of passionate intensity,"[49] must take care to protect it from the ignorance of some and the worst excesses of others. Theorists of spacepower, and practitioners who would read such theory, must always be mindful of the fact that strategy "is nothing if not pragmatic," and that "strategic theory is a theory for action."[50] A theory of spacepower that is disrespectful of the practicalities of spaceflight and orbitology, the limits of technology, and the eternal, universal workings of strategy could be worse than useless; it could be dangerous.

The Nature of Spacepower

To repeat, spacepower is not beyond the logic of strategy, nor can it be. Strategy is eternal in its nature and logic, and while the grammar and character of strategy evolve because of changes in their many dimensions such as society, politics, and technology, strategy's fundamental nature does not. Spacepower is subject to the nature of strategy and always will be. The nature of spacepower is simply the ability to use space for political purposes, and that too will never change. John G. Fox is only partially correct when he states, "The nature and character of space warfare 50 years from now may be wholly unrecognizable to those of us alive today."[51] Fox is probably correct in that the *character* of spacepower will change over the next 50 years, due perhaps to unforeseen technological developments. He is wrong, however, to state that the *nature* of spacepower is changeable; it is not. So long as humankind possesses the ability to exploit the space environment, then the nature of spacepower is immutable and impervious to societal, political, economic, technological, or any other kind of change.

Conclusion

This chapter has sought to elucidate the very real problems of creating and developing a theory of spacepower. The impediments are varied and tangible, but many of them apply equally to theorymaking for other military instruments. The crux of the matter is that strategy is difficult and so, therefore, is creating and developing a theory of spacepower. A true theory of spacepower will be able to account for its role in modern war and statecraft, as well as how it interacts with other instruments of power, and this chapter has sought to provide the would-be theorist with food for thought.

Notes

[1] Colin S. Gray, "The Influence of Space Power upon History," *Comparative Strategy* 15, no. 4 (October–December 1996), 307.

[2] Ibid., 304.

[3] Colin S. Gray, *Modern Strategy* (Oxford: Oxford University Press, 1999), 17.

[4] B.H. Liddell Hart, *Strategy*, 2ᵈ rev. ed. (New York: Signet, 1974), 322.

[5] Colin S. Gray and John B. Sheldon, "Spacepower and the Revolution in Military Affairs: A Glass Half-Full?" in *Spacepower for a New Millennium: Space and U.S. National Security*, ed. Peter L. Hays, James M. Smith, Alan R. Van Tassel, and Guy M. Walsh (New York: McGraw-Hill, 2000), 254.

[6] A growing number of countries are realizing the benefits and challenges of spacepower. Among them are the People's Republic of China, India, Brazil, South Korea, Israel, France, Germany, Italy, Nigeria, and Iran. See the special issue of *Astropolitics* 4, no. 2 (Summer 2006), for essays on the implications of rising spacepowers.

[7] With the exception of Sun Tzu, Thucydides, and Vegetius, of course. On the evolution of military theory in the modern period, see Azar Gat, *A History of Military Thought: From the Enlightenment to the Cold War* (Oxford: Oxford University Press, 2001).

[8] See Baron Antoine Henri de Jomini, *The Art of War* (London: Greenhill Books, 1992); and Carl von Clausewitz, *On War*, ed. and trans. Michael Howard and Peter Paret (Princeton: Princeton University Press, 1984).

[9] See, among his other works, Alfred Thayer Mahan, *The Influence of Sea Power Upon History, 1660–1783* (Boston: Little, Brown, 1890); Julian S. Corbett, *Some Principles of Maritime Strategy*, introduction and notes by Eric J. Grove (Annapolis, MD: Naval Institute Press, 1988); C.E. Callwell, *Military Operations and Maritime Preponderance*, ed. and introduced by Colin S. Gray (Annapolis, MD: Naval Institute Press, 1996); and Raoul Castex, *Strategic Theories*, trans., ed., and introduced by Eugenia C. Kiesling (Annapolis, MD: Naval Institute Press, 1993).

[10] See Giulio Douhet, *The Command of the Air*, trans. Dino Ferrari (Washington, DC: Air Force History and Museums Program, 1998); William Mitchell, *Winged Defense: The Development and Possibilities of Modern Air Power, Economic and Military* (Mineola, NY: Dover Publications, 1988); Wing Commander J.C. Slessor, RAF, *Air Power and Armies* (London: Oxford University Press, 1936); and Colonel John A. Warden III, USAF, *The Air Campaign: Planning for Combat* (Washington, DC: Brassey's, 1989).

[11] David MacIsaac, "Voices from the Central Blue: The Air Power Theorists," in *Makers of Modern Strategy: From Machiavelli to the Nuclear Age*, ed. Peter Paret (Princeton: Princeton University Press, 1986), 624.

[12] Harold R. Winton, "A Black Hole in the Wild Blue Yonder: The Need for a Comprehensive Theory of Air Power," *Air Power History* 39, no. 4 (Winter 1992), 32.

[13] Ibid., 32–33.

[14] MacIsaac, 625.

[15] Gray, *Modern Strategy*, 205. See also David Jablonsky, "Why Is Strategy Difficult," in *The Search for Strategy: Politics and Strategic Vision*, ed. Gary L. Guertner (Westport, CT: Greenwood Press, 1993), 3–45; and David J. Lonsdale, "Strategy: The Challenge of Complexity," *Defence Studies* 7, no. 1 (March 2007), 42–64.

[16] A point also made in Gray and Sheldon, "Spacepower and the Revolution in Military Affairs: A Glass Half Full?" 239–257.

[17] See, for example, Alan Beyerchen, "Clausewitz, Nonlinearity, and the Unpredictability of War," *International Security* 17, no. 3 (Winter 1992/1993), 59–90.

[18] See Colin S. Gray, *Weapons for Strategic Effect: How Important Is Technology?* Occasional Paper No. 21 (Maxwell Air Force Base, AL: Center for Strategy and Technology, Air War College, January 2001) for an exposition on the limits of technology.

[19] Clausewitz, *On War*, 119.

[20] Lonsdale, 42.

21 James Oberg, *Space Power Theory* (Washington, DC: U.S. Government Printing Office, 1999); Everett C. Dolman, *Astropolitik: Classical Geopolitics in the Space Age* (London: Frank Cass, 2002); and John J. Klein, *Space Warfare: Strategy, Principles, and Policy* (New York: Routledge, 2006).

22 Oberg, 1–22.

23 Ibid., 43–66.

24 Ibid., 67–86, but also the very useful appendices.

25 Ibid., 124.

26 Ibid.

27 Ibid.

28 Ibid., 126.

29 Ibid., 127.

30 Ibid.

31 Ibid., 128.

32 Ibid., 129.

33 Ibid., 130.

34 Ibid.

35 See, in particular, Dolman, 12–59.

36 Ibid., especially 60–85.

37 See G. Harry Stine, *Confrontation in Space* (Englewood Cliffs, NJ: Prentice-Hall, 1981), for a discussion of Dandridge Cole's "Panama Canal" spacepower theory, and Simon P. Worden and Bruce J. Jackson, "Space, Power, and Strategy," *The National Interest*, no. 13 (Fall 1988), 43–52, for a similar "High Ground" view.

38 Dolman, 86–112.

39 Ibid., 113–144.

40 Klein, 44–50.

41 David Hackett Fischer, *Historian's Fallacies: Toward a Logic of Historical Thought* (New York: Harper and Row, 1970), 243.

42 Robert Jervis, *Perception and Misperception in International Politics* (Princeton: Princeton University Press, 1976), 220.

43 Klein, 20.

44 Ibid., 107–115.

45 De Witt Douglas Kilgore, *Astrofuturism: Science, Race and Visions of Utopia in Space* (Philadelphia: University of Pennsylvania Press, 2003), 2.

46 Raymond Aron, *Peace and War: A Theory of International Relations*, trans. Richard Howard and Annette Baker Fox (London: Weidenfeld and Nicolson, 1966), 664.

47 Edward N. Luttwak, *Strategy: The Logic of War and Peace* (Cambridge: The Belknap Press of Harvard University Press, 1995), 156.

48 Corbett, 7.

49 With our sincerest apologies to the Bard of Sligo, see W.B. Yeats, "The Second Coming," in *The Collected Poems of W.B. Yeats* (New York: The Macmillan Company, 1952), 184–185.

50 Bernard Brodie, *War and Politics* (New York: The Macmillan Company, 1973), 452.

51 John G. Fox, "Some Principles of Space Strategy (or 'Corbett in Orbit')," *Space Policy* 17, no. 1 (February 2001), 7–11.

Chapter 2

On the Nature of Military Theory

Harold R. Winton

The quest for a theory of spacepower is a useful enterprise. It is based on the proposition that before one can intelligently develop and employ spacepower, one should understand its essence. It is also based on the historical belief that, over the long haul, military practice has generally benefited from military theory.[1] While such a conviction is generally true, this happy state has not always been realized. Faulty theory has led to faulty practice perhaps as often as enlightened theory has led to enlightened practice.[2] This does not necessarily call into question the utility of theory per se, but it does reinforce the need to get it about right. Taking the broader view, it is a trait of human nature to yearn for understanding of the world in which we live; and when a relatively new phenomenon such as spacepower appears on the scene, it is entirely natural to seek to comprehend it through the use of a conceptual construct. Thus, one can at least hope that the common defense will be better provided for by having a theory of spacepower than by not having one.

This chapter will deal only tangentially with spacepower. Its main task is to explore the nature of theory itself. First, it examines the general and somewhat problematic relationship between theory and the military profession. Next, it surveys what theorists and academics say about the utility of theory. It then seeks to determine what utility theory actually has for military institutions, particularly in the articulation of military doctrine. Finally, it offers a few implications that may be germane to a theory of spacepower.

Theory and the Military Profession

To examine the relationship between theory and the military profession, we must first assess the salient characteristics of each.[3]

Webster's definition of *theory* as "a coherent group of general propositions used as principles of explanation for a class of phenomena"[4] is a pretty good place to start. It highlights the essential task of explanation and the desirable criterion of coherence. But if we stand back a bit, we can tease out several other functions of theory. The first two occur before its explanatory function. Theory's first task is to define the field of study under investigation, or, in Webster's words, the "class of phenomena." In visual terms, this defining act draws a circle and declares that everything inside the circle is encompassed by the theory, while everything outside it is not. In the theory of war, for example, Carl von Clausewitz offers two definitions. The first states baldly, "War is thus an act of force to compel our enemy to do our will."[5] After introducing the limiting factor of rationality into the consideration of what war is, Clausewitz expands this definition as follows: "War is not a mere act of policy but a true political instrument, a continuation of political activity with other means."[6] A synthesis of these two definitions would be that war is the use of force to achieve the ends of policy. Although the utility of this definition has been argued at some length, it leaves no doubt as to what Clausewitz's theory is about.[7]

The next task of theory is to categorize—to break the field of study into its constituent parts. Here it may be helpful to visualize the subject of the theory as a spherical object rather than a circle. The sphere can be divided in many different ways: horizontally, vertically, diagonally, or, if it is a piece of citrus fruit, into sections that follow the natural internal segmentation. Again, reference to Clausewitz is instructive. War has two temporal phases—planning and conduct—and two levels—tactics and strategy—each with its own dynamics.[8] Furthermore, wars could also be categorized according to their purpose (offensive or defensive) and the amount of energy (limited or total) to be devoted to them.[9] A word about categorization is important here because it relates to the continuous evolution of theory. Theories tend to evolve in response to two stimuli: either new explanations are offered and subsequently verified that more accurately explain an existing reality, or the field of study itself changes, requiring either new explanations or new categories. An example of the former is the Copernican revolution in astronomy.[10] An example of the latter is the early 20th-century discovery of the *operation*, which emerged from the industrial revolution's influence on the conduct of war, as the connecting link between a battle and a campaign and subsequently led to the study of *operational art* as a new subdiscipline of military art and science.[11]

The third, and by far the most important, function of theory is to explain. Webster's definition cited above is correct in emphasizing theory's explanatory role, for, as Nicolaus Copernicus, Johannes Kepler, Albert Einstein, and scores of other theorists so clearly demonstrated, explanation is the soul of theory. In the military sphere, Alfred Thayer Mahan's statement that the sea is "a wide common, over which men may pass in all directions, but on which some well-worn paths show that controlling reasons have led them to choose certain lines of travel rather than others" explains the underlying logic of what are today called *sea lines of communication*.[12] Reading further in Mahan, one finds an extended explanation of the factors influencing the seapower of a state.[13] Explanation may be the product of repetitive observation and imaginative analysis, as Copernicus' was, or of "intuition, supported by being sympathetically in touch with experience," as Einstein's was.[14] In either case, theory without explanatory value is like salt without savor—it is worthy only of the dung heap.

But theory performs two additional functions. First, it connects the field of study to other related fields in the universe. This marks the great utility of Clausewitz's second definition of war, noted above. Although war had been used as a violent tool of political institutions dating to before the Peloponnesian War, Clausewitz's elegant formulation, which definitively *connected* violence with political intercourse, was perhaps his most important and enduring contribution to the theory of war.

Finally, theory anticipates. The choice of this verb is deliberate. In the physical realm, theory predicts. Isaac Newton's theory of gravitation and Kepler's laws of planetary motion, combined with detailed observations of perturbations in the orbit of Uranus and systematic hypothesis testing, allowed Urbain Jean Joseph Le Verrier and John Couch Adams independently to predict the location of Neptune in 1845.[15] But action and reaction in the human arena, and therefore in the study of war, are much less certain, and we must be content to live with a lesser standard. Nevertheless, anticipation can be almost as important as prediction. In the mid-1930s, Mikhail Tukhachevskii and a coterie of like-minded Soviet officers discovered that they had the technological capacity "not only to exercise pressure directly on the enemy's front line, but to penetrate his dispositions and to attack him simultaneously over the whole depth of his tactical layout."[16] They lacked both the means and the knowledge that would allow them to extend this "deep battle" capability to the level of "deep operations," where the problems of coordination on a large scale would become infinitely more complex. But the underlying conceptual construct—that is, what was practically feasible on a small level was theoretically achievable on a much larger scale—was a powerful notion that has only recently been fully realized in the performance of the U.S. Armed Forces in the Gulf Wars of 1991 and 2003.

But theory also has its limitations. No theory can fully replicate reality. There are simply too many variables in the real world for theory to contemplate them all. Thus, all theories are to some extent simplifications. Second, as alluded to earlier, things change. In the realm of military affairs, such change is uneven, varying between apparent stasis and virtual revolution. Nevertheless, military theory always lags behind the explanatory curve of contemporary developments. Thus, we can here paraphrase Michael Howard's famous stricture on doctrine, theory's handmaiden, and declare dogmatically that whatever theories exist (at least in the realm of human affairs), they are bound to be wrong—but it is the task of theorists to make them as little wrong as possible.[17]

This observation leads to a brief consideration of the several sources of theory. The first lies in the nature of the field of study about which the theory is being developed. As Clausewitz noted in his discussion of the theory of strategy, the ideas about the subject had to "logically derive from basic necessities."[18] These necessities are rooted in the nature of the thing itself, its phenomenology. As time passes, men accumulate experience related to the phenomenon, and this experience contributes to the refinement and further development of theory. As Mahan famously noted of naval strategy, "The teachings of the past have a value which is in no degree lessened."[19] But if theory has one foot firmly rooted in the empirical past, it also has the other planted in the world of concepts. In other words, theory draws from other relevant theory. It is no accident that Julian Corbett's instructive treatise *Some Principles of Maritime Strategy* begins with an extended recapitulation of *On War*, which might lightheartedly be characterized as "Clausewitz for Sailors."[20] Corbett was keenly aware that the theory of war at sea, while distinct in many ways from the theory of war on land, had to be rooted in a general conceptual framework of war itself. He also knew that Clausewitz provided a solid base upon which to build. But Corbett's work is also emblematic of another source of theory: dissatisfaction with existing theory. This notion of dissatisfaction runs like a brightly colored thread throughout almost all of military theory. Clausewitz wrote because he was fed up with theories that excluded moral factors and genius from war; Corbett wrote to correct Mahan's infatuation with concentration of the fleet and single-minded devotion to the capital ship; and J.F.C. Fuller railed against what he called the *alchemy of war*, whose poverty of thought and imagination had led to the horrors of World War I.[21]

To sum up, although theory is never complete and is always bound to be at least somewhat wrong, it performs several useful functions when it defines, categorizes, explains, connects, and anticipates. And it is primarily a product of the mind. There are good reasons that the world produces relatively few theorists worthy of the name. The formulation of useful theory demands intense powers of observation, ruthless intellectual honesty, clear thinking, mental stamina of the highest order, gifted imagination, and other attributes that defy easy description.[22] These are not qualities normally associated with the military profession.

Why is this so? First, war is an intensely practical activity and a ruthless auditor of both individuals and institutions. The business of controlled violence in the service of political interest demands real attention to detail and real results. Complex organizations of people with large amounts of equipment must be trained and conditioned to survive under conditions of significant privation and great stress, moved to the right place at the right time, and thrust into action against an adversary determined to kill or maim in frustrating the accomplishment of their goals. Those who cannot get things done in this brutal and unforgiving milieu soon fall by the wayside.

Second, war demands the disciplined acceptance of lawful orders even when such orders can lead to one's own death or disfigurement. A Soldier, Sailor, Marine, or Airman unwilling to follow orders is a contradiction in terms. Thus, there is an inherent bias in military personnel to obey rather than to question. On the whole, this tendency does more good than harm, but it tends to limit theoretical contemplation.

Finally, war is episodic. Copernicus could look at the movement of the planets on any clear night and at the sun on any clear day. But war comes and goes, rather like some inexplicable disease, and the resulting discontinuities make it a difficult phenomenon about which to theorize.

I do not mean to imply that the military profession is inherently antitheoretical. There are countervailing tendencies. As both Sun Tzu and Clausewitz cogently observed, the very seriousness of war provides a healthy stimulus to contemplation.[23] Its episodic nature, while restricting opportunity for direct observation, does provide opportunity for reflection. Furthermore, the very complexity of war, while limiting the ability of theorists to master it, creates incentives for military practitioners to discover simplifying notions that reduce its seeming intractability. And we would not have seen the appearance of institutions of higher military learning, societies for the study of the martial past, or a virtual explosion of military literature over the last 20 years were there not some glimmerings of intellectual activity surrounding the conduct of war.

But the larger point remains: there are underlying truths about both theory and the military profession that make the relationship between the two problematic at best. Despite this inherently uneasy relationship, there is sufficient evidence that theory has utility in military affairs to justify probing more deeply. In doing so, I would like to follow a dual track: to explore the question of what utility theory should have for military institutions and what utility it actually does have. In investigating the former, the study is confined to the opinions of theorists and educators. In the latter, it plumbs the empirical evidence. But an important caveat before proceeding: tracing connections between thought and action is intrinsically difficult. When the nature of the thought is conceptual, rather than pragmatic, as theory is bound to be, such sleuthing becomes even more challenging, and one frequently is forced to rely on inferential conjecture and even a bit of imagination to connect the deed to an antecedent proposition.

The Theorists Make Their Case

A narrow but rich body of discourse about theory's contribution to individual military judgment is densely packed in *On War*. Clausewitz's line of thought is most cogently revealed in book two, "On the Theory of War." He begins this discourse by classifying war into the related but distinct fields of tactics and strategy. He follows with a stinging critique of the theories of his day that seek to exclude from war three of its most important characteristics: the action of moral forces, the frustrating power of the enemy's will, and the endemic uncertainty of information. From this, he deduces that "a positive teaching is unattainable."[24] Clausewitz sees two ways out of this difficulty. The first is to admit baldly that whatever theory is developed will have decreasing validity at the higher levels of war where "almost all solutions must be left to imaginative intellect."[25] The second is to argue that theory is a tool to aid the contemplative mind rather than a guide for action.

This formulation leads to some of the most majestic passages of *On War*. Theory is "an analytical investigation leading to a close *acquaintance* with the subject; applied to experience—in our case, to military history—it leads to thorough familiarity with it." Clausewitz elaborates:

> Theory will have fulfilled its main task when it is used to ana-
> lyze the constituent elements of war, to distinguish precisely
> what at first seems fused, to explain in full the properties of the
> means employed and to show their probable effects, to define

clearly the nature of the ends in view, and to illuminate all phases of war through critical inquiry. Theory then becomes a guide to anyone who wants to learn about war from books; it will light his way, ease his progress, train his judgment, and help him avoid pitfalls. . . . Theory exists so that one need not start afresh each time sorting out the material and plowing through it, but will find it ready to hand and in good order. It is meant to educate the mind of the future commander, or, more accurately, to guide him in his self-education, not to accompany him to the battlefield; just as a wise teacher guides and stimulates a young man's intellectual development, but is careful not to lead him by the hand for the rest of his life.[26]

This view of theory has a particular implication for military peda-gogy. It requires that education begin with broad principles, rather than an accumulation of technical details. "Great things alone," Clausewitz argued, "can make a great mind, and petty things will make a petty mind unless a man rejects them as alien."[27] But Clausewitz also makes it abundantly clear that the cumulative insights derived from theory must ultimately find practical expression:

The knowledge needed by a senior commander is distin-guished by the fact that it can only be attained by a special talent, through the medium of reflection, study, and thought: an intellectual instinct which extracts the essence from the phenomena of life, as a bee sucks honey from a flower. In addi-tion to study and reflection, life itself serves as a source. Expe-rience, with its wealth of lessons, will never produce a *Newton* or an *Euler*, but it may well bring forth the higher calculations of a *Condé* or a *Frederick*. . . . By total assimilation with his mind and life, the commander's knowledge must be trans-formed into a genuine capability. . . . It [theory] will be suffi-cient if it helps the commander acquire those insights that, once absorbed into his way of thinking, will smooth and pro-tect his progress, and will never force him to abandon his convictions for the sake of any objective fact.[28]

Thus, a century before Carl Becker advanced the proposition that "Mr. Everyman" had to be his own historian in order to function effectively in daily life, Clausewitz argued that every commander had to be his own theorist in order to function effectively in war.[29] In Clausewitz's view, the essential role of theory was to aid the commander in his total learning, which synthesized study, experience, observation, and reflection into a coherent whole, manifested as an ever-alert, perceptive military judgment.

There is, however, another view of the utility of theory, most famously articulated by Baron Antoine Henri de Jomini, Clausewitz's chief competitor in this arena. Jomini indeed believed in the power of positive teaching. Although he was prepared to admit that war as a whole was an art, strategy—the main subject of his work—was "regulated by fixed laws resembling those of the positive sciences."[30] Following this point-counterpoint formula again, he conceded that bad morale and accidents could prevent victory, but:

> These truths need not lead to the conclusion that there can be
> no sound rules in war, the observance of which, the chances
> being equal, will lead to success. It is true that theories cannot
> teach men with mathematical precision what they should do
> in every possible case; but it is also certain that they will always
> point out the errors which should be avoided; and this is a
> highly important consideration, for these rules thus become,
> in the hands of skillful generals commanding brave troops,
> means of almost certain success.[31]

This fundamental belief in the efficacy of prescriptive theory led Jomini to formulate his theory itself much differently than Clausewitz. At the epicenter of Clausewitz's theory, we find a trinity of the elemental forces of war—violence, chance, and reason—acting on each other in multifarious ways, whose dynamics the statesman and commander must thoroughly consider before deciding whether to go to war and how to conduct it.[32] Jomini's central proposition consists of a series of four maxims about strategy that he summarized as "bringing the greatest part of the forces of an army upon the important point of a theater of war or of the zone of operations."[33] Jomini's principle-based approach to theory has had great endurance over the years. It perhaps found its most complete expression in J.F.C. Fuller's *The Foundations of the Science of War*, a treatise whose nine didactic imperatives, each expressed as a single word or short phrase, continue to resonate in contemporary doctrinal manuals.[34]

Clausewitz's and Jomini's views of theory were not mutually exclusive. Jomini addressed some of the wider considerations of policy central to Clausewitz, particularly in the opening chapter of *The Art of War*.[35] And Clausewitz occasionally engaged in formulaic statements, perhaps most notably in his observation that "destruction of the enemy force is always the superior, more effective means, with which others cannot compete."[36] Nevertheless, their two approaches—one descriptive, the other prescriptive—represent the two normative poles concerning the utility of theory.

But we find useful insights into the utility of theory from more modern observers as well. In his 1959 foreword to Henry E. Eccles's important but much-neglected work, *Logistics in the National Defense*, Henry M. Wriston, then president of the American Assembly at Columbia University, opined, "Theory is not just dreams or wishful thinking. It is the orderly interpretation of accumulated experience and its formal enunciation as a guide to future intelligent action to better that experience."[37] In this pithy and elegant formulation, Wriston captures an important truth: the fundamental social utility of theory is to help realize man's almost universal longing to make his future better than his past. The fact that the book that followed offered a theory of military logistics was but a particular manifestation of a general verity. Several years later, J.C. Wylie, a reflective, combat-experienced Sailor, developed a formulation similar to Wriston's that described the mechanics of translating theory into action:

> Theory serves a useful purpose to the extent that it can collect and organize the experiences and ideas of other men, sort out which of them may have a valid transfer value to a new and different situation, and help the practitioner to enlarge his vision in an orderly, manageable and useful fashion—and then apply it to the reality with which he is faced.[38]

In sum, there are two somewhat polar philosophies of how theory should influence practice. In the Clausewitzian view, it does so indirectly by educating the judgment of the practitioner; in the Jominian view, it does so directly by providing the practitioner concrete guides to action. Wriston and Wylie, both slightly more Clausewitzian than Jominian, provide a useful synthesis and update of Clausewitz and Jomini, rearticulating the value of theory to the military professional.

Influence of Theory on Military Institutions

In the modern age, theory has its most immediate influence on military institutions in the form of doctrine, a sort of stepping stone between theory and application. Along a scale stretching from the purely abstract to the purely concrete, doctrine occupies something of a middle ground representing a conceptual link between theory and practice. Having come much into vogue in the U.S. Armed Forces since the end of the Vietnam

War and with its popularity propagated to many other institutions as well, doctrine also represents, in a sense, sanctioned theory. In other words, there are two principal distinctions between theory and doctrine: the latter is decidedly more pragmatic, and it is stamped with an institutional imprimatur. How does theory influence doctrine? Generally speaking, we would expect theory to provide general propositions and doctrine to assess the extent to which these strictures apply, fail to apply, or apply with qualifications in particular eras and under particular conditions. In other words, the intellectual influence flows from the general to the particular. But at times, the relationship is reversed. This occurs when doctrine seeks to deal with new phenomena for which theory has not yet been well developed, such as for the employment of nuclear weapons in the 1950s, or when doctrine developers themselves formulate new ways of categorizing or new relational propositions. In cases such as these, doctrine may drive theory. In seeking to examine the relationship between the two in detail, we will explore the theoretical underpinnings of the 1982 and 1986 statements of U.S. Army doctrine and the 1992 articulation of U.S. Air Force doctrine.

Our first laboratory for exploring these relationships is the Army in the aftermath of the Vietnam War. In 1976, it promulgated Field Manual (FM) 100–5, *Operations.* This manual was deliberately crafted by its principal architect, General William E. DePuy, first commander of the U.S. Army Training and Doctrine Command (TRADOC), to shake the Army out of its post-Vietnam miasma and provide a conceptual framework for defeating a Soviet incursion into Western Europe.[39] It succeeded in the first but failed in the second. DePuy definitely got the Army's attention, and he culturally transformed it from being indifferent toward doctrine to taking it quite seriously. But his fundamental concept of piling on in front of Soviet penetrations, which he referred to as the "Active Defense," did not find favor. It was seen as reactive, rather than responsive; dealing with the first battle, but not the last; and insufficiently attentive to Soviet formations in the second operational and strategic echelons. Thus, the stage was set for a new manual, a new concept, and a new marketing label.

The new manual was the 1982 edition of FM 100–5; the new concept was to fight the Soviets in depth and hit them at unexpected times from unexpected directions; and the new marketing label was "AirLand Battle." The principal authors were two gifted officers, L.D. "Don" Holder and Huba Wass de Czege. Both had advanced degrees from Harvard University (Holder in history, Wass de Czege in public administration); both were combat veterans of the Vietnam War; and both were sound, practical soldiers. The manual they produced under the direction of General Donn A.

Starry, DePuy's successor at TRADOC, was clearly informed by theory as well as history. From Clausewitz came notions such as the manual's opening sentence, "There is no simple formula for winning wars"; a quotation to the effect that "the whole of military activity must . . . relate directly or indirectly to the engagement"; "The objective of all operations is to destroy the opposing force"; and another direct citation characterizing the defense as a "shield of [well-directed] blows."[40] But there was also a strong element of indirectness in the manual that one could trace to the ideas of Sun Tzu, who was mentioned by name, and Basil H. Liddell Hart, who was not. Sun Tzu was quoted to the effect that "rapidity is the essence of war; take advantage of the enemy's unreadiness, make your way by unexpected routes, and attack unguarded spots"; soldiers were adjured that "our tactics must appear formless to the enemy"; and one of the seven combat imperatives was to "direct friendly strengths against enemy weaknesses."[41] Additionally, the manual's extensive discussion of "Deep Battle," which advocated striking well behind enemy lines to disrupt the commitment of reinforcements and subject the opposing force to piecemeal defeat, drew heavily on the legacy of Mikhail Tukhachevskii, V.K. Triandafillov, A.A. Svechin, and other Soviet thinkers of the 1920s and 1930s.[42] Although it was politically infeasible to acknowledge this intellectual debt at the height of the Cold War, the apparent reasoning here was that one had to fight fire with fire. And the strong emphasis on "Deep Battle" was an outgrowth of an intensive study of Soviet military practices dating back to the earliest years of the Red Army. A further reflection of this debt was the introduction of a variation of the Soviet term *operational art* into the American military lexicon as the *operational level of war*.[43]

When the manual was updated 4 years later, a third author, Richard Hart Sinnreich, was brought into the work. Sinnreich's professional and academic credentials were just as sound as those of his two compatriots: combat time in Vietnam, an advanced degree in political science from The Ohio State University, and well-developed soldiering skills. Holder, Wass de Czege, and Sinnreich engaged in a collaborative effort that expanded and conceptualized the notion of operational art. But rather than associating the term *operational* strictly with large-scale operations, as had been done in the previous edition, the 1986 manual defined *operational art* as "the employment of military forces to attain strategic goals in a theater of war or theater of operations through the design, organization, and conduct of campaigns and major operations."[44] This depiction of operational art as a conceptual link between tactical events (the building blocks of major operations) and strategic results significantly broadened the Soviet concept and made it applicable to the wide variety of types of wars that the U.S. Army might have to fight. It also harkened back to Clausewitz's definition of strategy as "the use of an engagement for the purpose of the war."[45] The manual then ventured into some theory of its own in requiring the operational commander to address three issues: the conditions required to effect the strategic goal, the sequence of actions necessary to produce the conditions, and the resources required to generate the sequence of actions. The combination of a new definition of operational art and a framework for connecting resources, actions, and effects gave the manual an underlying coherence that made it an extremely valuable document in its day and an admirable example of the genre of doctrinal literature.

Roughly contemporaneously with the publication of the second expression of the Army's AirLand Battle doctrine, a group of Airmen with a scholastic bent was assembled at the Airpower Research Institute (ARI) of the U.S. Air Force College of Aerospace Doctrine, Research, and Education to launch a bold experiment in the formulation of Air Force basic doctrine. This effort was based on an idea put forth by the highly respected Air Force historian Robert Frank Futrell, who opined that doctrine should be published with footnotes to document the evidence supporting the doctrinal statements.[46] The ARI Director, Dennis M. Drew, a Strategic Air Command warrior who had served at Maxwell Air Force Base since the late 1970s and held an advanced degree in military history from the University of Alabama, decided to put Futrell's idea to the test. But he and his research/writing team ultimately determined to expand on Futrell's basic notion. They would publish the doctrine in two volumes. The first, relatively thin, document would contain the bare propositional inventory; the second, more substantial, tome would lay out the evidence upon which the statements in the first were based. The process involved a good deal of both research and argument; but by the eve of the 1991 Gulf War, Drew and his team had produced a workable first draft. Publication was delayed until 1992 to allow the Air Force to assimilate the experience of that war. The result was what Air Force Chief of Staff Merrill A. McPeak called "one of the most important documents published by the United States Air Force."[47] Arguably, he was correct. No other American military Service had ever mustered the intellectual courage to put its analysis where its propositions were. It was potentially, in form alone, a paradigm for a new, analytically rigorous approach to the articulation of doctrine.[48]

As one would suspect, the primary influence on the manual was empirical. Historical essays addressed issues such as the environment, capabilities, force composition, roles and missions, and employment of aerospace power as well as the sustainment, training, organizing, and equipping of aerospace forces.[49] But there was a notable conceptual cant as well. The opening pages either paraphrased or quoted Clausewitz: "War is an instrument of political policy"; "the military objective in war is to compel the adversary to do our will"; and "war is characterized by 'fog, friction, and chance.'"[50] And the notion that "an airman, acting as an air component commander, should be responsible for employing all air and space assets in the theater" was right out of Giulio Douhet and Billy Mitchell.[51] There was also, like the 1982 version of FM 100–5, a nod in the direction of Sun Tzu and Liddell Hart: "Any enemy with the capacity to be a threat is likely to have strategic vulnerabilities susceptible to air attack; discerning those vulnerabilities is an airman's task."[52] The only place that the propositional inventory appeared to be but thinly supported by underlying concepts or evidence was a page-and-a-quarter insert titled "An Airman's View," which contained a series of statements that could perhaps be summed up in a single aphorism: airpower does it better.[53] Nevertheless, the 1992 statement of Air Force basic doctrine represented a bold, promising new approach to doctrinal formulation and articulation. Given this strong dose of intellectual rigor, it is not surprising that the experiment was short-lived.[54]

Nevertheless, in summing up the actual interplay between theory and the military profession, we can conclude that the institutional relationship between military theory on the one hand and military doctrine on the other is fairly direct.

Implications for a Theory of Spacepower

Having surveyed the nature of military theory, the general relation between theory and the military profession, and the particular relationship between theory and doctrine, it remains to suggest a few implications of this analysis for the theory of spacepower.

First, great care and extended debate should be devoted to articulating the central proposition, or main idea, of spacepower theory. One that is cast narrowly to focus only on spacepower's contributions to national security will take the theory in one direction. One that is cast more broadly to acknowledge spacepower's contributions to the expansion of man's knowledge of the universe will take it in another. Within the narrower ambit of national security, the construct of the theory should be informed by its purpose, which is related to the target audience. Here, Clausewitz's admonition is germane. In this author's opinion, one should not aim at some sort of positivist teaching that will spell out in precise and unambiguous fashion exactly what some future space forces commander or policymaker influencing the development of spacepower should do in a given situation. Rather, the theory should aim to *assist the self-education* of such individuals. To do this, it should focus on *explanatory relationships* within categories of spacepower itself and among spacepower and other related fields in the military-political universe. Given the relative newness of spacepower as both an instrument of military force and a vehicle for scientific exploration, and given as well the speed at which technological developments are likely to alter the physics of relationships among space-power subfields, it should be the tenor of a spacepower theory to develop a fairly firm list of questions that will inform the development and employ-ment of spacepower but to recognize that the answers to those questions can change both rapidly and unexpectedly and must, therefore, remain rather tentative. Finally, it would be helpful to use the five-fold functions of definition, categorization, explanation, connection, and anticipation as a heuristic device to check the work for its efficacy and relevance. Such a review will not guarantee a useful product. It may, however, help to reduce errors and to sharpen the analysis of relevant issues.

In summary, both the nature and history of military theory indicate that the task of developing a comprehensive, constructive theory of space-power will not be easy. Nor can the present attempt be considered the final word on the subject. It can, nevertheless, move the dialogue on spacepower to a new and more informed level and thus make a worthwhile contribu-tion to the enhancement of national security and perhaps to the conduct of broader pursuits as well.

Notes

[1] The terms of reference establishing the need for a theory of spacepower specifically alluded to this rationale, noting that "the lack of a space power theory is most notable to the national security sector. Military theorists such as Clausewitz, Mahan, and Douhet have produced definitive works for land, sea, and air, but there is not such comparable resource for circumterrestrial space." Thomas G. Behling, Deputy Under Secretary of Defense (Preparation and Warning), "Space Power Theory Terms of Reference," enclosure to memorandum to President, National Defense University, February 13, 2006, Subject: Space Power Theory, 1.

[2] Perhaps the most apposite example of this contrast is the difference between French and Ger-man military concepts in the years between World Wars I and II and the resultant campaign outcomes. On the French, see Robert Allan Doughty, *Seeds of Disaster: The Development of French Army Doctrine 1919–1939* (Hamden, CT: Archon Books, 1985); on the Germans, see James S. Corum, *The Roots of Blitzkrieg: Hans von Seeckt and German Military Reform* (Lawrence: University Press of Kansas, 1992).

[3] The argument here begins with a discussion of theory in a general sense. However, when the word *theory* is applied to the field of war, it becomes *military theory* in the classical sense of that term—that is, a systematic, codified body of propositions about the art and science of war and war preparation.

[4] *Webster's Encyclopedic Unabridged Dictionary of the English Language* (New York: Gramercy Books, 1996), 1967.

[5] Carl von Clausewitz, *On War*, ed. and trans. Michael Howard and Peter Paret (Princeton: Princeton University Press, 1989), 75.

[6] Ibid., 87.

[7] Perhaps the most spirited assault on Clausewitz's notion that war is an extension of politics is found in John Keegan, *A History of Warfare* (New York: Alfred A. Knopf, 1993), 3–60. For an equally spirited rejoinder, see Christopher Bassford, "John Keegan and the Grand Tradition of Trashing Clausewitz: A Polemic," *War in History* 1 (November 1994), 319–336.

[8] Clausewitz, 128.

[9] Ibid., 611–637.

[10] For a fascinating description of how Copernicus developed his new view of the universe, see Thomas S. Kuhn, *The Copernican Revolution: Planetary Astronomy in the Development of Western Thought* (1957; reprint, Cambridge: Harvard University Press, 1999), 134–184.

[11] The roots and early study of operational art are succinctly described in David M. Glantz, *Soviet Military Operational Art: In Pursuit of Deep Battle* (London: Frank Cass, 1991), 17–38.

[12] Alfred Thayer Mahan, *The Influence of Sea Power upon History, 1660–1783*, 12th ed. (Boston: Little, Brown, 1918), 25.

[13] Ibid., 29–89. Mahan's factors include a country's geographical position, physical conformation, extent of territory, size of population, national character, and the character of its government.

[14] Albert Einstein's lead essay in the collection *Science et Synthèse* (Paris: Gallimard, 1967), 28, cited in Gerald Holton, *Thematic Origins of Scientific Thought: Kepler to Einstein* (Cambridge: Harvard University Press, 1980), 357.

[15] The MacTutor History of Mathematics Archive, "Mathematical Discovery of Planets," available at <www.gap.dcs.st-and.ac.uk/~history/HistTopics/Neptune_and_Pluto.html>.

[16] Mikhail Tukhachevskii, "The Red Army's New (1936) Field Service Regulations," in Richard Simpkin, Deep Battle: *The Brainchild of Marshal Tukhachevskii* (London: Brassey's Defence Publishers, 1987), 170.

[17] Michael Howard, "Military Science in an Age of Peace," *Journal of the Royal United Services Institute for Defence Studies* 119 (March 1974), 7.

[18] Clausewitz's unfinished note, presumably written in 1830; Clausewitz, *On War*, 70.

[19] Mahan, 9.

[20] Julian S. Corbett, *Some Principles of Maritime Strategy*, introduction and notes by Eric J. Grove (1911; reprint, Annapolis, MD: Naval Institute Press, 1988), 15–51.

[21] Clausewitz, 134–136; Corbett, 107–152; J.F.C. Fuller, *The Foundations of the Science of War* (London: Hutchinson, 1926), 19–47.

[22] Holton attempts to capture the essential qualities of scientific genius in *Thematic Origins of Scientific Thought*, 353–380. His major focus in this investigation is the genius's ability to work in the mental realm of apparent opposites. Although I am not equating the ability to formulate theory with genius, I am arguing that such formulation requires many of the same qualities that Holton describes.

[23] "War is a matter of vital importance to the State; the province of life or death; the road to survival or ruin. It is mandatory that it be thoroughly studied." Sun Tzu, *The Art of War*, trans. Samuel B. Griffith (New York: Oxford University Press, 1963), 63; "War is not pastime; it is no mere joy in daring and winning, no place for irresponsible enthusiasts. It is a serious means to a serious end," Clausewitz, 86.

[24] Clausewitz, 140. In the Paret-Howard translation, the phrase reads, "A Positive Doctrine is Unattainable." The text comes from a subchapter heading, "*Eine positive Lehre ist unmöglich.*" Carl von Clausewitz, *Vom Kriege*, 19th ed., ed. Werner Hahlweg (Bonn: Ferd. Dümmlers Verlag, 1991), 289. The rendering of the German Lehre as doctrine is certainly acceptable. However, in light of the very specific military connotation that the term doctrine has developed since the early 1970s as being officially sanctioned principles that guide the actions of armed forces, I have chosen to render Lehre as the somewhat more general term teaching.

[25] Clausewitz, *On War*, 140.

[26] Ibid., 141.

²⁷ Ibid., 145.

²⁸ Ibid., 146–147.

²⁹ Carl Becker, "Everyman His Own Historian," *American Historical Review* XXXVII (January 1932), 221–236; reprinted in Carl L. Becker, *Everyman His Own Historian: Essays on History and Politics* (New York: F.S. Crofts, 1935), 233–255.

³⁰ Baron Antoine Henri de Jomini, *The Art of War*, trans. G.H. Mendell and W.P. Craighill (1862; reprint, Westport, CT: Greenwood Press, 1971), 321.

³¹ Ibid., 323.

³² Clausewitz, *On War*, 89. Clausewitz's description of the three elements provides a strong indication of his lack of dogmatism: "These three tendencies are like three different codes of law, deep-rooted in their subject and yet variable in their relationship to one another. A theory that ignores any one of them or seeks to fix an arbitrary relationship between them would conflict with reality to such an extent that for this reason alone it would be totally useless."

³³ Jomini, 322. The maxims themselves are found on page 70.

³⁴ The derivation of these nine principles is laid out in Fuller, 208–229. Fuller named them Direction, Concentration, Distribution, Determination, Surprise, Endurance, Mobility, Offensive Action, and Security. The U.S. Air Force's current list of principles of war includes Unity of Command, Objective, Offensive, Mass, Maneuver, Economy of Force, Security, Surprise, and Simplicity. *Air Force Basic Doctrine: AF Doctrine Document 1*, November 17, 2003, 19–26, available at <www.dtic.mil/doc-trine/jel/service_pubs/afdd1.pdf>. Contemporary joint doctrine contains precisely the same list of the principles of war as the Air Force's but adds three "Other Principles": Restraint, Perseverance, and Legitimacy. Joint Publication 3–0, *Joint Operations*, September 17, 2006, II–2, available at <www.dtic.mil/doctrine/jel/new_pubs/jp3_0.pdf>.

³⁵ Jomini, 16–39. The chapter is titled "The Relation of Diplomacy to War."

³⁶ Clausewitz, *On War*, 97.

³⁷ Henry M. Wriston, foreword to Henry E. Eccles, *Logistics in the National Defense* (1959; reprint, Washington, DC: Headquarters, United States Marine Corps, 1989), vii.

³⁸ J.C. Wylie, *Military Strategy: A General Theory of Power Control* (1967; reprint, Annapolis, MD: Naval Institute Press, n.d.), 31.

³⁹ For DePuy's pivotal role in the formulation of the 1976 edition of FM 100–5 and the reaction thereto, see Romie L. Brownlee and William J. Mullen III, *Changing an Army: An Oral History of General William E. DePuy, USA Retired* (Carlisle Barracks, PA: United States Military History Institute, n.d.), 187–189, and John L. Romjue, *From Active Defense to AirLand Battle: The Development of Army Doctrine 1973–1982* (Fort Monroe, VA: United States Army Training and Doctrine Command, 1984), 3–21.

⁴⁰ Department of the Army, Field Manual 100–5, *Operations* (Washington, DC: Department of the Army, 1982), 1–1, 1–4, 2–1, and 11–1.

⁴¹ Ibid., 2–1, 2–8.

⁴² Ibid., 7–13 through 7–17.

⁴³ Ibid., 2–3.

⁴⁴ Department of the Army, Field Manual 100–5, *Operations* (Washington, DC: Department of the Army, 1986), 10.

⁴⁵ Clausewitz, *On War*, 76. This definition, as the drafters of the manual were well aware, was much more conceptual than Jomini's description of strategy as "the art of making war upon the map." Jomini, *Art of War*, 69.

⁴⁶ Interview with Professor Dennis M. Drew, School of Advanced Air and Space Studies, March 11, 2004. In addition to an extremely detailed history of U.S. Air Force operations in the Korean War, Futrell produced a two-volume compilation titled *Ideas, Concepts, Doctrine: Basic Thinking in the United States Air Force* (Maxwell Air Force Base, AL: Air University Press, 1989).

⁴⁷ Department of the Air Force, Air Force Manual 1–1, *Basic Aerospace Doctrine of the United States Air Force*, 2 vols. (Washington, DC: Department of the Air Force, 1992), 1:v.

⁴⁸ For a detailed assessment of this groundbreaking work, see Harold R. Winton, "Reflections on the Air Force's New Manual," *Military Review* 72 (November 1992), 20–31.

[49] Air Force Manual 1–1, 2:i.

[50] Ibid., 1:1–2.

[51] Ibid., 1:9.

[52] Ibid., 1:12.

[53] Ibid., 1:15–16.

[54] The subsequent statement of Air Force basic doctrine, published in 1997, reverted to the traditional format. See Department of the Air Force, Air Force Doctrine Document 1, *Air Force Basic Doctrine* (Maxwell Air Force Base, AL: Headquarters, Air Force Doctrine Center, 1997).

Chapter 3

International Relations Theory and Spacepower

Robert L. Pfaltzgraff, Jr.

The traditional focus of international relations (IR) theory has been peace and war, cooperation and competition, among the political units into which the world is divided—principally states, but also increasingly nonstate actors in the 21st century. Until the advent of technologies for air- and spacepower, all interaction took place on the Earth's surface. With the development of manned flight, followed by our ability to venture into space, international relations expanded to include the new dimension provided by the air and space environment. Just as terrestrial geography framed the historic setting for international relations, space is already being factored more fully into 21st-century IR theory, especially as rivalries on Earth, together with perceived requirements for cooperation, are projected into space. The foundations for the explicit consideration of space exist in IR theory. In all likelihood, new theories eventually will emerge to take account of the novel features of space as we come to know more about this environment. For the moment, however, we will think about space with our theories about Earth-bound political relationships as our essential point of departure. Just as we have extended Eurocentric IR theory to the global setting of the 21st century, such theories will be tested in space. Because all IR theories either *describe* or *prescribe* interactions and relationships, space becomes yet another arena in which to theorize about the behavior of the world's political units. The assumption that theories developed for Earth-bound relationships apply in space will be reinforced, modified, or rejected as we come to know more about human interaction in space. We may theorize about IR theory as it applies to the relationships between entities in space as well as how space affects the relationship between political units on Earth. We may also speculate about the extent to which space would eliminate or mitigate conflicts or promote cooperation between formerly hostile Earthly units if they found it necessary to confront an extraterrestrial foe. Such issues open other areas for speculation and discussion, including the potential implications of IR theory as space becomes an arena in which Earthly units attempt to enhance their position on Earth and eventually to establish themselves more extensively in space.

We need not live in fantasyland to think about the extension of Earthly life to space. This could include orbiting space stations building on the achievements of recent decades as well as colonies of people whose forebears originated on Earth but who have established themselves far from Earth. The need for IR theory about space could also arise from the development of transportation and communication routes among space colonies and space stations, and between peoples living on asteroids and the Moon as well as other planets. We may think of asteroids as either fragmenting objects that could destroy or alter Earth or as a basis for extending man's reach into space. As Martin Ira Glassner points out, such activities in space environments "will inevitably generate questions of nationality and nationalism and sovereignty, of ownership and use of resources, of the distribution of costs and benefits, of social stratification and cultural differences, of law and loyalties and rivalries and politics, of frontiers and boundaries and power, and perhaps of colonial empires and wars of independence."[1] This will provide a fertile environment for theorizing about existing and potential political relationships. We will come to understand more fully the extent to which Earthly theories can be projected onto space or the need to evolve entirely new ways of thinking about space. Because space is not the exclusive domain of governments, theories will include private sector entities as well. In this respect, the present IR theory emphasis on states as well as actors other than states has direct applicability.

Colonization of the Moon, asteroids, and planets would present humans with challenges to survival in space not encountered on Earth. We would greatly enhance scientific knowledge in a setting with greater or lesser levels of gravity and potentially lethal cosmic ray exposure, to mention only the most obvious differences with Earthly life. At the same time, we would face far different circumstances related to political and social relationships. For example, the challenges to survival would probably be so great that the rights of the individual might be sacrificed to the needs of the collective, or rugged individualism and self-reliance would be essential. Space colonies would be dependent for a time on their mother country on Earth but increasingly would be compelled by vast distances and time measured by years from Earth to fend for themselves. Barring dramatic technological advances that compress such travel time, the interactive capability of space colonies, whether with each other or with Earth, would be extremely limited. A premium would be placed on independence, and leadership would be measured by the ability to adapt to new and harsh circumstances.

There are many other unknowns concerning political and social relationships in space. We literally do not know what we do not know. Would Earthly religions be strengthened or weakened by space knowledge? It cannot be known in advance whether space colonization would reinforce existing social science theory about the behavior of individuals or groups with each other or lead to dramatic differences. For example, under what conditions in space would there be a propensity for greater conflict or for greater cooperation? In the absence of such experience in space, we have little choice but to extrapolate from existing IR theory to help us understand such relationships in space. In any event, the testing of theory about interaction of humans in space lies in the future. Our more immediate goal is to gain a greater understanding of how IR theory can (and does) inform our thinking about the near-term space issues, notably how space shapes the power of Earthly states, while we also speculate about the longer term issue of social science theory and relationships within and between groups in space. Thus, we think first about the extension of capabilities of states into space as a basis for enhancing their position on Earth and only subsequently about how sociopolitical relationships might evolve between space-based entities far from Earth.

The huge expanse of space provides a rich basis for theory development about relations between the Earth and the other bodies of the solar system and ultimately perhaps between these entities themselves. If social science theorizing is based on our images about the world surrounding us, how we imagine, or develop images about, the evolution of such relationships can only give new meaning to the word *imagination* as a basis for future IR theory. What is unique about space is the fact that we are dealing with infinity. Whereas the terrestrial land mass and the seas have knowable finite bounds, we literally do not know where space ends or understand the implications of infinity for how we theorize about space. In its space dimension, IR theory will evolve as emerging and future technologies permit the more extensive exploration, and perhaps even the colonization, of parts of the solar system and the exploitation of its natural resources, beginning with the Moon and ultimately extending beyond our solar system. As in the case of Earth-bound geopolitical theorizing, the significance of space will be determined by technologies that facilitate the movement of people, resources, and other capabilities. Those technologies may be developed as a result of our assumptions about the geopolitical or strategic significance of space extrapolated from IR theory and the requirements that are set forth in our spacepower strategy.

From IR theory we derive the notion, building on geography, that a new arena becomes first an adjunct to the security and well-being of the primary unit and, later, a setting to be controlled for its own sake. Airpower was first envisaged as a basis for enhancing ground operations but subsequently became an arena that had to be defended for its own sake because of the deployment of vulnerable assets such as heavy bombers. As technologies become more widely available, they are acquired by increasing numbers of actors. Such technologies proliferate from the core to the periphery, from the most advanced states to others. Space becomes first an environment for superpower competition, as during the Cold War, to be followed by larger numbers of states developing space programs. At least 35 countries now have space research programs that are designed to either augment existing space capabilities or lead to deployments in space. Others are likely to emerge in the decades ahead.

IR theory has long emphasized power relationships, including the extent to which power is the most important variable for understanding the behavior of the political units into which the world is divided. The theory addresses questions such as: How pervasive is the quest for power, and how should power be defined? Given its centrality to IR theory, power in the form of spacepower represents a logical extension of this concept. Spacepower consists of capabilities whose most basic purpose is to control and regulate the use of space. This includes the ability, in the words of the 2006 U.S. National Space Policy, to maintain "freedom of action in space" as vital to national interests. According to the National Space Policy, "United States national security is critically dependent upon space capabilities, and this dependence will grow."

All Presidents since Dwight Eisenhower have stated that preserving freedom of passage in space is a vital U.S. interest that should be protected for all of humankind. Freedom of passage through space represents a norm embodied in the 1967 Outer Space Treaty. This is analogous to sea control, which encompasses freedom of passage in peacetime and the ability to deny an enemy the use of the seas during wartime. In the future, the interests of space powers will be in assuring safe passage for themselves and for their allies, while denying such access to their enemies. In practice, this means that, like the seas, space will become an arena for both competition and cooperation as political issues, including security, are extended from their terrestrial environment into space. Because IR theory has both a descriptive and prescriptive focus on competition and cooperation, it inevitably becomes the basis for speculation and theorization about such relationships in space, including spacepower.

Definitions of spacepower focus on the ability, as Colin Gray points out, to use space and to deny its use to enemies.[2] Spacepower is a multifaceted concept that, like power in IR theory, is "complex, indeterminate, and intangible," as Peter L. Hays put it.[3] Spacepower includes the possession of capabilities to conduct military operations in and from space and to utilize space for commercial and other peaceful purposes. Such capabilities have been increasing in the decades since the first German V2 rockets passed through the outer edge of space en route to their targets in England in the final months of World War II and the Soviets launched the first *Sputnik* in 1957. These events made space a military arena. In recent decades, space has become an essential setting for precision, stealth, command and control, intelligence collection, and maneuverability of weapons systems. In addition to its military uses, space has also become indispensable to civilian communications and a host of other commercial applications. Strategies for dissuasion and deterrence in the 21st century depend heavily on the deployment of capabilities in space. As a concept, spacepower broadens the domain of IR theory from the traditional horizontal geographical configuration of the Earth divided into land and the seas to include the vertical dimension that extends from airspace to outer space.

Because spacepower enables and enhances a state's ability to achieve national security, IR theory will be deficient if it does not give space more prominent consideration. In the decades ahead, spacepower theory and IR theory will draw symbiotically on each other. It is increasingly impossible to envisage one without the other. Space is an arena in which competition and cooperation are already set forth in terms and issues reminiscent of Earth-bound phenomena. Spacepower includes assumptions drawn from IR theory. Our theories about the political behavior of states and other entities in space are extensions of our hypotheses about terrestrial power. To the extent that our theories emphasize competition on Earth, we theorize in similar fashion about such interactions in the domain of space. If we emphasize the need for regimes to codify and regulate Earth-bound relationships, we extend such thinking to the dimension represented by space. Indeed, the ongoing debates about space, including its militarization and weaponization, have direct reference points to IR theory. The inclusion of space in IR theory will evolve as we incorporate space into national security because IR theory, like social science theory in general, is contextual. As E.H. Carr has written: "Purpose, whether we are conscious of it or not, is a condition of thought; and thinking for thinking's sake is as abnormal and barren as the miser's accumulation of money for its own sake."[4] We theorize, or speculate, about relationships among the variables that constitute the world that exists at any time.

However, states in some instances work with other states to develop cooperative arrangements that govern their relationships. It is to be expected that they would undertake efforts to regulate their operations in space as they do on Earth by developing legal and political regimes based on normative standards. Cooperative arrangements are already deemed necessary to prevent the stationing of weapons of mass destruction in space. It is the goal of our adversaries to place limits on U.S. terrestrial activities, and it would be unusual to expect them to try to do otherwise in space. Space becomes another arena for states to attempt to limit the activities of other states and to develop "rules of the road" favorable to their interests and activities. Thus, we have the basis for theory that *prescribes* how political entities in space should possibly interact with each other, including the kinds of regimes and regulations states may seek to develop in space.

At this early stage in space, we have already devoted extensive intellectual energy to prescribing how such entities *should* relate to each other. According to E.H. Carr, because "purpose, or teleology, precedes and conditions thought, at the beginning of the establishment of a new field of inquiry the element of wish is overwhelmingly strong."[5] This leads to normative thinking about how we would like human behavior to evolve in space. Carr was describing IR theory as it developed in the early decades of the 20th century. However, IR theory was erected on a rich base of historical experience dating from the Westphalian state system that had arisen in the mid-17th century. There is as yet no comparable basis for developing and testing theories about political relationships in space. With this important caveat in mind, we turn first to IR theory and spacepower in its geopolitical, or geostrategic, setting and then to other efforts, existing and potential, to theorize about space and to link IR theory to spacepower. Subsequent sections deal with geopolitics, realist theory, liberal theory, and constructivism.

Geopolitics and IR Theory

The process of theorizing about space is most advanced in the area of the geopolitics of the domain. This is a derivative of classical geopolitical theory. According to Everett C. Dolman, geopolitical theory developed for the Earth and its geographical setting can be transferred to outer space with the "strategic application of new and emerging technologies within a framework of geographic, topographic, and positional knowledge."[6] He has developed a construct that he terms *Astropolitik*, defined as "the extension of primarily nineteenth- and twentieth-century theories of global geopolitics into the vast context of the human conquest of outer space."[7] Although space has a unique geography, strategic principles that govern terrestrial geopolitical relationships nevertheless can be applied. States have behavioral characteristics, notably a quest for national security, that exist on Earth but that may also govern state behavior in space, thus opening the way for consideration of those theories about national interest as states acquire interests and capabilities in space. Dolman suggests that geopolitical analysis can be folded into the realist image of interstate competition extended into space.

Geopolitical theory represents a rich and enduring part of the literature of IR theory. In fact, all IR theory is based on environing factors that are physical (geography) and nonphysical (social or cultural), as Harold and Margaret Sprout have pointed out.[8] As the Sprouts recognized, all human behavior takes place in a geographic setting whose features shape what humans do or cannot do. Although geography pertains to the mapping of the Earth's surface, its physical differentiation has important implications for the behavior of the units that inhabit the various parts of the world, for example, as land or sea powers and now space powers. Thus, geography is crucially important. However, the significance of specific aspects of geography, or geographic location, changes as technology changes. For example, technology has exerted a direct influence on how wars are fought and how commercial activity has developed. As the seas became the dominant medium for the movement of trade and commerce, port cities developed. As land transportation evolved, junctions and highway intersections shaped land values. As resource needs changed, the importance of the geographical locations of resources such as reserves of coal or oil rose. If vitally important natural resources are found in abundance in certain locations in space, their geopolitical importance will be enhanced. The exploitation of such resources may become the basis for international cooperation or competition in order to secure or preserve access.

Central in the writings of classical geopolitical theorists such as Alfred Thayer Mahan and Sir Halford Mackinder is the direct relationship between technology and power projection. As long as technology favored the extension of power over the oceans (Mahan), those states most fully able to build and deploy naval forces were preeminent. The advent of the technological means for rapid movement of large forces over land (Mackinder), and subsequently for flight through the Earth's atmosphere, transformed not only the ways in which war could be waged, but also the hierarchy of states with the necessary capabilities. Thus, there was a close relationship between technology and the utilization, both for military and civilian purposes, of the Earth's surfaces— maritime and land—as well as the surrounding atmosphere and exosphere. Such a frame of reference emerges from the analysis of historic technological-strategic-economic relationships. Similarly, the existence of technologies for the transport of formerly Earth-bound objects into outer space has implications for both military and civilian activities at least as great as those changes that accompanied the great technological innovations of the past.

Historically, geopolitical theorists tell us, technology has had the effect of altering the significance of specific spatial relationships. The advent of the airplane, and subsequently the means to penetrate outer space, provided a whole new dimension to geopolitics. As long as human activities were restricted to the Earth's surface, they were subject to constraints imposed by the terrain. Although the seas are uniform in character, human mobility via the oceans is limited by the coastlines that surround them. No such constraints exist above the Earth's surface, in airspace or in outer space. In this environment, the possibilities of unprecedented mobility and speed enable states to seek either to protect their interests or project their power. For such purposes, they may exploit opportunities for surveillance, reconnaissance, and verification, as well as the potential afforded by space as an arena for offensive and defensive operations.

Just as geopolitical theorists have set forth their ideas about the political significance of specific geographical features, comparable efforts have been made to address "geography" in space. Writing on the geopolitics of space focuses on gravity and orbits. Gravity is said to be the most important factor in the topography of space because it shapes the "hills and valleys" of space, which are known as *gravity wells*. A simple astropolitical (geopolitical) proposition has been set forth: the more massive the body, such as a planet or moon, the deeper the gravity well. The expenditure of energy in travel from one point to another in space is less dependent on distance than on the effort expended to break out of gravitational pull to get from one point to another. The geographical regions of space have been divided into near Earth orbit, extending about 22,300 miles from the Earth's surface; cislunar space, extending from geosynchronous orbit to the Moon's orbit and including the geopolitically important Lagrange libration points, discussed below; and translinear space, extending from an orbit beyond the Moon, where the gravitational pull of the Sun becomes greater than that of the Earth, to the edge of the solar system.[9]

As with the Earth, an understanding of the geopolitics of space emerges initially from efforts to delineate the physical dimensions of the space environment. We need not review in great detail the literature on this important topic. What should be immediately obvious, however, is the limited applicability of the national sovereignty concept that governs nation-state relationships on Earth. The farther one ventures into space, the more difficult it becomes to determine what is above any one point on Earth. States can assert exclusive jurisdiction within their airspace because it lies in close proximity to their sovereign territory and they are more likely to have the means to enforce their claim to exclusive jurisdiction. Of course, this calculation could be changed by the development and deployment of capabilities constituting spacepower. The Earth and its atmosphere have been likened to the coastal areas of the seas on Earth. The high sea of Earth space is accessible only after we are able to break through the Earth's atmosphere or, in the case of the high seas, to pass beyond the coastal waters.

Earth space is the environment in which reconnaissance and navigation satellites currently operate. It is the setting in which space-based military systems, including space-based missile defense, would be deployed. Beyond this segment of space lies the lunar region encompassing the Moon's orbit. It is of special importance because it contains the Lagrange libration points where the gravitational effects of the Earth and Moon would cancel each other out. As Marc Vaucher pointed out in a seminal paper on the geopolitics of space, the military and commercial importance of these points is vast.[10] They are at the top of the gravity well of cislunar space, meaning that structures placed there could remain permanently in place. Because of the effects of the Sun, however, only two of the five Lagrange libration points (L4 and L5) are regarded as stable.

Finally, as we venture from lunar space, we would enter the solar space that lies beyond the Moon's orbit, encompasses the planets and asteroids of the solar system, and exists within the gravity well of the Sun. As already noted, the asteroids are feared as objects that could eventually collide with the Earth and end life as we know it. Alternatively, they could represent the new frontier of space exploration. In this latter case, asteroids become the basis for stations in space en route to the Moon or from Earth or Moon to other planets. Asteroids are said to acquire geostrategic importance as their potential for enhancing space travel increases.

Realist Theory and Spacepower

In order to understand its implications for spacepower, realist theory can be examined in each of its three major variations. These include *classical* realist theory as set forth by Hans Morgenthau;[11] *structural* realist theory developed by Kenneth Waltz;[12] and *neoclassical* realist theory.[13] What has made realist theory as a whole such a prominent part of the IR theory landscape is its multidimensionality, including hypotheses that can be generated at each of the levels of analysis of IR theorizing: the international system, the units that comprise the international system, and the behavioral characteristics of the units themselves. Among the key variables of realist theory, in addition to power, is the concept of competing national interests in a world of anarchy, with states comprising an international system that requires them to rely extensively on their own means of survival or to join alliances or coalitions with others sharing their interests. Although realist theory does not (yet) contain an extensive emphasis on space, it is possible to derive from its variants numerous ideas as a basis for further IR theory development. We begin with national interest.

According to classical realist theory, the territorial state pursues national interest, which is defined by a variety of factors such as geography, ideology, resources, and capabilities based on the need to ensure its survival in a world of anarchy. Because international politics is a struggle for power, it can easily be inferred that spacepower is a manifestation of such a struggle. With the advent of space technologies, national interest now includes space. If international rivalries on Earth are being projected into space, theories about how states deal with them on Earth can also be extended into space. Because technologically advanced states are heavily dependent on space-based assets, the ability to defend or destroy such assets becomes a key national security concern, as in the case of the United States. Although states are the current entities that may threaten the space capabilities of other states, not-so-distant future challenges may come from terrorist groups capable, for example, of launching an electromagnetic pulse attack that would destroy or disable vital electronic infrastructures, including telecommunications, transportation, and banking and other financial infrastructures, and food production and distribution systems.[14] Such a threat would arise from a nuclear weapon detonated 80 to 400 kilometers above the Earth's surface directly over the United States or adjacent to its territory. However, those entities best able to safeguard their Earth-bound interests through the exploitation of new technologies are also likely to be able to utilize space for that purpose.

Space is a new frontier that will be exploited as part of an inevitable and enduring struggle for power. This is the obvious lens through which adherents of the realist theory would view space. More than 40 years ago, President John F. Kennedy expressed this idea when he declared, "The exploration of space will go ahead, whether we join in it or not, and it is one of the great adventures of all time, and no nation which expects to be the leader of other nations can expect to stay behind in the race for space."[15] In the absence of space leadership, states will lose preeminence on Earth. In recognition of this essential fact, competition in space began as soon as technologies became feasible. During the Cold War, the Soviet Union challenged the United States in space. Such statements are fully in keeping with classical realist theory.

In the 21st century, the United States faces increasing numbers of states whose power and prestige will be enhanced by their space programs. Therefore, with the advent of space technologies, a new dimension has been added to the national interest concept of realist theory. The fact that several states have developed national space programs highlights the relevance of realist theory in helping to explain why states acquire those programs. As already noted, space has begun to be utilized in support of the national interest. That the competition characteristic of terrestrial political relationships would be extended to space as soon as technologies for this purpose became feasible is implicit in realist theory. This includes the ballistic missiles dating from World War II and satellites that had their origins in the national security needs for reconnaissance, surveillance, and communications during the Cold War. The U.S.-Soviet competition included an increasingly important space component that would only have grown more intense if the rivalry had gone on for many more years. The dependence of technologically advanced states on space, together with their resulting vulnerability to attack in and from space, contributes to the relevance of realist theory to the analysis of space and national security.

Realist theory also contains the assumption that states rely ultimately on themselves for survival in the anarchical world of international politics. As sovereign entities, states (more accurately, their decisionmakers) determine for themselves how they will ensure their survival based on perceptions of national interest. Central to such theory is independence, including capabilities that increase the latitude available to states to help themselves to survive without outside assistance. Such theory may describe well the problems that entities in space will confront, perhaps only mitigated by vast distances separating them from each other and minimizing the contact that is essential for conflict, while also rendering impossible substantial levels of outside help. What is assumed in realist theory about self-help on Earth may be amply magnified in space if and when its colonization moves forward. Nevertheless, the vast distances that separate entities in space may drastically limit the possibility of armed conflict, as we have known it on Earth, between space-based entities on distant planets or asteroids. Even to begin to speculate about such behavior is to demonstrate the great latitude for divergent perspectives about conflict and cooperation.

Because national interest can best be understood within a geographical setting, the political dimension of geography is integral to realist theory. It has been noted that IR theorizing about spacepower begins with space-related geopolitical analysis that cannot be separated from national interest. Realist theory thus provides insights into the basis for national space policies. According to realist theory, states that are able to develop vast terrestrial capabilities are likely to extend their reach into space as technologies for this purpose become available. The private sector becomes a vital source of innovation in the most advanced economies. Because developed states, and especially the United States, have greater technological capabilities to operate in space, they are likely to favor a substantial role for the private sector, together with international regimes that regulate the use of space and protect the ability of public and private sector entities to operate there. Developing countries that cannot afford to divert resources to space or simply lack such capabilities are more likely to favor the extension of the common heritage principle to space while attempting to place drastic limits on developed countries and perhaps calling for mandatory transfers of space technology to developing countries. Such countries view space through a different prism of national interest, seeking to restrict or retard more developed states from exercising full control or from maximizing spacepower. Such behavior on the part of states large and small with regard to space issues is in keeping with realist theory. Each state operates according to perceptions of national interest.

Structural realist theory offers other insights into future space relationships. According to Kenneth Waltz, the international structure shapes the options available to units (in this case, states). In particular, the international structure is key to understanding unit-level behavior. *Structure* is defined as the type and number of units and their respective capabilities. The type and number of states have changed dramatically over time. New technologies have conferred unprecedented capabilities, including interactive capacity, on the states comprising the international system. Levels of interdependence have increased greatly. The foreign policy options available to states differ between bipolar and multipolar international systems.

Structure shapes how states align with or against each other. We have already begun to consider the structural characteristics of space if we assume that the planets and their lunar satellites constitute the principal units. The geography of space, including where units are strategically situated, provides an important basis for theorizing about their relative importance, first, to states and other units on Earth and, eventually, perhaps with each other. The physical sciences, including astronomy, have already provided vast knowledge about how these units of the solar system relate to each other and to the Sun. IR theories will be enriched as we move into space and develop political relationships that become the basis for theorizing about the sociopolitical entities that will comprise space-based actors. Earlier, the suggestion was made that the unique characteristics of space, including distances and other features, will shape interactive patterns within and among space-based political units. Space colonies may have to operate with great independence because they cannot rely on a Mother Earth that would be possibly light years distant. If such assertions are true, they provide insights into how structure, extrapolated from structural realist theory, would shape unit behavior in space. Perhaps this would resemble in some ways the extremely limited preindustrial interactive capacity on Earth when communications between widely separated groups were few and often nonexistent.

Compared to present terrestrial international structures, space structures are likely to remain at a very rudimentary level. As technology develops, however, it is not fanciful to anticipate that parts of the solar system will be linked in unprecedented fashion as the ability to project spacepower rises, thus giving new meaning to space structure. Like the proliferation of capabilities leading to new power centers and globalization on Earth, it is possible to envisage such an analogy in space someday. This might include space stations or capabilities in space controlled from Earth. It might also encompass space colonization and the creation of new interactive capacity and patterns in space such as those that take place among Earth-based units. In the absence of colonization from Earth as took place in the age of European expansion, structural analogies in outer space are obviously premature.

However, a major theme of this chapter is that space exploration and exploitation will create interactive patterns that in themselves become the basis for theory and its testing. What constitutes those capabilities and how they are distributed among political units will be essential to understanding space structures. This may eventually become another level of analysis supplementing the existing levels for understanding the source of unit behavior. For example, as already discussed, we have begun to factor space into IR theory about power relationships. Space control is held by many to be indispensable to power on Earth. The extent to which options available to states at one or more levels are shaped by spacepower providing for space control contributes to space as an increasingly important level of analysis in itself. According to such theory, spacepower becomes the essential basis for Earthpower. If entities are to be dominant on Earth, they must control space. If space control shapes the foreign policy options available to states on Earth, then such theorizing about space replaces or supplements the international system level as the key echelon of analysis if we move beyond the structural realist theory of Kenneth Waltz.

Structural realist theory attaches great importance to the numbers and types of actors, the distribution of capabilities among them, and their interactive capabilities. For example, to think about globalization today is to understand the growing importance of telecommunications, including the Internet and broadband. Only recently has the Earth been wired for instantaneous communications. Interactive capacity translates into greater interaction that, in turn, creates systemic relationships leading to higher levels of specialization and interdependence. Systems as the outgrowth of structures represent a major focal point of IR theory. Astronomers have accumulated great knowledge about the behavior of the units comprising the solar system, including how such units relate to each other and how they are arranged in the solar system. Our theories about the social-political behavior of such units will evolve as social or political systems. This means that space first will affect interactive patterns, as we already see, of Earthly units with each other. Subsequently, the space-based interactive patterns that will become the object of theorizing are likely to differ dramatically from those on Earth because of factors such as vast distances measured in light years. The social-political solar system will remain far more primitive in its development than Earthly international systems, barring major advances in space technologies. Nevertheless, it is possible to make use of IR theory focused on structure and system to speculate about such space relationships.

Neoclassical realist theory also provides a basis for discussing spacepower and IR theory. The effort to refine neorealist theory includes an understanding of the conditions under which states choose whether competition or cooperation is the preferred option. Although its overall power and the place of the state in the international system decisively shape actor choices, foreign policy, potentially including spacepower, is the result of choices based on perceptions, values, and other domestic-level factors. Thus, the neoclassical realist literature brings together international systems and unit-level variables based on the assumption that foreign policy is the result of complex patterns of interaction within and between both levels. Neoclassical realist theory rethinks power in its offensive and defensive components, including the circumstances under which states seek security in an anarchic setting by developing military forces to deter or defend against an adversary as well as the level and types of capabilities that are deemed sufficient to ensure one state's security without threatening the other side's ability to deter or defend. Such issues are easily identifiable in discussions about spacepower.

A variant of neoclassical realist theory, called contingent-realist theory, emphasizes what is termed the *offense-defense balance*, defined as the ratio of the cost of offensive forces to the cost of defensive capabilities. Contingent-realist theory provides a theoretical basis for examining when and how states, in a self-help system, decide to cooperate as a means of resolving the security dilemma. Entirely consistent with such IR theory, space affords yet another setting for states to develop cooperative or competitive relationships. To the extent that domestic preferences shape the foreign policy of democratic states, we also come close to democratic peace theory. Domestic factors help mold foreign policy preferences, including support for cooperation or competition. Such neoclassical realist thought leads logically to a discussion about, and possible integration of, other IR theories into theory about space, including neoliberal and especially democratic peace theory.

Neoliberal Theories and Space

Just as space can be viewed as an area for competition, so can it also be the basis for cooperation. Such an assertion opens for consideration a spectrum of IR theory beyond neoclassical realist theory to be applied to our thinking about space. For example, democratic peace theory (DPT) posits that states defined as liberal democracies do not go to war with other liberal democracies. Such states are more likely to cooperate with each other in space activities than they are with totalitarian governments in space or in other endeavors—although the United States and the Soviet Union developed cooperative relationships with each other during the Cold War. Liberal democracies in disputes with other liberal democracies are likely to resolve their disagreements by means other than armed conflict. It is primarily in democracies that debates about the militarization and weaponization of space take place. Presumably, democracies that provide the basis for colonization or other interactive patterns in space would carry with them the values that could shape their behavior in space, just as the seeds of American democracy were planted by the British colonists who settled in the New World. Could we conceive of the colonization of space leading to forms of government pitting democratic colonies against those from nondemocratic states on Earth? Such is the logic of DPT extended into space. However, it is plausible to suggest that the rigors of space will test Earthly values in environments drastically different than those that exist on Earth, necessitating dramatic changes in political and social relationships. Such a suggestion is fully in keeping with the assumption that environing factors shape the options available to humans, whether on Earth or in space, just as humans make concerted efforts to alter the environment to meet their needs. The interactive process between humans and their environment has provided an enduring focal point for IR theory and other social science theory.

As they develop a presence in space as an adjunct to their terrestrial interests, democracies and other states have already begun to form regimes that codify normative standards designed to facilitate cooperation based on agreed procedures and processes as well as common interests and shared values about space-related activities. Those regimes may be formal or informal. Formal regimes may be the result of legislation by international organizations that are themselves established by democracies and other states having an interest in such arrangements. Such formal regimes may possess governing councils and bureaucratic structures. In contrast, informal regimes may be based simply on consensus about objectives and the interests of the participants. Therefore, it is possible to envisage regimes in space or on space issues based on a convergence of interests in keeping with realist theory or as the outgrowth of the cooperative values of democracies.

The liberal world vision holds that states and their actors engage in mutually rewarding exchanges, including trade based on specialization and comparative advantage. Cooperation benefits states as well as individuals and groups that become increasingly interdependent. Order emerges as self-interested units in an anarchic setting cooperate for mutual benefit. In other words, cooperation may be based on national interests, an idea that is compatible with realist theory. Liberal theory holds that cooperation in one sector may produce satisfaction that enhances incentives to collaborate in additional sectors, leading to what Ernst Haas termed "spillover" or the "expansive logic of sector integration."[16] Just as advances in technology have led to the emergence of a single global system and international society, neo-liberal theory posits that the extension of man's reach into the solar system and ultimately the broader universe will enhance the need for cooperation. Both as an expression of the values of a liberal democracy set forth in DPT and as a matter of self interest, cooperation becomes an essential part of liberal IR theory about space relationships. We do not currently know whether outer space will reinforce the competitive dimension or create the need for greater cooperation within and among the emerging entities that will populate space. We may hypothesize that the demands of life in outer space may enhance the need for cooperation, but we may also consider the pursuit of clashing interests between contending groups for control of key space geopolitical positions and assets. The answer to such questions, of course, holds important implications for the relevance of one IR theory or another to space. At this point in time, however, neoliberal theory, like realist theory, has much to offer as we speculate about space relationships.

Constructivism

Another approach (and a fertile one) to theorizing about space flows from constructivism. Whereas much of IR theory usually focuses on relationships among structures that shape the behavior of units or agents, and how interactive capacity leads to interactive patterns (systems), constructivism views the world in a fundamentally different way. In the constructivist image, the building blocks of international society can be best understood by analysis of rules, practices, agents, statements, social arrangements, and relationships. Constructivism is not a theory, but instead an ontology, an understanding of the nature of being, a way of looking at the world. The world is constantly being "constructed" and therefore changed as new geopolitical, geoeconomic, or geostrategic changes take place. Such changes occur in a setting in which a "vast part of the planet [is] also changing 'internal' ways of running [its] political, economic, and social affairs. No part of the world can avoid these changes or their consequences; the entire world is continuously 'under construction.'"[17] What this means is that theories based on phenomena such as states, balances of power, anarchy, or national interest are inadequate, if not misleading, because they are abstractions that are "constructed" in our minds rather than being objects having concrete reality. Instead, human relationships are inherently social in that they are defined by the social arrangements made by individuals or groups who are endowed with free will. What is acceptable in the form of human behavior at one point in time may not be acceptable in a subsequent phase. For example, the role of women in Western society has been altered dramatically in the past century. Practices that were once commonplace are no longer deemed acceptable. People are constantly changing and redefining their relationships based on the practices and rules that they create. Therefore, they are free of the material inanimate factor termed *structure*. Translated into IR theory and space, this means that we have the ability to create, or construct, the types of arrangements that we may wish to have for space. What is important is how we think about and construct "rules rather than imaginary, artificially unified entities such as states or structures. Rules have ontological substance; they are there for anybody to see."[18]

Rules of behavior are the result of a changing intersubjective consensus that arises over time from discussions, thought, and action. Just as geopolitics addresses the physical environment, constructivism deals with the ideational setting. What we have, according to Nicholas Onuf, a leader in constructivist thought, is a continuous "two way process" in which "people make society, and society makes people."[19] As a result of such interaction, we develop rules of behavior within institutions and elsewhere. In other words, we construct reality as well as our respective individual, group, and national identities. It is not a great leap in logic to consider space as an arena in which rules of behavior, first derived from Earthly experience and subsequently evolving in light of new factors, lead to the construction of newer rules governing behavior as well as identities. According to constructivism, new values and expectations are created that become embedded in growing numbers of people and spread to broader epistemic communities, defined as elites with a shared understanding of a particular subject. Presumably, the organizers of this project and its participants fall within this category as they develop an ideational basis for thinking about and developing strategies for spacepower. Such epistemic communities create a strategy for achieving their goals and play a major innovative role. For the constructivist, the essential issue is how such a process will play itself out in sectors of importance such as space. Whoever constructs rules of behavior that can be applied to space will determine what those rules are, at least to the extent that we are dealing with political/social relationships.

Conclusion

This chapter has briefly surveyed four major perspectives or IR theories. Greater depth and analysis are required to encompass the more extensive IR theory. This includes theories of conflict and war, deterrence and dissuasion, cooperation, integration, and political community. To what extent, for example, will the clashes that take place on Earth have counterparts in space, and what can conflict theory suggest to us about their parameters? By the same token, what can be hypothesized about the forces making for greater community and integration, including nationalism and identity, that would have direct relevance to space? Although we can only speculate about the answers to such questions, IR theory provides a useful point of departure for such an exercise.

IR theory rests on contending and contrasting assumptions about relationships between international units, including states and other actors. Even having far less knowledge of space than we have about the Earth, we have already begun to transfer beliefs about Earth-bound interactions into our thinking about the behavior of states in space. However, space has already become an arena for competition and cooperation. IR theory offers alternative explanations about international competition and cooperation. The emphasis that we place on competition or cooperation may depend on the IR theory or theories on which we choose to rely. This we already do in the case of terrestrial international relationships. To the extent that we envisage space as an arena for growing competition based on an inevitable quest for power, we will be drawn to realist theory. If we emphasize the cooperative dimension, we will likely embrace assumptions derived from liberal theory. Because the stakes are immense, how we theorize about space, drawing on existing and yet-to-be-developed IR and other social science theories, will have major implications for strategies and policies. Because no single IR theory capable of describing, explaining, or prescribing political behavior on Earth exists, we cannot expect to find otherwise in space. Therefore, it is important to recognize the inherent limitations in extrapolating from Earthly IR theory to space, while also drawing wherever possible on such theory as we probe farther into space.

Notes

[1] Martin Ira Glassner, *Political Geography* (New York: John Wiley and Sons, Inc., 1993), 519.

[2] Colin S. Gray, "The Influence of Space Power upon History," *Comparative Strategy* 15, no. 4 (October–December 1996), 293–308.

[3] Peter L. Hays, *United States Military Space: Into the Twenty-first Century* (Maxwell Air Force Base, AL: Air University Press, 2002).

[4] E.H. Carr, *The Twenty Years' Crisis 1919–1939: An Introduction to the Study of International Relations* (New York: Palgrave, 2001), 4.

[5] Ibid., 6.

[6] Everett C. Dolman, "Geostrategy in the Space Age: An Astropolitical Analysis," in *Geopolitics: Geography and Strategy*, ed. Colin S. Gray and Geoffrey Sloan (London and Portland, OR: Frank Cass, 1999), 83.

[7] Everett C. Dolman, *Astropolitik: Classical Geopolitics in the Space Age* (London and Portland, OR: Frank Cass, 2002), 1.

[8] Harold and Margaret Sprout, *The Ecological Perspective on Human Affairs with Special Reference to International Politics* (Princeton: Princeton University Press, 1965), 27.

⁹ Marc E. Vaucher, "Geographical Parameters for Military Doctrine in Space and the Defense of the Space-Based Enterprise," in *International Security Dimensions of Space*, ed. Uri Ra'anan and Robert L. Pfaltzgraff, Jr. (Hamden, CT: Archon Books, 1984), 34.

¹⁰ Ibid., 32–46.

¹¹ See especially Hans Morgenthau, *Politics among Nations: The Struggle for Power and Peace* (New York: Alfred A. Knopf, 1960), 3–15.

¹² Kenneth M. Waltz, *Theory of International Politics* (Reading, MA: Addison-Wesley, 1979).

¹³ See, for example, Gideon Rose, "Neoclassical Realism and Theories of Foreign Policy," *World Politics* (October 1998), 144–172. See also Fareed Zakaria, "Realism and Domestic Politics," *International Security* 17, no. 1 (Summer 1997), 162–183; Charles L. Glaser, "Realists as Optimists: Cooperation as Self-Help," *International Security* 19, no. 3 (Winter 1994/1995), 50–90.

¹⁴ This type of threat is described and discussed in the *Report of the Commission to Assess the Threat to the United States from Electromagnetic Pulse (EMP) Attack*, vol. 1, Executive Report (2004).

¹⁵ John F. Kennedy, address at Rice University on the Nation's Space Effort, Houston, Texas, September 12, 1962, available at <www.jfklibrary.org/Historical+Resources/Archives/Reference+Desk/Speeches/JFK/003POF03SpaceEffort09121962.htm>.

¹⁶ Ernst Haas, *Beyond the Nation-State* (Stanford: Stanford University Press, 1964), 48.

¹⁷ Vendulka Kubalokova, Nicholas Onuf, and Paul Kowert, eds., *International Relations in a Constructed World* (Armonk, NY: M.E. Sharpe, 1998).

¹⁸ Ibid., xii.

¹⁹ Nicholas Onuf, "Constructivism: A User's Manual," in *International Relations in a Constructed World*, 59.

Chapter 4

Real Constraints on Spacepower

Martin E.B. France and Jerry Jon Sellers

Any discussion of the bases and tenets of spacepower must begin with a solid understanding of the governing physical laws, environment, advantages, and difficulties inherent in space systems and their operations.[1] While conferring significant advantages on those who can operate there effectively, space presents unique challenges and high development costs, both monetarily and experientially. After all, it *is* rocket science. Beyond the equations, too, there exist the complex systems definition and engineering needed to "operationalize" space and bring its effects to the user in a timely and affordable fashion. From definition of the basic need to delivery of a given capability, the variety of technical, programmatic, and acceptable risk issues that must be defined before any spacepower can be sustained or developed is daunting. Theorists and users must realize that, even on the strategic level, there are irreducible sets of knowledge, understanding, and trades that form the foundation of space competency. The purpose of this chapter is to highlight these key concepts, serving as a review for some readers, an overview for others, and (we hope) a motivation for all to continue to hone their space expertise.

Advantages of Space

Getting into space is dangerous and expensive. So why bother? The five primary advantages space offers for modern society are:

- global perspective

- clear view of the heavens

- free-fall environment

- abundant resources

■ unique challenge as the final frontier.

While each of these benefits plays a role in defining a nation's space-power, they may not be equally valued.

Clearly, the global perspective provided by space is a primary motivator for deploying commercial, civil, military, and scientific systems there. Space takes the quest for greater perspective to its ultimate end, allowing access to large areas of the Earth's surface depending upon orbital specifics. Orbiting spacecraft can thus serve as "eyes and ears in the sky" to provide a variety of useful services.

The high ground, once achieved, makes possible several other capabilities that may reinforce a nation's space and economic power. Scientifically, space offers a clear view of the heavens. From the Earth's surface, the atmosphere blurs, blocks, and disturbs (scintillates) visible light and other electromagnetic radiation, frustrating astronomers who need access to all the regions of the electromagnetic spectrum to explore the universe. Spacecraft such as the Hubble Space Telescope and the Gamma Ray Observatory overcome this restriction and have revolutionized our understanding of the cosmos.

Space offers a free-fall environment enabling manufacturing processes not possible on the Earth's surface. Though certainly not exploited to date for other than experimental value, the potential to manufacture exotic compounds for computer components or pharmaceutical products exists.

Further downstream, space offers abundant resources. While spacecraft now use only one of these abundant resources—solar energy—the bounty of the solar system offers an untapped reserve of minerals and energy to sustain future exploration and colonization. In the not-too-distant future, lunar resources, or even those from the asteroids, might fuel a growing space-based economy.

Finally, space serves simply as a frontier. The human condition has always improved as new frontiers were challenged. As a stimulus for technological advances and a crucible for creating economic expansion, space offers a limitless challenge that compels national and global attention. The act of exploration—across oceans or prairies in the past, and in this case pushing back the frontiers of space—has long been a wellspring of pride and an expression of power.

Turning Need into Capability

From an engineer's perspective, spacepower can be viewed as the exploitation of space-based systems (and the natural laws governing them) to achieve national political or economic ends. Maintaining and expanding a nation's spacepower hinges on the ability to define the need for new systems and turn those needs into capabilities that policymakers and warfighters can exploit. The purpose of the space systems acquisition process is to translate those needs into capable systems. The technical foundation of space systems acquisition is systems engineering. Fundamentally, the space systems engineering process leverages one or more of the advantages of space outlined above to turn needs, as defined by policymakers and warfighters, into operational capabilities. The more clearly the needs for these systems are articulated in terms of performance, cost, and schedule goals, the better systems engineers can make realistic tradeoffs to achieve those goals with acceptable risk.

Ultimately, the intended goals and objectives of the system become defined in terms of *requirements*—single, testable *shall* statements that define what the system will be or shall do and how well. Bounding the universe of possible solutions for any problem are *constraints*. The difference between a requirement and a constraint is really a matter of perspective. One person's requirement for a given mechanical interface as defined by a specific bolt pattern becomes a constraint from the standpoint of the designer of the interface plate. Some requirements are imposed on a system for practical, political, or economic reasons and are arguably negotiable at some pay grade, while some constraints, such as the laws of physics or the real state of the art, are not subject to negotiation. The remainder of this chapter will focus on understanding the source of requirements and constraints on space systems—and thus ultimately on spacepower—that form the realm of the possible. Fortunately, this realm is vast, offering many as-yet-untapped capabilities. But the better we understand the limits of this realm, the better we will manage scarce resources to achieve best systems—and hence capabilities—to enhance spacepower.

Mission Architectures

The increasing complexity and interoperability of space systems have lead to discussions of "systems of systems" or, more broadly, *mission architectures*. A space mission architecture includes all of the space and ground elements needed to make the mission successful. A mission architecture includes the spacecraft (including payload and bus), operating in a specific orbit, interacting with some subject (see figure 4–1). The spacecraft is placed into orbit by a launch vehicle and is operated using a defined communication architecture that uses ground stations and operators. At the heart of the architecture are the objectives, requirements, and other factors that define the mission concept.

Figure 4–1. Mission Architecture

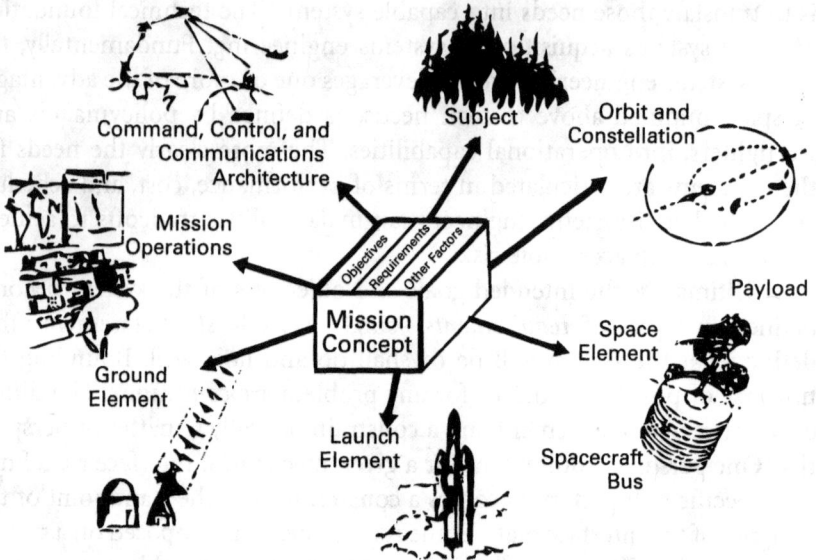

Command, Control, and Communications Architecture

Subject

Orbit and Constellation

Mission Operations

Objectives Requirements Other Factors

Mission Concept

Payload

Space Element

Ground Element

Launch Element

Spacecraft Bus

Source: James R. Wertz and Wiley J. Larson, eds., *Space Mission Analysis and Design*, 3ᵈ ed. (Dordrecht, Netherlands: Kluwer Academic Publishers, 1999).

Defining Requirements, Understanding Constraints

As stated earlier, the need desired by the policymaker or warfighter must eventually be articulated as a set of design-to, build-to, and test-to requirements by the systems engineer during the acquisition process. If we consider only technical requirements (the focus of this chapter), we can divide these requirements into a number of basic categories (similar to those specified by Military Standard-961c, "Preparation of Military Specifications and Associated Documents"). Within these broad categories, we can further define a number of typical requirements identified for military missions. These requirements are in turn specified by some number of detailed performance parameters. Finally, these parameters are constrained by a number of factors (see table 4–1). The point of this exercise is to distill the broad operational requirements normally levied on space systems down to a handful of constraining factors that affect them. The reader will notice a number of recurring themes that affect myriad types of requirements—for example, orbital mechanics. The balance of this chapter will explore these constraining factors to understand the possibilities and limits they pose on spacepower capabilities.

Table 4–1. Space Mission and Constraints

Requirement Category	Typical Requirement	Specified by	Constrained by
Performance	Resolution	Spatial resolution Spectral resolution Radiometric resolution Temporal resolution	Orbital mechanics Remote sensing physics
	Data rate	Bits per second	Communication physics
	Coverage	Latitude/longitude ranges	Orbital mechanics
	Maneuverability	Delta-V	Orbital mechanics Space launch and rocket propulsion
Interfaces	Spacecraft-to-launch vehicle	Mechanical bolt pattern, connectors pin in/out description	Space launch and rocket propulsion
	Spacecraft-to-ground segment	Data rates, frequencies, modulation schemes, encryption methods	Communication physics
	Spacecraft-to-spacecraft	Data rates, frequencies, modulation schemes, encryption methods, Doppler shifts	Communication physics
Physical Characteristics	Spacecraft mass, volume Constellation Description	Mass, volume, number of satellites, number of orbit planes, spacing of orbit planes	Spacecraft state of the art Orbital mechanics

(continued)

Requirement Category	Typical Requirement	Specified by	Constrained by
Operational Environments	Launch environment Space environment	Vibration, thermal, acoustic, radio frequency gravitational, vacuum, neutral atmospheric, charged particles, radiation, micrometeoroid/orbital debris	Space launch and rocket propulsion Space environment
System Quality	Lifetime operability	Reliability Orbit lifetime Autonomy, interfaces	Spacecraft state of the art Orbital mechanics Space launch and rocket propulsion
Design	Technical risk	Technology readiness levels Design standards	Spacecraft state of the art

Orbital Mechanics

Simply put, an orbit is achieved when an object is moving fast enough that the Earth's curved surface is falling away from it faster than the object itself is pulled to the Earth by gravity. The velocity of the object (or spacecraft, for our purposes) and its position relative to the Earth define the specific orbit in which it moves. At ground level, an object would need a velocity of approximately 7.9 kilometers (km) per second (tangent to the Earth's surface) to effectively "fall" around the Earth—neglecting aerodynamic drag, of course. This motion is governed by Newton's second law of motion and law of gravitation and assumes that the spacecraft acts as a constant point mass, its mass is insignificant relative to the Earth's, the Earth is a perfect sphere, and no other forces (drag, thrust, solar, or lunar gravity, and so forth) are acting upon our spacecraft. These assumptions represent the requirements for the "restricted two-body problem," for which Newton's solution describes the spacecraft's location using two constants and a polar angle and represents a general relationship for any conic section (circle, ellipse, parabola, or hyperbola).

Describing Orbits

For the most useful case in this study, we consider the elliptical Earth orbit defined by the parameters shown in figure 4–2.

Figure 4–2. Elliptical Orbit Parameters

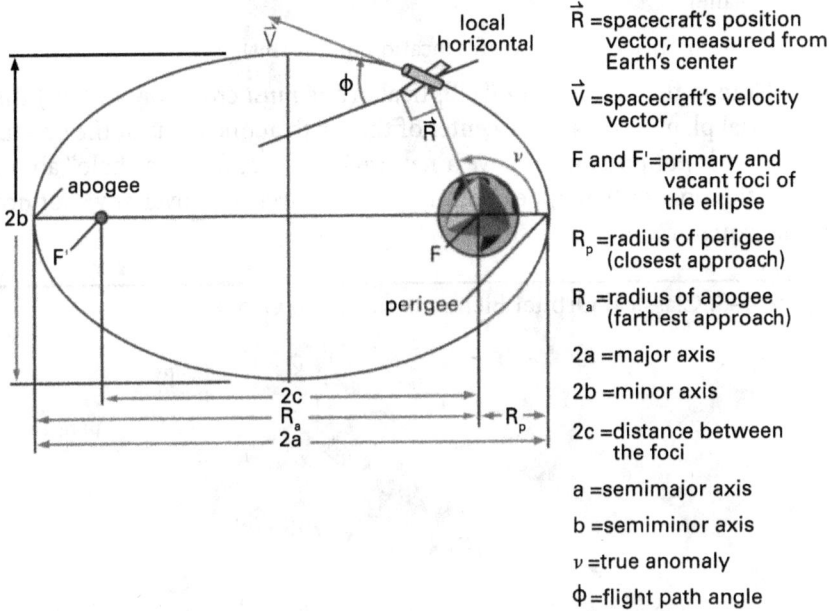

$\vec{R}$ =spacecraft's position vector, measured from Earth's center

$\vec{V}$ =spacecraft's velocity vector

F and F'=primary and vacant foci of the ellipse

R_p =radius of perigee (closest approach)

R_a =radius of apogee (farthest approach)

2a =major axis

2b =minor axis

2c =distance between the foci

a =semimajor axis

b =semiminor axis

ν =true anomaly

ϕ =flight path angle

Source: Jerry J. Sellers et al., *Understanding Space: An Introduction to Astronautics*, 3ᵈ ed. (New York: McGraw-Hill, 2005), figure 4–33.

With no other forces acting upon the satellite, both total mechanical energy and angular momentum of the spacecraft remain constant throughout its orbit—consistent with Newton's laws of motion and the fact that gravity is a conservative force field. While in elliptical orbit, then, the satellite is constantly exchanging potential energy and kinetic energy, moving from apogee to perigee and back. At *apogee*—the highest point in an orbit—the satellite is moving slowest, while at *perigee*, the lowest point, it is moving fastest.

Operational orbits can be described in terms of six classical orbital elements (COEs) that describe their physical properties (see figure 4–3):

- semimajor axis, a (orbital size)

- eccentricity, e (orbital shape)

- inclination, I (orientation of the orbital plane with respect to the equatorial plane)

- right ascension of the ascending node, Ω (orientation of the orbital plane with respect to the Earth-centered reference frame)

- argument of perigee, ω (orientation of the orbit within its orbital plane)

- true anomaly, n (spacecraft's location in its orbit).

Note in the figure that *all* elliptical orbits *must* cross (or contain) the equatorial plane and have the center of the Earth at one focus of the orbital ellipse.[2] It is *not* possible to have a natural orbit that forms a "halo" above the Earth's pole or that appears motionless ("hovering") over any spot not on the equator.

Figure 4–3. Classical Orbital Elements for Earth Orbits

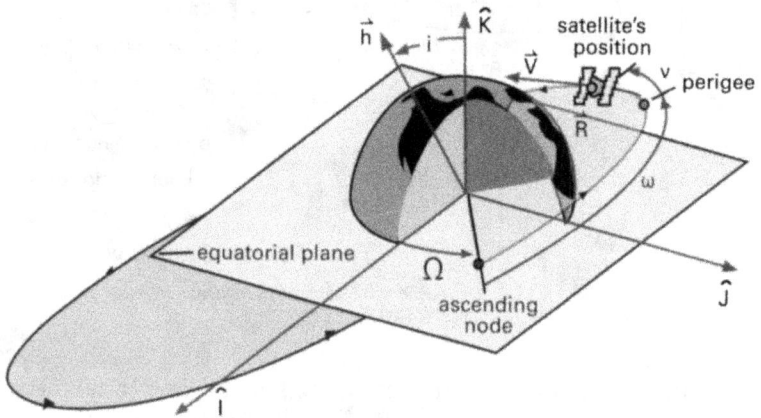

Source: Jerry J. Sellers et al., *Understanding Space: An Introduction to Astronautics,* 3[d] ed. (New York: McGraw-Hill, 2005), figure 5–9.

Earth-orbiting space missions supporting civil, commercial, and military objectives generally fall into one of four categories: communications, remote sensing, navigation and timing, and scientific. The previously presented physical laws governing spacecraft motion form the realm of the possible for which specific mission requirements can be met. The orbit's size, shape, and orientation determine whether the spacecraft payload can observe its target subjects and carry out other mission objectives. The orbit's size (height) determines how much of the Earth's surface the space-craft's instruments can see, as well as how often it might pass overhead. Naturally, the higher the orbit, the more the total area that can be seen at once. But just as our eyes are limited in how much of a scene we can see without moving them or turning our head, a spacecraft payload has similar limitations. We define the payload's *field of view* as the cone of visibility for a particular sensor (see figure 4–4). Depending on the sensor's field of view and the height of its orbit, a specific total area on the Earth's surface is visible at any one time, with the linear width or diameter of this area defined as the *swath width*. Some missions require continuous coverage of a point on Earth or the ability to communicate simultaneously with every point on Earth. When this happens, a single spacecraft may not be able to satisfy the mission need, requiring a constellation of identical spacecraft placed in different (but often similar) orbits to provide the necessary coverage. The global positioning system (GPS) mission requirement, for example, requires a constellation of satellites because the mission requirements call for every point on Earth to be in view of at least four GPS satellites at any one time—an impossibility with only four satellites at any altitude.

Figure 4–4. Satellite Field of View

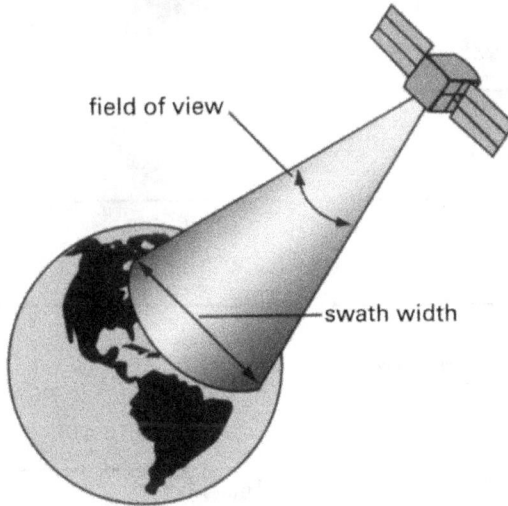

Source: Jerry J. Sellers et al., *Understanding Space: An Introduction to Astronautics*, 3ᵈ ed. (New York: McGraw-Hill, 2005), figure 1–25.

Figure 4–5 and table 4–2 show various types of missions and their typical orbits. A geostationary orbit is a circular orbit with a period of about 24 hours and inclination of 0°. Geostationary orbits are particularly useful for communications satellites because a spacecraft in this orbit appears motionless to an Earth-based observer, such as a fixed ground station. Geosynchronous orbits are inclined orbits with a period of about 24 hours. Ground-based observers above about 70° latitude (north or south) cannot see a satellite at geostationary altitude as it is actually below the horizon. A semisynchronous orbit (used by the GPS constellation) has a period of 12 hours. Sun-synchronous orbits are retrograde (westbound) low Earth orbits (LEOs) typically inclined 95° to 105° and most often used for remote sensing missions because they pass over locations on Earth with the same Sun angle each time. A Molniya orbit is a semisynchronous, eccentric orbit used for missions requiring coverage of high latitudes, those that cannot access a geostationary orbit as described above.

Figure 4–5. Types of Orbits and their Inclinations

Inclination	Orbital Type	Diagram
0° or 180°	Equatorial	
90°	Polar	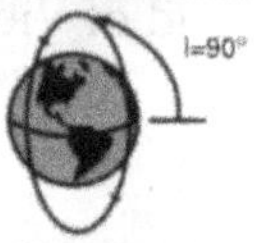 i=90°
0° ≤ i < 90°	Direct or Prograde (moves in the direction of Earth's rotation)	 ascending node
90° < i ≤ 90°	Indirect or Retrograde (moves against the direction of Earth's rotation)	 ascending node

Source: Jerry J. Sellers et al., *Understanding Space: An Introduction to Astronautics*, 3ᵈ ed. (New York: McGraw-Hill, 2005), table 5–2.

Table 4–2. Satellite Missions and Orbits

Mission	Orbital Type	Semimajor Axis (Altitude)	Period	Inclination	Other
Communication Early warning Nuclear detection	Geostationary	42,158 km (35,780 km)	~24 hr	~0°	$e \cong 0$
Remote sensing	Sun-synchronous	~6,500–7,300 km (~150–900 km)	~90 min	~95°	$e \cong 0$
—Weather	Geostationary	42,158 km (35,780 km)	~24 hr	~0°	$e \cong 0$

(continued)

Mission	Orbital Type	Semimajor Axis (Altitude)	Period	Inclination	Other
Navigation —GPS	Semi-syn- chronous	26,610 km (20,232 km)	12 hr	55°	$e \cong 0$
Space Shuttle	Low-Earth orbit	~6,700 km (~300 km)	~90 min	28.5°, 39°, 51°, or 57°	$e \cong 0$
Communication/ intelligence	Molniya	26,571 km (R_p = 7,971 km; R_a = 45,170 km)	12 hr	63.4°	$\omega = 270°$ $e \cong 0.7$

Source: Jerry J. Sellers et al., *Understanding Space: An Introduction to Astronautics*, 3ᵈ ed. (New York: McGraw-Hill, 2005), table 5–4.

Spacecraft users often need to know what part of Earth their spacecraft is overlying at any given time. For instance, remote sensing satellites must be over precise locations to get the coverage they need. A spacecraft's ground track is a trace of the spacecraft's path over the Earth's surface while the Earth rotates beneath the satellite on its axis. Ground tracks are presented to the user on a flat (Mercator) projection of the Earth (see figure 4–6).

Figure 4–6. Satellite Ground Tracks

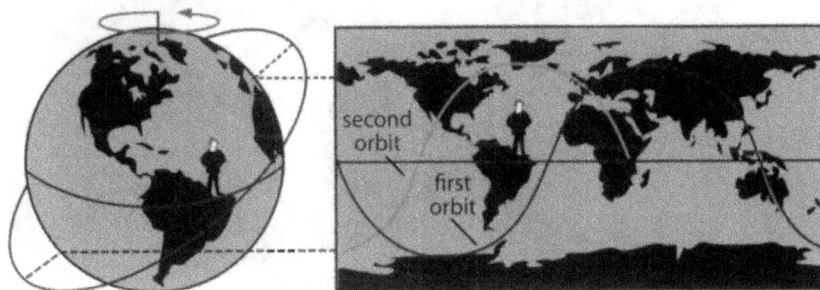

Source: Jerry J. Sellers et al., *Understanding Space: An Introduction to Astronautics*, 3ᵈ ed. (New York: McGraw-Hill, 2005), figure 5–33.

The impact of variation in orbital elements such as semi-major axis, inclination, and argument of perigee is shown in figures 4–7, 4–8, and 4–9.[3]

Figure 4–7. Orbital Ground Tracks with Different Periods

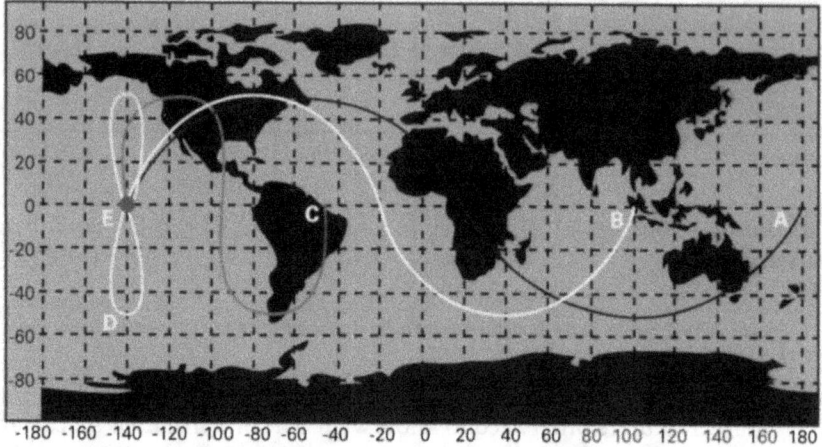

A = 2.67 hours; B = 8 hours; C =18 hours; D = E = 24 hours.

Source: Jerry J. Sellers et al., *Understanding Space: An Introduction to Astronautics*, 3ᵈ ed. (New York: McGraw-Hill, 2005), figure 5–33.

Figure 4–8. Orbital Ground Tracks with Different Inclinations

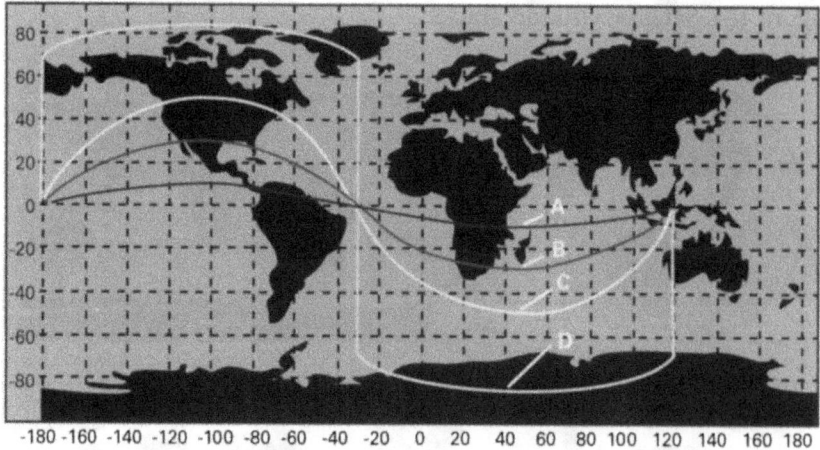

A = 10°; B = 30°; C = 50°; D = 85°.

Source: Jerry J. Sellers et al., *Understanding Space: An Introduction to Astronautics*, 3ᵈ ed. (New York: McGraw-Hill, 2005), figure 5–35.

Figure 4–9. Orbital Ground Tracks with Different Perigee Locations

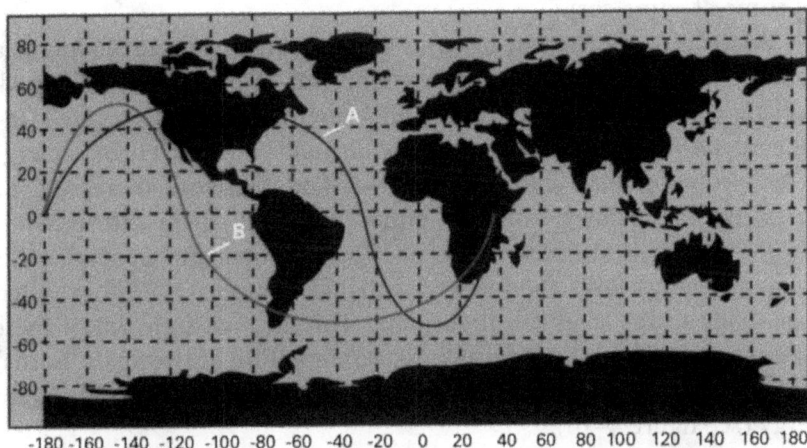

Both orbits have period of 9.3 hours, inclination of 50°, highly elliptical; orbit A perigee is in Northern Hemisphere, orbit B perigee is in Southern Hemisphere.

Source: Jerry J. Sellers et al., *Understanding Space: An Introduction to Astronautics*, 3[d] ed. (New York: McGraw-Hill, 2005), figure 5–36.

Maneuvers and Rendezvous

The ability to maintain a desired orbit and orientation within that orbit, to maneuver to possibly more useful orbits, or to rendezvous with other objects in space can be critical to overall space capability and survivability. Once a spacecraft achieves its assigned, desired orbit, it seldom remains there. Most space missions require changes to one or more of the classic orbital elements at least once. Geosynchronous satellites, for example, are sometimes first launched into a low perigee (~300 km) "parking orbit" due to launch vehicle limitations before transferring to their final orbit, requiring a large change in semi-major axis as well as shifting the satellite's inclination from that of the parking orbit to 0°. After achieving their desired mission orbit, many satellites regularly make small adjustments to compensate for small perturbations (for example, drag, solar wind, gravitational variations) to stay in that orbit. Spacecraft may also need to perform maneuvers to rendezvous with other spacecraft, as when the space shuttle maneuvers to dock with the International Space Station. The ability to maneuver in space differentiates more capable space systems from simpler buoy-like satellites with limited operational flexibility—but these extra capabilities come at some cost.

Spacecraft maneuvers, beyond simple adjustments to maintain a current orbit, can be classified as in-plane, out-of-plane, and combined, referring to the orbital plane into which the maneuver is executed. In-plane maneuvers primarily affect the semi-major axis of an orbit, enlarging or reducing the "size" of the orbit and therefore increasing or decreasing the orbit period. In either case, the spacecraft expends energy—usually in the form of burned rocket propellant. Generally, this change in energy takes the form of a change in velocity (DV) executed tangentially to the satellite's flight path. The most well known of these maneuvers, the Hohmann transfer, is a combination of two such "burns" that moves a satellite from one circular orbit to another using minimum energy (see figure 4–10).

Figure 4–10. Hohmann Transfer

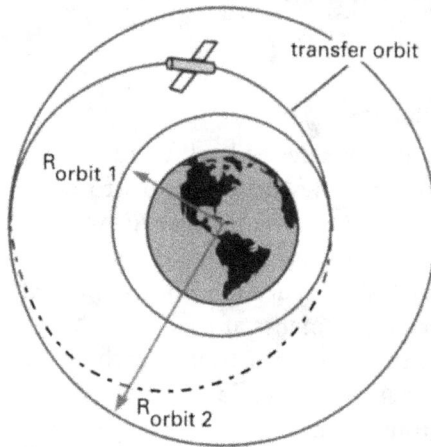

Source: Jerry J. Sellers et al., *Understanding Space: An Introduction to Astronautics*, 3ᵈ ed. (New York: McGraw-Hill, 2005), figure 6–4.

For the case where a satellite is moved from a lower to a higher orbit, the first burn (all burns are assumed to be impulsive) moves the satellite from the initial orbit to the point of perigee in the transfer orbit. The transfer ellipse's semi-major axis is the average of the semi-major axes of the initial and target circular orbits, and the DV needed to accomplish this first phase is the difference in the velocity at that point between the circular and elliptical orbits. Once the satellite reaches apogee of the transfer orbit, another burn is required to circularize its path into the final orbit. Again, this DV will be the difference between the velocity of the two orbits (transfer and final) at that point, and the total DV required for the mission is the sum of these two burns.[4]

Operationally, relatively small in-plane adjustments can change overhead passage time of LEO satellites by changing orbital period, can be used for collision avoidance, or can extend the on-orbit life of a LEO satellite whose orbit has slowly degraded due to atmospheric drag. Conversely, maneuvers can accelerate reentry by dropping the perigee of a satellite into a region where atmospheric drag increases, park an unused or nearly dead satellite into a safe orbit away from other operational systems, or initiate rendezvous with another spacecraft.

On-orbit rendezvous or interception maneuvers fall into two general categories: co-planar and co-orbital. In the former, a Hohmann transfer approach combines with appropriate phasing in order to time the burns correctly. The initial phase angle between the interceptor and target as well as the different speeds of each spacecraft in its particular orbit determines timing of the maneuver (see figures 4–11 and 4–12).

Figure 4–11. Coplanar Rendezvous

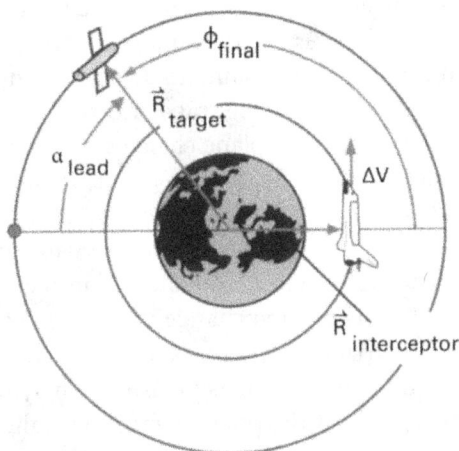

Source: Jerry J. Sellers et al., *Understanding Space: An Introduction to Astronautics*, 3[d] ed. (New York: McGraw-Hill, 2005), figure 6–12.

Figure 4–12. Co-orbital Rendezvous

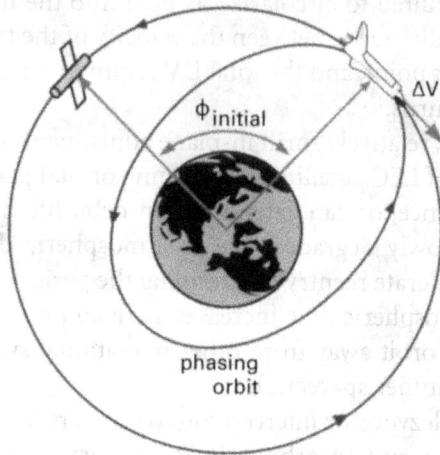

Source: Jerry J. Sellers et al., *Understanding Space: An Introduction to Astronautics,* 3ᵈ ed. (New York: McGraw-Hill, 2005), figure 6–14.

Co-orbital rendezvous occurs when both the target and interceptor are in the same orbit, though at different positions (true anomaly). In this case, the interceptor must maneuver into a phasing orbit, "speeding up to slow down" (or the converse) in order to meet the target after completing one phasing orbit. In both cases (co-planar and co-orbital), the interceptor must burn again at rendezvous to maintain its position near the target and not remain in its intercept or phasing transfer orbit.[5]

Out-of-plane maneuvers, or plane changes, occur when the satellite's direction of motion changes—usually by a nontangential burn. Operationally, plane changes to adjust the inclination of an orbit (see figure 4–13) are most commonly used when satellites launched into parking orbits from nonequatorial launch sites maneuver into geostationary orbits (a = 42,160 km, i = 0°). The plane change itself often combines with the apogee burn that circularizes the satellite's orbit at that altitude. For satellites in high inclination orbits (such as polar or Sun-synchronous), plane changes executed over one of the poles change the right ascension of the ascending node for the orbit (see figure 4–14), thus altering the overhead passage time and sun angle for that satellite. Since the burn is performed perpendicular to the spacecraft's flight path, the magnitudes of the spacecraft's initial and final velocities are identical.

Figure 4–13. Simple Inclination Plane Change

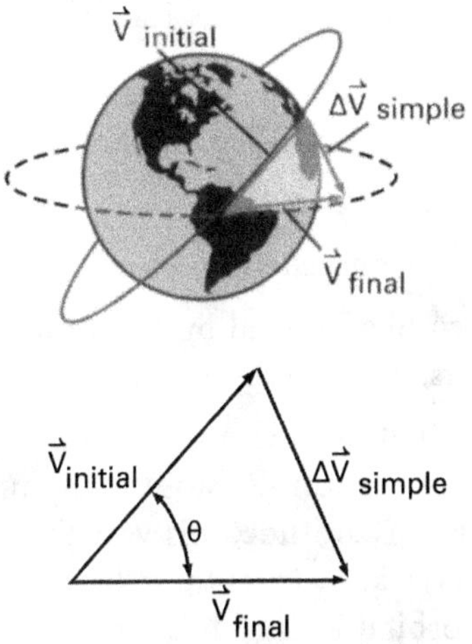

Figure 4–14. Simple Ω Plane Change

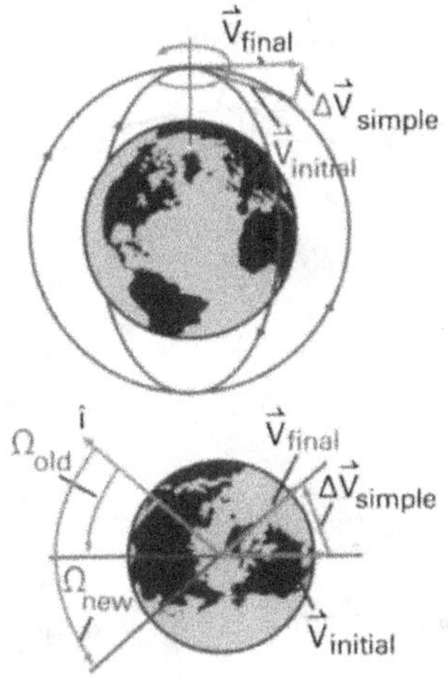

Orbit Perturbations

If some of the original simplifying assumptions for orbits are changed to include a more complete view of the forces acting on a spacecraft, COEs other than just the true anomaly will begin to change over time. The primary perturbations to simplified, classical orbital motion are:

- atmospheric drag
- Earth's oblateness (or nonsphericity in general)
- solar radiation pressure
- third-body gravitational effects (Moon, Sun, planets, and so forth)
- unexpected thrusting—caused by either outgassing or malfunctioning thrusters; can perturb orbits or cause spacecraft rotation.

While the Earth's atmosphere gets thinner with altitude, it still has some effect as high as 600 km. Because many important space missions occur in orbits below this altitude, this very thin air causes drag on these spacecraft, taking energy away from the orbit in the form of friction on the spacecraft. Because orbital energy is a function of semi-major axis, the semi-major axis will decrease over time. For noncircular orbits, the eccentricity also decreases since the drag at lower altitudes (near perigee) is higher than at apogee (see figure 4–15).

Figure 4–15. Effects of Drag on Eccentric Low Earth Orbit

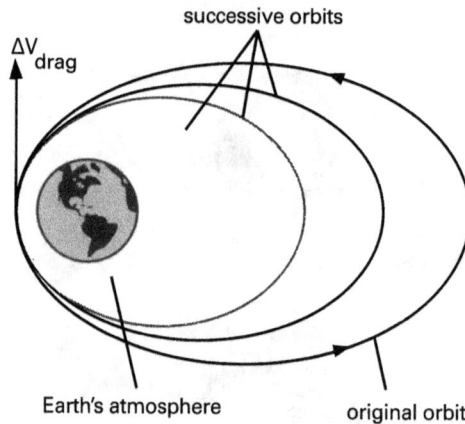

Source: Jerry J. Sellers et al., *Understanding Space: An Introduction to Astronautics,* 3ᵈ ed. (New York: McGraw-Hill, 2005), figure 8–7.

Factors such as the Earth's day-night cycle, seasonal tilt, variable solar distance, and fluctuating magnetic field, as well as the Sun's 27-day rotation and 11-year cycle for sunspots, make precise real-time drag modeling nearly impossible. Further complicating the modeling problem is the fact that the force of drag also depends on the spacecraft's coefficient of drag and frontal area, which can vary widely depending upon spacecraft orientation.

In addition, the Earth is not a perfect sphere, affecting the earlier point mass assumption. The most pronounced nonspheroidal characteristic is oblateness, meaning that the Earth bulges at the equator and is somewhat flattened at the poles, modeled using the constant J2. Unlike drag, which is a nonconservative force, the J2 effect is gravitational and does not change a spacecraft's total mechanical energy (that is, constant semi-major axis). Instead, J2 acts as a torque on the orbit since the Earth's gravitational pull is no longer directed from the Earth's exact center, causing the right ascension of the ascending node (RAAN, or Ω) to shift or precess with each orbit[6] and the perigee to rotate through an elliptical orbit. J2 effect is a function of orbit inclination and altitude as shown in figures 4–16 and 4–17 describing its effect on RAAN and argument of perigee.[7]

Figure 4–16. Perigee Rotation Rate

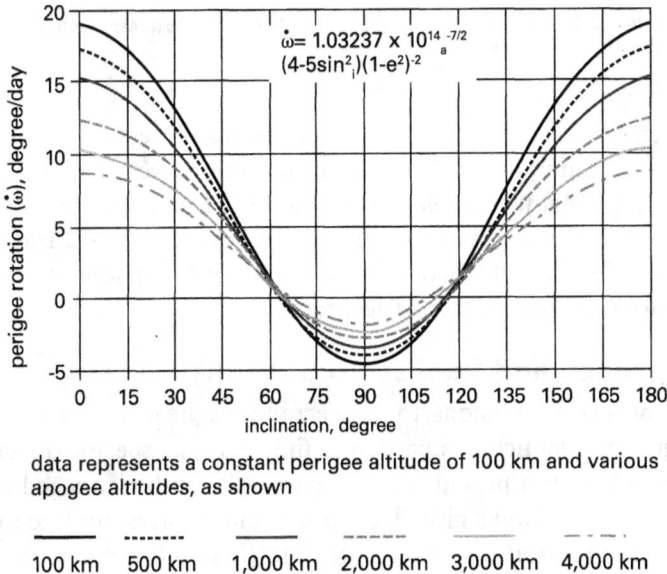

$$\dot{\omega} = 1.03237 \times 10^{14} \, a^{-7/2} (4-5\sin^2_i)(1-e^2)^{-2}$$

data represents a constant perigee altitude of 100 km and various apogee altitudes, as shown

100 km   500 km   1,000 km   2,000 km   3,000 km   4,000 km

Source: Jerry J. Sellers et al., *Understanding Space: An Introduction to Astronautics*, 3[d] ed. (New York: McGraw-Hill, 2005), figure 8–11.

Figure 4–17. Nodal Regression Rate

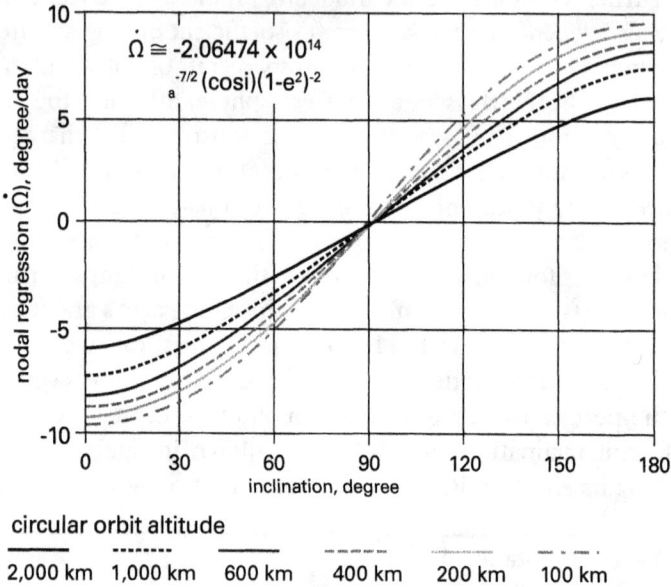

circular orbit altitude

| 2,000 km | 1,000 km | 600 km | 400 km | 200 km | 100 km |

Source: Jerry J. Sellers et al., *Understanding Space: An Introduction to Astronautics*, 3[d] ed. (New York: McGraw-Hill, 2005), figure 8–10.

Other, smaller perturbing forces also affect a spacecraft's orbit and its orientation within it, including solar radiation pressure, third-body gravitational effects (Moon, Sun, planets, and so forth), and unexpected thrusting—caused by either outgassing or malfunctioning thrusters. The importance of each perturbation is a function of the spacecraft's mission and need for orbital and attitude accuracy.

Space Launch and Rocket Propulsion

For most space missions, the spacecraft must be placed into a specific orbit, requiring a launch at a particular time and in a specific direction. A "launch window" is a period when a spacecraft can be launched directly into its initial orbit from a given launch site, and it corresponds to the time when the chosen orbit passes over the launch site. In practice, a launch window normally covers several minutes or even hours around this exact time since mission planners have some flexibility in the orbital elements they can accept, and launch vehicles usually can steer enough to expand the length of the window somewhat. However, to launch directly into an orbit, the launch site and orbital plane must intersect at least once per day.

Physically, that means that the inclination of the desired orbit must be equal to or greater than the latitude of the launch site. If the two are equal, then there will be one launch opportunity per day. If the inclination is greater than the latitude, there will be two potential opportunities since, in this case, the spacecraft may be launched toward either the ascending or descending node (see figure 4–18). However, due to practical restrictions at a given launch site, only one of these opportunities may be used. For example, launches from Cape Canaveral are restricted to the east and northeast only due to overflight considerations.

Figure 4–18. Launch Windows

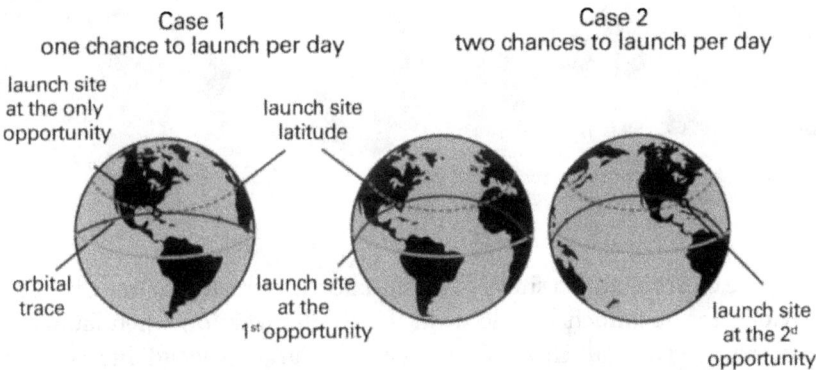

Case 1
one chance to launch per day

Case 2
two chances to launch per day

launch site at the only opportunity

launch site latitude

orbital trace

launch site at the 1st opportunity

launch site at the 2d opportunity

Source: Jerry J. Sellers et al., *Understanding Space: An Introduction to Astronautics,* 3d ed. (New York: McGraw-Hill, 2005), figure 9–7.

During liftoff, a launch vehicle goes through four distinct phases from the launch pad into orbit (see figure 4–19). During vertical ascent, the vehicle gains altitude quickly to escape the dense, high-drag lower atmosphere. The vehicle then executes a slow pitch maneuver to gain velocity downrange (horizontally), followed by a turn in which gravity pulls the launch vehicle's trajectory toward horizontal. In the final vacuum phase, the launch vehicle is effectively out of the Earth's atmosphere and continues accelerating to gain the necessary velocity to achieve orbit. The vehicle's on-board flight control system works to deliver the vehicle to the desired burnout conditions: velocity, altitude, and flight-path angle. The velocity needed to get to orbit consists of the launch vehicle's burnout velocity and the tangential velocity that exists at its launch site due to the Earth's rotation.

Figure 4–19. Phases of Launch Vehicle Ascent

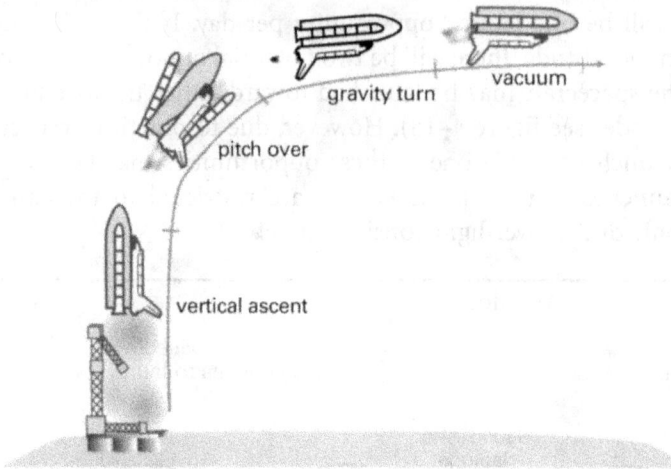

vacuum

gravity turn

pitch over

vertical ascent

Source: Jerry J. Sellers et al., *Understanding Space: An Introduction to Astronautics*, 3ᵈ ed. (New York: McGraw-Hill, 2005), figure 9–14.

The closer a launch site is to the equator, the greater the velocity assist provided to the launch vehicle from the Earth's rotation when launching eastward.[8] A given launch vehicle can launch a larger payload due east from a launch site at a lower latitude. For westerly launches into retrograde orbits, this same tangential velocity reduces launch capability.

Determining the total velocity needed to launch a spacecraft is a very complex problem requiring numerical integration in sophisticated trajectory modeling programs that incorporate launch vehicle properties, atmospheric density models, and other factors. To determine the overall design velocity, the mission designer must consider velocity needed to overcome gravity and reach the correct altitude, inertial velocity needed at burnout for the desired orbit, velocity of the launch pad due to Earth's rotation, and velocity losses due to air drag, back pressure, and steering losses. The difference between the launch vehicle's actual design velocity for a specific payload mass and the design velocity is the launch margin.

Rocket propulsion is responsible for not only launching spacecraft into orbit, but also maneuvering them once they are in space and adjusting their attitude to accomplish their mission as needed (see table 4–3). While there are many forms of rocket propulsion, they all depend upon Newton's laws to apply forces (thrust) or moments (torque). Rockets operate by expelling high-speed exhaust in one direction, causing the spacecraft to accelerate in another. The only types of rockets currently in use are thermodynamic and electrodynamic. Thermodynamic rockets rely on heat and pressure to accelerate a propellant (for example, the chemical reaction of fuel and oxidizer burning, or the heat generated by electrical heating or a nuclear reaction) using converging/diverging nozzles to convert the thermal energy to kinetic energy. Examples of thermodynamic rockets include chemical (liquid, solid, and hybrid); nuclear-thermal; solar-thermal; and electro-thermal. Electrodynamic rockets use electric and/or magnetic fields to accelerate charged particles to high velocities and include ion or electrostatic, Hall effect, and pulsed plasma thrusters.

Table 4–3. Rocket Propulsion Types and Performance Comparison

Type	Propellant Examples	I_{sp} (sec)	Thrust Range (N)	Advantages	Disadvantages
Thermodynamic					
Chemical					
Liquid					
Bipropellant	LO_2/LH_2 LO_2/Kerosene Hydrazine/ Nitrogen Tetroxide	334–455	$10–10^6$	• High I_{sp} • Throttleable • Restartable	• Must manage two propellants • Requires thermal control for chamber and nozzle
Mono-propellant	Hydrazine Hydrogen Peroxide	180–240	10–1,000	• Simple • Large flight heritage • One propellant to manage	• Lower I_{sp} than bipropellant • Toxic
Solid	Ammonium Perchlorate/ Aluminum/Binder	300	$1–10^6$	• Simple, reliable • No propellant management needed • Higher thrust	• Modest I_{sp} • Susceptible to propellant grain cracks • Difficult to stop; can't restart

(continued)

Type	Propellant Examples	I_{sp} (sec)	Thrust Range (N)	Advantages	Disadvantages
Thermodynamic					
Chemical					
Liquid					
Hybrid	Hydrogen Peroxide/ Polyethylene	333	$10\text{--}10^6$	• Simpler than bi-propellant • Safer, more flexible than solids; restartable	• Limited heritage • Modest I_{sp}
Nuclear-thermal	H_2	1,000	$1\text{--}10^6$	• Long-term energy supply • Refuelable, reusable • High I_{sp}, high thrust	• No flight heritage • Environmental/ political concerns
Electro-thermal	Ammonia (NH_3)	800	$0.1\text{--}1$	• Simple, reliable • High I_{sp}	• Requires large amounts of on-board electrical power • Low thrust
Solar-thermal	Ammonia	800	$0.1\text{--}10$	• High I_{sp} • Long-term energy supply	• Requires solar energy collection • Low thrust
Electrostatic					
Ion	Xenon	$10^3\text{--}10^4$	$0.1\text{--}1$	• High I_{sp} • Long-term use	• Low thrust
Electrodynamic					
Hall effect	Xenon	2,000	$0.1\text{--}1$	• High I_{sp} • Long-term use	• Low thrust
Pulsed Plasma	Teflon	1,500	$10^{-5}\text{--}10^{-3}$	• High I_{sp} • Long-term use	• Low thrust

Source: Jerry J. Sellers et al., *Understanding Space: An Introduction to Astronautics*, 3d ed. (New York: McGraw-Hill, 2005), table 14–6.

In all cases, the efficiency of a rocket is measured in terms of specific impulse (I_{sp}). Specific impulse gives us an effective "miles per gallon" rating as it relates the amount of thrust produced for a given weight flow rate of the propellant. Higher I_{sp} rockets produce more total V for the same amount of propellant than low I_{sp} rockets. However, high I_{sp} rockets (such as ion thrusters) are typically low thrust and not suited for some uses. The Rocket Equation[9] relates the initial and final masses of a spacecraft with the specific impulse of the propulsion system to determine the total V available. It is the mission designer's job to determine a space mission's many propulsion needs and select the appropriate system for each phase.

The total cost of a specific spacecraft's on-board propulsion system includes several factors, in addition to the bottom-line price tag, before making a final selection.[10] These factors include mass performance (measured by I_{sp}), volume required, time (how fast it completes the needed DV), power requirements, safety costs (how safe the system and its propellant are and how difficult it is to protect people working with the system), logistics (system and propellant transport to launch), integration cost with other spacecraft subsystems, and technical risk (what flight experience does it have or how did it perform in testing). Different mission planners naturally place a higher value on some of these factors than on others. A complex commercial mission may place high priority on reducing technical risk—for example, a new type of plasma rocket, even if it offers lower mass cost, may be too risky when all other factors are considered.

A basic understanding of rocket propulsion informs mission planners and space experts who next consider one of the most obvious manifestations of spacepower—space launch systems. While more widely open international access to launch has provided some level of space presence and power to dozens of nations, a space launch capability defines a unique level of spacepower and is possessed by many fewer states. Requirements for an operational launch system are technical, geographic, and financial. Development of a new space launch system consumes hundreds of millions to many billions of dollars[11] and requires broad expertise in propulsion systems, avionics, logistics, manufacturing, and integration processes. Testing during system development also requires extensive infrastructure and range facilities (often consisting of thousands of square miles of controlled airspace) that can assure public safety, while operational launch facilities must also include payload processing and mission control centers.

The physical, financial, and technical difficulties of launch are evident in the relatively small number of launch vehicles developed in the world's 50 years of space launch experience. Contrasted with the first 50 years of powered atmospheric flight, today's launch vehicles represent relatively small advances in capability from the Russian and American boosters of the late 1950s and early 1960s that trace their development to intercontinental ballistic missiles of the Cold War. All based on chemical (liquid and/or solid) propulsion, today's boosters can lift little more than 4 percent of their lift-off mass to LEO and much less than half that amount to geosynchronous transfer orbit from which a final apogee burn can place a spacecraft into a geostationary orbit. All vehicles use a minimum of two stages to achieve orbit (and some as many as four) with costs on the order of $10,000 per pound to LEO and $12,000 per pound to geostationary orbit.

Several attempts to incrementally or drastically reduce launch costs and improve responsiveness have not significantly altered the status quo. The space shuttle, originally intended as a "space truck" to access space routinely and cheaply, suffered from its immense complexity, resulting in enormous per-launch cost growth. After completing its support of the International Space Station construction in 2010, it will be retired, largely due to safety and high cost of ownership. Small launch vehicles such as Orbital Sciences' Pegasus air-launched vehicle (~$22 million per launch for about 500 kilograms [kg] to LEO) have served niche markets without reducing overall costs, as have refurbished Russian and American intercontinental ballistic missiles (for example, Minotaur). SpaceX's Falcon 1 (with an advertised cost of roughly $6 million per launch as of this writing) and the larger follow-on Falcon 9 may achieve some cost savings, but nothing near the order of magnitude or greater savings that might transform space access to a more aviation-like paradigm. More exotic attempts to change the launch industry—such as the NASA-funded/Lockheed Martin–developed VentureStar single-stage-to-orbit, fully reusable launch vehicle—have not been successful beyond the PowerPoint slide.[12] In fact, current technology makes it very difficult to reduce space launch costs or turnaround time for launch vehicles or to build cost-effective reusable launch systems. With no new rocket propulsion technologies for space launch available in the foreseeable future, savings in launch costs and processing time will be incremental and depend on gains in reliability, manufacturing techniques, and miniaturization of payloads.

Whatever the state of launch, mission planners and space experts considering launch systems must consider the following factors:

- performance capability (whether the launch vehicle can take the desired mass to the mission orbit)
- vehicle availability (whether the vehicle will be available and ready to launch when needed)

■ spacecraft compatibility (whether the payload will fit in the launch vehicle fairing and survive the launch environment imposed by the launch vehicle) cost.

Space Environment

Once in space, the unique environment presents several challenges to mission accomplishment, affecting not only spacecraft but also the signals received and transmitted in the course of that mission. The primary space environmental challenges are:

■ free-fall gravitational conditions

■ atmospheric effects

■ vacuum

■ collision hazards

■ radiation and charged particles.

The free-fall environment gives rise to problems with fluid management—measuring and pumping—typically related to on-board liquid propulsion systems. For manned spaceflight, the physiological issues can be quite severe, marked by fluid shift within the body (lower body edema), altered vestibular function (motion sickness), and reduced load on weight-bearing tissues resulting in bone decalcification and muscle tissue loss.

In addition to the effect of drag on spacecraft (mentioned earlier as a perturbation), the upper reaches of the atmosphere contain atomic oxygen caused when radiation splits molecular oxygen (O_2). Much more reactive than O_2, atomic oxygen can cause significant degradation of spacecraft materials, weakening components, changing thermal characteristics, and degrading sensor performance.

The vacuum of space creates three potential problems for spacecraft: outgassing, cold welding, and heat transfer. Outgassing occurs when materials, such as plastics or composites, release trapped gasses (volatiles) upon exposure to vacuum—particularly problematic if the released molecules coat delicate sensors, such as lenses, or cause electronic components to arc, damaging them. Prior to launch, spacecraft are usually tested in a thermal-vacuum chamber to reduce or eliminate potential outgassing sources. Cold welding occurs between mechanical parts having very little separation between them. After launch, with the small cushion of air molecules between components eliminated, parts may effectively "weld" together. The potential for cold welding can be mitigated by avoiding the use of moving parts or by using lubricants carefully selected to avoid evaporation or outgassing. Heat transfer via conduction, convection, and especially radiation may also complicate spacecraft operation—for example, causing temperatures to drop below acceptable operating levels—and must be considered in any spacecraft design.

The chances that a spacecraft will be hit by very small pieces of debris (natural or manmade) grow with each new space mission. Twenty thousand tons of natural materials—dust, meteoroids, asteroids, and comets—hit Earth every year, and estimates of the amount of manmade space debris approach 2,200 tons.[13] Air Force Space Command, headquartered in Colorado Springs, Colorado, uses a worldwide network of radar and optical telescopes to track more than 13,000 baseball-sized and larger objects in Earth orbit, and some estimate that at least 40,000 golf ball–sized pieces (too small for the Air Force to track) are also in orbit,[14] not including smaller pieces such as paint flakes and slivers of metal.

The energy of (and thus potential damage caused by) even a very small piece of debris hitting a spacecraft at relative speeds of up to 15 km per second makes the debris environment in Earth orbit a serious issue.[15] For a spacecraft with a cross-sectional area of 50 to 200 square meters at an altitude of 300 km (typical for space shuttle missions), the chance of getting hit by an object larger than a baseball during a year in orbit is about 1 in 100,000 or less.[16] The chance of getting hit by something only 1 millimeter or less in diameter, however, is about 100 times more likely, or about 1 in 1,000 during a year in orbit. The collision between two medium-sized spacecraft would result in an enormous amount of high-velocity debris, and the resulting cloud would expand as it orbited, greatly increasing the likelihood of impacting another spacecraft. The domino effect could ruin an important orbital band for decades.

Electromagnetic (EM) radiation from the Sun, while primarily in the visible and near-infrared parts of the EM spectrum, also contains significant higher energy radiation, such as X-rays and gamma rays. While solar cells generate needed electrical power from this radiation, spacecraft and astronauts well above the atmosphere face negative consequences from it depending on the wavelength of the radiation. The Sun's radiation heats exposed surfaces, which can degrade or damage surfaces and electronic components, and the resulting solar pressure can perturb orbits. Prolonged exposure to ultraviolet radiation degrades spacecraft coatings and is especially harmful to solar cells, reducing their efficiency and possibly limiting the useful life of the spacecraft they power. In addition, during intense solar flares, bursts of energy in the radio region of the spectrum can interfere with onboard communications equipment. Solar radiation pressure, though only 5 Newtons of force for 1 square kilometer of surface, can also disturb spacecraft orientation.

Perhaps the most dangerous aspect of the space environment is the pervasive influence of charged particles caused by solar activity and galactic cosmic rays. The Sun expels a stream of charged particles (protons and electrons) at a rate of 10^9 kg per second as part of the solar wind. During intense solar flares, the number of particles ejected can increase dramatically. Galactic cosmic rays are similar to those found in the solar wind or in solar flares, but they originate outside of the solar system—the solar wind from distant stars and remnants of exploded stars—and are much more energetic than solar radiation.

The solar wind's charged particles and cosmic particles form streams that hit the Earth's magnetic field. The point of contact between the solar wind and the magnetic field is the shock front or bow shock. Inside the shock front, the point of contact between the charged particles of the solar wind and the magnetic field lines is the magnetopause, and the area directly behind the Earth is the magnetotail (see figure 4–20). In the electromagnetic spectrum, many lower energy solar particles are deflected by the Earth's magnetic field, while some high-energy particles may become trapped and concentrated between field lines, forming the Van Allen radiation belts. Additionally, high-energy gamma and X-rays may ionize particles in the upper atmosphere that also populate the Van Allen belts.

Figure 4–20. Interaction between Solar Wind and Earth's Magnetic Field

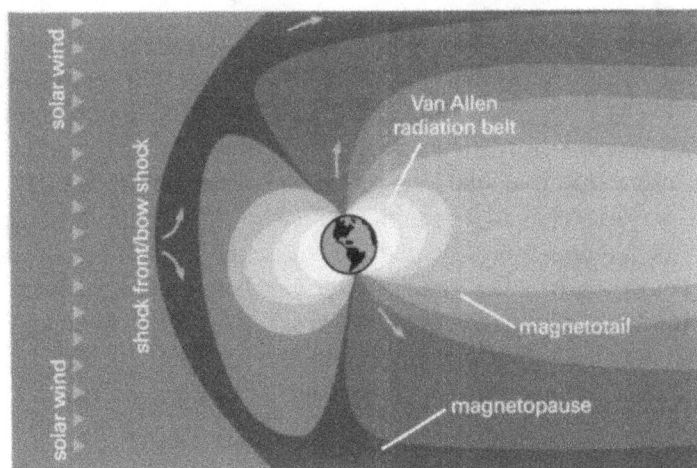

Source: Jerry J. Sellers et al., *Understanding Space: An Introduction to Astronautics*, 3ᵈ ed. (New York: McGraw-Hill, 2005), figure 3–29.

Whether charged particles come directly from the solar wind, indirectly from the Van Allen belts, or from the other side of the galaxy, they can harm spacecraft in four ways: charging, sputtering, single-event phenomenon, and total dose effects. Spacecraft charging results when charges build up on different parts of a spacecraft as it moves through concentrated areas of charged particles. Discharge can seriously damage surface coatings, degrade solar panels, cause loss of power, and switch off or permanently damage electronics. Sputtering damages thermal coatings and sensors simply by high-speed impact, in effect sandblasting the spacecraft. Single charged particles penetrating deeply into spacecraft electronics systems may cause a single event phenomenon. For example, a single event upset (SEU) or "bit flip" results when a high-energy particle impact resets one part of a computer's memory from 1 to 0, or vice versa, causing potentially significant changes to spacecraft functions. Total dose effects are long-term damage to the crystal structure of semiconductors within a spacecraft's computer caused by electrons and protons in the solar wind and the Van Allen belts. Over time, the cumulative damage lowers the efficiency of the material, causing computer problems. Orbits that pass through an area of higher radiation levels known as the South Atlantic anomaly increase the total dose damage during a spacecraft's lifetime. Spacecraft shielding and the use of hardened components offer some protection for these effects, as does software coding to negate the SEU effects by storing each bit multiple times and comparing them during each read operation. But all of these steps come at a cost of increased weight, testing requirements, and development time and cost.

Spacecraft State of the Art

A spacecraft consists of a payload and its supporting subsystems, also known as the bus. Overall payload requirements are defined in terms of the subject with which it must interact, and its components are designed to make this interaction possible. Using a remote sensing example, the payload could consist of a single simple camera to detect light from some ground-based phenomenon or could include a collection of sensors, each tuned to detect a particular characteristic (such as wavelength) of that light. The number and type of sensors chosen, and how they work together to form the spacecraft's payload, determine the spacecraft's design, which in turn generates requirements for the spacecraft bus that dictate:

- payload accommodation mass, volume, and interfaces
- spacecraft pointing precision

- data processing and transmission needs
- electrical power needs
- acceptable operating temperature ranges.

Spacecraft Subsystems

Mission designers define these requirements in terms of subsystem performance budgets such as the amount of velocity change, electrical power, or other limited resource that it must "spend" to accomplish some activity (for example, achieving operational orbit or turning on the payload). Six distinct spacecraft bus subsystems support the payload with all the necessary functions to keep it healthy and safe:

- space vehicle control: "steers" the vehicle to control its attitude and orbit, attaining and maintaining its operational orbit as well as pointing cameras and antennas toward targets on Earth or in space; on-board rockets control the orbit, while rockets and other devices rotate it around its center of mass to provide stability and precise pointing

- communication and data handling: monitors payload activities and environmental conditions, tracks and controls spacecraft location and attitude, communicates with ground controllers or other spacecraft, and warns of anomalies; communication requirements analysis produces a link budget that specifies communications parameters and the data rate

- electrical power: converts and conditions energy sources (such as solar) into usable electrical power and also stores energy to run the entire spacecraft; electrical power requirements for each of the other bus subsystems determine the total electrical power budget

- environmental control (and life support for manned missions): regulates component temperatures for proper operation, transferring or eliminating heat energy as needed; for manned missions, astronauts must be protected from the harsh space environment; provides a breathable atmosphere at a comfortable temperature, humidity, and pressure, along with water and food to sustain life

- structure and mechanisms: protect the payload and subsystems from high launch loads; deploy and maintain orientation of spacecraft components (such as solar panels and antennas)

■ propulsion: produces thrust to maneuver the spacecraft between orbits and control its altitude; highly dependent on altitude and orbital control needs.

Remote Sensing and Communications Physics

The most common general categories of spacecraft payloads perform remote sensing and communications missions and, as such, represent the variety of technical and operational trades and constraints typically found in space mission design. Remote sensing systems collect EM radiation reflected or emitted from objects on the Earth's surface, in the atmosphere, or in space—including space-based astronomy and space surveillance. Radio waves (also EM) are used to communicate to and from the Earth's surface, through the atmosphere, and between objects in space. For missions involving Earth sensing or communications, then, the transmission characteristics of the Earth's atmosphere—which frequencies are blocked, attenuated, or pass freely—drive payload performance and design decisions. Figures 4–21 and 4–22 describe the electromagnetic spectrum (in terms of EM wavelength and frequency) and the transmission of that spectrum through the atmosphere.

Figure 4–21. Electromagnetic Spectrum

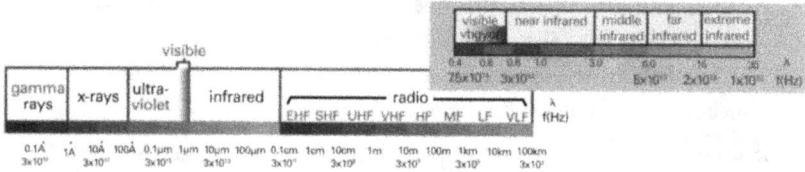

Source: Jerry J. Sellers et al., *Understanding Space: An Introduction to Astronautics*, 3ᵈ ed. (New York: McGraw-Hill, 2005), figure 11–29.

Figure 4–22. Atmospheric Windows

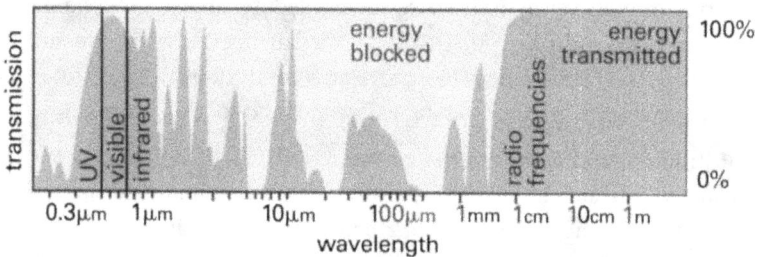

Source: Jerry J. Sellers et al., *Understanding Space: An Introduction to Astronautics*, 3ᵈ ed. (New York: McGraw-Hill, 2005), figure 11–32.

While some wavelengths (such as visible light) are completely transmitted, others are almost completely blocked. Spacecraft instruments have access to Earth from space through various atmospheric windows—wavelength bands in which 80 to 100 percent of the available energy is transmitted through the atmosphere. The most notable atmospheric windows are the visible, infrared, and radio wavelengths.

Passive remote sensing systems depend on reflected or emitted EM radiation passing through the atmosphere to the space-based sensor. Because objects reflect different wavelengths of EM radiation, measuring the amount and type of radiation can describe characteristics such as soil properties, moisture content, vegetation types, and many other important details. Objects also emit EM radiation at different wavelengths depending on their material properties and temperature. The relationship between temperature and wavelength of peak emission is well known,[17] and coupled with knowledge of the total energy output from the target object,[18] payload sensors can be designed to sense particular phenomena.

Given the physics of EM radiation, a workable sensor can then be designed. To observe an object, however, the spacecraft sensor must be able to point the sensor at the target, collect EM radiation from the target, transform the detected radiation into usable data, and process the usable data into usable information. First, the object must fall within the sensor's field of view—defined as the angular width within which the sensor can see. Projected onto the Earth's surface, the field of view translates into the swath width, the size of which is determined by the sensor's field of view and the spacecraft's altitude (as shown in figure 4–4). Next, the resolution of the sensor—the size of the smallest object it can detect—is a function of the wavelength of the radiation sensed, the sensor's aperture diameter, and the distance between the sensor and the target.[19]

Active remote sensors such as radar transmit their own radiation that reflects from the target and returns to the sensor for processing. Space-based radar, for example, permits accurate terrain measurement of features to construct a three-dimensional picture of a planet's surface. Because resolution relates directly to the wavelength of the transmitted and reflected signal, shorter wavelengths yield better resolution than longer wavelengths. Optical sensors measure EM wavelengths on the order of 0.5 micrometers (mm), while radar systems operate at about 240,000 mm. Thus, for optical and radar systems with the same size aperture, the optical system has almost 500,000 times better resolution. For conventional radar to have the same resolution as an optical system, the size of the radar's aperture must be increased.[20]

Space communications systems serve as the backbone for all other space missions in addition to being a mission in their own right. The primary goal, of course, is to get data to the users, whether that means relaying remote sensing data obtained from space sensors to ground systems and users, sending and receiving command and control data between spacecraft and ground control centers, or acting as a relay to receive and then transmit data from one point on the globe (or in space) to another. Communications payloads use a transmitted EM signal to carry data to a receiver. The communications link—what happens between the transmitter and the receiver—is the critical feature of any communications systems and is characterized by several critical parameters:

- signal-to-noise ratio
- bit error rate (signal quality)
- coverage
- data rate
- signal security.

The signal-to-noise ratio (SNR) is a function of transmitter power and gain, receiver bandwidth, temperature and gain, signal wavelength, and range between transmitter and receiver. For effective communication, SNR must be greater than or equal to one.[21] The bit error rate (BER) defines the likelihood of misinterpreting bits in a data stream, typically expressed in terms of single bit errors per power of 10 bits.[22] Increasing signal strength improves BER and can be accomplished by increasing transmitter power and antenna size, increasing receiver antenna size, improving receiver characteristics, using higher frequencies, or reducing the distance between the transmitter and the receiver. All of these factors impact the overall cost of the system. The system designer must investigate all available alternatives to obtain the desired signal-to-noise ratio at minimum system cost.

Coverage directly affects communications availability and is a function of satellite altitude and orbit, elevation angle of communicating satellites, satellite constellation configuration (number of satellites, orbital planes used, and so forth), ground station (receiver) location, and cross-linking capability. The simplest satellite communications architecture uses a "store-and-forward" approach (figure 4–23, case A) whereby it transmits or receives data only passing overhead of a single ground station. Between passes, it stores any collected data to be transmitted at the next pass. Adding well-placed ground stations improves coverage, as does adding satellites with a cross-link capability that would forward data to one or more ground stations, effectively increasing the frequency of overhead passes (figure 4–23, case D). Geostationary architectures employ three or more satellites along with terrestrial ground sites and cross-linking for global coverage (except for high latitudes) (figure 4–23, case B), while Molniya orbits with two or more satellites can provide stable, continuous coverage of polar regions (figure 4–23, case C). At low altitudes, larger numbers of cross-linked satellites in a properly arranged constellation can provide continuous coverage of the Earth (figure 4–23, case E), with the most well-known example being the Iridium satellite telephone system.

Figure 4–23. Satellite Coverage Strategies

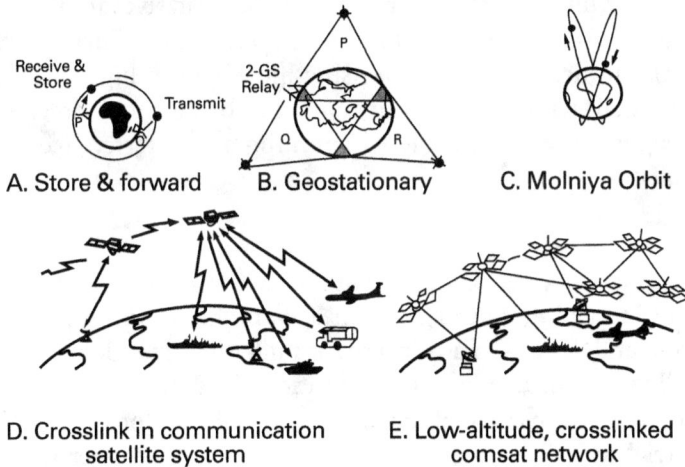

A. Store & forward

B. Geostationary

C. Molniya Orbit

D. Crosslink in communication satellite system

E. Low-altitude, crosslinked comsat network

Source: James R. Wertz and Wiley J. Larson, eds., *Space Mission Analysis and Design*, 3ᵈ ed. (Dordrecht, Netherlands: Kluwer Academic Publishers, 1999).

Data rate is the number of bits per second of information that must be transferred over the communications link and is a function of the signal frequency—higher frequency signals can better support higher data rates. Enhanced capabilities to support global operations such as unmanned aircraft systems, video teleconferencing, or simply providing Super Bowl broadcasts to deployed troops create greater demand for higher and higher data rates. Signal security and availability include communications security—disguising the actual transmitted data and typically including data encryption—and transmission security—disguising the transmitted signal, usually by generating security keys and variables that support spread spectrum techniques. Availability, on the other hand, depends upon the environment's effect on the transmission channel. Communications links are typically designed to create an SNR that produces the required BER for the anticipated environment (no hostile effects on the transmission channel). Link margin is then added to compensate for other expected (and unexpected) operating conditions. Signal jamming is an intentional means of corrupting the otherwise benign environment by introducing noise into the communications path, resulting in an SNR of less than one. Of course, simple interference from other systems operating at the same frequency may have a similar, less sinister effect on communications, making frequency deconfliction an important factor in insuring effective communications.

All of these factors will impact the overall cost of the system. The system designer must investigate all available alternatives to obtain the desired signal-to-noise ratio at minimum system cost. Current trends in space communications focus on using more power, higher frequencies, and phased-array antennas to point the beam more precisely to make the signals less susceptible to jamming and interference and to increase data rates.

Conclusion

Space offers society advantages that have revolutionized modern life since the launch of Sputnik 50 years ago and has motivated scientific investigation and dreams of adventure for millennia. The global perspective has allowed worldwide communications and remote sensing (in many forms) and transformed navigation and timing for civil, military, and industrial uses. The challenge of space as a final frontier has lured huge investments by nations seeking to increase their international stature while improving their ability to provide services to their citizens, motivating the technical progress and patriotism of those same citizens, enlarging their international economic influence, and, in many cases, increasing their military power. The clear view space provides causes astronomers and other scientists to dream of future discoveries about the fundamental nature of life and our universe, while the unlimited and largely untapped wealth of space tantalizes citizens of the Earth, who are increasingly aware of finite terrestrial resources.

Realizing these advantages and leveraging the power conferred on those who best exploit them, however, require an appreciation of the physics, engineering, and operational knowledge unique to space, space systems, and missions. It is precisely because so few citizens of Earth have first-hand experience with space—unlike previous terrestrial, maritime, and aeronautical "frontiers"—that we must stress some technical understanding of these characteristics of space. This chapter may serve as a summary or review of some of the key concepts necessary for a firm understanding of the realm of space. Further in-depth study, beginning with the references cited within, is de rigueur for anyone interested in a better understanding of space policy and power and is especially important for space decisionmakers. Making policy and power decisions without this understanding would be akin to formulating a maritime strategy using a team of "experts" who had never seen the ocean or experienced tides, had no concept of buoyancy, or seen sail or shore.

Notes

[1] For in-depth development of the concepts introduced in this chapter, refer to Jerry J. Sellers et al., *Understanding Space: An Introduction to Astronautics*, 3[d] ed. (New York: McGraw-Hill, 2005), from which much of this material has been excerpted or summarized. The classic text in this field is Roger R. Bate, Donald D. Mueller, and Jerry E. White, *Fundamentals of Astrodynamics* (New York: Dover Publications, 1971). Another excellent reference geared toward those not technically trained is David Wright et al., *The Physics of Space Security: A Reference Manual* (Cambridge: American Academy of Arts and Sciences, 2005).

[2] Kepler's First Law applied to Earth-orbiting satellites: the orbit of each planet is an ellipse with the Sun at one focus.

[3] Sellers et al., 182–184.

[4] A simple example: to move a satellite from a circular orbit at an altitude of 300 km (a = 6,678 km, V total= 7.726 km/sec) to a higher, 1,000 km altitude orbit (a = 7,378 km, V = 7.350 km/sec) requires a ΔV total of 378 m/sec. For a 1,000 kg satellite (initial mass on orbit), this would require approximately 155 kg of fuel using a common monopropellant rocket propulsion system.

[5] The same process can be used to disperse several satellites placed into an initial, identical orbit by a single launch vehicle—the effective reverse of a rendezvous maneuver. The satellites each perform well-timed "speed up and slow down" maneuvers to establish a constellation of equally spaced satellites (in time and angle) that might provide near-continuous coverage over the Earth.

[6] RAAN precession occurs westward for direct orbits (inclination < 90°), eastward for retrograde orbits (inclination > 90°), and zero for polar orbits (inclination = 90°) and equatorial orbits (inclination = 0°).

[7] Earth oblateness gives rise to two unique orbits with very practical applications: sun-synchronous and Molniya. The first case uses the eastward nodal progression when i > 90°. At i ≈ 98° (depending on spacecraft altitude), the ascending node moves eastward at the same rate as the Earth around the Sun (about 1° per day), keeping the spacecraft's orbital plane in the same orientation to the Sun throughout the year such that the spacecraft will always see the same Sun angle when it passes over a particular point on the Earth's surface. This is important for remote-sensing missions (such as reconnaissance) because observers can better track long-term changes in weather, terrain, and manmade features.

The Molniya (in Russian, *lightning*) orbit is usually a 12-hour orbit with high eccentricity (e ≈ 0.7), perigee location in the Southern Hemisphere, and i = 63.4. At this inclination, the perigee does not rotate, so the spacecraft "hangs" over the Northern Hemisphere for nearly 11 hours of its 12-hour period before it whips quickly through perigee in the Southern Hemisphere. Molniya orbits can provide communication coverage to areas of high latitude that could not practically use geostationary orbits.

[8] For example, the European Space Agency's launch site at Kourou (4°N latitude) gives launch vehicles an assist of 0.464 km/sec versus 0.4087 km/sec for the Kennedy Space Center at 28.5° latitude.

[9] $\Delta V = I_{sp}g_o ln \frac{mi}{mf}$ where g_o is the gravitational acceleration constant (9.81 m/sec²); m_i is the initial mass of the spacecraft (fully fueled); and m_f is the final mass (fuel empty).

[10] Jerry J. Sellers et al., "Investigation into Cost-Effective Propulsion System Options for Small Satellites," *Journal of Reducing Space Mission Cost* 1, no. 1 (1998).

[11] Recent bounding examples in the United States are Space Exploration (SpaceX) Incorporated's Falcon I vehicle (~1,000 pounds to low Earth orbit) on the low end and the two families of Evolved Expendable Launch Vehicles (EELV), Lockheed-Martin's Atlas V and Boeing's Delta IV. While exact figures on these are not available, low estimates for Falcon I are probably $100 million, while EELV developmental funding was several billion dollars.

[12] The VentureStar program was canceled in March 2001 after NASA canceled the suborbital X–33 technology demonstrator meant to reduce risk for full VentureStar development. NASA expenditures for X–33 totaled $912 million.

[13] Sellers, *Understanding Space*, 84.

[14] James R. Wertz and Wiley J. Larson, eds., *Space Mission Analysis and Design*, 3d ed. (Dordrecht, Netherlands: Kluwer Academic Publishers, 1999).

[15] The French Cerise spacecraft became the first certified victim of space junk when its 6-meter gravity-gradient boom was clipped during a collision with a leftover piece of an Ariane launch vehicle in 1996.

[16] Wertz and Larson, 1999.

[17] Given by Wien's Displacement Law, $\lambda m = \frac{2898}{T}$, where λ_m is the wavelength of maximum output in micrometers (mm) and T is the object's temperature in degrees Kelvin.

[18] Given by the Stefan-Boltzmann equation, $q_A = \varepsilon \sigma T^4$, where q_A is the object's power per unit area (W/m²), ε is the object's emissivity ($0 \leq \varepsilon \leq 1$), s is the Stefan-Boltzmann constant (5.67 x 10^{-8} W/m²K⁴), and T is the object's temperature in degrees Kelvin.

[19] Resolution = $\frac{2.44\lambda h}{D}$ where λ is the wavelength of the sensed radiation, h is the distance between the sensor and the target, and D is the instrument's aperture diameter.

[20] A conventional radar operating at a wavelength of 240,000 mm would need an aperture of more than 480 km (298 miles) to get the same resolution as an optical system with a mere 1-meter aperture! Fortunately, signal-processing techniques that enable synthetic aperture radar—effectively enlarging the radar aperture—can achieve much higher effective apertures and thus higher resolutions.

[21] $SNR = \left(\frac{P_t G_t}{kB}\right)\left(\frac{\lambda}{4\pi R}\right)^2\left(\frac{G_r}{T}\right)$, where P_t is transmitter power, G_t is transmitter gain, k is Boltzmann's constant, B is the receiver system's bandwidth, λ is the signal wavelength, R is the range to receiver, G_r is the receiver gain, and T is the receiver system's temperature.

[22] For example, a bit error rate of 10–3 implies an error rate of 1 bit out of every 1,000 bits; typical bit error rates are ~10–5 for voice and ~10–14 for data.

Part II: Space and National Security

Chapter 5

Increasing the Military Uses of Space

Everett C. Dolman and Henry F. Cooper, Jr.

America's reliance on space is so extensive that a widespread loss of space capabilities would prove disastrous for both its military security and its civilian welfare. The Armed Forces would be obliged to hunker down in a defensive crouch awaiting withdrawal from dozens of no-longer-tenable foreign deployments. America's economy, and along with it the rest of the world's, would collapse.

For these reasons, the Air Force is charged with protecting space capabilities from harm and ensuring reliable space operations for the foreseeable future. As a martial organization, the Air Force looks to military means to achieve these assigned ends—as well it should. The military means it seeks include the ability to apply force in, through, and from space, as well as enabling and enhancing terrestrially based forces. Is this not self-evident?

Consider for a moment that the Navy has a similar charge: to ensure freedom of access to international waters and, when directed in times of conflict, to ensure that other states cannot operate there. Now imagine how the Navy might achieve these objectives if it were denied the use of weapons, to include shore-based weapons or those owned by other Services. What if it were further denied the capacity or legal power to research, develop, or test weapons? How effective could it be? Such restrictions would be absurd, of course. And yet this scenario is almost perfectly parallel with the conundrum facing the Air Force in space.

In this chapter, we make the case that opposition to increasing the militarization and weaponization of space is a misapplied legacy of the Cold War and that dramatic policy shifts are necessary to free the scientific, academic, and military communities to develop and deploy an optimum array of space capabilities, including weapons in space, eventually under the control of a U.S. Space Force.

Creating the Myth of Space Sanctuary

During World War II—before the advent of the atomic bomb or intercontinental ballistic missiles (ICBMs)—the Chief of the U.S. Army Air Corps, General "Hap" Arnold, had a prescient view of the future:

> Someday, not too distant; there can come streaking out of somewhere (we won't be able to hear it, it will come so fast) some kind of gadget with an explosive so powerful that one projectile will be able to wipe out completely this city of Washington. . . . I think we will meet the attack alright [sic] and, of course, in the air. But I'll tell you one thing, there won't be a goddam pilot in the sky! That attack will be met by machines guided not by human brains, but by devices conjured up by human brains.[1]

Within about 15 years of Arnold's comments, Soviet ICBMs armed with nuclear warheads did indeed have the ability to threaten Washington, but over 40 years later, America's ability to reliably defend itself from ICBMs remains minimal—due not to technology limitations but to long-standing policy and political constraints.

To understand the passion of the current opposition to space weapons, one must look into the fundamental issue of the Cold War: nuclear weapons deployed at a scale to threaten the existence of all life on the planet. The specter of potential nuclear devastation was so horrendous that a neo-ideal of a world without war became a political imperative. Longstanding realist preference for peace through strength was stymied by the invulnerability of ballistic missiles traveling at suborbital velocities. Thus, America accepted a policy of *assured* and *mutual* destruction to deter its opponents in a horrible (if effective) balance of terror. This meant it became politically infeasible even to contemplate shooting down missiles aimed at America or its allies—especially from machines in space that might prove so efficient as to *force* an opponent to strike while it could, before such a system became operational.

With the coupling of space capabilities, including the extremely important roles of force monitoring and treaty verification, to nuclear policy, the unique characteristics of nuclear weapons and warfare became interconnected with military space. This is perhaps understandable, if fundamentally in error, but not only did space weapons become anathema for missile defense, but also weapons in space for the protection of interests there became a forbidden topic.

Ironically, elements of the elite scientific community in the 1950s and 1960s created the conditions that frustrated the second half of Arnold's vision, which called upon America's edge in technology to provide for the Nation's defense—because they believed reaching that objective was not achievable and that seeking to achieve it was not desirable. Perhaps because they were motivated by guilt for their complicity in bringing the nuclear bomb to fruition, these individuals preferred to rely solely on diplomacy and arms control and argued against exploiting technology, which they believed would only provoke an arms race. They advocated this point of view at the highest political levels—and they were very successful in meeting their objectives.

Whether by design or chance, the civilian leadership 40 to 50 years ago also imposed bureaucratic institutional constraints that limited the ability of the Services to exploit cutting-edge technologies to take advantage of space for traditional military purposes. When combined with arms control constraints and the current lack of vision among the military Services, this same dysfunctional space bureaucracy is simply not responsive to the growing threat from proliferating space technology among our adversaries as well as our friends.

What World Views Should Guide Space Exploration?

Current international relations political theory generally divides the panoply of world views into three broad outlooks: *Wilsonian idealism* or *liberalism, Marxist collectivism* or *socialism,* and *Hobbesian realism* (see figure 5–1). Arguably the most prevalent of these—certainly among practitioners if not academics—is the last, yet it has been conspicuously absent in the academic and theoretical debates concerning space exploration.

Wilsonian idealism is based on the tenets of a peaceful and democratic world order as espoused by Woodrow Wilson. It includes the notions that law and institutions are important factors leading to peace and that weapons are a basic cause of war. Hence, prevention of space weaponization through treaties and existing international organizations, completely eschewing any positive role for armed force, is its key pillar of space exploration. Equally prominent in the history of space development—due to the bipolar power structure of world politics through most of its developmental stage—has been the position of *Marxist-inspired collectivists*, who insist that space should not be appropriated by the nations or corporations of the Earth, and that whatever bounty is realized there must be shared by all peoples. Collectivist efforts are generally focused on legal and moral arguments binding states in a system of global wealth-sharing.

Figure 5–1. Triangulating the Space Exploitation Debate

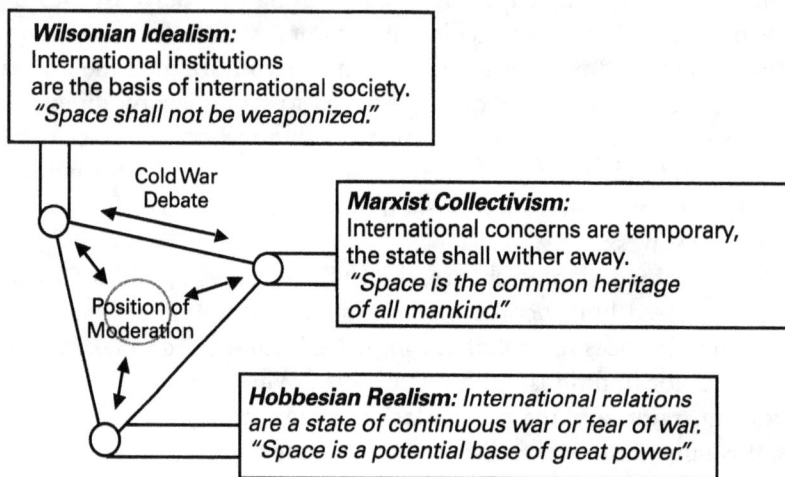

Wilsonian Idealism:
International institutions
are the basis of international society.
"Space shall not be weaponized."

Cold War
Debate

Marxist Collectivism:
International concerns are temporary,
the state shall wither away.
*"Space is the common heritage
of all mankind."*

Position of
Moderation

Hobbesian Realism: International relations
are a state of continuous war or fear of war.
"Space is a potential base of great power."

Hobbesian realists, inspired in part by the political teachings of Thomas Hobbes, generally perceive the condition known as *anarchy*—that awful time when no higher power constrains the base impulses of men and states, and both survive by strength and wit alone—to be the underlying condition of international relations. Might indeed makes right to these theorists, if not morally, certainly in fact. For them, states exist in a perpetual condition of war. Periods between combat are best understood as preparation for the inevitable next conflict. The harshest view in this group is called *realpolitik*.

We advocate a position far less harsh than that of Hobbes, an outlook increasingly known as *soft realism*, as we believe that proper use of military power within a framework of laws and rules can lead to greater security and welfare for all peoples, not just the wielders of that power. We do assert, however, that the state retains its position as the primary actor in international affairs and that violence has an indisputable and continuing influence on relations between states and nonstate actors.

Still, in most academic and policy debates, the realist view has been set aside (at least rhetorically) as states jockey for international space leadership. Those who even question the blanket prohibitions on weapons or market forces in space exploration are ostracized. To actually advocate weaponization in space brings full condemnation. Accordingly, the debate has not been whether space *should* be weaponized, but how best to *prevent* the weaponization of space; not whether space *should* be developed commercially, but how to ensure the spoils of space are nonappropriable and *distributed fairly* to all. There has been little room for the view that state interest persists as the prime motivator in international relations, or that state-based capitalist exploitation of outer space would more efficiently reap and distribute any riches found there. It is for these reasons, we insist here and in several other venues, that space exploration and exploitation have been artificially stunted from what might have been.[2]

Hence, a timely injection of realist thought may be precisely what is needed to jolt space exploration from its post-Apollo sluggishness. Our intent here, then, is to add the third point of a theoretical triangle in an arena where it had been missing, so as to center the debate on a true midpoint of beliefs, and not along the radical axis of two of the three world-views.

The Misplaced Logic of Antiweaponization

Opposition to the deployment of weapons in space clusters around two broad categories of dissent: that it *cannot* be done, and that it *should not* be done.

Space Weapons *Are* Possible

Arguments in the first category spill the most ink in opposition, but they are relatively easy to dispatch. Consider first that history is littered with prophesies of technical and scientific inadequacy, such as Lord Kelvin's famous retort, "Heavier-than-air flying machines are impossible." Kelvin, a leading physicist and president of the Royal Society, made this boast in 1895, and no less an inventor than Thomas Edison agreed. The possibility of spaceflight prompted even more gloomy pessimism. A *New York Times* editorial in 1921 excoriated Robert Goddard for his silly notions of rocket-propelled space exploration (an opinion it has since retracted): "Goddard does not know the relation between action and reaction and the need to have something better than a vacuum against which to react. He seems to lack the basic knowledge ladled out daily in high schools." Compounding its error in judgment, opining in 1936, the *Times* stated flatly, "A rocket will never be able to leave the Earth's atmosphere."[3]

Bluntly negative scientific opinion on the possibility of space weapons writ large has been weeded out over time. No credible scientist today makes the claim of impossibility, and so less encompassing arguments are now the rule. The debate has moved to more subtle and scientifically sustainable arguments that a *particular* space weapon is not feasible. Mountains of mathematical formulae have been piled high in an effort, one by one, simply to bury the concept. But these limitations on specific systems are less due to theoretical analysis than to assumptions about future funding and available technology.[4] The real objection, too often hidden from view, is that a *particular* weapons system or capability cannot be developed and deployed within the planned budget or within narrowly specified means. When one relaxes those assumptions, opposition on technical grounds generally falls away.

Furthermore, counterexamples exist—for example, the Brilliant Pebbles space-based interceptor system was the most advanced defense concept to emerge from the Strategic Defense Initiative (SDI). After a comprehensive series of technical reviews by even the strongest critics in 1989, it achieved major defense acquisition program status in 1990, was curtailed by congressional cuts in 1991 and 1992, and then was canceled by the Clinton administration in 1993. But the cancellation of the most advanced, least expensive, and most cost-effective missile defense system produced by the SDI program was for political, not technical, reasons.[5]

The devil may very well be in the details. But when critics oppose an entire *class* of weapons based upon analyses that show *particular* weapons will not work, their arguments fail to consider the inevitable arrival of fresh concepts or new technologies that change all notions of current capabilities. Have we thought out the details enough to say categorically that *no* technology will allow for a viable space weapons capability? If so, then the argument is pat; no counter is possible. But if there are technologies or conditions that *could* allow for the successful weaponization of space, then ought we not argue the policy details first, lest we be swept away by a course of action that merely chases the technology wherever it may go?

Space Weapons *Should* Be Deployed

Opponents of space weapons on technical or budgetary grounds are *not* advocating space weapons in the event their current assumptions or analyses are swept aside. Rather, they argue that we *ought* not to deploy space weapons. Granted, just because a thing *can* be done does not mean it *should* be. But prescience is imperfect, new technologies emerge unpredictably, and foolish policymakers eschew adapting to them until their utility is beyond doubt. In anticipation of coming technologies that would make space weaponization a most cost-effective option, moral opposition centers on six essential arguments.

Space weapons are expensive; alternatives are cheaper and just as effective. This is the first argument against space weaponization, although it is an easy one to set aside. Of course space weapons are expensive—very expensive, though not necessarily more expensive than terrestrially based systems that may accomplish the same objectives, not to mention objectives that cannot be met otherwise—but so are all revolutionary technologies, particularly those that pioneer a new medium. Furthermore, the state that achieves cutting-edge military technology first has historically been the recipient of tremendous battlefield advantage, and so pursuit of cutting-edge technology continues—despite the enormous cost. Moreover, the cultural and economic infrastructure that allows for and promotes innovation in the highest technologies *tends to remain at the forefront* of international influence.

All empires decline and eventually are subsumed, but it has not been their search for the newest technologies or desire to stay at the forefront of innovation that causes their declines. Rather, it has been the *policies* of those states, generally an overexpansion of imperial control or an economic decision to freeze technologies, that result in their stagnation and demise. Space and space technology represent both the resources and the innovation that can keep a liberal and responsible American hegemony in place for decades, if not centuries, to come; furthermore, unless America maintains this technological edge, it will likely lose its preeminence.

A follow-on argument is rhetorical and usually takes the form, "Wouldn't the money spent on space weapons be better spent elsewhere?" It would be lovely if the tens of billions of dollars necessary to effectively weaponize space could be spent on education, or the environment, or dozens of other worthy causes, but this is a moot argument. Money necessary for space weapons will not come from the Departments of the Interior or State or from any other department except Defense. Any windfall for *not* pursuing space weaponization is speculative only and is therefore not transitive. This means that the funds for space weaponization will come at the expense of other military projects, from within the budget of the Department of Defense. This observation is the basis for criticism among military traditionalists, who see the advent of space weapons as the beginning of the end for conventional warfare.

Current conventional military forces and means are enough to ensure America's security needs, so why risk weaponization of space? The

United States has the greatest military force the world has known; why change it when it is not broken? This argument is, obviously, tightly connected to the previous response, which points out that states failing to adapt to change eventually fall by the wayside. But more so, it shows a paucity of moral righteousness on the opposition's side. For the cost of deploying an effective space weapons program, America could buy and maintain 10 more heavy divisions (or, say, 6 more carrier battlegroups and 6 fighter wings). Let us suppose that is true. What would be more threatening to the international environment, to the sovereignty of states: a few hundred antiballistic missile satellites in low Earth orbit (LEO) backed by a handful of space lasers, or 10 heavy divisions with the support infrastructure to move and supply them anywhere on the globe?

This further highlights a common ethical omission of many space weaponization opponents. Most insist they are not opposed to weapons per se, only to weapons in space. Indeed, they insist a conventional strike against a threatening state's space facility would be just as effective as destroying satellites in space and a whole lot cheaper and more reliable to boot. But what does it say about an argument that asserts weapons cannot be in space, where no people reside, and insists that wars there would be terrible, while at the same time it advocates, even encourages, such violence on Earth? Why is it that weapons in *space* are so dreadful, but the same weapons on land, on sea, and in the air are perfectly fine?

Space is too vast to be controlled. If one state weaponizes, then all other states will follow suit, and a crippling arms race in space will ensue. Space is indeed vast, but a quick analysis of the fundamentals of space terrain and geography shows that control of just LEO would be tantamount to a global gate or checkpoint for entrance into space, a position that could not be flanked and would require an incredible exertion of military power to dislodge. Thus, the real question quickly becomes not whether the United States should weaponize space first, but whether it can afford to be the *second* to weaponize space.

Space has been dubbed the *ultimate high ground* (see figure 5–2). As with the high ground throughout history, whosoever sits ensconced upon it accrues incredible benefit on the terrestrial battlefield. This comes from the dual advantages of enhanced span of command acuity (visibility and control) and kinetic power. It is simply easier and more powerful to shoot down the hill than up it.

The pace of technological development, particularly in microsatellites and networked operations, could allow a major spacefaring state to quickly establish enough independent kinetic kill vehicles in LEO (through multiple payload launches) to effectively deny entry or transit to any other state. Currently, the United States has the infrastructure and capacity to do so; China may in the very near future. Russia is also a potential candidate for a space coup. Should any one of these states put enough weapons in orbit, they could engage and shoot down attempts to place counterspace assets in orbit, effectively taking control of outer space. Indeed, the potential to be gained from ensuring spacepower projection while denying that capability in others is so great that some state, some day, *will* make the attempt.

Figure 5–2. Gravitational Terrain of Earth-Moon Space

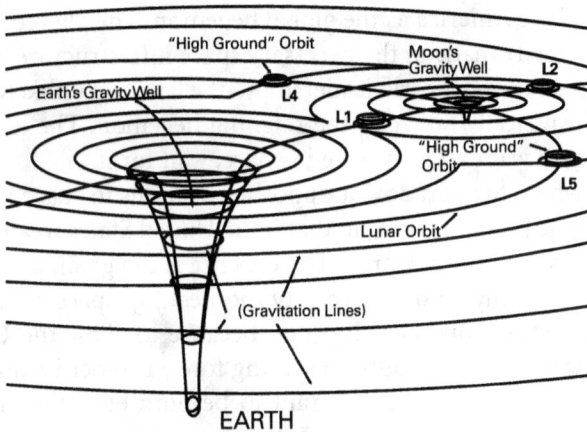

In order to ensure that no one tries, space weapons opponents argue that the best defense is a good example. So long as the United States does not make any effort to weaponize space, why would any competing state be tempted to do so? And even if another state does attempt it, the United States has the infrastructure to quickly follow suit and commence a campaign of retrieval in space. Not only does the logic escape us, but also it seems that by waiting, the United States is *guaranteeing* what space weapons opponents fear most: a space arms race.

All states will oppose an American military occupation of space, and their combined power will accelerate the demise of the United States. There is no doubt that the United States will be opposed in its efforts to dominate space militarily. There will always be fear that any state attempting to enhance its power may use it to act capriciously, but to suggest that the inevitable result is a space arms competition is the worst kind of mirror-imaging. If the United States, in the very near future, were to seize space, it would do so in an attempt to extend its current hegemonic power. Other states may feel threatened by this and will certainly begrudge it, but would any be willing to bankrupt their economies to develop the multi-trillion-dollar infrastructure necessary to defeat the United States *in* space, all the way up the daunting gravity well of Earth? Especially after the first billions were spent and a weapons system was launched, if the United States showed the will to destroy that rocket in flight (or the laser on the ground), how long would another state be willing to sustain its commitment to replacing America as controller of space?

On the other hand, any attempt by another power to seize and control space must be viewed as an attempt to overturn the extant international order, to replace America as the global hegemon. The United States, with investment already made in the necessary space infrastructure, would be forced to compete or cede world leadership—the latter an unlikely decision, one never historically taken by the reigning hegemon. The lesson is unambiguous; if you want an arms race in space, wait for it.

But here is where the paradox of opposing weapons in space is most apparent. On the one hand, we are told that if the United States weaponizes space, it will accelerate its own demise. The expense is too great, the ill will it fosters too encumbering, and the security too fleeting. Space cannot be controlled and therefore combat will occur, because to allow the United States to control space is tantamount to serving forever under its imperial thumb. Oddly, space weaponization is said to be both empowering and crippling—whichever argument appears most persuasive at the time.

Weaponization of space will create conditions that will make space travel risky if not impossible. Having extended the illogic of opposing space weapons to the limit, opponents then take on the mechanics of war and the evils of the military. As for the first argument, orbital debris is the challenge, which the recent Chinese antisatellite (ASAT) test confirms. The destruction of its own dying satellite in 2007 created thousands of bits of debris that are now floating at orbital velocity, an expanding cloud that poses a lasting navigational hazard to legitimate space flight. True, the Chinese test was criminal, especially since it *could have* engaged with almost no debris remnants if it had altered its engagement path. In over a dozen antisatellite tests that the Soviet Union held in the 1970s and 1980s, only the first left appreciable debris. After that, the massive co-orbital ASAT engaged in a kinetic direction toward the Earth, down the gravity well, causing all of the detritus of the ASAT and target to burn up in the atmosphere. Indeed, in a scenario where the United States is controlling space, most engagements would occur in launch phase, before the weapons even reach orbit. Any debris that is not burned up or destroyed will fall onto the launching state. Because tested weapons systems have maximized destruction to validate capabilities does not mean that future engagements must create long-lasting debris fields. Satellites are very fragile, and a bump or a push in the wrong direction is all that is necessary to send them spinning off into a useless or uncontrollable orbit—if you get to space first. Space war does not have to be dirty war, and in fact spacefaring nations will go out of their way to ensure that it is not (an argument that non-spacefaring powers may wish to fight dirty, and the only reliable defense against them would be *in* space, occurs below).

The second argument concerns commerce and tourism. Opponents say that space weapons would make individuals afraid to do business in space or travel there for pleasure, for fear of being blown to smithereens. This is an emotional appeal that has no basis in fact. Currently, for example, weapons are pervasive on the seas, in the air, and on land, but wherever there is a dominating power, commerce and travel are secure. America's Navy has dominated the open oceans for the last half-century, ensuring that commerce is fair and free for *all* nations, as has its Air Force in nonterritorial airspace. A ship leaving port today is more likely than ever to make it to its destination, safer from pirates, rogue states, navigational hazards, and even weather—all due to the enforcement of the rule of law on the seas and the assistance of sea- and space-based navigational assistance. Why would American dominance in space be different?

Space weapons advocates oppose treaties and obligations and want outer space ruled at the whim of whoever holds military power. This is a false argument, completely unsupportable. There is no dichotomy demanding law *or* order. Solutions lie in the most effective combination of law *and* order. There is no desire for a legal free-for-all or an arbitrary and capricious wielding of power by one state over all others. What we advocate is a *new* international legal regime that recognizes the lawful use of space by all nations, to include its commercial exploitation under appropriate rules of property and responsible free market values, to be enforced where necessary by the United States and its allies.

Beyond Theory: Military Space Realities

In 1991, U.S. forces defeated the world's fourth-largest military in just 10 days of ground combat. The Gulf War witnessed the public and operational debut of unfathomably complicated battle equipment, sleek new aircraft employing stealth technology, and promising new missile interceptors. Arthur C. Clarke went so far as to dub Operation *Desert Storm* the world's first space war, as none of the accomplishments of America's new-look military would have been possible without support from space.[6] Twelve years later, Operation *Iraqi Freedom* proved that the central role of spacepower could no longer be denied. America's military had made the transition from a space-supported to a fully space-enabled force, with astonishing results. The U.S. military successfully exercised most of its current spacepower functions, including space lift, command and control, rapid battle damage assessment, meteorological support, and timing and navigation techniques such as Blue Force tracking, which significantly reduced incidences of fratricide.

The tremendous growth in reliance on space from *Desert Storm* to *Iraqi Freedom* is evident in the raw numbers. The use of operational satellite communications increased four-fold, despite being used to support a much smaller force (fewer than 200,000 personnel compared with more than 500,000). New operational concepts such as *reach back* (intelligence analysts in the United States sending information directly to frontline units) and *reach forward* (rear-deployed commanders able to direct battlefield operations in real time) reconfigured the tactical concept of war. The value of Predator and Global Hawk unmanned aerial vehicles (UAVs), completely reliant on satellite communications and navigation for their operation, was confirmed. Satellite support also allowed Special Forces units to range across Iraq in extremely disruptive independent operations, practically unfettered in their silent movements.

But the paramount effect of space-enabled warfare was in the area of combat efficiency. Space assets allowed all-weather, day-night precision munitions to provide the bulk of America's striking power. Attacks from standoff platforms, including Vietnam-era B–52s, allowed maximum target devastation with extraordinarily low casualty rates and collateral damage. In *Desert Storm*, only 8 percent of munitions used were precision-guided, none of which were GPS-capable. By *Iraqi Freedom*, nearly 70 percent were precision-guided, more than half from GPS satellites.[7] In *Desert Storm*, fewer than 5 percent of aircraft were GPS-equipped. By *Iraqi Freedom*, *all* were. During *Desert Storm*, GPS proved so valuable that the Army procured and rushed into theater more than 4,500 commercial receivers to augment the meager 800 military-band ones it could deploy from stockpiles, an average of 1 per company (about 200 personnel). By *Iraqi Freedom*, each Army squad (6 to 10 Soldiers) had *at least* 1 military GPS receiver.

If, as it has been said, the 1990 Gulf War was the first space war—the birth of military enhancement and enabling space capabilities that had long gestated in the role of mission support—then the twin Operations

Enduring Freedom and *Iraqi Freedom* represent military spacepower's coming-out party. Space support enabled a level of precision, stealth, command and control, intelligence-gathering, speed, maneuverability, flexibility, and lethality heretofore unknown. U.S. combat capabilities were absolutely dominant in these conflicts—and the entire world now understands the significant military role played by space systems.

Unfortunately, the American military has bogged down in Phase IV operations in Iraq. An externally funded and supplied insurgency continues, and the death toll mounts. For critics of the George W. Bush administration's policies, the perceived inability of the U.S. Army to win this unconventional war is evidence that too much effort has been placed on conventional capabilities. A further argument persists that air and space forces are expensive luxuries that have no place in the retro-battlefield of counterterrorism. This is a position that ignores the cultural and political realities in Iraq and confuses policy for military capability.

Wherever America's ground troops engage in Iraq, they perform magnificently. In a nation as large as California with a population of more than 20 million, the 50,000 combat troops in Iraq are hard pressed to be in the right place at the right time. Support comes significantly from space and airborne assets, which are the first line of defense in the war on terror. The refuge of individuals whose intention is to spread violence randomly and without regard to the status of noncombatants is to blend into their surroundings. They are found out when they move in areas that are restricted, engage in Internet coordination or electronic communications, purchase or move incendiary materials or other weapons, or gather in significant numbers. When they do, they can be pinpointed, but with such a small force, it takes time for Soldiers to get into position and engage their targets.

Weapons in space could provide the global security needed to disrupt and counter small groups of terrorists wherever they operate, at the very moment they are identified. Currently, UAVs, dependent on space support for operations, fly persistent missions above areas of suspected terrorist activity in Iraq, providing real-time intelligence and, in some cases, onboard weapons to support ground forces in a specific area. Tactical units are informed of approaching hostiles, and due to all-weather and multi-spectral imaging systems, both friendly (Blue Force) and enemy tracking can occur throughout engagement operations. When ground troops are unable to respond to threatening situations beyond their line of sight or are unable to catch fleeing hostiles, armed UAVs can engage those threats.

The other option in a large-scale counterterror operation is to bring in an overwhelming number of troops, enough to create a line across the entire country that can move forward, rousting and checking every shack and hovel, every tree and ditch, with enough Soldiers in reserve to prevent enemy combatants from re-infiltrating the previously checked zones. America could in this manner combat low-tech terrorism with low-tech mass military maneuvers, perhaps at a cost savings over an effective space-based surveillance and engagement capability (if one does not count the value of a Soldier's life), but we do not think dollar value is the overriding consideration in this situation.

Terrorism in the form of limited, low-technology attacks is the most likely direct threat against America and its allies today, and space support is enabling the most sophisticated response ever seen. All-source intelligence has foiled dozens of attacks by al Qaeda and its associates. But what of the *most dangerous* threats today? Weapons of mass destruction, particularly nuclear but also chemical and biological ones, could be delivered in a variety of means vulnerable to interception if knowledge of their location is achieved in time for counteroperations to be effective. In situations where there is no defense available, or the need for one has not been anticipated, then time is the most precious commodity.

A limited strike capability from space would allow for the engagement of the highest threat and the most fleeting targets wherever they presented themselves on the globe, regardless of the intention of the perpetrator. The case of a ballistic missile carrying nuclear warheads is exemplary. Two decades ago, the most dangerous threat facing America (and the world) was a massive exchange of nuclear warheads that could destroy all life on the planet. Since a perfect defense was not achievable, negotiators agreed to no defense at all, on the assumption that reasonable leaders would restrain themselves from global catastrophe.

Today, a massive exchange is less likely than at any period of the Cold War, in part because of significant reductions in the primary nations' nuclear arsenals. The most likely *and* most dangerous threat comes from a single or limited missile launch, and from sources that are unlikely to be either rational or predictable. The first is an accidental launch, a threat we avoided making protections against due to the potentially destabilizing effect on the precarious Cold War balance. That an accidental launch, by definition undeterrable, would today hit its target is almost incomprehensible.

More likely than an accidental launch is the intentional launch of one or a few missiles, either by a nonstate actor (a terrorist or "rogue boat captain" as the scenario was described in the early 1980s) or a rogue state attempting to maximize damage as a prelude to broader conflict. This is especially likely in the underdeveloped theories pertaining to deterring third-party states. The United States can do nothing today to prevent India from launching a nuclear attack against Pakistan (or vice versa) except threaten retaliation. If Iran should launch a nuclear missile at Israel, or in a preemptory strike Israel should attempt the reverse, America and the world could only sit back and watch, hoping that a potentially world-destroying conflict did not spin out of control.

When President Reagan announced his desire for a missile shield in 1983, critics pointed out that even if a 99-percent-reliable defense from space could be achieved, a 10,000-warhead salvo by the Soviet Union still allowed for the detonation of 100 nuclear bombs in American cities—and both we and the Soviets had enough missiles to make such an attack plausible.

But if a single missile were launched out of the blue from deep within the Asian landmass today, for whatever reason, a space-based missile defense system with 99-percent reliability would be a godsend. And if a U.S. space defense could intercept a single Scud missile launched by terrorists from a ship near America's coasts before it detonated a nuclear warhead 100 miles up—creating an electromagnetic pulse that shuts down America's powergrid, halts America's banking and commerce, and reduces the battlefield for America's military to third world status[8]—it might provide for the very survival of our way of life.

Looking for Leadership

Such dire speculations call for enlightened leadership. Such a call is not new, but it is as yet unanswered. For example, in their February 2000 report, the co-chairmen of the Defense Science Board on Space Superiority wrote that:

> space superiority is absolutely essential in achieving global awareness on the battlefield, deterrence of potential conflict, and superior combat effectiveness of U.S. and Allied/Coalition military forces. . . . An essential part of the deterrence strategy is development of viable and visible (and perhaps demonstrated) capabilities to protect our space systems and to prevent the space capabilities being available to a potential adversary. . . . The Task Force recommends that improvements be made to our space surveillance system, higher priority and funding be placed on the "protection" of U.S. space systems, and that programs be started to create a viable and visible offensive space control capability.[9]

Despite this specific call for change near the beginning of the George W. Bush administration, one thought to be friendly to the idea of militarizing space, any move toward space superiority has so far been frustrated—as has consistently been the case during the past 50 years, when programs critical to obtaining an effective space force ran into a political/policy buzzsaw, particularly when space weapons were in any way involved. In 1983 and 1984, for example, the Reagan administration worked hard to reverse the so-called Tsongas amendment that held hostage the development and testing of the Air Force's F–15 hit-to-kill (HTK) ASAT system to a commitment that the United States would enter negotiations on a comprehensive ban of all ASAT systems. Congress, in response to the 1982 Reagan National Space Policy (which explicitly directed deployment of an ASAT system), was taken with testimony and arguments about the dangers of militarizing space and an associated arms race, the alleged lack of a requirement for an ASAT system, and suggested alternatives to developing an ASAT capability—especially including arms control.[10] A major component of the resistance came from members of the scientific community.

The Reagan administration's 1984 report to Congress and the administration's many meetings with Senators, Representatives, and their staffs eventually carried the day, and the Air Force was released to test successfully its prototype system on September 13, 1985—against a noncooperative target, which should be noted by those who claim all HTK tests have been against contrived targets.[11] An operational F–15 fighter used its prototype ASAT to shoot down a dying satellite that had been on orbit for years—against a cold space background. And that was over 20 years ago, using 25-year-old technology, in a program begun in the latter days of the Ford administration and carried through the Carter years into Reagan's second term.

So what happened? With fanfare about not militarizing space (responsive to criticism by the arms control elite and numerous nations, including the Soviet Union) and no serious Air Force advocacy, Congress defunded follow-on F–15 ASAT activities, and the United States has not built a hit-to-kill ASAT, in spite of the then- (and still-) operational Soviet/Russian co-orbital ASAT and China's recent test of its direct-ascent ASAT.[12]

The 1996 National Space Policies embed force application capabilities in euphemistic arms control language, for example, as discussed by Marc Berkowitz:

> [C]ritical capabilities necessary for executing space missions
> must be assured. Moreover, the policy directs that, consistent

with treaty obligations, the U.S. will develop, operate, and maintain space control capabilities to ensure freedom of action in space and, if directed, deny such freedom of action to adversaries. Such capabilities may also be enhanced by diplomatic, legal, or military measures to preclude an adversary's hostile use of space systems and services.[13]

The 2006 National Space Policy, released without fanfare on a Friday afternoon before a long holiday weekend, is consistent with the 1996 policy—and numerous preceding space policy statements as well.[14] Among other things, it states that "freedom of action in space is as important to the United States as air power and sea power"; notes that the exploration and use of outer space "for peaceful purposes" allows "U.S. defense and intelligence-related activities in pursuit of national interests"; states that "fundamental goals" are to "sustain the nation's leadership and ensure that space capabilities are available in time to further U.S. national security, homeland security and foreign policy objectives" and "enable U.S. operations in and through space to defend our interests there"; and directs the Secretary of Defense to "maintain the capabilities to execute space support, force enhancement, space control, and force application missions."

While the policy certainly can be interpreted to support an agenda to fully militarize space, decisive leadership to do so is lacking, presumably because of the political impedance illustrated by the above historical examples. Even military experts seem inclined to shrink from advocacy of fully exploiting space for military purposes—accepting that "space sensors are good, but space weapons are bad"—not a serious military perspective. Today, the Air Force contributes 90 percent of DOD's space personnel, 85 percent of DOD's space budget, 86 percent of DOD's space assets, and 90 percent of DOD's space infrastructure[15]—yet it has no comprehensive doctrine to guide the Nation's exploitation of space and assure U.S. supremacy—as the 2000 Defense Science Board stated should be the objective of the Nation's military space programs.[16]

Furthermore, the Defense establishment writ large also has taken little action to improve the situation, even under the leadership of former Defense Secretary Donald Rumsfeld, who in 2000 led a congressionally mandated Commission to Assess the United States National Security Space Management and Organization, fostered by former Senator Bob Smith (R–NH) to challenge the status quo of U.S. military space programs and move toward a needed U.S. Space Force.[17] The commission's unanimous bipartisan consensus conclusions and recommendations, which would move the Pentagon toward that desired objective, might have been expected to be guidelines under Secretary Rumsfeld—but, alas, there was little improvement on his watch. In fact, regressive steps, such as the disestablishment of U.S. Space Command, work in precisely the opposite direction. Meeting this challenge will rest with successor administrations.[18]

Astropolitical Realism

We aver that the application of space technology to military operations is simply the latest in a logical line of techno-innovations in the continuing process of developing military theory and strategy. In its narrowest construct, astropolitical realism comprises an extension of existing theories of global geopolitics into the vast context of the human conquest of outer space. In its more general and encompassing interpretation, it is the application of the prominent and refined realist visions of state political and military competition into outer space policy, particularly the development and evolution of a new legal and political regime that maximizes both global security and prosperity. Though historians have done an adequate job of describing the realist—even a harsh *realpolitik*—view of humanity's tendency toward confrontational diplomatic exchange in the chronology of space exploration, no similar effort has been made to place a stringent conceptual framework around and among the many vectors of space policies and chronicles.[19]

Thus, we propose fitting realist elements of space politics into their proper places in space strategy. While it may seem barbaric in this modern era to continue to assert the primacy of war and violence—"high politics" in the realist vernacular—in formulations of state strategy, it would be disingenuous and even reckless to try to deny the continued dominance of the terrestrial state and the place of military action in the short history and near future of space operations.

In the process, we advocate an open, honest debate about the future of American space intentions and the application of classical and emerging strategic theory to all realms of space exploration and exploitation—including:

- its protection as a domain for private investment and commercialization

- recognition of the emerging role of space as the critical, even quintessential, capacity for continuing American military preeminence in the international system

■ a thorough understanding of the astromechanical and physical properties of outer space essential for an optimum deployment of military space assets

■ a long-overdue development of a revamped legal and political regime based on current international realities and not Cold War fantasies.

Conclusion

With great power comes great responsibility. If the United States deploys and uses its military space force in concert with allies and friends to maintain effective control of space in a way that is perceived as tough, nonarbitrary, and efficient, adversaries would be discouraged from fielding opposing systems. Should the United States and its allies and friends use their advantage to police the heavens and allow unhindered peaceful use of space by any and all nations for economic and scientific development, control of low Earth orbit over time would be viewed as a global asset and a collective good. In much the same way it has maintained control of the high seas, enforcing international norms of innocent passage and property rights, the United States could prepare outer space for a long-overdue burst of economic expansion.

There is reasonable historic support for the notion that the most peaceful and prosperous periods in modern history coincide with the appearance of a strong, liberal hegemon. America has been essentially unchallenged in its naval dominance over the last 60 years and in global air supremacy for the last 15 or more. Today, there is more international commerce on the oceans and in the air than ever. Ships and aircraft of all nations worry more about running into bad weather than about being commandeered by a military vessel or set upon by pirates. Search and rescue is a far more common task than forced embargo, and the transfer of humanitarian aid is a regular mission. Lest one think this era of cooperation is predicated on intentions rather than military stability, recall that the policy of open skies advocated by every President since Eisenhower did not take effect until after the fall of the Soviet Union and the singular rise of American power to the fore of international politics. The legacy of American military domination of the sea and air has been positive, and the same should be expected for space.

As leader of the international community, the United States finds itself in the unenviable position of having to make decisions for the good of all. No matter the choice, some parties will benefit and others will suffer.

The tragedy of American power is that it must make a choice, and the worst choice is to do nothing. Fortunately, the United States has a great advantage: its people's moral ambiguity about the use of power. There is no question that corrupted power is dangerous, but perhaps only Americans are so concerned with the possibility that they themselves will be corrupted. They fear what they could become. No other state has such potential for self-restraint. It is this introspection, this angst, that makes America the best choice to lead the world today and tomorrow. America is not perfect, but perhaps it is perfectible, and it is preferable to other alternatives that will lead if America falters at the current crossroad.

Space weapons, along with the parallel development of information, precision, and stealth capabilities, represent a true revolution in military affairs. These technologies and capabilities will propel the world into an uncertain new age. Only a spasm of nuclear nihilism could curtail this future. By moving forward against the fears of the many, and harnessing these new technologies to a forward-looking strategy of cooperative advantage for all, the United States has the potential to initiate mankind's first global golden age. The nature of international relations and the lessons of history dictate that such a course begin with the vision and will of a few acting in the benefit of all. America must lead, for the benefit of all.

Notes

[1] Quoted from Jacob Neufeld, *Ballistic Missiles in the United States Air Force, 1945–1960* (Washington, DC: Office of Air Force History, 1990), 35.

[2] See, for example, Everett Dolman and John Hickman, "Resurrecting the Space Age: A State-Centered Commentary on the Outer Space Regime," *Comparative Strategy* 21 (Winter 2002), 1–45.

[3] Cited by Herbert London, "Piercing the Gloom and Doom," *American Outlook* (Spring 1999), available at <http://ao.hudson.org/index.cfm?fuseaction=article_detail&id=1270>.

[4] See, for example, Robert Preston, Dana J. Johnson, Sean J.A. Edwards, Michael D. Miller, and Calvin Shipbaugh, *Space Weapons: Earth Wars* (Santa Monica, CA: RAND Corporation, 2003).

[5] See Donald R. Baucomb, "The Rise and Fall of Brilliant Pebbles," *Journal of Social, Political, and Economic Studies* 29, no. 2 (2002), 145–190.

[6] Cited in John Burgess, "Satellites' Gaze Provides New Look at War," *The Washington Post*, February 19, 1991, A13.

[7] Testimony of Deputy Secretary of Defense Paul Wolfowitz, on U.S. Military Presence in Iraq: Implications for Global Defense Posture, for the House Armed Services Committee, Washington, DC, June 18, 2003. See also Department of Defense, *Conduct of the Persian Gulf War: Final Report to Congress* (Washington, DC: Department of Defense, April 1992), 227–228.

[8] While such a nuclear detonation would harm no one directly, the resulting electromagnetic pulse would wreak havoc on the U.S. powergrid, communication networks, and other critical infrastructure—with major national and international consequences. It could also cause significant upset and damage to satellite systems that are vital to U.S. terrestrial force operations and capabilities. See *Report of the Commission to Assess the Threat to the United States from Electromagnetic Pulse (EMP) Attack, Executive Report*, vol. I, 2004, pursuant to Public Law 201, 104th Congress, July 15, 1998.

⁹ Office of the Undersecretary of Defense for Acquisition and Technology, "Report of the Defense Science Board Task Force on Space Superiority," Washington, DC, February 2000. The board recommended that U.S. policymakers articulate two declaratory statements: "The United States will take all appropriate self-defense measures, including the use of force, to respond to the purposeful interference with U.S. or Allied space systems, or those systems critical in supporting national security interests"; and "The United States will take appropriate self-defense measures, including diplomatic and legal means as well as the flexible use of force, in response to the use of space by an adversary for purposes hostile to U.S. national interests." Among other things, the report concludes, "The use of space has become such a dominant factor in the outcome of future military conflict and in the protection of vital national and global interest that it should take on a priority and funding level similar to that which existed for U.S. strategic forces in the 1960s through 1980s."

¹⁰ See "Fact Sheet Outlining United States Space Policy," July 4, 1982, Public Papers of President Ronald W. Reagan, Ronald Reagan Presidential Library, available at <www.reaganutexas.edu/archives/speeches/1982/70482b.htm>.

¹¹ As argued in President Reagan's March 31, 1984, report to the Congress on U.S. Policy on ASAT Arms Control, such a comprehensive ban would not be verifiable and would be ineffective in precluding the development of a number of systems—including intercontinental ballistic missiles and various space systems—that would have inherent ASAT capability and, in any case, such a ban is not in the U.S. national security interest. President Reagan declared, "[N]o arrangements or agreements beyond those already governing military activities in outer space have been found to date that are judged to be in the overall interest of the United States or its Allies."

¹² The failure of the F–15 ASAT program, after a decade of research and development costing over $1.5 billion, can be traced to incoherence in program advocacy and related arms control initiatives during several administrations. See Henry F. Cooper, "Anti-Satellite Systems and Arms Control: Lessons from the Past," *Strategic Review* (Spring 1989), 40–48. For example, President Carter, while continuing the same F–15 ASAT program, proposed a comprehensive ASAT ban in 1977 in his first package of arms control initiatives—fortunately, the Soviets rejected it outright. Beginning with their 1981 UN proposal, the Soviets proposed a comprehensive ban—while conducting major military exercises including multiple tests of their co-orbital ASAT. The arms control community, including many in the scientific community, judged that the Reagan policy meant an end to arms control. See, for example, Paul B. Stares, *The Militarization of Space: U.S. Policy, 1945–1984* (Ithaca, NY: Cornell University, 1985).

¹³ A comprehensive discussion of the 1996 U.S. space policy is given by Marc J. Berkowitz, "National Space Policy and National Defense," *Spacepower for the New Millennium* (Colorado Springs: U.S. Air Force Institute for National Security Studies/McGraw-Hill, 2000), 37–59.

¹⁴ The unclassified summary of the 2006 National Space Policy, released by the White House on August 31, 2006, is available at <www.ostp.gov/html/US%20National%20Space%20Policy.pdf>.

¹⁵ Michael E. Ryan and F. Whitten Peters, *The Aerospace Force: Defending America in the 21ˢᵗ Century—A White Paper on Aerospace Integration* (Washington, DC: Department of the Air Force, May 2000), 5.

¹⁶ For a critical review of this lack of vision, see Peter L. Hays and Karl P. Mueller, "Going Boldly—Where? Aerospace Integration, the Space Commission, and the Air Force's Vision for Space," *Aerospace Power Journal* (Spring 2001).

¹⁷ The Commission's report, issued pursuant to Public Law 106–65 on January 11, 2001, is available at <www.defenselink.mil/pubs/space20010111.pdf>.

¹⁸ For a discussion of these considerations, see "What Do You Leave Behind? Evaluating the Bush Administration's National Security Space Policy," *George C. Marshall Institute Policy Outlook*, December 2006, available at <www.marshall.org/pdf/materials/490.pdf>.

¹⁹ See Walter McDougall's incomparable . . . *the Heavens and the Earth* (New York: Basic Books, 1986).

Chapter 6

Preserving Freedom of Action in Space: Realizing the Potential and Limits of U.S. Spacepower

Michael Krepon, Theresa Hitchens, and Michael Katz-Hyman

Our working definition of *spacepower* is the sum total of capabilities that contribute to a nation's ability to benefit from the use of space. Space-power, like other types of power, can wax or wane depending on a country's choices and those of its potential adversaries. Wise national decisions can lead to cumulative increases in spacepower, but even they can be negated, if, for example, significant debris-increasing events in space impair spacepower for all nations.

There is widespread agreement on what most of the key elements of spacepower are, but not all those elements are equal. Key elements would surely include possessing the relevant technology base, physical infrastructure, and workforce necessary to excel in space. Space prowess is also measured by how purposefully and successfully these essential elements are applied to specific missions. Many missions increase the sum total of a nation's capability in space. Metrics would include utilizing space for exploration and the advancement of knowledge; facilitating commercial transactions, resource planning, and terrestrial economic development; monitoring planetary health; mapping; providing a medium for telecommunications and broadcasting; assisting first responders, search and rescue operations, and disaster relief; providing early warning of consequential events; and utilizing space assets to enhance military and intelligence capabilities. The commercial, communication, and military uses of space have become less separable.

Since meaning is partly defined by circumstances—and since circumstances, with respect to the utilization of space, are so favorable for the United States—it is understandable why passionate and articulate American advocates of spacepower often define this term in a muscular way. Many forceful advocates equate spacepower with military missions because U.S. forces are extraordinarily dependent on space assets that confer significant advantages while saving countless lives on the battlefield, and because the negation of these assets would be so harmful.[1]

While the military uses of space are growing for the United States and other spacefaring nations, sweeping analogies between spacepower and terrestrial military power are unwise. In space, power is not accompanied by weapons—at least not yet. And in space, weapon-enabling technologies are widely applicable to nonmilitary pursuits. Weapon capabilities—or hard power—that can be utilized in space are currently confined to gravity-bound battlefields. In contrast, the soft power aspects of space prowess are unbounded, with satellites used for direct broadcasting and communication becoming conveyor belts for the projection of national culture and economic transactions. The long history of international cooperative research among civil space agencies reflects another element of soft spacepower. Collaborative efforts such as the Apollo-Soyuz mission, the International Space Station, and the space shuttle attest to the utility of soft spacepower as a diplomatic instrument. China, an emerging spacepower, is following this well-trodden path, at least in part, by forging space cooperation agreements with nations such as oil-rich Venezuela and Nigeria.

Nowhere is soft spacepower more evident than in the commercial realm, where economic competition is sometimes fierce but multinational cooperation is nonetheless required. The world relies at present on five major multinational corporations for the provision of global telecommunications. Global and national reliance on space assets has become intertwined not only for communications, but also for banking, disaster monitoring, weather forecasting, positioning, timing and navigation, and myriad other activities central to modern life. Many satellites primarily operated for commercial and civil uses can also serve military purposes. The use of space for commercial and economic development, as well as for other soft power applications, can be jeopardized if the deployment and use of weapons in space occur. This is because once weapons are used in space, their effects may not be controllable, as it is difficult to dictate strategy and tactics in asymmetric warfare. Consequently, weapons effects may not be limited to a small subset of satellites or those of a particular nation. In this sense, hard and soft spacepower cannot be decoupled. The misapplication of hard spacepower could therefore have indiscriminate effects, particularly if a destructive strike against a satellite produces significant and long-lasting debris.

The misapplication of hard power on Earth could also adversely affect relations between major powers, friends, and allies. However, the interconnectedness of hard and soft spacepower means that poor decisions by one spacefaring nation are more likely to negatively affect all other spacefaring nations, a situation that does not arise in nonnuclear, terrestrial conflict. Recovery from poor decisions in space also takes far longer than from nonnuclear, terrestrial conflict. For example, when conventional battles take place on the ground, sea, and air, debris is a temporary and geographically limited phenomenon. Minefields can be marked or cleared, and chemical spills can be contained or cleaned—although this may take large amounts of both time and money. Battlefield debris in space, however, can last for decades, centuries, or even millennia, thereby constituting an indiscriminate lethal hazard to space operations. Debris generated in space also tends to spread to other orbits over time, and environmental cleanup technologies in space do not appear promising at present.[2] In gravity-based warfare, the victor's spoils are gained through unhindered access. But such access is likely to be lost in the event that weapons are used in or from space, even for the "victor."

Battlefields in space are therefore fundamentally different from those on land, at sea, or in the air. The potentially disabling problem of space debris is now well recognized even by advocates of hard spacepower. Therefore, hit-to-kill kinetic energy antisatellite (ASAT) weapons that have been tested occasionally constitute a significant potential danger to space operations, as was most evident in China's test in January 2007, which created the worst debris-generating event in the history of the space age.[3] The earliest ASAT weapons—nuclear warheads atop ballistic missiles—would produce indiscriminate and lethal effects, as the United States learned after conducting a series of atmospheric nuclear tests in 1962. Nonetheless, this method of space warfare could still be employed. Currently, the preferred U.S. methods of using force to maintain "space control" entail nondestructive techniques (although U.S. officials and military leaders have not ruled out destructive methods). But bounding the unintended negative consequences of warfare in space depends on questionable assumptions, beginning with the dictation of rules of warfare against weaker foes. In unfair fights, however, weaker foes typically play by different rules. And if debris-causing space warfare hurts the United States severely, it is reasonable to expect that U.S. fastidiousness in engaging in warfare in space may not be reciprocated—as the Chinese kinetic-kill ASAT test seemed to indicate.

While appreciation of soft spacepower has expanded, arguments over the military uses of space have actually narrowed over time. In an earlier era, there were heated debates over the propriety of using space for monitoring secret military activities. Beginning in the 1970s, national technical means used to monitor nuclear forces received formal treaty protection. Subsequent debates focused on the propriety of using space to assist military operations. During the administrations of Presidents Jimmy Carter and Ronald Reagan, Soviet negotiators sought expansive definitions of space weapons (including the space shuttle) to constrain perceived U.S. military advantages in space. These negotiating gambits have long since lost their audience. The use of satellites to assist military operations on Earth is no longer controversial; instead, it has become the primary (and widely envied) metric of spacepower.

While debates over spacepower and its advancement have become more narrowly drawn, they continue to be quite heated. Current debates focus not on the military uses of space but rather on its weaponization. This dividing line is admittedly not clear-cut and is fuzziest on the issue of jamming, when disruptive energy is applied not against satellites per se, but against satellite communication links. Another gray area in the spectrum leading from militarization to weaponization relates to lasing objects in space.

While acknowledging gray areas (and discussing them further below), we submit that they do not absolve or oblige us to obliterate useful distinctions between the militarization and weaponization of space. It is true, for example, that long-range ballistic missiles that carry deadly weapons transit space en route to their targets. But ballistic trajectories constitute ground-based weapons aimed at ground-based targets, rather than being weapons based in space or aimed at space-based targets. Thus, we distinguish between transitory phenomena and permanent conditions. Similarly, we differentiate between the use of lasers for range finding, space tracking, and communication purposes, and the use of lasers to temporarily disable or destroy satellites. One type of activity provides substantial benefit while the other invites great risk. We further argue that U.S. national security and economic interests are advanced by working to clarify this distinction and by seeking the concurrence with and reinforcement of it by other key spacefaring nations.

By distinguishing between the militarization and the weaponization of space, we argue that analogies between spacepower and other forms of military power have only limited utility. In other realms of military affairs, we measure power by metrics such as the number of weapons available, various characteristics that make them more effective, and their readiness for employment. Accordingly, the distinction between militarization and weaponization is meaningless when we discuss air, ground, and naval forces. In contrast, spacepower is defined at present in the absence of the deployment and use of weapons in space. We argue that the absence of "dedicated" space weapons is favorable to the United States.

While some have compared space to another "global commons," the high seas, we believe this analogy to be deeply flawed. Warships provide backup for sea-based commerce, but they are essentially instruments of warfighting. Satellites, on the other hand, usually serve multiple purposes in both military and nonmilitary domains. A ship damaged in combat can seek safety and repairs at a friendly port. The debris from combat at sea sinks and rarely constitutes a lingering hazard. Defensive measures are easier to undertake at sea than in space. If space weapons are deployed and used, no nation can expect there to be safe havens in space. And if the most indiscriminate means of space warfare are employed, debris will become a long-lasting hazard to military and nonmilitary satellite operations.

All countries would be victimized if a new precedent is set and satellites are attacked in a crisis or in warfare. As the preeminent space power, the United States has the most to lose if space were to become a shooting gallery. The best offense can serve as an effective defense in combat at sea, but this nostrum does not apply in space, since essential satellites remain extremely vulnerable to rudimentary forms of attack. The introduction of dedicated and deployed weapons in space by one nation would be followed by others that feel threatened by such actions. The first attack against a satellite in crisis or warfare is therefore unlikely to be a stand-alone event, and nations may choose different rules of engagement for space warfare and different means of attack once this threshold has been crossed.

Our analysis thus leads to the conclusion that the introduction and repeated flight-testing of dedicated ASAT weapons would greatly subtract from U.S. spacepower, placing at greater risk the military, commercial, civil, and lifesaving benefits that satellites provide. Instead, we propose that the United States seek to avoid further flight testing of ASATs while hedging against hostile acts by other spacefaring nations.

We argue that realizing the benefits of spacepower requires acknowledgment of four related and unavoidable dilemmas. First, the satellites upon which spacepower depends are extremely vulnerable. To be sure, advanced spacefaring nations can take various steps to reduce satellite vulnerability, but the limits of protection will surely pale beside available means of disruption and destruction, especially in low Earth orbit (LEO). Vulnerabilities can be mitigated, but not eliminated.

Second, the dilemma of the profound vulnerability of essential satellites has been reinforced by another dilemma of the space age: satellites have been linked with the nuclear forces of major powers. Nuclear deterrence has long depended on satellites that provide early warning, communications, and targeting information to national command authorities. Even nuclear powers that do not rely on satellites for ballistic missile warning may still rely on them for communications, forecasting, and targeting. To interfere with the satellites of major powers has meant—and continues to mean—the possible use of nuclear weapons, since major powers could view attacks on satellites as precursors to attacks on their nuclear forces.

The third dilemma of spacepower is that space disruption is far more achievable than space control. A strong offense might constitute the best defense on the ground, in the air, and at sea, but this principle holds little promise in space since a strong offense in this domain could still be negated by asymmetric means. Space control requires exquisitely correct, timely, and publicly compelling intelligence; the readiness to initiate war and to prevent another nation from shooting back; as well as the ability to dictate the choice of strategy and tactics in space. It takes great hubris to believe that even the world's sole superpower would be able to fulfill the requirements of space control when a $1 bag of marbles, properly inserted into LEO, could destroy a $1 billion satellite. The ability of the United States to dictate military strategy and tactics in asymmetric, gravity-bound warfare has proven to be challenging; it is likely to be even more challenging in space, where there is less margin for error.

The fourth overarching dilemma relating to spacepower therefore rests on the realization that hard military power does not ensure space control, particularly if other nations make unwise choices and if these choices are then emulated by others. The United States has unparalleled agenda-setting powers, but Washington does not have the power to dictate or control the choices of other nations.

These dilemmas are widely, but not universally, recognized. Together with the widespread public antipathy to elevating humankind's worst practices into space, they help explain why the flight-testing and deployment of dedicated space weapons have not become commonplace. These capabilities are certainly not difficult to acquire, as they are decades old. Indeed, tests of dedicated ASAT weapons have periodically occurred, and such systems were deployed for short periods during the Cold War. If the weaponization of space were inevitable, it surely would have occurred when the United States and the Soviet Union went to extraordinary lengths to compete in so many other realms. The weaponization of space has not occurred to date and is not inevitable in the future because of strong public resistance to the idea of weapons in space, and because most national leaders have long recognized that this would open a Pandora's box that would be difficult to close.

Much has changed since the end of the Cold War, but the fundamental dilemmas of space control, including the linkage of satellites to nuclear deterrence among major powers, have not changed. The increased post–Cold War U.S. dependence on satellites makes the introduction of dedicated space weapons even more hazardous for national and economic security. Advocates of muscular space control must therefore take refuge in the fallacy of the last move, since warfighting plans in space make sense only in the absence of successful countermoves. Offensive counterforce operations in space do not come to grips with the dilemmas of spacepower, since proposed remedies are far more likely to accentuate than reduce satellite vulnerability.

This analysis leads inexorably to a deeply unsatisfactory and yet inescapable conclusion: Realizing the enormous benefits of spacepower depends on recognizing the limits of power. The United States now enjoys unparalleled benefits from the use of space to advance national and economic security. These benefits would be placed at risk if essential zones in space become unusable as a result of warfare. Spacepower depends on the preservation and growth of U.S. capabilities in space. Paradoxically, the preservation and growth of U.S. spacepower will be undercut by the use of force in space.

Because the use of weapons in or from space can lead to the loss or impairment of satellites of all major space powers, all of whom depend on satellites for military and economic security, we believe it is possible to craft a regime based on self-interest to avoid turning space into a shooting gallery. This outcome is far more difficult to achieve if major space powers engage in the flight-testing and deployment of dedicated ASAT weapons or space-to-Earth weapons. We therefore argue that it would be most unwise for the United States, as the spacepower with the most to lose from the impairment of its satellites, to initiate these steps. Similar restraint, however, needs to be exercised by other major spacefaring nations, some of which may feel that the preservation and growth of U.S. spacepower are a threat, or that it is necessary to hold U.S. space assets at risk. The United States is therefore obliged to clarify to others the risks of initiating actions harmful to U.S. satellites without prompting other spacefaring nations to take the very steps we seek to avoid. Consequently, a preservation and growth strategy for U.S. spacepower also requires a hedging strategy because, even if the United States makes prudent decisions in space, others may still make foolish choices.

Hedging

The exercise of restraint from using weapons in space is not easy for the world's most powerful nation or for other nations fearing catastrophic losses that they believe might be averted by disabling U.S. satellites. How, then, might U.S. spacepower influence the decisions of other nations to leave vulnerable satellites alone?

We maintain that a prudent space posture would clarify America's ability to respond purposefully if another nation interferes with, disables, disrupts, or destroys U.S. satellites, without being the first to take the actions that we wish others to refrain from taking. Thus, our proposed hedging strategy would not include the flight-testing and deployment of dedicated ASAT or on-orbit weapons because such steps would surely be emulated by others and would increase risks to vital U.S. space assets. Whatever preparations the United States takes to hedge against attacks on its satellites must be calibrated to maximize freedom of action and access in space. Hedging moves that create an environment where the flight-testing and deployment of space weapons would be a common occurrence would thus be contrary to U.S. military and economic security.

Responsible hedges by the United States include increased situational awareness, redundancy, and cost-effective hardening of satellites and their links. The strongest hedge the United States possesses is its superior conventional military capabilities, including long-range strike and special operations capabilities. Since an attack on a satellite can be considered an act of war, the United States could respond to such an attack by targeting the ground links and launch facilities of the offending nation or the nation that harbors a group carrying out such hostile acts. Far more punishing responses might be applicable. A hedging strategy is also likely to include ground-based research and development into space weapons technologies, activities that are under way in major spacefaring nations.

The demonstration of dual- or multi-use space technologies that could be adapted, if needed, to respond to provocative acts would constitute another element of a responsible hedging strategy. Such technologies could include on-orbit rendezvous, repair, and refueling technologies and other proximity operations. These activities are also essential for expanded scientific and commercial use of space and would be key enabling technologies for long-duration missions such as the return to the Moon and the exploration of Mars.

A prudent hedging strategy would also align U.S. military doctrine and declaratory policy with America's national security and economic interest in preventing weapons in space and ASAT tests. In the context of a proactive Air Force counterspace operations doctrine and official disdain for negotiations that might constrain U.S. military options in space, the hedging strategy we advocate might be perceived as preliminary steps toward the weaponization of space, which we would oppose. Wise hedging strategies would also be accompanied by constructive diplomatic initiatives.

The flight-testing of multipurpose technologies, the possession of dominant power projection capabilities, and the growing residual U.S. military capabilities to engage in space warfare should provide a sufficient deterrent posture against a "space Pearl Harbor."[4] These capabilities would also clarify that the United States possesses the means to defend its interests in a competition that other major space powers claim not to want, as well as to react in a prompt and punishing way against hostile acts against U.S. space assets.

If all responsible spacefaring nations adhere to a "no further ASAT test" regime, and an adversary still carries out a "space Pearl Harbor" by using military capabilities designed for other purposes, the United States has the means to respond in kind. U.S. latent or residual space warfare capabilities exceed those of other spacefaring nations and are growing with the advent of ballistic missile defenses. We maintain that the existence of such capabilities constitutes another element of a hedging strategy, while providing further support for our contention that dedicated ASAT tests and deployments are both unwise and unnecessary.

Space Preservation and Growth Strategy

A successful hedging strategy preserves and grows U.S. spacepower. In contrast, the flight-testing and deployment of dedicated ASAT and on-orbit weapons produce conditions whereby U.S. space assets are unlikely to be available or could be gravely impaired when needed. Space control operations that foster the preservation and growth of U.S. spacepower are to be welcomed; space control operations that would have the net effect of placing U.S. satellites at greater risk are to be avoided.

The U.S. Air Force's doctrine on space control operations, *Counterspace Operations*, requires the identification of adversary space assets and space-related capabilities on Earth. Identified targets include on-orbit satellites (including third-party assets), communication links, launch facilities, ground stations, and command, control, computers, communications, intelligence, surveillance, and reconnaissance (C⁴ISR) resources.[5] Many of these satellites or space-related assets can be targeted using multipurpose conventional capabilities. For example, launch facilities and ground stations can be targeted by ground forces, warships, and airpower. Communication links can be jammed using proven systems, and elements of C⁴ISR can be neutralized using cyber attacks. Many space powers possess these capabilities to varying degrees, which may help explain why dedicated systems to attack satellites have rarely been flight-tested or deployed.

The vulnerability of terrestrial space assets can be mitigated in a number of ways. Equipment can be hidden, hardened, or operated stealthily. Depending on the order of battle and opposing military capabilities, some assets could be protected by overwhelming force, and assets lost in battle can sometimes be replaced. These considerations are quite different in space, where force replacement is usually problematic and protection measures operate, at best, on the margins of economic and technical possibility.

Major space powers should be adept at locating satellites in Earth orbit. Maneuvering in space, unlike terrestrial warfare, is usually very limited. While satellites can be placed in orbits that pass over regions with limited space surveillance capabilities, the nature of orbital mechanics dictates that, at some point, satellites will be visible to ground observers.[6] Fuel is a more precious commodity in space due to its weight and very limited prospects for refueling. Maneuvering for most spacecraft is limited to normal station-keeping operations. Moreover, satellites, unlike tanks, cannot be suitably armored for combat. They can be hardened to withstand some types of electromagnetic interference and small impacts, but it is not feasible to shield against an impact from even a marble-sized debris hit, much less an intentional physical attack. Spacecraft shielding increases launch weight and costs by approximately $10,000 per pound.[7]

Operating satellites in formations is quite different from operating aircraft carrier battlegroups. Valuable warships can survive direct hits of various kinds, and the debris from losses at sea sinks to the bottom of the ocean. In contrast, the debris from satellite warfare could impair constellations in space, placing at risk the orbit of the high-value satellites meant to be protected. Arming satellites with defensive weapons is not a satisfactory solution for many reasons. Unlike warships or tanks that can maneuver and fire many weapons, satellites have little carrying capacity beyond that required to perform their missions. The fundamentals of space warfare described above—including the difficulties in dictating tactics and the choice of weapons, as well as the consequences of space debris—appear immutable. The marginal cost of attack will always be less than the marginal cost of defense, since attacking does not necessarily require technological sophistication and limited attacks can cause grievous injury.

If essential but vulnerable satellites cannot be effectively defended by space weapons, their protection rests largely on deterrence. When offense is too lethal to use because its net effect would be to harm vital national assets and interests, the default option for freedom of action in space is to accept mutual vulnerability. Nuclear deterrence had many detractors during the Cold War, even though it helped prevent nuclear exchanges between well-armed foes. The more power a nation possesses, the harder it is to accept vulnerability. But the benefits of hard and soft spacepower inescapably depend on satellites that are far easier to attack than to defend.

Asymmetric capabilities and vulnerabilities in space do not negate the precepts of deterrence or the essence of mutual vulnerability. During the Cold War, for example, Beijing faced not one but two hostile superpowers and yet chose to maintain nuclear forces that were significantly inferior to those of the United States and the Soviet Union. Presumably, China's leadership concluded that relatively few mushroom clouds were needed to clarify superpower vulnerability.

We argue, by analogy, that asymmetries related to dependence on space and capabilities in space do not alter the fundamentals of vulnerability and deterrence. The country with the most to lose from attacks on satellites, the United States, also has the most capabilities to respond with lethal force, which would be more indiscriminate because of the impairment or loss of its satellites. We have argued elsewhere that space warfare and its effects are unlikely to be country-specific. Because space warfare can be more indiscriminate than terrestrial warfare, and because all spacefaring nations are increasingly dependent on space assets for national and economic security, all major powers face the same fundamental dilemma that satellites are both essential and extraordinarily vulnerable, and that the use of weapons in space is likely to have unintended, negative consequences. Mechanical objects may be the initial victims of space warfare, but satellites are unlikely to be the only victims, since they are directly linked to soldiers, noncombatants, and nuclear weapons.

Nuclear deterrence was based on the repeated testing of nuclear weapons and their means of delivery, as well as on the deployment of many dedicated weapons systems in a high state of launch readiness. If we were to adopt such practices for dedicated ASAT or space-to-Earth weapons, satellite security would be greatly diminished, and relations among major powers, along with international space cooperation, would deteriorate. At best, a very uneasy standoff in space could result from the flight-testing and deployment of dedicated ASAT weapons. In our view, no further ASAT testing is required because, for all practical purposes, this uneasy standoff already exists. Major spacefaring nations have already clarified their ability to disrupt or destroy satellites. Since these capabilities are well understood, they do not need to be demonstrated by further testing, the net effect of which would be more worrisome than reassuring.

Mutual assured destruction in space is therefore far easier to maintain than nuclear deterrence was during the Cold War, because mutual vulnerability from the use of weapons in or from space does not require repeated demonstrations of the weapons in question. And unlike nuclear deterrence, which had the practical effect of limiting freedom of action, acceptance of mutual vulnerability in space would maximize freedom of action and access. Despite these significant differences, there are two principal connecting threads between the acceptance of mutual vulnerability between major nuclear powers and major space powers. First, attacks on satellites in crises between major powers risk the use of nuclear weapons. And second, existential vulnerability to nuclear and satellite attacks is not solvable by military means.

Code of Conduct

We view a code of conduct for responsible spacefaring nations as a necessary complement to a hedging strategy and as an essential element of a space posture that provides for the preservation and growth of U.S. space capabilities. A code of conduct makes sense because, with the increased utilization and importance of space for national and economic security, there is increased need for space operators and spacefaring nations to act responsibly. While some rules and treaty obligations exist, there are many gaps in coverage, including how best to avoid collisions and harmful interference, appropriate uses of lasers, and notifications related to potentially dangerous maneuvers. Because the increased utilization of space for security and economic purposes could lead to friction and diminished space assurance, it serves the interests of all responsible spacefaring nations to establish rules of the road to help prevent misunderstandings, catastrophic actions in space, and grievances.

Another reason for pursuing rules of the road is that interactive hedging strategies could generate actions in space that diminish space security by nations concerned about the import of technology demonstrations and flight tests. We have therefore argued that hedging strategies are best accompanied by diplomatic initiatives to set norms that increase the safety and security of satellites vital to U.S. national and economic security. A code of conduct would serve these purposes.

No codes of conduct or rules of the road are self-enforcing. Despite traffic laws, some drivers still speed. But having rules of the road reduces the incidence of misbehavior and facilitates action against reckless drivers. We acknowledge that there are no traffic courts for misbehavior in space, but we nonetheless argue that having agreed rules of the road in this domain will also reduce the incidence of misbehavior, while facilitating the isolation of the miscreant as well as the application of necessary remedies. Without rules, there are no rule breakers.

Traditional arms control was devised to prevent arms racing between the superpowers. With the demise of the Soviet Union, concerns over arms racing have been replaced by concerns over proliferation and nuclear terrorism. Cooperative threat reduction initiatives have been designed to deal with contemporary threats. These arrangements have taken myriad forms, including rules of the road to prevent proliferation. Since the flight-testing, deployment, and use of weapons in space would increase security concerns, and since security concerns are drivers for proliferation, agreed rules of the road for space could supplement other codes of conduct that seek to prevent proliferation.

Codes of conduct supplement, but differ from, traditional arms control remedies. Skeptics of new arms control treaties to prevent ASAT tests and space-based weapons argue that it would be difficult to arrive at an agreed definition of space weapons, and that even if this were possible, it would be hard to monitor compliance with treaty obligations. A code of conduct would focus on responsible and irresponsible activities in space that, in turn, would obviate the need for an agreed definition of space weapons. For example, a code of conduct might seek to prohibit the deliberate creation of persistent space debris. Again, our focus is on behavior, not an agreed definition of space weapons. Moreover, the deliberate creation of persistent space debris is very hard to hide and can be monitored by existing technical means.

The United States has championed codes of conduct governing militaries operating in close proximity at sea in the 1972 Incidents at Sea Agreement, as well as in the air and on the ground, in the 1989 Dangerous Military Practices Agreement. More recently, the United States has championed codes of conduct to reduce proliferation threats, including The Hague Code of Conduct (2002) and the Proliferation Security Initiative

(2003). The 2001 Space Commission Report chaired by Donald Rumsfeld also endorsed rules of the road for space.[8]

Codes of conduct typically take the form of executive agreements in the United States. They can begin as bilateral or multilateral compacts and they can expand with subsequent membership. Codes of conduct are either an alternative to, or a way station toward, more formal treaty-based constraints that often take extended effort.[9]

Some rules of the road, formal agreements, and elements of a code of conduct already exist for space. The foundation document that defines the responsibilities of spacefaring nations is the Outer Space Treaty (1967). Other key international agreements and institutions include the Liability Convention and the International Telecommunications Union.

There is growing sentiment among space operators to develop and implement several key elements of a code of conduct, including improved data sharing on space situational awareness; debris mitigation measures; and improved space traffic management to avoid unintentional interference or collisions in increasingly crowded orbits. A more comprehensive code of conduct might include elements such as notification and consultation measures; provisions for special caution areas; constraints against the harmful use of lasers; and measures that increase the safety, and reduce the likelihood, of damaging actions against manmade space objects, such as harmful interference against satellites that create persistent space debris. Key elements of a code of conduct are useful individually, but they are even more useful when drawn together as a coherent regime.

Situational Awareness

Space situational awareness (SSA)—the ability to monitor and understand the constantly changing environment in space—is one of the most important factors in ensuring the safety and security of all operational satellites and spacecraft. SSA provides individual actors with the ability to monitor the health of their own assets, as well as an awareness of the actions of others in space. Transparency measures can be particularly helpful in providing early warning of troubling developments and in dampening threat perceptions. One measure of U.S. spacepower and space prowess is America's unparalleled space situational awareness capabilities. Thus, the United States is in a position to become a leader in building space transparency, which is the foundation stone of norm setting and rules of the road in space.

Traffic Management

The International Academy of Astronautics (IAA) "Cosmic Study on Space Traffic Management" defines *space traffic management* as:

> the set of technical and regulatory provisions for promoting safe access into outer space, operations in outer space and return from outer space to Earth free from physical or radio-frequency interference.[10]

We also endorse intermediate steps toward this outcome and advocate empowering or creating an industry advisory group that could recommend actions and participate in the work of international bodies.

Notification and Consultations

The development of more formal processes for notification of satellite maneuvers is critical for ensuring space situational awareness; without such notification, satellite tracking and collision avoidance become much more difficult. Prelaunch notification could assist space surveillance as well as traffic management. Models for prelaunch notification could be the 2000 U.S.-Russian Joint Data Exchange Center[11] and the 2000 U.S.-Russian Pre- and Post-Launch Notification Agreement.[12] Elements from these agreements—as well as other ideas for data provision—might be studied by the United Nations Committee on the Peaceful Use of Outer Space's (COPUOS's) Scientific and Technical Subcommittee and translated into recommendations for either a voluntary regime or a possible multilateral accord.

Special Caution Areas

The IAA Cosmic Study mentions two different approaches to what the Dangerous Military Practices Agreement has termed *special caution areas*. In space, these might consist of provisions for safe distances or zones around satellites or more general "zoning" rules that restrict certain activities in certain orbital planes. Further in-depth study of the technical requirements and legal considerations surrounding the establishment of special caution areas is required before judgments can be made on the practicality and utility of such approaches; this is work that the IAA or other organizations could easily pursue.

Debris Mitigation

The deliberate generation of persistent space debris constitutes a hazard to space operations. Debris mitigation is therefore a pressing problem related to space traffic management. It is also the code of conduct element that has been furthest developed. The Inter-Agency Space Debris Coordination Committee (IADC), comprised of the space agencies of the world's major space powers, has developed a number of debris mitigation guidelines. Several nations have incorporated the agreed measures into their national laws and regulatory systems, and others are moving to do so. The United States is a leader in codifying strong debris mitigation guidelines. Thus, the United States is well placed to use this element of its soft spacepower to set strong international norms and work toward legally binding, formal international accords.

No Harmful Use of Lasers

There are at least two precedents for restricting the use of lasers during peacetime: the Prevention of Dangerous Military Activities Agreement and the Incidents at Sea Agreement.[13] The multiple applications of lasers highlight the utility of establishing rules of the road that distinguish between acceptable uses—such as range-finding, communication, and information-gathering—and uses that could be considered acts of war, such as dazzling, blinding, and damaging satellites. Norms regarding laser power/configuration for tracking purposes might be discussed to reduce the likelihood of damage to satellites and to reduce miscalculation. We endorse the convening of a panel of technical specialists, perhaps under the auspices of the IAA, to discuss this. COPUOS might usefully propose procedures for dealing with laser incidents.

Increasing Satellite Safety and Reducing the Likelihood of Satellite Damage

A national space strategy designed to preserve and grow U.S. capabilities in space would benefit from steps to increase satellite safety and reduce the potential damage to satellites upon which that strategy rests. This would, of course, include technical protection measures. However, it would also entail proactive diplomatic measures to prevent weapons-related creation of space debris. As advocates of U.S. spacepower, we therefore believe it would be wise to set rules of the road against the further testing of ASATs or other weapons based in space that would create debris by applying energy against targets. The use of weapons that produce indiscriminate and long-lasting damage in ground combat has justifiably earned widespread opprobrium. The use of certain weapons in space could be doubly injurious, since they could produce indiscriminate and long-lasting damage in orbit that, in turn, could prompt similar damage on Earth.

Conclusion

We have argued that spacepower rests on a broad foundation, building upward to the orbital dance of satellites. We further argue that spacepower is inextricably linked to, but different from, other forms of military power. The fundamental paradox of spacepower is that satellite effectiveness and vulnerability are inseparable, which makes hard power projection in and from space an extraordinarily risky undertaking. The preservation and growth of U.S. spacepower therefore requires the protection of satellites—vital assets that can readily be lost and quite difficult to replace in combat—by other means. We propose to address this dilemma through a variety of initiatives, including a hedging strategy and diplomatic initiatives centered on a code of conduct for responsible spacefaring nations.

Notes

[1] See, for example, David E. Lupton, *On Space Warfare: A Spacepower Doctrine* (Maxwell Air Force Base, AL: Air University Press, June 1998); Colin S. Gray, "The Influence of Spacepower upon History," *Comparative Strategy* 15, no. 4 (October–December 1996), 293–308; James Oberg, *Spacepower Theory* (Washington, DC: U.S. Government Printing Office, 1999); and Air Force Doctrine Document 2–2, *Space Operations* (Maxwell Air Force Base, AL: Air Force Doctrine Center, November 27, 2001).

[2] J.C. Liou and N.L. Johnson, "Risks in Space from Orbiting Debris," *Science* 311 (January 20, 2006), 340.

[3] Frank Morring, Jr., "Worst Ever: Chinese Anti-satellite Test Boosted Space-debris Population by 10% in an Instant," *Aviation Week and Space Technology*, February 12, 2007, 20.

[4] Department of Defense, "Report of the Commission to Assess United States National Security Space Management and Organization" (Washington, DC: Department of Defense, 2001), 22.

[5] Air Force Doctrine Document 2.2–1, *Counterspace Operations* (Washington, DC: Department of the Air Force, August 2, 2004), 32–33.

[6] Even classified satellites, for which no orbital data is publicly available, have been tracked by amateur ground observers using nothing more than a camera and a stopwatch. See, for example, the *Visual Satellite Observer's Home Page* Web site at <www.satobs.org/>.

[7] Futron Corporation, "Space Transportation Costs: Trends in Price per Pound to Orbit 1990–2000," available at <www.futron.com/pdf/resource_center/white_papers/FutronLaunchCostWP.pdf>.

[8] "Report of the Commission to Assess United States National Security Space Management and Organization," 18.

[9] For more information regarding space code of conduct approaches, see Michael Krepon and Christopher Clary, *Space Assurance or Space Dominance: The Case Against Weaponizing Space* (Washington, DC: The Henry L. Stimson Center, 2003), and Theresa Hitchens, *Future Security in Space: Charting a Cooperative Course* (Washington, DC: Center for Defense Information, September 2004).

[10] Corrine Contant-Jorgenson, Petr Lála, and Kai-Uwe Schrogl, eds., "Cosmic Study on Space Traffic Management" (Paris: International Academy of Astronautics, 2006), 10, available at <http://iaaweb.org/iaa/Studies/spacetraffic.pdf>.

[11] Peter L. Hays, "United States Military Space into the Twenty-first Century," Institute for National Security Studies Occasional Paper 42 (Colorado Springs: U.S. Air Force Academy, September 2002), 115–116.

[12] U.S. Department of State Fact Sheet, "Memorandum of Understanding on Notification of Missile Launches," December 16, 2000, available at <www.state.gov/t/ac/trt/4954.htm>; Philipp C.

Bleek, "U.S., Russia Sign Missile- and Space-Launch Notification Deal," *Arms Control Today* (January–February 2001), available at <www.armscontrol.org/act/2001_01_02/usruslaunch.asp>; Hays, 116.

[13] The Prevention of Dangerous Military Activities Agreement prohibits uses of lasers that might harm personnel or equipment; text of the agreement can be found in *International Legal Materials* 28, no. 2 (1989), 877–895. The Incidents at Sea accord prohibits the illumination of the bridges of the other parties' ships; see "Agreement Between the Government of the United States of America and the Government of the Union of Soviet Socialist Republics on the Prevention of Incidents on and over the High Seas," available at <http://dosfan.lib.uic.edu/acda/treaties/sea1.htm>.

Chapter 7

Balancing U.S. Security Interests in Space

Michael E. O'Hanlon

What should the United States do with its future space policy? Available options range from hastening to develop and deploy space weapons that could destroy ballistic missiles, other satellites, or ground targets, to banning the weaponization of space altogether through international treaty. This chapter takes a middle path, not in the interest of triangulation or compromise for its own sake, but because the extreme options would poorly serve American security interests. At some point, a clearer decision in favor of one end of the weaponization/arms control spectrum or the other could be appropriate. But in light of strategic and technological realities, this is not the time.

Space systems were a focus of arms control debate during the Cold War, and many would still like outer space, the last physical frontier of the human experience, to be a sanctuary from military competition.[1] These proponents favor binding, permanent, multilateral bans on space weaponry. Beyond their philosophical motivation, American opponents of the weaponization of space make a practical national-interest argument: as the world's principal space power today, the United States stands to lose the most from weaponization, since it could jeopardize the communications and reconnaissance systems on which the U.S. military and economy so disproportionately depend.[2] Opponents of weaponizing space also point to the world's growing economic dependence on space assets and to the risk of damaging those assets should weaponry be based in or used outside of the atmosphere.

Non-American opponents of weaponizing space also worry about a unilateralist America pursuing its own military advantage at the expense of other countries, most of which do not favor putting weapons in space. This dispute has much of its origins and motivation in the history of the ballistic missile defense debate, as well as in the antisatellite weapons debate of the 1980s. But it has taken on a new tone in what many view as an era of American unipolarity or hegemony. In recent years, China and Russia have been consistent in their opposition to the weaponization of space and in their desire for a treaty banning the testing, deployment, and use of weapons in space.[3] So have a number of U.S. allies, including Canada, which proposed in 1998 that the United Nations (UN) convene a committee on outer space during its conference on disarmament in Geneva.[4] The UN General Assembly passed resolutions for more than 20 straight years opposing the weaponization of space.

In contrast, developing more military applications for outer space is an important imperative for most American defense planners today. Much thinking about the so-called revolution in military affairs and transformation of defense emphasizes space capabilities. Ensuring American military dominance in the coming years—something proponents tend to see as critical for global stability as well as for unilateral advantage—will require the United States to remain well ahead of its potential adversaries technologically. For some defense futurists, the key requirement will be to control space, denying its effective use to U.S. adversaries while preserving the unfettered operation of American satellites that help make up a "reconnaissance-strike complex." Others favor an even more ambitious approach. Given that fixed bases on land and large assets such as ships are increasingly vulnerable to precision-strike weaponry and other enemy capabilities—or to the political opposition of allies such as Turkey, Saudi Arabia, and France, which have sometimes opposed use of their territories or airspace for military operations (as in the 2003 war in Iraq and in the 1986 U.S. bombing of Libya)—these advocates favor greater U.S. reliance on long-range strike systems, including platforms in space.[5]

Advocates of space weaponry also argue that, in effect, space is already weaponized, at least in subtle ways. Most medium- and long-range rockets capable of carrying nuclear weapons already constitute latent antisatellite (ASAT) weapons. Likewise, rockets and space-launch vehicles could probably be used to launch small homing satellites equipped with explosives and capable of approaching and destroying another satellite. Such capabilities may not even require testing, or at least testing that is not easily detectable from Earth. Advocates of weaponization further note that the United States is willing to use weapons to deny other countries' wartime use of the atmosphere, the oceans, and land, raising the question of why space should be a sanctuary when these other realms are not. As Barry

Watts put it, "Satellites may have owners and operators, but, in contrast to sailors, they do not have mothers."[6]

And of course, not all countries that publicly oppose putting weapons in space are true to their rhetoric in practice. The People's Republic of China (PRC) is the most notable example, with its early 2007 ASAT test destroying an old PRC weather satellite, increasing low Earth orbit space debris by 10 percent and shattering an effective moratorium on the testing of ASAT systems that was more than two decades old. In fairness to Beijing, it could be argued that it had a right to "catch up" with the United States— not only with the ASAT technology the Pentagon had developed in the 1970s and 1980s, but also with latent modern ASAT capabilities in the form of American ballistic missile defense systems. That said, it was China and only China that ended the effective international moratorium on actual testing of antisatellite systems, and it was the PRC that chose to take actions at blatant odds with its own official negotiating position in international talks over space weaponry. The point of this assessment is not to vilify China's behavior; in fact, in many ways, such a demonstration of capability is consistent with how a rising power historically would be expected to handle such a situation. Its behavior fits squarely within the trajectory that realists at least would predict. That is true even if it may have reflected poor coordination and communications within the PRC government (since the blow to China's international image may not be offset by the acquisition of useful new capabilities).[7] But whatever one's views on that point, China's ASAT test would seem to reaffirm that the United States must fashion its military space policy based more on a hard-headed assessment of capabilities and potential capabilities than on ideological positions, be they of the pro–arms control or pro–space weaponization variety.

Specific military scenarios can bring these more abstract arguments into clearer focus. Consider just one possibility. If, in a future Taiwan Strait crisis, China could locate and target American aircraft carriers using satellite technology, the case for somehow countering those satellites through direct offensive action would be powerful. This decision might be made easier if China itself initiated the use of ASATs, perhaps against Taiwan, but it could be an option the United States would have to consider seriously even if China had not. If jamming or other means of temporary disruption could not be shown to reliably interrupt China's satellite activities, outright destruction would probably be seriously proposed. This scenario is investigated in greater detail below, not out of any conviction that the United States and China are headed for military rivalry or conflict, but out of the belief that such scenarios must concern American force planners as they think through the pros and cons of various policy options.

No space-based missile defense or antisatellite weapons (with the possible exception of an isolated experimental launcher or two) were deployed during the Cold War. That did not, however, reflect any decision to keep space forever free from weaponry. Nor do existing arms control treaties ban such weapons. Instead, they ban the deployment or use of nuclear weapons in outer space, prevent colonization of heavenly bodies for military purposes, and protect the rights of countries to use space to verify arms control accords and to conduct peaceful activities.[8] In addition, in 2000, the United States and Russia agreed to notify each other of most space launches and ballistic missile tests in advance.[9] Most other matters are still unresolved. And the concept of space as a sanctuary will be more difficult to defend or justify as the advanced targeting and communications capabilities of space systems are increasingly used to help deliver lethal ordnance on target.[10]

Some scholars do argue that the Strategic Arms Reduction, Intermediate-Range Nuclear Forces, and Conventional Armed Forces in Europe treaties effectively ban the use of ASATs by one signatory of these treaties against any and all others, given the protection provided to satellite verification missions in the accords. But these treaties were signed before imaging satellites came into their own as targeting devices for tactical warfighting purposes, raising the legal and political question of whether a satellite originally protected for one generally nonprovocative and stabilizing purpose can be guaranteed protection when used in a more competitive fashion. Moreover, no one argues that these treaties ban the development, testing, production, or deployment of ASATs.[11] Nor do any involve China.

The United States currently conducts few space weapons activities, but that could change quickly. From time to time, a Pentagon official speaks of the need to be forward-leaning on the space weaponization issue, and periodically, the open press reports consideration of at least small amounts of research and development funding for dedicated antisatellite weapons. As best as one can tell from the outside, such programs do not appear to have much momentum as of now. Yet it is hard to be sure and very hard to predict the future.

In this light, should the United States agree to restraints on future military uses of outer space, in particular the weaponization of outer space? Any useful formal treaties would have to be multilateral in scope. It makes little sense to consider bilateral treaties because it is unclear what country should be the other party to a treaty. At this point, any space treaty worth the effort to negotiate would have to include as many other space-faring countries as possible, ranging from Russia and the European powers to China, India, and Japan. To be sure, that accords would be multilateral does not mean that they should be negotiated at the United Nations, where many space arms control discussions have occurred to date. There is a strong and perhaps ideological pro–arms control bias in the UN Conference on Disarmament, where these discussions have taken place. In addition, some countries may be using those fora to score political points against the United States rather than to genuinely pursue long-term accords for promoting international stability. The United Nations might ultimately be involved to bless any treaty, but it might be best to negotiate elsewhere.

On the other hand, should the United States accelerate any space weaponization programs? Here again, my conclusion is one of caution. Although opposed to most types of binding arms control (which would deprive the United States of options that may someday be necessary), I do not believe that the United States would benefit from exercising most of those options at present. Some additional capabilities, such as improved space situational awareness, make sense, as do more hardening for key satellites and more redundancy in communications and reconnaissance systems. But weapons, at present, do not make sense—with the exception of certain ballistic missile defense capabilities designed for a different purpose (even if they admittedly often have some inherent ASAT potential).

Before going into these issues in more detail, it is useful to provide clear strategic and military context to the discussion with a fuller examination of what a space-related military contingency could entail in the future. It is along these lines that a China scenario merits further study.

Scenario: Possible War Against China Over Taiwan

Given trends in military reconnaissance, information processing, and precision-strike technologies, large assets (such as aircraft carriers and land bases) on which the United States depends are likely to be increasingly vulnerable to attack in the years ahead. Land bases can to an extent be protected, hardened, and made more numerous and redundant, but ships are a different matter. How fast, and whether, China can exploit these trends remains unclear. But the trends are real nonetheless. As a recent example, China reportedly has tested an antiship cruise missile with a 155-mile range—more than twice that originally expected by U.S. intelligence. And its space assets are surely growing in scope. Even if it does not have an extensive imaging satellite network in a decade or so, it may be able to orbit one or two reconnaissance satellites that could occasionally detect large ships near Taiwan. That might be good enough. If China could find major U.S. naval assets with satellites, it would only need to sneak a single airplane, ship, or submarine into the region east of Taiwan to have a good chance of sinking a ship.

Knowing the U.S. reluctance to risk casualties in combat, China might convince itself that its plausible ability to kill many hundreds or even thousands of U.S. military personnel in a single attack would deter the United States from entering the war in the first place. Such a perception by China might well be wrong (just as Argentina was wrong to think in 1982, in a somewhat analogous situation, that it could deter Britain from deciding to take back the Falkland Islands); but it could still be quite dangerous, given the resulting risks of deterrence failure and war.

China is certainly taking steps to improve its capabilities in space operations. According to a Pentagon assessment, "Exploitation of space and acquisition of related technologies remain high priorities in Beijing. China is placing major emphasis on improving space-based reconnaissance and surveillance. . . . China is cooperating with a number of countries, including Russia, Ukraine, Brazil, Great Britain, France, Germany, and Italy, in order to advance its objectives in space." China will also surely focus on trying to neutralize U.S. space assets in any future such conflict; no prudent military planner could do anything else, and the early 2007 ASAT test would seem to confirm this logic. According to the Pentagon, in language written before that 2007 test:

> Publicly, China opposes the militarization of space, and seeks to prevent or slow the development of anti-satellite (ASAT) systems and space-based ballistic missile defenses. Privately, however, China's leaders probably view ASATs—and offensive counterspace systems, in general—as well as space-based missile defenses as inevitabilities. . . . Given China's current level of interest in laser technology, Beijing probably could develop a weapon that could destroy satellites in the future.[12]

Exactly how many U.S. satellites, and of what type, China might be able to damage or destroy is hard to predict. But it seems likely that low-altitude satellites as well as higher altitude commercial communications satellites would be vulnerable. Low-altitude imaging satellites are vulnerable to direct attack by nuclear-armed missiles, at a minimum, by high-energy lasers on the ground, and quite possibly by rapidly orbited or predeployed microsatellites as well. They are sufficiently hardened that they would have to be attacked one by one to ensure their rapid elimination. And they are sufficiently capable of transmitting signals through or around jamming that China probably could not stop their effective operation in that way. But they are few enough in number, and sufficiently valuable, that China might well find the means to go after each one.

For higher altitude military satellite constellations, including the global positioning system (GPS), military communications, and electronic intelligence systems, China's task would be much harder. Such constellations often have greater numbers of satellites than do low-altitude imagery systems. They are probably out of range of most plausible laser weapons, as well as ballistic missiles carrying nuclear weapons. They might, however, be reached by microsatellites deployed as hunter-killer weapons, particularly if those microsatellites had been predeployed (a few might be orbited quickly just before a war, but launch constraints could limit their number, since microsatellites headed to different orbits would probably require different boosters). They might also be reachable by an ASAT similar to what China tested in 2007, once placed on a larger rocket.[13]

Finally, high-altitude commercial communications satellites are quite likely to be vulnerable. Their transmissions to Earth might well be interrupted for a critical period of hours or days by jamming or a nuclear burst in the atmosphere. For example, disruption of ultra-high-frequency radio signals due to a nuclear burst can last for many hours over a ground area of hundreds or even thousands of kilometers per dimension. Unhardened satellites might be damaged by a large nuclear weapon at distances of 20,000 to 30,000 kilometers. They might even be vulnerable to laser blinding.

So it appears that China will remain quite far behind the United States in military capability, relatively rudimentary in its space capabilities and lacking in sophisticated electronic warfare techniques and similar means of disrupting command and communications. But it could hamper some satellite operations, and it could have an "asymmetric capability" to find, target, and attack U.S. Navy ships (not to mention commercial ships trying to survive the postulated blockade of Taiwan).

Some might argue that the above analysis overstates the potential role of satellites. For example, even if China would have a hard time getting aircraft close enough to track U.S. ships, given American air supremacy, it might have other means. For example, it may be able to use a sea-based acoustic network. Such a system most likely would be deployed on the seabed, as with the U.S. sound surveillance system (SOSUS) array. On that logic, China may have so many options and capabilities that it need not depend on any one type, such as space assets.

Or China may not be able to make good use of any improvements it can achieve in its satellite capabilities. To use a reconnaissance-strike complex to attack a U.S. carrier, one needs not only periodic localization of the carrier, but also real-time tracking and dissemination of that information to a missile that is capable of reaching the carrier and defeating its defenses. The reconnaissance-strike complex must also be resilient in the face of enemy action. The PRC is not close to having such a capability either in its constituent parts or as part of an integrated real-time network.

But the case for concern in general, and for special concern about Chinese satellite capabilities in particular, is still rather strong. If China does improve its satellite capabilities for imaging and communications, the United States could be quite hard-pressed to defeat them without ASAT capabilities. Destroying ground stations could require deep inland strikes—and may not work if China builds mobile stations. The sheer size of the PRC also makes it difficult to jam downlinks; the United States cannot flood all of China continuously with high-energy radio waves. (Although the United States may be able to jam links to antiship cruise missiles already in flight, if it can detect them, it would be imprudent to count on this defense alone.) Jamming uplinks may be difficult as well if China anticipates the possibility and develops good encryption technology or a satellite mode of operations in which incoming signals are ignored for certain periods of time. Jamming any PRC radar-imaging satellites may work better, since such satellites must transmit and receive signals continuously to function. But that method would work only if China relied on radar, as opposed to optical, systems.

In regard to the argument that China could use SOSUS arrays or other such capabilities to target U.S. carriers, making satellites superfluous, it should be noted that the United States has potential means for countering any such efforts. To deploy a fixed sonar array in the vast waters east of Taiwan where U.S. ships would operate in wartime, China would need to pre-deploy sensors in a region many hundreds of kilometers on a lateral dimension at least. This could be technically quite difficult in such deep waters. Although the United States has laid sonar sensors in waters more than 10,000 feet deep, the procedure is usually carried out remotely from a ship or by a special submarine, and hence becomes more difficult as depth increases. In addition, the United States would have a very good chance of recognizing what China was doing. Even though peacetime protocols would prohibit preemptive attacks, the United States could be expected to know where many of China's underwater assets had been deployed, allowing attacks of one kind or another in wartime. The United States is devoting considerable assets to intelligence operations in the region already, for example, with its attack submarine force. It would similarly have a good chance of detecting and destroying Chinese airborne platforms, including even small unmanned aircraft systems, used for reconnaissance purposes.

On balance, growing Chinese satellite capabilities for targeting and communications could be an important ingredient in what Beijing might take (or mistake) for a war-winning capability in the future. China would not need to think it had matched the U.S. Armed Forces in most military categories, only that it had an asymmetric ability to pose greater risks to the United States than Washington might consider acceptable in the event of a future Taiwan Strait crisis.

China might also have the means to attack U.S. space assets, particularly lower-flying reconnaissance satellites, by 2010 (if it does not already). It is not entirely out of the question that China might use nuclear weapons to do so systematically, knowing that such a strike might greatly weaken U.S. military capabilities without killing many, if any, Americans. China attaches enough political importance to holding onto Taiwan that it might well prove quite willing to run some risk of escalation in order to do so—especially if its leaders thought they had deduced a clever way to escalate without inviting massive retaliation. Whether it could disrupt or destroy most satellites is unclear. Whether it could reach large numbers of GPS and communications assets in medium Earth orbit and geosynchronous orbit is doubtful. But for these and other reasons, it is also doubtful that the United States could operate its space assets with impunity, or count on completely dominating military space operations, in such a scenario.

The United States is not in danger of falling behind China, Iran, or any other country in military capability in the coming years and decades, and its own capabilities will probably grow, in absolute terms, faster than those of any other country. But its relative position could still suffer in a number of military spheres, including space-related activities. Its satellites will be less dependable in conflict than they are today or have been in recent years. Other countries may also mimic the U.S. ability to use satellites and accompanying ground assets for targeting and real-time attack missions. The trends are not so unfavorable or so rapid as to require urgent remedial action. Indeed, the United States has military and political reasons to show restraint in most areas of space weaponry. But passive defensive measures should be expanded and some potential offensive capabilities investigated so as to retain the option of weaponizing them in the future, if necessary.

Arms Control and Weaponization Options

Proposals for space arms control may be grouped into three broad categories. First are outright prohibitions of indefinite duration and broad scope. Second are confidence-building measures, such as requirements for advance notification of space launches and keep-out zones around deployed satellites. Third are informal understandings, worked out in talks or more likely established through the unilateral but mutual actions of major powers.

Overall, space arms control should not be a top priority for the United States in the future, contrary to what many arms control traditionalists have concluded. Some specific accords of limited scope, such as a treaty banning collisions or explosions that would produce debris above a certain (low) altitude, and confidence-building measures such as keep-out zones near deployed satellites, do make sense. But the inability to verify compliance with more sweeping prohibitions, the inherent antisatellite capabilities of many missile defense systems, and the military need to counter efforts by other countries to use satellites to target American military assets all suggest that comprehensive accords banning the weaponization of space are both impractical and undesirable. That said, the United States should not want to hasten the weaponization of space and indeed should want to avoid such an eventuality. It benefits from its own military uses of space greatly and disproportionately at present. It should take unilateral action, such as by declaring that it has no dedicated antisatellite weapons programs, to help buttress the status quo as much as possible.

One type of arms control accord on activities in space would be quite comprehensive, calling for no testing, production, or deployment of ASATs of any kind, based in space or on the ground, at any time; no Earth-attack weapons stationed in space, ever; and formal, permanent treaties codifying these prohibitions. These provisions are in line with those in proposals made by the Chinese and Russian delegations to the UN Conference on Disarmament in Geneva. They also are supported by some traditional arms control proponents who argue that space should be a sanctuary from weaponization and that the Outer Space Treaty already strongly suggests as much.[14]

These provisions suffer from three main flaws. To begin, it is difficult to be sure that other countries' satellite payloads are not ASATs. This is especially true in regard to microsatellites, which are hard to track. Some have proposed inspections of all payloads going into orbit, but this would not prevent a "breakout," in which a country on the verge of war would simply refuse to continue to abide by the provisions. Since microsats can be tested for maneuverability without making them look like ASATs and are being so tested, it will be difficult to preclude this scenario. A similar problem arises with the idea of banning specific types of experimentation, such as outdoor experiments or flight testing.[15] A laser can be tested for beam strength and pointing accuracy as a ballistic missile defense device without being identified as an ASAT. A microsat can be tested for maneuverability as a scientific probe, even if its real purpose is different, since maneuvering microsats capable of colliding with other satellites may have no visible features clearly revealing their intended purpose. Bans on outdoor testing of declared ASAT devices would do little to impede their development.

Second, more broadly, it is not possible to prevent certain types of weapons designed for ballistic missile defense from being used as ASATs. This is in essence a problem of verification. However, the issue is less of verification per se than of knowing the intent of the country building a given system—and ensuring that its intent never changes. The latter goals are unrealistic. Some systems designed for missile defense have inherent ASAT capabilities and will retain them, due to the laws of physics, regardless of what arms control prohibitions are developed, and countries possessing these systems will recognize their latent capabilities.[16] For example, the American midcourse missile defense system and the airborne laser would both have inherent capabilities against low Earth orbit (LEO) satellites, if given good information on a satellite's location—easy to obtain—and perhaps some software modifications. The United States could declare for the time being that it will not link these missile defense systems to satellite networks or give them the necessary communications and software capabilities to accept such data. But such restraints, while currently worthwhile as informal, nonbinding measures, are difficult to verify and easy to reverse. Thus, no robust, long-term formal treaty regime should be based on them. Indeed, the problem goes beyond missile defense systems. Even the space shuttle, with its ability to maneuver and approach satellites in low Earth orbit, has inherent ASAT potential. So do any country's nuclear weapons deployed atop ballistic missiles. Explicit testing in ASAT modes can be prohibited, but any prohibition could have limited meaning.

Third, it is not clear that the United States will benefit militarily from an ASAT ban forever. The scenario of a war in the Taiwan Strait is a good example of how, someday, the United States could be put at serious risk by another country's satellites.[17] That day is not near, and there are many other possible ways to deal with the worry in the near term besides developing destructive ASATs. But over time, a possible need for such a weapon cannot be ruled out.

There is a stronger argument for banning Earth-attack weapons based in space. Most such weapons would probably require considerable testing. That means that testing might well be verifiable (especially if testing via ballistic missile were also prohibited). Furthermore, prohibitions on such weapons will cost the United States little, since it will retain other possible recourses to delivering weapons quickly over long distances (as may other countries). So a ban may make sense. The most powerful counterargument to banning ground-attack weapons in space is that the long-term need for them cannot be easily assessed now. But physical realities do suggest that the United States will be able to make do without them or to find alternatives.

A number of specific prohibitions, fairly narrowly construed, are worth considering as well. They could be carefully tailored so as not to preclude development of various capabilities in the future, given the realities and security requirements noted. But they nevertheless could help to reassure other countries about U.S. intentions at a time of still-unsettled great power relations and help protect space against the creation of excessive debris or other hazards to safe use over the longer term. Measures could include the following:

- temporary prohibitions, possibly renewable, on the development, testing, and deployment of ASATs, Earth-attack weapons, or both

- bans on testing or deployment of ASATs above set altitudes in space

- bans on debris-producing ASATs

- no first use of ASATs and space weapons.

Compliance with temporary formal treaty prohibitions would be no more verifiable than permanent bans. But they could make sense when future strategic and technological circumstances cannot easily be predicted.

There are downsides to signing accords from which one might very well withdraw, of course. If and when the United States could no longer support the prohibitions involved, it would likely suffer in the court of international public opinion by its unwillingness to extend the accord, even if the accord was specifically designed to be nonpermanent. The experience of the United States in withdrawing from the Anti-Ballistic Missile Treaty suggests that the damage from such decisions can be limited. But that experience also suggests that it requires a great deal of effort to lay the diplomatic foundation for withdrawal, that bitterness about such a decision can persist thereafter, and that withdrawal from one treaty regimen—however outdated—might be used as a justification by other states to withdraw from more important and less outdated treaties that they find undesirable. On balance, accords of indefinite duration should not be entered into unless one expects to remain part of them indefinitely, so I tend to oppose most such accords.

Bans on testing or employing ASATs that produce debris make sense and could well be codified by binding international treaty. Destructive testing of weapons such as the Clinton administration's midcourse missile defense system or other hit-to-kill or explosive devices against objects in satellite orbital zones would not only increase the risks of an ASAT competition, it would also create debris in LEO regions that would remain in orbit indefinitely (that is, unless the testing occurred in what are effectively the higher parts of the Earth's atmosphere, where air resistance would ultimately bring down debris and where few if any satellites fly in any case). The U.S. military worries about this debris-producing effect of testing. To date, tests of the midcourse system have occurred at roughly 140 miles altitude, producing debris that deorbits within roughly 20 minutes, but future tests will be higher. A ceiling of 300 to 500 miles might be placed on such tests and a ban placed on using targets that are in orbit.

Another category of arms accords includes those that do not limit the weapons capabilities of states but instead seek to establish rules or guidelines for how states use their military assets. The goals would be to reduce tension, improve communications, and build safety mechanisms into how countries make military use of outer space. This arms control concept would build on some of the agreements that the nuclear superpowers signed to reduce the potential for unintentional nuclear confrontation during the Cold War, including the 1972 Incidents at Sea Agreement and agreements to set up communications hotlines.[18] Here the stakes might not be so great, but they could still be great enough to justify some straightforward measures and rules of the road—as long as no great effort has to be expended to work out some commonly accepted practices.

One such idea is that of establishing keep-out zones around deployed satellites. There is no reason for a satellite to approach within a few tens of kilometers—or, in some orbits, within even hundreds of kilometers—of another satellite. Any close approach can thus be assumed to be hostile and ruled out as an acceptable action. States might consider formalizing this understanding of keep-out zones. The idea makes particularly good sense if there is a way to monitor compliance. Future American satellites are expected to have more sensors capable of surveying the environment around them, so this approach may work.[19]

What real strategic purpose would be served by such zones? Unless satellites were themselves given self-defense capabilities—making them difficult to distinguish from offensive ASATs—the zones could not be enforced. And any country wishing to develop a close-approach capability for the purpose of ultimately launching a large-scale ASAT surprise attack could develop that capability despite the existence of keep-out zones, by testing against its own space assets or even against empty points in space.

That said, the idea may still make sense, even though keep-out zones would not substantially limit military capabilities. First, creating such zones would add another step that any state planning an attack would have to address. ASATs could not easily be predeployed near other satellites without arousing suspicion (especially if the United States and other countries deployed satellites with sensors capable of monitoring their neighborhoods). Second, any state violating the keep-out zones would tend to tip off the targeted country about its likely intentions; conversely, respecting the zones would constitute a form of restraint that could calm nerves to some modest but perhaps worthwhile degree. And the United States has no need to place satellites near other countries' space assets in any case, so it would not be giving up anything to endorse such a rule of the road. On balance, this idea is a worthy one for a treaty regime, though not worth a great deal of top-level time to negotiate.

What of advance notice of space launches? Again, this type of accord, such as that reached between the United States and Russia during the Clinton administration, would not prevent a country from breaking out suddenly, nor would it place a meaningful constraint on capabilities. But as long as it was observed, countries would have additional reassurance that others were playing by the rules. They would also have time to prepare to observe the deployment of satellites from any launch, allowing slightly greater confidence that ASATs were not being deployed. As a peacetime rule of the road at least, it makes sense. Some have also suggested allowing international monitoring of space payloads prior to their launch.[20] This seems questionable, though, since satellites could be effective ASATs without carrying payloads that made that obvious.

On balance, several of these confidence-building measures are marginally useful. They will not prevent the United States from retaining its hedges against a future need for ASATs, whether in the form of dual-purpose ballistic missile defense programs or even dedicated antisatellite systems. They will not prevent China or another country from quietly building inherent ASAT capability either. But they will add an extra step or two that other countries choosing to weaponize space would need to deal with before threatening American interests.

A final category of measures would not involve arms control at all—in the formal sense of signed treaties and binding commitments—but rather unofficial and unilateral restraints. Such restraints would not force the United States to tie one hand behind its back and leave other countries free to develop space weapons; rather, by adopting the restraints and thereby setting a precedent and a tone, the United States would aim to encourage other countries to reciprocate. To the extent others did not show restraint, the policy could be reconsidered. This approach has several precedents in international affairs. For example, during the first Bush administration, the United States reduced the alert levels of some nuclear forces and took tactical nuclear weapons off naval vessels in part to encourage similar Soviet actions, which followed.[21] This approach can work more quickly than formal arms control; it can also preserve flexibility should circumstances change. It is perhaps most useful when it is not absolutely critical that all countries immediately comply with a given set of rules or restraints. In other words, if the United States would have ample time to change its policy in the event that other countries failed to cooperate, without doing harm to its security interests in the interim, there is much to be said for this approach.

Since the United States is not presently building or deploying space weapons, informal restraint would presumably apply to research and development and testing activities. As one example, if a treaty to accomplish this goal could not be quickly negotiated, the United States could make a unilateral pledge not to create space debris through testing of any ASAT.[22] The flexibility associated with such a pledge might permit it to go further and also pledge not to produce any ASAT that would ever create debris, given that even if the United States needs a future ASAT, it would have alternative technological options.

The United States might also consider making a clear statement that it has no dedicated ASAT programs and no intention of initiating development or deployment of any, if that is true. It could also declare that it will not test any systems, including high-powered lasers, microsatellites, and ballistic missile defenses, in an ASAT mode. The latter approach would have the greatest chance of eliciting verifiable reciprocation by other countries.

The downsides to such statements are that if and when U.S. policy requirements changed, the statements would have to be repudiated, raising alarms abroad and risking a greater diplomatic problem than would occur if the United States had never held itself to informal restraints. The advantages are that they might buy the United States some time, allowing it to play its part in stigmatizing space weapons it has no strategic interest in developing or seeing developed any time soon.

Conclusion

While I have spent considerable time on arms control options, it is worth concluding with an observation on which military measures do make some sense now (even as options are preserved for considering others in the future). First, improved American space surveillance is needed, largely to know what other countries are doing with their microsatellites. Second, individual American satellites would also benefit from local situational awareness so that Department of Defense officials will know if satellites are approached closely. Third, and most of all, the vulnerability of key U.S. satellites to a Rumsfeldian Space Pearl Harbor—admittedly a melodramatic and exaggerated image, but still a useful caution and reminder—should be mitigated. This requires hardening against electromagnetic pulse and shielding optical components against blinding lasers. Someday, it could require creating mechanisms to deal with excess heat from lasers with prolonged dwell times. It also argues strongly in favor of redundancy. That need not mean rapid-launch satellite replenishment capability. But it does argue for a portfolio of reconnaissance capabilities, including airbreathing capabilities.

Military space policy is and will remain complex, with judgments constantly required about which programs make strategic sense and serve American national security objectives. To be sure, that argument is frustrating for those who would prefer the analytical and rhetorical simplicity of the argument that space must remain man's last unmilitarized frontier or that space, like all other frontiers, will eventually be militarized, so we may as well get on with it first. But a balanced approach reflects reality and the complex web of interests that the United States needs to advance in the years ahead.

Notes

[1] This section draws heavily on Michael E. O'Hanlon, *Neither Star Wars nor Sanctuary: Constraining the Military Use of Space* (Washington, DC: Brookings Institution, 2004).

[2] See, for example, Theresa Hitchens, "Monsters and Shadows: Left Unchecked, American Fears Regarding Threats to Space Assets Will Drive Weaponization," *Disarmament Forum* 1 (2003), 24.

[3] See transcript of the panel discussion held in the United Nations on October 19, 2000, by the NGO Committee on Disarmament, available at <www.igc.org/disarm/T191000outerspace.htm>; and

statement by Hu Xiaodi, ambassador for disarmament affairs of China, at the Plenary of the Conference on Disarmament, June 7, 2001, available at <www3.itu.int/missions/China/disarmament/2001files/disarmdoc010607.htm>; and "China, Russia Want Space Weapons Banned," *Philadelphia Inquirer*, August 23, 2002.

[4] See Canadian Working Paper Concerning Conference on Disarmament Action on Outer Space, January 21, 1998, available at <www.fas.org/nuke/control/paros/docs/1487.htm>; James Clay Moltz, "Breaking the Deadlock on Space Arms Control," *Arms Control Today* (April 2002), available at <www.armscontrol.org/act/2002_04/moltzapril02.asp?print>.

[5] Peter L. Hays, *United States Military Space: Into the Twenty-first Century* (Montgomery, AL: Air University Press, 2002), 11–13; Alvin and Heidi Toffler, *War and Anti-War: Survival at the Dawn of the 21st Century* (Boston: Little, Brown, 1993); Stuart E. Johnson and Martin C. Libicki, eds., *Dominant Battlespace Knowledge* (Washington, DC: National Defense University Press, 1996); Thomas A. Keaney and Eliot A. Cohen, *Gulf War Air Power Survey Summary Report* (Washington, DC: U.S. Government Printing Office, 1993); William Owens, *Lifting the Fog of War* (New York: Farrar, Straus and Giroux, 2000); Daniel Goure and Christopher M. Szara, eds., *Air and Space Power in the New Millennium* (Washington, DC: Center for Strategic and International Studies, 1997); Defense Science Board 1996 Summer Study Task Force, *Tactics and Technology for 21st Century Military Superiority* (Washington, DC: Department of Defense, 1996); James P. Wade and Harlan K. Ullman, *Shock and Awe: Achieving Rapid Dominance* (Washington, DC: National Defense University Press, 1996); George and Meredith Friedman, *The Future of War: Power, Technology, and American World Dominance in the 21st Century* (New York: Crown Publishers, 1996); John Arquilla and David Ronfeldt, eds., *In Athena's Camp: Preparing for Conflict in the Information Age* (Santa Monica, CA: RAND Corporation, 1997); National Defense Panel, *Transforming Defense: National Security in the 21st Century* (Arlington, VA: The Pentagon, December 1997); and Joint Chiefs of Staff, *Joint Vision 2010* (Washington, DC: Department of Defense, 1996) and *Joint Vision 2020* (Washington, DC: Department of Defense, 2000).

[6] Barry D. Watts, *The Military Use of Space: A Diagnostic Assessment* (Washington, DC: Center for Strategic and Budgetary Assessments, 2001), 29–30.

[7] Bates Gill and Martin Kleiber, "China's Space Odyssey," *Foreign Affairs* 86, no. 3 (May–June 2007), 2–6.

[8] Paul B. Stares, *Space and National Security* (Washington, DC: Brookings Institution, 1987), 147.

[9] Peter L. Hays, "Military Space Cooperation: Opportunities and Challenges," in *Future Security in Space: Commercial, Military, and Arms Control Trade-Offs*, ed. James Clay Moltz, Occasional Paper No. 10 (Monterey, CA: Monterey Institute of International Studies, 2002), 37.

[10] This view is hardly confined to conservatives; see, for example, Ashton Carter, "Satellites and Anti-Satellites: The Limits of the Possible," *International Security* 10, no. 4 (Spring 1986), 47.

[11] Jonathan Dean, "Defenses in Space: Treaty Issues," in Moltz, 4.

[12] Department of Defense, *Annual Report to Congress: The Military Power of the People's Republic of China*, July 28, 2003, 36, available at <www.defenselink.mil/pubs/2003chinaex.pdf>.

[13] Geoffrey Forden, "After China's Test: Time for a Limited Ban on Anti-Satellite Weapons," *Arms Control Today* 37, no. 3 (April 2007), 19–23.

[14] See Rebecca Johnson, *Missile Defence and the Weaponisation of Space*, International Security Information Service Policy Paper on Ballistic Missile Defense No. 11 (London: International Security Information Service, January 2003), available at <www.isisuk.demon.co.uk>; Jonathan Dean, "Defenses in Space: Treaty Issues," in Moltz, 4; George Bunn and John B. Rhinelander, "Outer Space Treaty May Ban Strike Weapons," *Arms Control Today* 32, no. 5 (June 2002), 24; and Bruce M. Deblois, "Space Sanctuary: A Viable National Strategy," *Aerospace Power Journal* (Winter 1998), 41.

[15] For a proposal along these lines, see Michael Krepon with Christopher Clary, "Space Assurance or Space Dominance? The Case against Weaponizing Space," Henry L. Stimson Center, 2003, 109–110.

[16] For an earlier, highly sophisticated argument along these lines, see John Tirman, ed., *The Fallacy of Star Wars* (New York: Vintage Books, 1984).

[17] See O'Hanlon.

[18] For a good discussion, see Krepon and Clary, 114–124.

[19] For an example of a specific proposal along these lines, see Michael Krepon, "Model Code of Conduct for the Prevention of Incidents and Dangerous Military Practices in Outer Space," Henry L. Stimson Center, 2004, available at <www.stimson.org/wos/pdf/codeofconduct.pdf>.

[20] Krepon and Clary, 93.

[21] For a summary, see David Mosher and Michael O'Hanlon, *The START Treaty and Beyond* (Washington, DC: Congressional Budget Office, October 1991), 34–35; Ivo H. Daalder, *Cooperative Arms Control: A New Agenda for the Post–Cold War Era*, CISSM Papers No. 1, University of Maryland at College Park (October 1992), 23–27.

[22] Hays, "Military Space Cooperation: Opportunities and Challenges," in Moltz, 42.

Chapter 8
Airpower, Spacepower, and Cyberpower

Benjamin S. Lambeth

When American airpower played such a central role in driving Iraq's occupying forces from Kuwait in early 1991, many doubters of its seemingly demonstrated capacity to shape the course and outcome of a major showdown independently of ground action tended to dismiss that remarkable performance as a one-of-a-kind force employment anomaly. It was, the doubters said, the clear and open desert environment, or the unusual vulnerability of Iraq's concentrated armored formations to precision air attacks, or any number of other unique geographic and operational circumstances that somehow made the Persian Gulf War an exception to the general rule that it takes "boots on the ground" in large numbers, and ultimately in head-to-head combat, to defeat well-endowed enemy forces in high-intensity warfare.

To many, that line of argument had a reasonable ring of plausibility when airpower's almost singular contribution to the defeat of Saddam Hussein's forces was an unprecedented historical achievement. During the 12 years that ensued in the wake of Operation *Desert Storm*, however, the world again saw American airpower prevail in broadly comparable fashion in four dissimilar subsequent cases, starting with the North Atlantic Treaty Organization's two air-centric contests over the Balkans in Operations *Deliberate Force* in 1995 and *Allied Force* in 1999 and followed soon thereafter by Operation *Enduring Freedom* against terrorist elements in Afghanistan in 2001–2002 and by the 3-week period of major combat in Operation *Iraqi Freedom* that ended Saddam Hussein's rule in 2003. Granted, in none of those five instances did the air weapon produce the ultimate outcome all by itself. However, one can fairly argue that in each case, successful aerial combat and support operations were the pivotal enablers of all else that followed in producing the sought-after results at a relatively low cost in friendly and noncombatant enemy lives lost.

In light of those collective achievements, what was demonstrated by American air assets between 1991 and 2003 was arguably *not* a succession of anomalies, but rather the bow wave of a fundamentally new American approach to force employment in which the air weapon consistently turned in a radically improved level of performance compared to what it had previously delivered to joint force commanders. Indeed, that newly emergent pattern has now become so pronounced and persistent as to suggest that American airpower has finally reached the brink of maturity and become the tool of first resort by combatant commanders, at least with respect to defeating large enemy force concentrations in high-intensity warfare. Yet in each of the five instances noted above, what figured so importantly in determining the course and outcome of events was not just *airpower* narrowly defined, but rather operations conducted in, through, and from the Earth's atmosphere backstopped and enabled, in some cases decisively, by the Nation's diverse additional assets in space and by operations conducted within cyberspace (that is, the electromagnetic spectrum).

Accordingly, any effort to understand the evolving essence of American *airpower* must take into account not only our aerial warfare assets, but also those vitally important space and cyberspace adjuncts that, taken together, have made possible the new American way of war. By the same token, any successful effort to build a theoretical framework for better charting the future direction and use of American air, space, and cyberspace warfare capability must first take due measure of the Nation's current state of advancement in each domain. Toward that end, the discussion that follows will offer a brief overview of where the United States stands today in each of the three operating mediums. It will then consider some pertinent lessons from the airpower experience that bear on the development of spacepower and cyberpower theory, along with the sorts of cross-domain synergies that should be pursued in the many areas where the air, space, and cyberspace arenas overlap. Finally, it will consider some essential steps that will need to be taken toward that end before a holistic theory of warfare in all three domains, let alone any separate and distinct theory of spacepower, can realistically be developed.

Recent Achievements in Airpower Application

By any measure, the role of airpower in shaping the course and outcome of the 1991 Persian Gulf War reflected a major breakthrough in the effectiveness of the Nation's air arm after a promising start in World War

II and more than 3 years of misuse in the Rolling Thunder bombing campaign against North Vietnam from 1965 to 1968. At bottom, the *Desert Storm* experience confirmed that since Vietnam, American airpower had undergone a nonlinear growth in its ability to contribute to the outcome of joint campaigns at the operational and strategic levels thanks to a convergence of low observability to enemy sensors in the F–117 stealth attack aircraft, the ability to attack fixed targets consistently with high accuracy from relatively safe standoff distances using precision-guided munitions, and the expanded battlespace awareness that had been made possible by recent developments in command, control, communications, and computers, and intelligence, surveillance, and reconnaissance (ISR).[1]

As a result of those developments, American airpower had finally acquired the capabilities needed to fulfill the longstanding promise of its pioneers of being able to set the conditions for winning in joint warfare— yet *not* through the classic imposition of brute force, as had been the case throughout most of airpower's history, but rather through the *functional* effects that were now achievable by targeting an enemy's vulnerabilities and taking away his capacity for organized action. The combination of real-time surveillance and precision target–attack capability that was exercised to such telling effect by airpower against Iraq's fielded ground forces in particular heralded a new relationship between air- and surface-delivered firepower, in which friendly ground forces did the fixing and friendly airpower, now the predominant maneuver element, did the killing of enemy troops rather than the other way around.

During the years immediately after the 1991 Gulf War, further qualitative improvements rendered the Nation's air weapon even more capable than it had been. For one thing, almost every American combat aircraft now possessed the ability to deliver precision-guided weapons. For another, the advent of stealth, as was first demonstrated on a significant scale by the F–117 during the Gulf War, was further advanced by the subsequent deployment of the Air Force's second-generation B–2 stealth bomber that entered operational service in 1993. Finally, the advent of the satellite-aided GBU–31 Joint Direct Attack Munition (JDAM) gave joint force commanders the ability to conduct accurate target attacks with near impunity, around the clock and in any weather, against an opponent's core concentrations of power, whether they be deployed forces or infrastructure assets.

In the three subsequent major wars that saw American combat involvement (Operations *Allied Force, Enduring Freedom,* and the major combat phase of *Iraqi Freedom*), the dominant features of allied air operations were persistence of pressure on the enemy and rapidity of execution, thanks to the improved data fusion that had been enabled by linking the inputs of various air- and space-based sensor platforms around the clock. Greater communications connectivity and substantially increased available bandwidth enabled constant surveillance of enemy activity and contributed significantly to shortening the sensor-to-shooter data cycle time. Throughout each campaign, persistent ISR and growing use of precision munitions gave the United States the ability to deny the enemy a sanctuary. More important, they also reflected an ongoing paradigm shift in American combat style that now promises to be of greater moment than was the introduction of the tank at the beginning of the 20th century.[2]

Unlike the earlier joint campaigns that preceded it since *Desert Storm*, the second Gulf War involving the United States in 2003 was not mainly an air war, even though offensive air operations played a pivotal role in setting the conditions for its highly successful immediate outcome. Neither, however, was the campaign predominantly a *ground* combat affair, despite the fact that nearly all subsequent assessments of it have tended to misrepresent it in such a manner. That misrepresentation largely resulted from host-nation sensitivities that precluded correspondents from being embedded with forward-deployed allied flying units, and especially in the coalition's Combined Air Operations Center at Prince Sultan Air Base, Saudi Arabia, from which most of the air war was commanded and conducted. As a result, most of the journalists who provided first-hand reporting on the campaign were attached to allied ground formations.

Yet the ground offensive could not have been conducted with such speed and relatively small loss of friendly life (only 108 American military personnel lost to direct enemy action) without the indispensable contribution of the air component in establishing air supremacy over Iraq and then beating down enemy ground forces until they lost both the capacity and the will to continue fighting. By the same token, the rapid allied ground advance could not have progressed from Kuwait to Baghdad in just 3 weeks without the air component giving ground commanders the confidence that their exposed flanks were free of enemy threats on either side, thanks to the success of allied air attacks in keeping the enemy pinned down, exposed to relentless hammering from above, and unable to fight as a coherent entity. That omnipresent ISR eye over the war zone gave allied ground commanders not just the proverbial ability to "see over the next hill," but also a high-fidelity picture of the entire Iraqi battlespace.

In its execution of the major combat phase of *Iraqi Freedom*, U.S. Central Command (USCENTCOM) enjoyed air and information dominance essentially from the campaign's opening moments. Moreover, during the ensuing 3 weeks of joint and combined combat, allied air operations featured the application of mass precision as a matter of course. In the initial attack waves, every air-delivered weapon was precision-guided. Even well into the war's first week, 80 percent of USCENTCOM's air-delivered munitions had been either satellite-aided or laser-guided. In addition, the 3-week campaign featured a more closely linked joint and combined force than ever before. Persistent ISR coupled with a precision strike capability by all participating combat aircraft allowed the air component to deliver discriminant effects throughout the battlespace, essentially on demand. In contributing to the campaign, allied airpower did not just "support" allied land operations by "softening up" enemy forces. More often than not, it conducted wholesale destruction of Iraqi ground forces both prior to and independently of allied ground action. The intended net effect of allied air operations, which was ultimately achieved, was to facilitate the quickest possible capture of Baghdad without the occurrence of any major head-to-head land battles between allied and Iraqi ground forces.

As attested by its consistently effective performance from *Desert Storm* onward, American airpower has been steadily transformed since Vietnam to a point where it has finally become truly strategic in its potential effects. That was not the case before the advent of stealth, highly accurate target attack capability, and substantially improved information availability. Earlier air offensives were of limited effectiveness at the operational and strategic levels because it took too many aircraft and too high a loss rate to achieve too few results. Today, in contrast, American airpower can make its presence felt quickly and from the outset of combat and can impose effects on an enemy that can have a determining influence on the subsequent course and outcome of a joint campaign.

To begin with, thanks to the newly acquired capabilities of American airpower, there is no longer a need to mass force as there was even in the recent past. Today, improved battlespace awareness, heightened aircraft survivability, and increased weapons accuracy have made possible the *effects* of massing without an air component actually having to do so. As a result, airpower can now produce effects in major combat that were previously unattainable. The only question remaining, unlike in earlier eras, is *when* those effects will be registered, not *whether* they will be.

Of course, all force elements—land and maritime as well as air—have increasingly gained the opportunity in principle, at the theater commander's discretion, to achieve such effects by making the most of new technologies and concepts of operations. What is distinctive about contemporary fixed-wing airpower in all Services, however, is that it has pulled ahead of surface force elements in both the land and maritime arenas in its *relative* capacity to do this, thanks not only to its lately acquired advantages of stealth, precision, and information dominance, but also to its abiding characteristics of speed, range, and flexibility. Current and emerging air employment options now offer theater commanders the possibility of neutralizing an enemy's military forces from standoff ranges with virtual impunity, thus reducing the threat to U.S. troops who might otherwise have to engage undegraded enemy forces directly and risk sustaining high casualties as a result. They also offer the potential for achieving strategic effects from the earliest moments of a joint campaign through their ability to attack an enemy's core vulnerabilities with both shock and simultaneity.

In sum, a variety of distinctive features of American airpower have converged over the past two decades to make the Nation's air arm fairly describable as transformed in comparison to what it could offer joint force commanders throughout most of its previous history. Those distinctive features include such tangible and intangible equities as:

- intercontinental-range bombers and fighters with persistence
- a tanker force that can sustain global strike
- a sustainable global mobility capability
- surgeable carrier strike groups able to operate as a massed force[3]
- an increasingly digitized and interlinked force
- unsurpassed ISR and a common operating picture for all
- air operations centers as weapons systems in themselves
- operator competence and skill second to none.

These airpower equities have, in turn, enabled the following unique operational qualities and performance capabilities:

- freedom *from* attack and freedom *to* attack
- situation awareness dominance
- independence from shore basing for many theater strike requirements
- unobserved target approach and attack through stealth
- consistently accurate target attack day or night and in any weather
- the ability to maintain constant pressure on an enemy, perform time-sensitive targeting routinely, and avoid causing collateral damage routinely.

As borne out by their pivotal contributions to the Nation's five major combat experiences over the preceding decade and a half, these and related developments have made possible a new way of war for the United States, at least with respect to high-intensity operations against organized and concentrated enemy forces in land and maritime theaters. As has become increasingly clear since the successful conclusion of the 3-week major combat phase of *Iraqi Freedom* in April 2003, however, mastering the sorts of lower intensity counterinsurgency challenges that have dominated more recent headlines with regard to continuing combat operations in Iraq and Afghanistan remains another matter, and one that highlights modern airpower's limitations as well as strengths. Although today's instruments of air warfare have thoroughly transformed the Nation's ability to excel in conventional warfare, those instruments and their associated concepts of operations have not yet shown comparable potential in irregular warfare, since irregular opponents, given their composition and tactics, are less vulnerable to airpower as currently configured and employed. (On the other side of the coin, it should be noted in this regard that the recent rise of irregular warfare by the Nation's opponents has been substantially a result of airpower's proven effectiveness in conventional warfare, a fact that attests to modern airpower's unprecedented leverage at the same time that it illuminates the continuing challenges that airpower faces.)

Space Contributions and Near-term Priorities

Thus far in this discussion, the space medium and its associated mission areas have not been examined in any detail. Yet both have figured prominently and indispensably in the steady maturation of American airpower that has occurred since Vietnam. If there is a single fundamental and distinctive advantage that mature American airpower has conferred upon theater commanders in recent years, it has been an increasingly pronounced degree of freedom *from* attack and freedom *to* attack for all force elements, both in the air and on the ground, in major combat operations. The contributions of the Nation's space systems with respect to both ISR and precision attack have figured prominently in making those two force-employment virtues possible. Although still in its adolescence compared to our more mature air warfare posture, the Nation's ever-improving space capability has nonetheless become the enabler that has made possible the new strategy of precision engagement.

Despite that and other contributions from the multitude of military assets now on orbit, however, the Nation's air warfare repertoire still has a way to go before its post-Vietnam maturation can be considered complete.

Advances in space-based capabilities on the ISR front will lie at the heart of the full and final transformation of American airpower. It is now almost a cliché to say that airpower can kill essentially anything it can see, identify, and engage. To note one of the few persistent and unrectified shortfalls in airpower's leverage, however, it can kill *only* what it can see, identify, and engage. Airpower and actionable real-time target intelligence are thus opposite sides of the same coin. If the latter is unavailing in circumstances in which having it is essential for mission success, the former will likely be unavailing also. For that reason, accurate, timely, and comprehensive information about an enemy and his military assets is not only a crucial enabler for airpower to produce pivotal results in joint warfare, it also is an indispensable precondition for ensuring such results. In this regard, it will be in substantial measure through near-term improvements in space-based capabilities that the Air Force's long-sought ability to find, fix, track, target, engage, and assess any target of interest on the face of the Earth will become an established reality rather than merely a catchy vision statement with great promise.[4]

The spectrum of military space missions starts with *space support*, which essentially entails the launching of satellites and the day-to-day management of on-orbit assets that underpin all military space operations. It next includes *force enhancement*, a broader category of operations involving all space-based activities aimed at increasing the effectiveness of terrestrial military operations. This second mission area embraces the range of space-related enabling services that the Nation's various on-orbit assets now provide to U.S. joint force commanders worldwide. Activities in this second area include missile attack warning and characterization, navigation, weather forecasting, communication, ISR, and around-the-clock global positioning system (GPS) operations. A particularly notable aspect of space force enhancement in recent years has been the growing use of space-based systems for directly enabling, rather than merely enhancing, terrestrial military operations, as attested by the increasing reliance by all four Services on GPS signals for accurate, all-weather delivery of satellite-aided JDAMs.

To date, the American defense establishment has largely limited its space operations to these two rather basic and purely enabling mission areas. Once the third mission area, *space control*, develops into a routine operational practice, it will involve the direct imposition of kinetic and nonkinetic effects both within and through space. Conceptually, space control is analogous to the familiar notions of sea and air control, both of which likewise involve ensuring friendly access and denying enemy access to those mediums. Viewed purely from a tactical and technical perspective, there is no difference in principle between defensive and offensive space control operations and similar operations conducted in any other medium of warfare. It is simply a matter of desirability, technical feasibility, and cost-effectiveness for the payoff being sought.

Unlike the related cases of sea and air control, however, serious investment in space control has been slow to take place in the United States, in part due to a persistent lack of governmental and public consensus as to whether actual combat, as opposed to merely passive surveillance and other terrestrial enabling functions, should be allowed to migrate into space and thus violate its presumed status as a weapons-free sanctuary. The delay also has had to do with the fact that the United States has not, at least until recently, faced direct threats to its on-orbit assets that have needed to be met by determined investment in active space control measures, all the more so in light of more immediate and pressing research and development and systems procurement priorities. For both reasons, the space control mission area remains almost completely undeveloped. About all the United States can do today to deny enemy access to the data stream from space is through electronic jamming or by physically destroying satellite uplinks and downlinks on the ground.

Finally, the *force application* mission, which thus far remains completely undeveloped due to both widespread international disapprobation and a general absence of political and popular domestic support, will eventually entail the direct defensive and offensive imposition of kinetic and nonkinetic measures from space in pursuit of joint terrestrial combat objectives. In its ultimate hardware manifestations, it could include the development, deployment, and use of space-based nonnuclear, hyperkinetic weapons against such terrestrial aim points as fixed high-value targets (hardened bunkers, munitions storage depots, underground command posts, and other heavily defended objectives), as well as against surface naval vessels, armored vehicles, and such other targets of interest as enemy leadership. How many years or decades into the future it may be before such capabilities are developed and fielded by the United States has been a topic of debate among military space professionals for many years. For the time being, it seems safe to conclude that any such developments will be heavily threat-determined and will not occur, if only from a cost-effectiveness viewpoint, as long as effective air-breathing or other terrestrial alternatives for performing the same missions are available.

Fortunately, as the Nation's defense community looks toward further developing these mission areas in an orderly sequence, it can claim the benefit of a substantial foundation on which to build. In February 2000, the Defense Science Board (DSB) concluded that the United States enjoyed undisputed space dominance, thanks in large part to what the Air Force had done in the space support and force enhancement mission areas over the preceding four decades to build a thriving military space infrastructure. Air Force contributions toward that end expressly cited by the DSB included a robust space launch and support infrastructure, an effective indications and warning and attack-assessment capability, a unique ground-based space surveillance capability, global near-real-time surveillance of denied areas, the ability to disseminate the products of that capability rapidly, and a strong command, control, and communications infrastructure for exploiting space systems.[5]

In looking to build on these existing capabilities with the goal of extracting greater leverage from the military promise of space, the Air Force now faces an urgent need to prioritize its investment alternatives in an orderly and manageable way. It cannot pursue every appealing investment opportunity concurrently, since some capability upgrade needs are more urgent than others. These appropriately rank-ordered priorities, moreover, must be embraced squarely and unsentimentally by the Nation's leadership. If the experience with the successful transformation of American *airpower* since Vietnam is ever to become a prologue to the next steps in the expansion of the Nation's military space repertoire, then it follows that the Air Force, as the lead service in space operations, will need to get its hierarchy of operational requirements in space right if near-Earth space is to be exploited for the greatest gains per cost in the service of theater commanders. Because an early working template for an overarching theory of spacepower might help impose a rational discipline on the determination of that hierarchy, perhaps the pursuit of such a focusing device should be undertaken as one of the first building blocks for such a theory.

Furthermore, a case can reasonably be made that the Nation's next moves with respect to military space exploitation should first seek to ensure the further integration of space with the needs of terrestrial warfighters, however much that might appear, at least for the near term, to shortchange the interests of those who are ready *now* to make space the fourth medium of warfare. More to the point, one can reasonably suggest that if the Nation's leadership deems a current space-based capability to be particularly important to the effective conduct of joint warfare and that it is either facing block obsolescence or otherwise at the threshold of failing, then it should be replaced as a first order of business before any other major space investment programs are pursued. Once those most pressing recapitalization needs are attended to, then all else by way of investment opportunities can be approached in appropriate sequence, including such space-based multispectral ISR assets as electro-optical, infrared, and signals intelligence satellites, followed by space-based radar once the requisite technology has proven itself ready for major resources to be committed to it.

Moreover, in considering an orderly transfer of such ISR functions from the atmosphere to space, planners should exercise special caution not to try to change too much too quickly. For example, such legacy air-breathing systems as the E–3 Airborne Warning and Control System (AWACS) and E–8 Joint Surveillance Target Attack Radar System (JSTARS), which have been acquired through billions of dollars of investment, cannot be summarily written off with substantial service life remaining, however well intended the various arguments for mission migration to space may be. Thus, it may make greater sense to think of space not as a venue within which to replace existing surveillance functions wholesale, but rather as a medium offering the potential for expanding the Nation's existing ISR capability by more fully exploiting both the air *and* space environments. It also may help to think in terms of windows of time in which to commence the migration of ISR missions to space. A challenge the Air Force faces now in this respect is to determine how to divest itself of existing legacy programs in a measured way so as to generate the funds needed for taking on tomorrow's challenges one manageable step at a time. That will require careful tradeoff assessments to determine the most appropriate technology and medium—air or space—toward which its resources should be vectored for any mission at any given time.

Finally, it will be essential that the survivability of any new ISR assets migrated to space be assured by appropriate protective measures that are developed and put into place first. American investment in appropriate first-generation space control measures has become increasingly essential in order for the Nation to remain secure in the space enabling game. Having been active in space operations for more than four decades, the United States is more heavily invested in space and more dependent on its on-orbit assets than ever before, and both real and potential adversaries are closing in on the ability to threaten our space-based assets by means ranging from harassment to neutralization to outright destruction, as attested by China's demonstration in January 2007 of a direct-ascent antisatellite kinetic kill capability against one of its own obsolete weather satellites 500 miles above the Earth's surface.[6] As the Nation places more satellites on orbit and comes to rely more on them for military applications, it is only a matter of time until our enemies become tempted to challenge our freedom of operations in space by attempting to undermine them.

In light of that fact, it would make no sense to migrate the JSTARS and AWACS functions to space should the resultant on-orbit assets prove to be any less survivable than JSTARS and AWACS are today. It follows that getting more serious about space control is not an issue apart from force-enhancement migration, but rather represents a sine qua non for such migration. Otherwise, in transferring our asymmetric technological advantages to space, we will also run the risk of burdening ourselves with new asymmetric vulnerabilities.

Exploiting the Cyberspace Arena

If the case for proceeding with timely initiatives to ensure the continued enabling functions of the Nation's space-based assets sounds reasonable enough in principle, then the argument for pursuing similar measures by way of vouchsafing our continued freedom of movement in cyberspace can be said to be downright compelling. The latter arena, far more than today's military space environment, is one in which the Nation faces clear and present threats that could be completely debilitating when it comes to conducting effective military operations. Not only that, opponents who would exploit opportunities in cyberspace with hostile intent have every possibility for adversely affecting the very livelihood of the Nation, since that arena has increasingly become not just the global connective tissue, but also the Nation's central nervous system and center of gravity.

Just a few generations ago, any American loss of unimpeded access to cyberspace would have been mainly an inconvenience. Today, however, given the Nation's ever-expanding dependence on that medium, the isolation, corruption, or elimination of electrical power supply, financial transactions, key communications links, and other essential Web-based functions could bring life as we know it to a halt. Furthermore, given the unprecedented reliance of the United States today on computers and the Internet, cyberspace has arguably become the Nation's center of gravity not just for military operations, but for *all* aspects of national activity, to include economic, financial, diplomatic, and other transactions. Our heightened vulnerability in this arena stems from the fact that we have moved beyond the era of physical information and financial exchanges through paper and hard currency and rely instead on the movement of digital representations of information and wealth. By one informed account, more than 90 percent of American business in all sectors, to say nothing of key institutions of governance and national defense, connects and conducts essential communications within the cyberspace arena.[7] Accordingly, that arena has become an American Achilles heel to a greater extent than any of our current opponents.

The term *cyberspace* derives from the Greek word *kubernetes*, or "steersman." Reduced to basics, it is the proverbial ether within and through which electromagnetic radiation is propagated in connection with the operation and control of mechanical and electronic transmission systems. Properly understood, cyberspace is not a "mission," but rather an operating domain just like the atmosphere and space, and it embraces all systems that incorporate software as a key element. It is a medium, moreover, in which information can be created and acted on at any time, anywhere, and by essentially anyone. It is qualitatively different from the land, sea, air, and space domains, yet it both overlaps and continuously operates within all four. It also is the only domain in which all instruments of national power (diplomatic, informational, military, and economic) can be concurrently exercised through the manipulation of data and gateways. Cyberspace can be thought of as a "digital commons" analogous to the more familiar maritime, aerial, and exoatmospheric commons. Moreover, just like the other three commons, it is one in which our continued uninhibited access can never be taken for granted as a natural and assured right. Yet uniquely among the other three, it is a domain in which the classic constraints of distance, space, time, and investment are reduced, in some cases dramatically, both for ourselves and for potential enemies.

There is nothing new in principle about cyberspace as a military operating domain. On the contrary, it has existed for as long as radio frequency emanations have been a routine part of military operations. As far back as the late 1970s, the commander in chief of the Soviet Navy, Admiral Sergei Gorshkov, declared famously that "the next war will be won by the country that is able to exploit the electromagnetic spectrum to the fullest."[8] Furthermore, the Soviets for decades expounded repeatedly, and with considerable sophistication and seriousness, on a mission area that they referred to as *REB* (for *radioelektronaya bor'ba*, or radio-electronic combat). However, only more recently has it been explicitly recognized as an operating arena on a par with the atmosphere and space and begun to be systematically explored as a medium of combat in and of itself.

At present, theorizing about airpower and its uses and limitations has the most deeply rooted tradition in the United States, with conceptualizing about military space occupying second place in that regard. In contrast, focused thinking about operations in cyberspace remains in its infancy. Yet cyberspace-related threats to American interests are currently at hand to a degree that potentially catastrophic air and space threats are not—at least yet. Accordingly, the U.S. defense establishment should have every incentive to get serious about this domain now, when new terrorist, fourth-generation warfare, and information operations challengers have increasingly moved to the forefront alongside traditional peer-adversary threats.[9]

In light of that emergent reality, it is essential to include cyberspace in any consideration of air and space capabilities. Like the air and space domains, cyberspace is part and parcel of the third dimension (the first two being the land and maritime environments). Also like those other two domains, it is a setting in which organized attacks on critical infrastructure and other targets of interest can be conducted from a distance, on a wide variety of "fronts," and on a global scale—except in this case, at the speed of light. Moreover, it is the principal domain in which the Nation's air services exercise their command, control, communications, and ISR capabilities that enable global mobility and rapid long-range strike.

In thinking about cyberspace as a military operating arena, a number of the medium's distinguishing characteristics are worth noting. First and foremost, control of cyberspace is a sine qua non for operating effectively in the other two domains. Were unimpeded access to the electromagnetic spectrum denied to us through hostile actions, satellite-aided munitions would become useless, command and control mechanisms would be disrupted, and the ensuing effects could be paralyzing. Accordingly, cyberspace has become an emergent theater of operations that will almost surely be contested in any future fight. Successful exploitation of this domain through network warfare operations can allow an opponent to dominate or hold at risk any or all of the global commons. For that reason, not only American superiority but also American dominance must be assured.

One reason for the imminent and broad-based nature of the cyberspace challenge is the low buy-in cost compared to the vastly more complex and expensive appurtenances of air and space warfare, along with the growing ability of present and prospective Lilliputian adversaries to generate what one expert called "catastrophic cascading effects" through asymmetric operations against the American Gulliver.[10] Because the price of entry is fairly minimal compared to the massive investments that would be required for any competitor to prevail in the air and space domains, the cyberspace warfare arena naturally favors the offense. It does so, moreover, not only for us, but also for any opponents who might use the medium for conducting organized attacks on critical nodes of the Nation's infrastructure. Such attacks can be conducted both instantaneously and from a safe haven anywhere in the world, with every possibility of achieving high impact and a low likelihood of attribution and, accordingly, of timely and effective U.S. retribution.

Indeed, America's vulnerabilities in cyberspace are open to the entire world and are accessible by anyone with the wherewithal and determination to exploit them. Without appropriate defensive firewalls and countermeasures in place, anything we might do to exploit cyberspace can be done to us as well, and relatively inexpensively. Worse yet, threat trends and possibilities in the cyberspace domain put in immediate jeopardy much, if not all, of what the Nation has accomplished in the other two domains in recent decades. Our continued prevalence in cyberspace can help ensure our prevalence in combat operations both within and beyond the atmosphere, which, in turn, will enable our prevalence in overall joint and combined battlespace. On the other side of the coin, any loss of cyberspace dominance on our part can negate our most cherished gains in air and space in virtually an instant. Technologies that can enable offensive cyberspace operations, moreover, are evolving not only within the most well-endowed military establishments around the world, but also even more so in the various innovative activities now under way in other government, private sector, and academic settings. The United States commands no natural advantage in this domain, and its leaders cannot assume that the next breakthrough will always be ours. All of this has rendered offensive cyberspace operations an attractive asymmetric option not only for mainstream opponents and other potential exploiters of the medium in ways inimical to the Nation's interests, but also for state and nonstate rogue actors with sufficient resources to cause us real harm.

Moreover, unlike the air and space environments, cyberspace is the *only* military operating area in which the United States already has peer competitors in place and hard at work. As for specific challengers, U.S. officials have recently suggested that the most sophisticated threat may come from China, which unquestionably is already a peer competitor with ample financial resources and technological expertise. There is more than tangential evidence to suggest that cyberwar specialists in China's People's Liberation Army have already focused hostile efforts against nonsecure U.S. transmissions.[11] Such evidence bears strong witness to the fact that state-sponsored cyberspace intrusion is now an established fact and that accurate and timely attack characterization has come to present a major challenge.

In light of its relative newness as a recognized and well-understood medium of combat, detailed and validated concepts of operations for offensive and defensive counter–cyber warfare and cyberspace interdiction have most likely yet to be worked out and formally incorporated into the Nation's combat repertoire. Interestingly, some of the most promising initial tactical insights toward that end may come from accessible sources in the nonmilitary domain, including from the business world, the intelligence world, the high-end amateur hacker world, and even perhaps segments of the underworld that have already pioneered the malicious exploitation of cyberspace. Ultimately, such efforts can help inform the development of a full-fledged theory of cyberspace power, which, at bottom, "is about dominating the electromagnetic spectrum—from wired and unwired networks to radio waves, microwaves, infrared, x-rays, and directed energy."[12]

With a full-court press of creative thought toward the development of new capabilities, the possibility of what a future cyberspace weapons array might include is almost limitless. Cyber weapons can be both surgical and mass-based in their intended effects, ranging from what one Air Force cyber warrior recently portrayed as "the ultimate precision weapon—the electron," all the way to measures aimed at causing mass disruption and full system breakdowns by means of both enabling and direct attacks.[13] The first and most important step toward dealing effectively with the cyberspace warfare challenge in both threat categories will be erecting impenetrable firewalls for ourselves and taking down those of the enemy. Of course, with respect to plausible techniques and procedures for tomorrow's cyberspace world, it will be essential never to lose sight of the timeless rule among airmen that a tactic tried twice is no longer a tactic but a procedure.

As the newly emerging cyberspace warfare community increasingly sets its sights on such goals, it would do well to consider taking a page from the recent experience of the military space community in charting next steps by way of organizational and implementation measures. For example, just as the military space community eventually emulated to good effect many conventions of the air warfare community, so might the cyberspace community usefully study the proven best practices of the space community in gaining increased relevance in the joint warfare world. Some possible first steps toward that end might include a systematic stocktaking of the Nation's cyberspace warfare posture, with a view toward identifying gaps, shortfalls, and redundancies in existing offensive and defensive capabilities.

Similarly, those now tasked with developing and validating cyberspace concepts of operations might find great value in reflecting on the many parallels between space and cyberspace as domains of offensive and defensive activity. For example, both domains, at least today, are principally about collecting and transmitting information. Both play pivotal roles in enabling and facilitating lethal combat operations by other force elements. Both, again at least today, have more to do with the pursuit of functional effects than with the physical destruction of enemy equities, even though both can materially aid in the accomplishment of the latter. Moreover, in both domains, operations are conducted remotely by warfighters sitting before consoles and keyboards, not only outside the medium itself, but also in almost every case out of harm's way. Both domains are global rather than regional in their breadth of coverage and operational impact. And both domains overlap—for example, the jamming of a GPS signal to a satellite-aided munition guiding to a target is both a counterspace and a cyberwar operation insofar as the desired effect is sought simultaneously in both combat arenas.[14] To that extent, it seems reasonable to suggest that at least some tactics, techniques, procedures, and rules of thumb that have been found useful by military space professionals might also offer promising points of departure from which to explore comparable ways of exploiting the cyberspace medium.

Finally, as cyberspace professionals become more conversant with the operational imperatives of joint warfighting, they also will have a collective obligation to rise above the fragmented subcultures that unfortunately still persist within their *own* community and become a more coherent and interconnected center of cyberspace excellence able to speak credibly about what the exploitation of that medium brings to joint force employment. Moreover, cyberspace warfare professionals will need to learn and accept as gospel that any "cyberspace culture" that may ultimately emerge from such efforts must not be isolated from mainstream combat forces in all Services, as the Air Force's space sector was when it was in the clutches of the systems and acquisition communities, but instead must be rooted from the start in an unerring focus on the art and conduct of war.

Toward a Cross-domain Synthesis

As long as military space activity remains limited to enabling rather than actually conducting combat operations, as will continue to be the case for at least the near-term future, it will arguably remain premature even to *think* of the notion of space "power," strictly speaking, let alone suggest that the time has come to begin crafting a self-standing theory of spacepower comparable in ambitiousness and scope to the competing (and still-evolving) theories of land-, sea-, and airpower that were developed over the course of the 20th century. Only when desired operational effects can be achieved by means of imposition options exercised directly through and from space to space-based, air-breathing, and terrestrial targets of interest (or, more to the point, when we can directly inflict harm on our adversaries from space) will it become defensible to entertain thoughts about space "power" as a fact of life rather than as merely a prospective and desirable goal.

To be sure, it scarcely follows from this observation that today's space professionals have no choice but to wait patiently for the day when they become force appliers on a par with their air, land, and maritime power contemporaries before they can legitimately claim that they are true warfighters. On the contrary, the Nation's space capabilities have long since matured to a point where they have become just as important a contributor to the overall *national* power equation as has what one might call mobility power, information power, and all other such adjuncts of the Nation's military strength that are indispensable to joint force commanders for achieving desired effects at all levels of warfare. To that extent, insisting that it remains premature to speak of spacepower solely because our space assets cannot yet deliver such combat effects directly may, in the end, be little more than an exercise in word play when one considers what space already has done toward transforming the Nation's airpower into something vastly more capable than it ever was before U.S. on-orbit equities had attained their current breadth of enabling potential.

Until the day comes when military space activity is more than "merely" about enabling terrestrial combat operations, however, a more useful exercise in theory-building in the service of combat operators at all levels might be to move beyond the *air*-power theorizing that has taken place to date in pursuit of something akin to a working "unified field theory" that explicates the connections, interactions, and overlaps among the air, space, and cyberspace domains in quest of synergies between and among them in the interest of achieving a joint force commander's objectives more efficiently and effectively. A major pitfall to be avoided in this regard is the pursuit of separate theory sets for each medium. To borrow from Clausewitz on this point, space, like the earth's atmosphere and the electromagnetic spectrum, may have its own grammar, but it does not have its own logic. Each of the three environments explored in the preceding pages has distinctive physical features and operating rules that demand respect. By one characterization in this regard, "air permits freedom of movement not possible on land or sea. . . . Space yields an overarching capability to view globally and attack with precision from the orbital perspective. Cyberspace provides the capability to conduct combat on a global scale simultaneously on a virtually infinite number of 'fronts.'"[15] Yet while the air, space, and cyberspace mediums are all separate and unique physical environments, taken together, they present a common warfighting challenge in that operations in each are mutually supportive of those in the other two. For example, the pursuit of air supremacy does not simply entail combat operations in the atmosphere, but also hinges critically on ISR functions and on GPS targeting from both air-breathing and space-based platforms that transmit through cyberspace.

Another pitfall from the earliest days of airpower theorizing to be avoided is that of overreaching with respect to promises and expectations of what any ensuing theory should encompass and seek to make possible. Since airpower, spacepower, cyberpower, or any combination thereof can be everything from totally decisive to only marginally relevant to a commander's needs at any given moment, any insistence that these dimensions of military power be the centerpieces of overall national strategy will almost certainly fail to resonate and take lasting root in the joint arena. The single greatest failure of airpower's most revered founts of presumed insight and foresight, Generals Giulio Douhet and Billy Mitchell, was their passionate espousal not simply of a theory of *airpower*, but an overarching theory of *war* that hinged everything on the air weapon to the virtual exclusion of all other instruments of military power. As retired Air Vice Marshal Tony Mason of Great Britain's Royal Air Force insightfully noted in this regard, any truly effective theory of airpower (and, by the same token, of spacepower and cyberpower) must endeavor to emphasize not just the unique characteristics of the instrument, but also "the features it shares, to a greater or lesser degree, with other forms of warfare." Mason added that the preeminence of the instrument "will stand or fall not by promises and abstract theories, but, like any other kind of military power, by its relevance to, and ability to secure, political objectives at a cost acceptable to the government of the day."[16]

In light of the foregoing, the most immediate task for those seeking to build a better theory for leveraging capabilities in the third dimension may be to develop a point of departure for thinking systematically and holistically about synergies and best uses of the Nation's capabilities and prospects in all three domains, since all are key to the Nation's transforming joint strike warfare repertoire. Furthermore, it would be helpful to have a seamless body of applied and actionable theory that encompasses all three domains and that focuses more on functions and effects than on the physical locations of the instruments of power, with a view toward rank-ordering the many priorities in each and across all three, with the goal of charting a course for achieving cross-domain dominance. Another useful step toward managing the existing seams between and among the air, space, and cyberspace communities within the American defense establishment would be a perspective focused on *operational integration* accompanied by *organizational differentiation*. Through such a bifurcated approach, each medium can be harnessed to serve the needs of all components in the joint arena while, at the same time, being treated rightly as its own domain when it comes to program and infrastructure management, funding, cadre building, and career development.[17] Such organizational differentiation will be essential for the orderly growth of core competencies, discrete career fields, and mature professionalism in each medium. However, operational integration should be the abiding concern and goal for all three mediums, since it is only from synergies among the three that each can work to its best and highest use.

This is *not* a call for the Air Force, as the Nation's main repository of air, space, and cyberspace warfare capabilities today, to make the same mistake in a new guise that it made in 1959 when it conjured up the false artifice of "aerospace" to suggest that the air and space mediums were somehow undifferentiated just because they happened to be coextensive. Nothing could be further from the truth. It is, rather, to spotlight the unifying purpose of operations in all three mediums working in harmony, namely, to deliver desired combat effects in, through, and from the third dimension as quickly as possible and at the least possible cost in friendly lives lost and unintended damage incurred. Only after that crucial transitional stage of conceptualization has passed and when military space operations have come into their own as an independent producer, rather than just an enabler, of combat effects will it be possible to start giving serious thought to coming to grips with the prerequisites for a self-standing theory of spacepower.

Notes

[1] For an overview of the Air Force's pivotal contribution to this transformation, see Benjamin S. Lambeth, "The Air Force Renaissance," in *The Air Force*, ed. General James P. McCarthy, USAF (Ret.), and Colonel Drue L. DeBerry, USAF (Ret.) (Andrews Air Force Base, MD: The Air Force Historical Foundation, 2002), 190–217. A fuller assessment of post-Vietnam developments in fixed-wing air warfare capability in all of the Services may be found in Benjamin S. Lambeth, *The Transformation of American Airpower* (Ithaca, NY: Cornell University Press, 2000).

[2] These major air operations are examined in detail in Benjamin S. Lambeth, NATO's *Air War for Kosovo: A Strategic and Operational Assessment* (Santa Monica, CA: RAND Corporation, 2001); *Airpower Against Terror: America's Conduct of Operation Enduring Freedom* (Santa Monica, CA: RAND Corporation, 2005); and *The Unseen War: Airpower's Role in the Takedown of Saddam Hussein* (Santa Monica, CA: RAND Corporation, forthcoming).

[3] For more on this point, see Benjamin S. Lambeth, *American Carrier Airpower at the Dawn of a New Century* (Santa Monica, CA: RAND Corporation, 2005).

[4] Of course, space plays a larger role in the "fixing" of targets than just providing space-based ISR. Space-based communications and the Global Positioning System are both essential enablers of unmanned aerial vehicle operations, which are also a critical contributor to the "fix, find, track, target, engage, assess" equation.

[5] Cited in E.C. Aldridge, Jr., "Thoughts on the Management of National Security Space Activities of the Department of Defense," unpublished paper, July 6, 2000, 3.

[6] For the essential known details of the test, see Craig Covault, "Space Control: Chinese Anti-satellite Weapon Test Will Intensify Funding and Global Policy Debate on the Military Uses of Space," *Aviation Week and Space Technology*, January 22, 2007, 24–25.

[7] General James Cartwright, USMC, Commander, U.S. Strategic Command, remarks at the Air Force Association's Warfare Symposium, Orlando, Florida, February 8, 2007.

[8] Admiral of the Fleet Sergei G. Gorshkov, *The Sea Power of the State* (Annapolis, MD: Naval Institute Press, 1979).

[9] Among the classic articles in the airpower theory literature are Edward Warner, "Douhet, Mitchell, Seversky: Theories of Air Warfare," in *Makers of Modern Strategy*, ed. Edward Mead Earle (Princeton: Princeton University Press, 1943), and David MacIsaac, "Voices from the Central Blue: The Airpower Theorists," in *Makers of Modern Strategy: From Machiavelli to the Nuclear Age*, ed. Peter Paret (Princeton: Princeton University Press, 1986). See also the collection of essays in Phillip S. Meilinger, ed., *The Paths of Heaven: The Evolution of Airpower Theory* (Maxwell Air Force Base, AL: Air University Press, 1997). One of the better synopses of spacepower thinking to date is presented in Peter L. Hays et al., *Spacepower for a New Millennium: Space and U.S. National Security* (New York: McGraw Hill, 2000). For the most serious and thorough treatise thus far to have expounded about the cyberspace domain, its boundaries, and its potential, see George J. Rattray, *Strategic Warfare in Cyberspace* (Cambridge: MIT Press, 2001). The book is the doctoral dissertation of an Air Force lieutenant colonel who commanded the 23[d] Information Operations Squadron in the Air Force Information Warfare Center.

[10] Colonel Glenn Zimmerman, USAF, "The United States Air Force and Cyberspace: Ultimate Warfighting Domain and the USAF's Destiny," unpublished paper.

[11] See Carlo Munoz, "Air Force Official Sees China as Biggest U.S. Threat in Cyberspace," *Inside the Air Force*, November 17, 2006.

[12] "Ten Propositions Regarding Cyber Power," Air Force Cyberspace Task Force, unpublished briefing chart, no date.

[13] Zimmerman.

[14] I am grateful to my RAND colleague Karl Mueller for suggesting these and other thought-provoking parallels between the two media.

[15] Zimmerman.

[16] Air Vice Marshal Tony Mason, RAF (Ret.), *Airpower: A Centennial Appraisal* (London: Brassey's, 1994), 273–274.

[17] For an earlier development of this line of argument with respect to the Air Force's space community, see Benjamin S. Lambeth, *Mastering the Ultimate High Ground: Next Steps in the Military Uses of Space* (Santa Monica, CA: RAND Corporation, 2003).

Part III: Civil, Commercial, and Economic Space Perspectives

Chapter 9

History of Civil Space Activity and Spacepower

Roger D. Launius

The U.S. civil space program emerged in large part because of the pressures of national security during the Cold War.[1] In general, it has remained tightly interwoven with the national security aspects of space. As space policy analyst Dwayne A. Day noted, "The history of American civil and military cooperation in space is one of competing interests, priorities and justifications at the upper policy levels combined with a remarkable degree of cooperation and coordination at virtually all operational levels."[2] This has been the case throughout the first 50 years of the space age for myriad reasons. First, space employs dual-use technologies that are necessary for both military and civil applications. These technologies are developed mostly at government expense and sometimes with significant in-house government laboratory research by U.S.-owned and -based high technology firms, euphemistically called the military-industrial complex. Those firms do not much care whether the technologies' end uses are for civil or national security purposes, and indeed the same essential knowledge, skills, and technologies are required for both human spaceflight missions and national security space operations. The overlap of technologies and the related activities necessary to operate them explains much about the interwoven nature of civil-military space efforts.[3]

A second issue, closely related to the first, is that the military and civil space programs have represented essentially two central aspects of a concerted effort over the long haul to project national strength. The military component has represented "bare-knuckle" force, while the civil space program represented a form of soft power in which pride at home and prestige abroad accrued to the United States through successful space activities conducted with a sense of peace. Civil space operations also served, in the words of R. Cargill Hall, as a "stalking horse" for a clandestine national security effort in space. That cover served well the needs of the United States during the Cold War, diverting attention from reconnaissance and other national security satellites placed in Earth orbit.[4]

Observers certainly recognized the national prestige issue from the beginning of the space age. Vernon Van Dyke commented on it in his 1964 book, *Pride and Power: The Rationale of the Space Program,* making the case with scholarly detachment that prestige was one of the primary reasons for the United States to undertake its expansive civil space effort.[5] In the words of reviewer John P. Lovell, "Van Dyke marshals convincing evidence in support of the thesis that 'national pride' has served as the goal value most central to the motivation of those who have given the space program its major impetus."[6] Although his research is certainly dated, Van Dyke's conclusions hold up surprisingly well after the passage of more than 45 years. At a fundamental level, American Presidents have consciously used these activities as a symbol of national excellence to enhance the prestige of the United States throughout the world.[7]

Third, the gradual process whereby the political leadership of the United States—especially the Dwight D. Eisenhower and John F. Kennedy administrations—decided which governmental organizations should take responsibility for which space missions led to persistent and sometime sharp difficulties.[8] Several military entities, especially U.S. Air Force leaders, had visions of dominating the new arena of space, visions that were only partially realized. This proved especially troubling in the context of human spaceflight, when early advocates believed military personnel would be required. In essence, they thought of space as a new theater of conflict just like land, sea, and air and chafed under the decision of Eisenhower, reaffirmed to the present, to make space a sanctuary from armed operations. One important result of that decision was the elimination of military human missions in space, a bitter pill for national security space adherents even today. Indeed, the insistence on flying military astronauts on the space shuttle until the *Challenger* accident in 1986 represented an important marker for future developments. It may also be that in some advocates' minds, the current debate over space weaponization represents an opportunity to gain a human military mission in space.[9]

After a brief introduction to the space policy arena in the early years of the space age, the remainder of this chapter will explore these three themes—dual-use technology, the role of soft power and the prestige and pride issue in national security affairs, and the quest for military personnel in space.

National Security and the Space Program during the Cold War

Since the latter 1940s, the Department of Defense (DOD) has pur-sued research in rocketry and upper atmospheric sciences as a means of assuring American leadership in technology. The civilian side of the space effort can be said to have begun in 1952 when the International Council of Scientific Unions established a committee to arrange an International Geo-physical Year (IGY) for the period of July 1, 1957, to December 31, 1958. After years of preparation, on July 29, 1955, the U.S. scientific community persuaded President Eisenhower to approve a plan to orbit a scientific sat-ellite as part of the IGY effort. With the launch of Sputnik I and II by the Soviet Union in the fall of 1957 and the American orbiting of Explorer 1 in January 1958, the space race commenced and did not abate until the end of the Cold War—although there were lulls in the competition.[10] The most visible part of this competition was the human spaceflight program—with the Moon landings by Apollo astronauts as de rigueur—but the effort also entailed robotic missions to several planets of the solar system, military and commercial satellite activities, and other scientific and technological labors.[11] In the post–Cold War era, the space exploration agenda under-went significant restructuring and led to such cooperative ventures as the International Space Station and the development of launchers, science missions, and applications satellites through international consortia.[12]

Role of Adventure and Discovery

Undoubtedly, adventure, discovery, and the promise of exploration and colonization were the motivating forces behind the small cadre of early space program advocates in the United States prior to the 1950s. Most advocates of aggressive space exploration efforts invoked an extension of the popular notion of the American frontier with its then-attendant positive images of territorial discovery, scientific discovery, exploration, colonization, and use.[13] Indeed, the image of the American frontier has been an especially evocative and somewhat romantic, as well as popular, argument to support the aggres-sive exploration of space. It plays to the popular conception of "westering" and the settlement of the American continent by Europeans from the East that was a powerful metaphor of national identity until the 1970s.

The space promoters of the 1950s and 1960s intuited that this set of symbols provided a vigorous explanation for and justification of their efforts. The metaphor was probably appropriate for what they wanted to accomplish. It conjured up an image of self-reliant Americans moving west-ward in sweeping waves of discovery, exploration, conquest, and settlement of an untamed wilderness. In the process of movement, the Europeans who settled North America became, in their own eyes, a people imbued with virtue and justness, unique from all the others of the Earth. The frontier ideal has always carried with it the principles of optimism, democracy, and right relationships. It has been almost utopian in its expression, and it should come as no surprise that those people seeking to create perfect societies in the 17th, 18th, and 19th centuries—the Puritans, the Mormons, the Shakers, the Moravians, the Fourians, the Icarians, the followers of Horace Greeley— often went to the frontier to carry out their visions.

It also summoned in the popular mind a wide range of vivid and memorable tales of heroism, each a morally justified step of progress toward the modern democratic state. While the frontier ideal reduced the complexity of events to a relatively static morality play, avoided matters that challenged or contradicted the myth, viewed Americans moving westward as inherently good and their opponents as evil, and ignored the cultural context of westward migration, it served a critical unifying purpose for the Nation. Those who were persuaded by this metaphor—and most white Americans in 1960 did not challenge it—embraced the vision of space exploration.[14]

Role of Popular Conceptions of Space Travel

If the frontier metaphor of space exploration conjured up romantic images of an American nation progressing to something for the greater good, the space advocates of the Eisenhower era also sought to convince the public that space exploration was an immediate possibility. Science fiction books and films portrayed space exploration, but more importantly, its possibility was fostered by serious and respected scientists, engineers, and politicians. Deliberate efforts on the part of space boosters during the late 1940s and early 1950s helped to reshape the popular culture of space and to influence government policy. In particular, these advocates worked hard to overcome the level of disbelief that had been generated by two decades of "Buck Rogers"–type fantasies and to convince the American public that space travel might actually, for the first time in human history, be possible.[15]

The decade following World War II brought a sea change in perceptions, as most Americans moved from being skeptical about the probability of spaceflight to accepting it as a near-term reality. This shift can be seen in the public opinion polls of the era. For instance, in December 1949, Gallup pollsters found that only 15 percent of Americans believed humans would reach the Moon within 50 years, while a whopping 70 percent believed that it would not happen within that time. By 1957, 41 percent believed firmly that it would not take longer than 25 years for humans to reach the Moon, while only 25 percent believed that it would. An important shift in perceptions had taken place during that era, and it was largely the result of a public relations campaign based on the real possibility of spaceflight coupled with the well-known advances in rocket technology.[16]

The American public became aware of the possibility of spaceflight through sources ranging from science fiction literature and film that were closer to reality than ever before, to speculations by science fiction writers about possibilities already real, to serious discussions of the subject in respected popular magazines. Among the most important serious efforts were those of German émigré Wernher von Braun, who was working for the U.S. Army at Huntsville, Alabama. Von Braun, in addition to being a superbly effective technological entrepreneur, managed to seize the powerful print and communications media that the science fiction writers and filmmakers had been using in the early 1950s and became a highly effective promoter of space exploration to the public.[17]

In 1952, von Braun burst on the public stage with a series of articles in *Collier's* magazine about the possibilities of spaceflight. The first issue of *Collier's* devoted to space appeared on March 22, 1952. An editorial in that issue suggested that spaceflight was possible, not just science fiction, and that it was inevitable that mankind would venture outward. In his articles, von Braun advocated the orbiting of humans, development of a reusable spacecraft for travel to and from Earth orbit, construction of a permanently inhabited space station, and human exploration of the Moon and Mars by spacecraft departing from the space station. The series concluded with a special issue of the magazine devoted to Mars, in which von Braun and others described how to get there and predicted what might be found based on recent scientific data.[18]

The merging of the public perception of spaceflight as a near-term reality with the technological developments then being seen at White Sands and other experimental facilities created an environment conducive to the establishment of an aggressive space program. Convincing the American public that spaceflight was *possible* was one of the most critical components of the space policy debate of the 1950s. Without it, the aggressive exploration programs of the 1960s would never have been approved. For a concept to be approved in the public policy arena, the public must have both an appropriate vision of the phenomenon with which the society seeks to grapple and confidence in the attainability of the goal. Indeed, space enthusiasts were so successful in promoting their image of human spaceflight as being imminent that when other developments forced public policymakers to consider the space program seriously, alternative visions of space exploration remained ill formed, and even advocates of different futures emphasizing robotic probes and applications satellites were obliged to discuss space exploration using the symbols of the human space travel vision that its promoters had established so well in the minds of Americans.[19]

Role of Foreign Policy and National Security Issues

At the same time that space exploration advocates, both amateurs and scientists, were generating an image of spaceflight as a genuine possibility and proposing how to accomplish a far-reaching program of lunar and planetary exploration, another critical element entered the picture: the role of spaceflight in national defense and international relations. Space partisans early began hitching their exploration vision to the political requirements of the Cold War, in particular to the belief that the nation that occupied the "high ground" of space would dominate the territories underneath it. In the first of the *Collier's* articles in 1952, the exploration of space was framed in the context of the Cold War rivalry with the Soviet Union and concluded that "the time has come for Washington to give priority of attention to the matter of space superiority. The rearmament gap between the East and West has been steadily closing. And nothing, in our opinion, should be left undone that might guarantee the peace of the world. It's as simple as that." The magazine's editors argued "that the U.S. must immediately embark on a long-range development program to secure for the West 'space superiority.' If we do not, somebody else will. That somebody else very probably would be the Soviet Union."[20]

The synthesis of the idea of progress manifested through the frontier, the selling of spaceflight as a reality in American popular culture, and the Cold War rivalries between the United States and the Soviet Union made possible the adoption of an aggressive space program by the early 1960s. The National Aeronautics and Space Administration (NASA) effort through Project Apollo, with its emphasis upon human spaceflight and extraterrestrial exploration, emerged from these three major ingredients, with Cold War concerns the dominant driver behind monetary appropriations for space efforts.

The Heroic Age of Space Exploration

Rivalry with the Soviet Union was the key that opened the door to aggressive space exploration, not as an end in itself, but as a means to achieving technological superiority in the eyes of the world. From the perspective of the 21st century, it is difficult to appreciate Americans' near-hysterical preoccupation with nuclear attack in the 1950s. Far from being the idyll portrayed in the television show "Happy Days," the United States was a dysfunctional nation preoccupied with death by nuclear war. Schools required children to practice civil defense techniques and shield themselves from nuclear blasts, in some cases by simply crawling under their desks. Communities practiced civil defense drills, and families built personal bomb shelters in their backyards.[21] In the popular culture, nuclear attack was inexorably linked to the space above the United States, from which the attack would come.

After an arms race with its nuclear component, a series of hot and cold crises in the Eisenhower era, and the launching of Sputniks I and II in 1957, the threat of holocaust felt by most Americans and Soviets seemed increasingly probable. For the first time, enemies could reach the United States with a radical new technology. In the contest over the ideologies and allegiances of the world's nonaligned nations, space exploration became contested ground.[22] Even while U.S. officials congratulated the Soviet Union for this accomplishment, many Americans thought that the Soviet Union had staged a tremendous coup for the communist system at U.S. expense. It was a shock, introducing the illusion of a technological gap and leading directly to several critical efforts aimed at catching up to the Soviet Union's space achievements. Among these efforts were:

- a full-scale review of both the civil and military programs of the United States (scientific satellite efforts and ballistic missile development)

- establishment of a Presidential science advisor in the White House who would oversee the activities of the Federal Government in science and technology

- creation of the Advanced Research Projects Agency (ARPA) in the Department of Defense, and the consolidation of several space activities under centralized management

- establishment of NASA to manage civil space operations

- passage of the National Defense Education Act to provide Federal funding for education in the scientific and technical disciplines.[23]

More immediately, the United States launched its first Earth satellite on January 31, 1958, when Explorer I documented the existence of radiation zones encircling the Earth. Shaped by the Earth's magnetic field, what came to be called the Van Allen radiation belt partially dictates the electrical charges in the atmosphere and the solar radiation that reaches Earth. It also began a series of scientific missions to the Moon and planets in the latter 1950s and early 1960s.[24]

Congress passed and President Eisenhower signed the National Aeronautics and Space Act of 1958, which established NASA with a broad mandate to explore and use space for "peaceful purposes for the benefit of all mankind."[25] The core of NASA came from the earlier National Advisory Committee for Aeronautics, which had 8,000 employees, an annual budget of $100 million, and research laboratories. It quickly incorporated other organizations into the new agency, notably the space science group of the Naval Research Laboratory in Maryland, the Jet Propulsion Laboratory managed by the California Institute of Technology for the Army, and the Army Ballistic Missile Agency in Huntsville, Alabama.[26]

The Soviet Union, while not creating a separate organization dedicated to space exploration, infused money into its various rocket design bureaus and scientific research institutions. The chief beneficiaries of Soviet spaceflight enthusiasm were the design bureau of Sergei P. Korolev (the chief designer of the first Soviet rockets used for the Sputnik program) and the Soviet Academy of Sciences, which devised experiments and built the instruments that were launched into orbit. With huge investments in spaceflight technology urged by premier Nikita Khrushchev, the Soviet Union accomplished one public relations coup after another against the United States during the late 1950s and early 1960s.[27]

Within a short time of its formal organization, NASA also took over management of space exploration projects from other Federal agencies and began to conduct space science missions, such as Project Ranger to send probes to the Moon, Project Echo to test the possibility of satellite communications, and Project Mercury to ascertain the possibilities of human spaceflight. Even so, these activities were constrained by a modest budget and a measured pace on the part of NASA leadership.

In an irony of the first magnitude, Eisenhower believed that the creation of NASA and the placing of so much power in its hands by the Kennedy administration during the Apollo program of the 1960s was a mistake. He remarked in a 1962 article: "Why the great hurry to get to the moon and the planets? We have already demonstrated that in everything except the power of our booster rockets we are leading the world in scientific space exploration. From here on, I think we should proceed in an orderly, scientific way, building one accomplishment on another."[28] He later cautioned that the Moon race "has diverted a disproportionate share of our brain-power and research facilities from equally significant problems, including education and automation."[29] He believed that Americans had overreacted to the perceived threat.

During the first 15 years of the space age, the United States emphasized a civilian exploration program consisting of several major components. The capstone of this effort was, of course, the human expedition to the Moon, Project Apollo. A unique confluence of political necessity, personal commitment and activism, scientific and technological ability, economic prosperity, and public mood made possible the May 25, 1961, announcement by President John F. Kennedy of the intent to carry out a lunar landing program before the end of the decade as a means of demonstrating the Nation's technological virtuosity.[30]

Project Apollo was the tangible result of an early national commitment in response to a perceived threat from the Soviet Union. NASA leaders recognized that while the size of the task was enormous, it was technologically and financially within their grasp, but they had to move forward quickly. Accordingly, the space agency's annual budget increased from $500 million in 1960 to a high point of $5.2 billion in 1965. NASA's budget began to decline beginning in 1966 and continued on a downward trend until 1975. With the exception of a few years during the Apollo era, the NASA budget has hovered at slightly less than one percent of all money expended by the U.S. Treasury (see figure 9–1).[31]

Figure 9–1. NASA Budget as a Percentage of Federal Budget

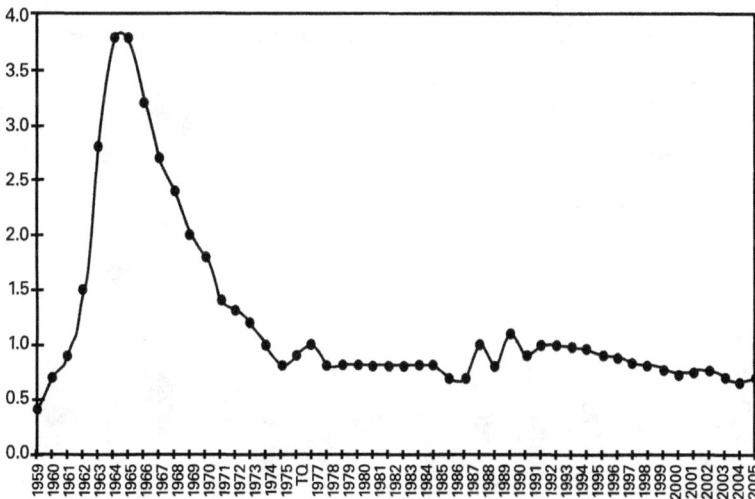

While there may be reason to accept that Apollo was transcendentally important at some sublime level, assuming a rosy public acceptance of it is at best a simplistic and ultimately unsatisfactory conclusion. Indeed, the public's support for space funding has remained remarkably stable at approximately 80 percent in favor of the status quo since 1965, with only one significant dip in support in the early 1970s. However, responses to funding questions on public opinion polls are extremely sensitive to question wording and must be used cautiously.[32] Polls in the 1960s consistently ranked spaceflight near the top of those programs to be cut in the Federal budget. Most Americans seemingly preferred doing something about air and water pollution, job training for unskilled workers, national beautification, and poverty before spending Federal funds on human spaceflight. In 1967, *Newsweek* stated: "The U.S. space program is in decline. The Vietnam war and the desperate conditions of the nation's poor and its cities—which make spaceflight seem, in comparison, like an embarrassing national self-indulgence—have combined to drag down a program where the sky was no longer the limit."[33]

Nor did lunar exploration in and of itself inspire a groundswell of popular support from the general public, which during the 1960s largely showed hesitancy to "race" the Soviets to the Moon (see figure 9–2). Polls asked, "Would you favor or oppose U.S. government spending to send astronauts to the moon?" and in virtually all cases, a majority opposed doing so, even during the height of Apollo. At only one point, October 1965, did more than half of the public favor continuing human lunar exploration. In the post-Apollo era, the American public has continued to question the validity of undertaking human expeditions to the Moon.[34]

Figure 9–2. Public Attitudes about Government Funding for Space Trips

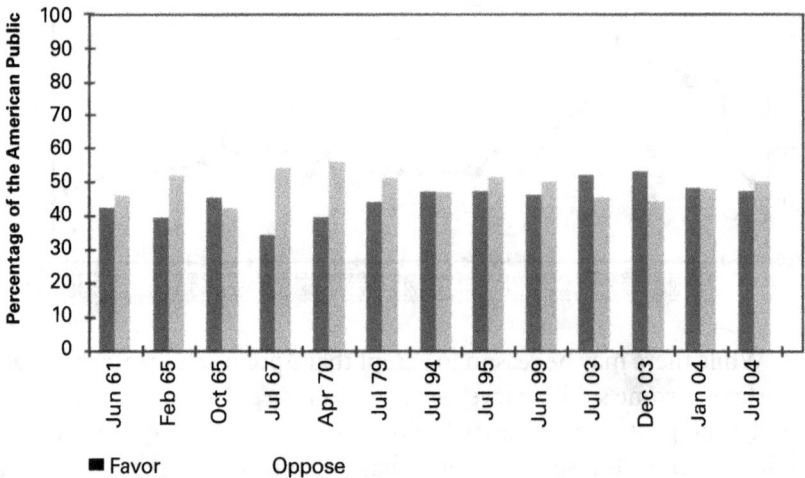

SHOULD THE GOVERNMENT FUND HUMAN TRIPS TO THE MOON?

These statistics do not demonstrate unqualified support for NASA's effort to reach the Moon in the 1960s. They suggest, instead, that the Cold War national security crisis that brought public support to the initial lunar landing decision was fleeting, and within a short period the coalition that announced it had to retrench.[35] It also suggests that the public was never enthusiastic about human lunar exploration, and especially about the costs associated with it. What enthusiasm it may have enjoyed waned over time, until by the end of the Apollo program in December 1972, the program was akin to a limping marathoner straining with every muscle to reach the finish line before collapsing.

The Space Program and Dual-use Technology

The reality, if not the definition, of dual-use technology has existed since humanity first fashioned a weapon and then used it for some other nonviolent purpose. Certainly, spears, bows and arrows, swords, clubs, firearms, and a host of other implements have dual uses for both destructive and constructive purposes. Even as nondescript a tool as a shovel has a military use as an implement for digging fortifications and as a crude weapon in hand-to-hand combat. During the Cold War, this concept of dual-use technology reached a crescendo in the context of nuclear weapons in general and their delivery systems in particular. It also found explicit situating within international agreements such as the Nonproliferation Treaty, the 1987 Missile Technology Control Regime, and the Wassenaar Arrangement on Export Controls for Conventional Arms and Dual-Use Goods and Technologies.[36] The Wassenaar accord is by far the most sweeping in its attempt to govern the transfer of dual-use space technologies. Interestingly, remote sensing, navigation, and communications satellite policies emerged first as the technologies requiring governance, with launch vehicle technology being added later. This was in no small part because of the perception that nuclear weapons launchers did not present a problem for the enhancement of military capability. Only later in the 20th century did U.S. officials wake up to the realization that the spread of launcher technology to so-called rogue states such as North Korea, Iraq, and other potential enemies posed a threat to national interests.[37]

Launch vehicles developed for the delivery of nuclear weapons unquestionably had dual use as civil space launchers with minimum, if any, alteration. Most of the launchers used by NASA during its formative years originated as military ballistic missiles that DOD had developed (see figure 9–3). It was, and remains, the fundamental technology necessary for civil space exploration, and it came largely from the military. Throughout the late 1940s and early 1950s, rocket technicians working for DOD conducted ever more demanding test flights, and scientists conducted increasingly complex scientific investigations made possible by this new dual-use technology.[38] The Army developed the Redstone rocket during this period, a missile capable of sending a small warhead a maximum of 500 miles, and its dual use became obvious when NASA used it to send the first U.S. suborbital Mercury missions with astronauts Alan B. Shepard and Gus Grissom into space in 1961.[39] The same was true for the Air Force's Atlas and Titan intercontinental ballistic missiles (ICBMs), originally developed to deliver nuclear warheads to targets half a world away. The Atlas found important uses as the launcher for the Mercury program's orbital missions, and the Titan served well as the launcher for the Gemini program human spaceflights in 1965–1966.[40]

Figure 9–3. Launch Vehicles, 1953–2000

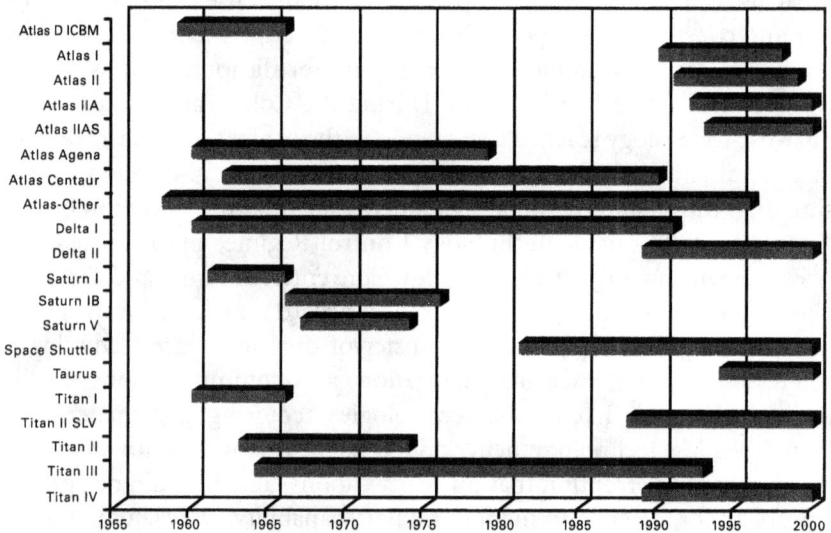

But the application of military rocket technology to the civil space program was neither automatic nor especially easy. As a converted ICBM, for example, the Atlas had undergone on-again, off-again development since 1946. Canceled once and underfunded thereafter, the Air Force had been unable until the Sputnik crisis of 1957–1958 to secure sufficient resources to make serious progress on it. Because of this difficulty, U.S. Air Force officials had accepted a 20 percent failure rate. This rate offered the fundamental argument against using the Atlas in the civil space program;

no one was willing to accept the loss of one out of five missions with astronauts aboard. But even that rate proved higher in the early going. By 1959, seven out of eight launches had failed. That would most assuredly not do with astronauts aboard. NASA's Robert R. Gilruth testified to Congress about this problem in mid-1959: "The Atlas . . . has enough performance . . . and the guidance system is accurate enough, but there is the matter of reliability. You don't want to put a man in a device unless it has a very good chance of working every time." Gilruth added, "Reliability is something that comes with practice."[41]

Incrementally, NASA, Air Force, and contract engineers improved the performance of the Atlas. They placed a fiberglass shield around the liquid oxygen tank to keep the engines from igniting it in a massive explosion, a rather spectacular failure that seemed to happen at least half the time. They changed out almost every system on the vehicle, substituting tried and true technology wherever possible to minimize problems. They altered procedures and developed new telemetry to monitor the operations of the system. Most important, they developed an abort sensing system (labeled ASS by everyone but the people involved in developing it) to monitor vehicle performance and to provide early escape for astronauts from the Mercury capsule.[42]

Transition to the Titan launcher for the Gemini program was also far from automatic. It experienced longitudinal oscillations, called the "pogo" effect because it resembled the behavior of a child on a pogo stick. Overcoming this problem required engineering imagination and long hours of overtime to stabilize fuel flow and maintain vehicle control. Other problems also led to costly modifications, increasing the estimated $350 million program cost to over $1 billion. The overruns were successfully justified by the space agency, however, as necessities to meet the Apollo landing commitment, but not without some sustained criticism.[43]

The dual-use nature of this launch technology has long presented serious challenges for the interrelations of the civil and national security space programs. Moreover, this reliance on the descendants of the three major ballistic missiles—Atlas, Titan, and what became the Delta—developed in the 1950s and 1960s for the bulk of the Nation's space access requirements has hampered space access to the present. Even though the three families of expendable space boosters—each with numerous variants—have enjoyed incremental improvement since first flight, there seems no way to escape their beginnings in technology (dating back to the 1950s) and their primary task of launching nuclear warheads. National defense requirements prompted the developers to emphasize schedule and operational reliability over launch costs.

Movement beyond these first-generation launchers is critical for the opening of space access to more activities. Like the earlier experience with propeller-driven aircraft, launchers have been incrementally improved for the last 40 years without making a major breakthrough in technology. Accordingly, the United States today has a very efficient and mature expendable launch vehicle (ELV) launch capability that is still unable to overcome the limitations of the first-generation ICBM launch vehicles.[44]

The overpowering legacy of the space shuttle has also dominated the issue of space access since Project Apollo, and it has enjoyed dual use as both a military and civil launcher. Approved in 1972 by President Richard M. Nixon as the major NASA follow-on program to the highly successful Moon landings, the space shuttle would provide routine, economical, and reliable indefinite access to space for the U.S. human spaceflight program.[45] With the first spaceflight of the *Columbia* in 1981, NASA's human space-flight capability became wedded to the space shuttle, and moving beyond that basic coupling has required 20 years. In addition to forestalling debate on a shuttle replacement, the decision to build the space shuttle in 1972 short-circuited debate on the desirability of investment in new ELVs. At first, NASA and most other space policy analysts agreed that the shuttle would become the "one-size-fits-all" space launcher of the U.S. fleet. There would be, simply put, no need for another vehicle since the shuttle could satisfy all launch requirements, be they scientific, commercial, or military, human or robotic.[46] The military Services at first agreed to launch all of their payloads on the shuttle, and NASA aggressively marketed the shuttle as a commercial vehicle that could place any satellite into orbit.[47]

This was never a perfect situation, for in the truest sense of dual usage, the shuttle was shouldering the responsibility for all government launches and many commercial ones during the early Reagan years. It was, sadly, ill equipped to satisfy these demands. Even with the best of intentions and with attractive payload pricing policies, the space shuttle remained what it had been intended to be in the first place: a research and development vehicle that would push the frontiers of spaceflight and knowledge about the universe. The desire for the shuttle to be all things to all people—research and development aerospace vehicle, operational space truck, commercial carrier, scientific platform—ensured that it would satisfy none of these singular and mutually exclusive missions.[48]

Only with the loss of the *Challenger* on January 28, 1986, did this reliance on the space shuttle begin to change. It reinvigorated a debate over the use of the space shuttle to launch all U.S. satellites. In August 1986, President Reagan announced that the shuttle would no longer carry commercial satellites, a policy formalized in December 1986 in National Security Decision Directive 254, "United States Space Launch Strategy." A total of 44 commercial and foreign payloads that had been manifested on the space shuttle were forced to find new launchers.[49]

For the next 3 years, the U.S. Government worked to reinvigorate the American ELV production lines and to redesign and modify satellites to be launched on ELVs instead of the shuttle. The shift back to ELVs required additional government funding to fix the problems that had resulted from years of planning to retire these systems. The United States practically ceased commercial launch activities for several years, conducting just three commercial satellite launches (one just prior to the *Challenger* flight) for only 6 percent of U.S. space launches from 1986 to 1989.[50]

During this period, however, two actions were initiated that enabled the emergence of a legitimate U.S. launch industry. First, DOD committed to purchasing a large number of ELVs as part of a strategy to maintain access to space using a mixed fleet of both the space shuttle and ELVs. This reopened the dormant U.S. ELV production lines at government expense and helped provide economies of scale necessary to enable U.S. companies to effectively compete against Ariane. Second, in 1988, Congress amended the Commercial Space Launch Act (CSLA) to establish new insurance requirements whose effect was to limit liability for U.S. companies in case their launches caused damage to government property or third parties. The revised CSLA also established protections against government preemption of commercial launches on government ranges.[51]

As a result, the first U.S. commercial space launch took place in 1989—nearly 5 years after the CSLA was passed. Beginning in 1989, U.S. launches of commercial satellites were conducted by commercial launch companies (in most cases, the same companies providing launch services for DOD and NASA payloads as government contractors), not the U.S. Government.[52]

There is much more to this story of space access and the nature of dual-use technology, but I will conclude with these observations. The commonality of this technology has meant one of two things for both military and civil space efforts: either a competition for knowledge and capability among a limited pool of suppliers, or a cooperation to achieve a fleet of dual-use machines that satisfy all users. In many cases this has never happened, and the differences between NASA and DOD have been persistent and at times quite combative.

Only when there has been clear delineation of responsibilities has this absence of collaboration not been the case. For example, on April 16, 1991, the National Space Council directed NASA and DOD to jointly fund and develop the National Launch System to meet civil and military space access by the beginning of the 21st century at a cost of between $10.5 billion and $12 billion.[53] This effort failed. Most of the other efforts to cooperate have not been much more successful. It seems that the best results have come when either the civil or the military side of the space program develops its own technologies, at least in space launch, and the other adapts it for its own use. That was the case with NASA employing launchers originally designed as ballistic missiles in the 1960s and DOD using the space shuttle built by NASA in the 1980s. The landscape is littered with failed cooperative projects in space access.[54]

Prestige and Soft Power on the International Stage

From the early days of thought about the potential of flight in space, theorists believed that the activity would garner worldwide prestige for those accomplishing it. For example, in 1946, the newly established RAND Corporation published the study "Preliminary Design of an Experimental World-Circling Spaceship." This publication explored the viability of orbital satellites and outlined the technologies necessary for its success. Among its many observations, its comment on the prestige factor proved especially prescient: "A satellite vehicle with appropriate instrumentation can be expected to be one of the most potent scientific tools of the Twentieth Century. The achievement of a satellite craft would produce repercussions comparable to the explosion of the atomic bomb."[55]

This perspective is a classic application of what analysts often refer to as *soft power*. The term, coined by Harvard University professor Joseph Nye, gave a name to an alternative to threats and other forms of hard power in international relations.[56] As Nye contends:

> Soft power is the ability to get what you want by attracting and persuading others to adopt your goals. It differs from hard power, the ability to use the carrots and sticks of economic and military might to make others follow your will. Both hard and soft power are important . . . but attraction is much cheaper than coercion, and an asset that needs to be nourished.[57]

In essence, such activities as Apollo represented a form of soft power, the ability to influence other nations through intangibles such as an impressive show of technological capability. It granted to the nation achieving it first an authenticity and gravitas not previously enjoyed among the world community. In sum, this was an argument buttressing the role of spaceflight as a means of enhancing a nation's standing on the international stage.

Even so, few appreciated the potential of spaceflight to enhance national prestige until the Sputnik crisis of 1957–1958. Some have characterized this as an event that had a "Pearl Harbor" effect on American public opinion, creating an illusion of a technological gap and providing the impetus for increased spending for aerospace endeavors, technical and scientific educational programs, and the chartering of new Federal agencies to manage air and space research and development. This Cold War rivalry with the Soviet Union provided the key that opened the door to aggressive space exploration, not as an end in itself, but as a means to achieving technological superiority in the eyes of the world. From the perspective of the 21st century, it is difficult to appreciate the importance of the prestige factor in national thinking at the time. Although the initial response was congratulatory, American political and opinion leaders soon expressed a belief in the loss of national prestige. As the *Chicago Daily News* editorialized on October 7, 1957, "It must be obvious to everyone by now that the situation relative to Russian technology and our own has changed drastically. There can be no more underestimating Russia's scientific potential, either for war or for peace."[58]

Political leaders also used the satellite as an object lesson in prestige. Senate majority leader Lyndon B. Johnson recalled of the Soviet launch, "Now, somehow, in some new way, the sky seemed almost alien. I also remember the profound shock of realizing that it might be possible for another nation to achieve technological superiority over this great country of ours."[59]

One of Johnson's aides, George E. Reedy, wrote to him on October 17, 1957, about how they could use the Sputnik issue to the party's advantage: "The issue is one which, if properly handled, would blast the Republicans out of the water, unify the Democratic Party, and elect you President." He suggested that "it is unpleasant to feel that there is something floating around in the air which the Russians can put up and we can't."[60]

Unquestionably, the Apollo program in particular and all of U.S. human spaceflight efforts in general were mainly about establishing U.S. primacy in technology. Apollo served as a surrogate for war, challenging the Soviet Union head on in a demonstration of technological virtuosity. The desire to win international support for the "American way" became the raison d'etre for the Apollo program, and it served that purpose far better than anyone imagined when first envisioned. Apollo became first and foremost a Cold War initiative and aided in demonstrating the mastery of the United States before the world. This motivation may be seen in a succession of Gallup polls conducted during the 1960s that asked, "Is the Soviet Union ahead of the United States in space?" Until the middle part of the decade—about the time that the Gemini program began to demonstrate American prowess in space—the answer was always *yes*. At the height of the Apollo Moon landings, world opinion had shifted overwhelmingly in favor of the United States.[61] The importance of Apollo as an instrument of U.S. foreign policy—which is closely allied to but not necessarily identical with national prestige and geopolitics—should not be mislaid in this discussion. It served, and continues to serve, as an instrument for projecting the image of a positive, open, dynamic American society abroad.

For decades, the United States launched humans into space for prestige, measured against similar Soviet accomplishments, rather than for practical scientific or research goals. This was in essence positive symbolism—each new space achievement acquired political capital for the United States, primarily on the international stage. As Caspar Weinberger noted in 1971, space achievements gave "the people of the world an equally needed look at American superiority."[62]

In this context, the civil space program, both its human and robotic components, was fully about national security. Demonstrations of U.S. scientific and technological capability were about the need to establish the credibility and reliability of nuclear deterrence in this new type of standoff with the Soviet Union (see figure 9–4). If the Soviets did not believe that credibility was real, if the rest of the world thought it bogus, the American rivalry with the Soviet Union portended a dire future for humankind. American success in space offered a perception of credibility worldwide about its military might. "This contest was rooted in proving to the world the superiority of capitalism over communism, of the American and communist ways of life, and of cultural, economic, and scientific achievements," according to historian Kenneth Osgood. American civil space successes served to counteract those questioning the nature of the future.[63]

Figure 9–4. Is the Soviet Union Ahead of the United States in Space?

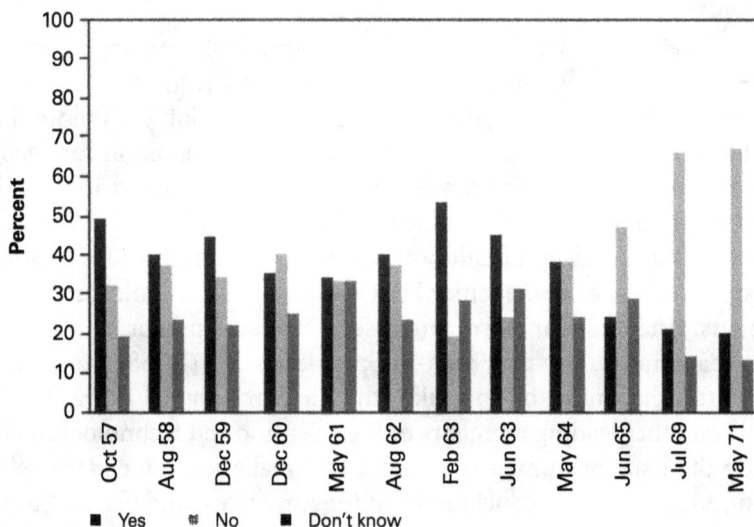

The importance of this prestige issue for civil space also worked at home. It conjured images of the best in the human spirit and served, in the words of journalist Greg Easterbrook, as "a metaphor of national inspiration: majestic, technologically advanced, produced at dear cost and entrusted with precious cargo, rising above the constraints of the earth." It "carries our secret hope that there is something better out there—a world where we may someday go and leave the sorrows of the past behind."[64] It may well be that space achievements, particularly those involving direct human presence, remain a potent source of national pride and that such pride is why the U.S. public continues to support human spaceflight. Certainly, space images— an astronaut on the Moon or the space shuttle rising majestically into orbit—rank just below the American flag and the bald eagle as patriotic symbols. The self-image of the United States as a successful nation is threatened when we fail in our space efforts, as we have seen from the collective loss when astronauts die before our eyes in space shuttle accidents. Americans expect a successful program of civil spaceflight as part of what the United States does as a nation. Americans are not overly concerned with the content or objectives of specific programs. But they are concerned that what is done seems worth doing and is done well. It is that sense of pride in space accomplishment that has been missing in recent years.[65]

The Military and the Quest for a Human Mission in Space

Even before the beginning of the space age, DOD had angled for the mission of placing humans in space for myriad tasks. In the early 1950s, Wernher von Braun had proposed a massive space station with more than 50 military personnel aboard to undertake Earth observation for reconnaissance and as an orbiting battle station. He even believed it could be used to launch nuclear missile strikes against the Soviet Union.[66] While von Braun could not get any Eisenhower administration authorities to adopt his space station plan, some senior DOD officials did see a role for military astronauts. The U.S. Air Force proposed the development of a piloted orbital spacecraft under the "Man-in-Space-Soonest" (MISS) program in 1957.[67] After the launch of Sputnik I, the Air Force invited Edward Teller and several other leading members of the scientific and technological elite to study the issue of human spaceflight and make recommendations for the future. Teller's group concluded that the Air Force could place a human in orbit within 2 years and urged that the department pursue this effort. Teller understood, however, that there was essentially no military reason for undertaking this mission and chose not to tie his recommendation to any specific rationale, falling back on a basic belief that the first nation to accomplish human spaceflight would accrue national prestige and advance, in a general manner, science and technology.[68]

Soon after the new year, Lieutenant General Donald L. Putt, the Air Force Deputy Chief of Staff for Development, informed National Advisory Committee for Aeronautics (NACA) Director Hugh L. Dryden of the Service's intention to pursue aggressively "a research vehicle program having as its objective the earliest possible manned orbital flight which will contribute substantially and essentially to follow-on scientific and military space systems." Putt asked Dryden to collaborate in this effort, but with the NACA as a decidedly junior partner.[69] Dryden agreed; however, by the end of the summer, Putt would find the newly created NASA leading the human spaceflight effort for the United States, with the Air Force being the junior player.[70]

Notwithstanding the lack of clear-cut military purpose, the Air Force pressed for MISS throughout the first part of 1958, clearly expecting to become the lead agency in any space program of the United States. Specifically, it believed hypersonic space planes and lunar bases would serve national security needs well in the coming decades. To help make that a reality, it requested $133 million for the MISS program and secured approval for the effort from the Joint Chiefs of Staff.[71] Throughout this period, a series of disagreements between Air Force and NACA officials rankled both sides. The difficulties reverberated all the way to the White House, prompting a review of the roles of the two organizations.[72] The normally staid and proper Hugh Dryden complained in July 1958 to the President's science advisor, James R. Killian, of the lack of clarity on the role of the Air Force versus the NACA. He asserted that:

> The current objective for a manned satellite program is the determination of man's basic capability in a space environment as a prelude to the human exploration of space and to possible military applications of manned satellites. Although it is clear that both the National Aeronautics and Space Administration and the Department of Defense should cooperate in the conduct of the program, I feel that the responsibility for and the direction of the program should rest with NASA.

He urged that the President state a clear division between the two organizations on the human spaceflight mission.[73]

As historians David N. Spires and Rick W. Sturdevant have pointed out, the MISS program became derailed within the Department of Defense at essentially the same time because of funding concerns and a lack of clear military mission:

> Throughout the spring and summer of 1958 the Air Force's Air Research and Development Command had mounted an aggressive campaign to have ARPA convince administration officials to approve its Man-in-Space-Soonest development plan. But ARPA balked at the high cost, technical challenges, and uncertainties surrounding the future direction of the civilian space agency.[74]

Dwight D. Eisenhower signed the National Aeronautics and Space Act of 1958 into law at the end of July and the next month assigned the Air Force's human spaceflight mission to NASA. Thereafter, the MISS program was folded into what became Project Mercury. By early November 1958, DOD had acceded to the President's desire that the human spaceflight program be a civilian effort under the management of NASA. For its part, NASA invited Air Force officials to appoint liaison personnel to the Mercury program office at Langley Research Center, and they did so.[75]

Everyone recognized that time was of the essence in undertaking the human spaceflight project that NASA would now lead. Roy Johnson, director of ARPA for DOD, noted in September 1958 that competition with the Soviet Union precluded taking a cautious approach to the human spaceflight initiative and advocated additional funding to ensure its timely completion. As he wrote to the Secretary of Defense and the NASA administrator:

> I am troubled, however, with respect to one of the projects in which there is general agreement that it should be a joint undertaking. This is the so-called "Man-in-Space" project for which $10 million has been allocated to ARPA and $30 million to NASA. My concern over this project is due (1) to a firm conviction, backed by intelligence briefings, that the Soviets' next spectacular effort in space will be to orbit a human, and (2) that the amount of $40 million for FY 1959 is woefully inadequate to compete with the Russian program. As you know our best estimates (based on some 12–15 plans) were $100 to $150 million for an optimum FY 1959 program.
>
> I am convinced that the military and psychological impact on the United States and its Allies of a successful Soviet man-in-space "first" program would be far reaching and of great consequence.
>
> Because of this deep conviction, I feel that no time should be lost in launching an aggressive Man-in-Space program and that we should be prepared if the situation warrants, to request supplemental appropriations of the Congress in January to pursue the program with the utmost urgency.[76]

Johnson agreed to transfer a series of space projects from ARPA to NASA but urged more timely progress on development of the space vehicle itself. Two weeks later, ARPA and NASA established protocols for cooperating in the aggressive development of the capsule that would be used in the human spaceflight program.[77]

To aid in the conduct of this program, ARPA and NASA created a panel for Manned Space Flight, also referred to as the Joint Manned Satellite Panel, on September 18, 1958. At its first meeting on September 24, the panel established goals and strategy for the program. Chaired by Robert Gilruth and including such NASA leaders as Max Faget and George Low, the panel focused on a wide range of technical requirements necessary to complete the effort. Under this panel's auspices, final specifications for the piloted capsule emerged in October 1958, as did procurement of both modified Redstone (for suborbital flights) and Atlas (for orbital missions) boosters.[78]

Even while cooperating with NASA on Project Mercury, DOD remained committed to the eventual achievement of human spaceflight. It pursued several programs aimed in that direction. The first was the X–20 Dynasoar, a military spaceplane to be launched atop a Titan launcher—a narrow mission, to be sure. The Air Force believed that the X–20 would provide a long-range bombardment and reconnaissance capability by flying at the edge of space and skipping off the Earth's atmosphere to reach targets anywhere in the world. The Air Force design for the Dynasoar project, which began on December 11, 1961, required the Titan IIIC to launch its military orbital spaceplane.[79] This winged, recoverable spacecraft did not possess as large a payload as NASA's capsule-type spacecraft and was always troubled by the absence of a clearly defined military mission. Accordingly, in September 1961, Defense Secretary Robert S. McNamara questioned whether Dynasoar represented the best expenditure of funds. This resulted in numerous studies of the program, but in 1963, McNamara canceled the program in favor of a Manned Orbiting Laboratory (MOL). This military space station, along with a modified capsule known as Gemini-B, would be launched into orbit aboard a Titan IIIM vehicle that used seven-segment solids and was human-rated. As an example of the seriousness with which the Air Force pursued the MOL program, the third Titan IIIC test flight boosted a prototype Gemini-B (previously used as GT–2 in the Gemini test program) and an aerodynamic mockup of the MOL laboratory into orbit. It was as close as MOL would come to reality. The new military space station plan ran into numerous technical and fiscal problems, and in June 1969, Secretary of Defense Melvin R. Laird informed Congress that MOL would be canceled.[80]

Military space policy analyst Paul Stares summarized the fallout from the loss of the X–20 and MOL programs upon the Air Force during the 1960s:

> With the cancellation of the Dynasoar and MOL, many believed in the Air Force that they had made their "pitch" and failed. This in turn reduced the incentives to try again and reinforced the bias towards the traditional mission of the Air Force, namely flying. As a result, the Air Force's space activities remained a poor relation to tactical and strategic airpower in its organizational hierarchy and inevitably in its funding priorities. This

undoubtedly influenced the Air Force's negative attitude towards the various ASAT modernization proposals put forward by Air Defense Command and others in the early 1970s. The provision of satellite survivability measures also suffered because the Air Force was reluctant to propose initiatives that would require the use of its own budget to defend the space assets of other services and agencies.[81]

This setback did not dissuade DOD from further attempts to enter the realm of human spaceflight, although the next effort involved persuading NASA to alter its space shuttle concept and to include a military mission in its planning scenarios.

After Apollo, the human element of the U.S. civil space program went into a holding pattern for nearly a decade. During that time, it moved from its earlier heroic age to one characterized by more routine activities, perspectives, and processes; it was an institutionalizing of critical elements from a remarkably fertile heroic time.[82]

The space shuttle became the sine qua non of NASA during the 1970s, intended as it was to make spaceflight routine, safe, and relatively inexpensive. Although NASA considered a variety of configurations, some of them quite exotic, it settled on a stage-and-a-half partially reusable vehicle with an approved development price tag of $5.15 billion. On January 5, 1972, President Richard Nixon announced the decision to build a space shuttle. He did so for both political reasons and national prestige purposes. Politically, it would help a lagging aerospace industry in key states he wanted to carry in the next election, especially California, Texas, and Florida.[83] Supporters—especially Caspar Weinberger, who later became Reagan's defense secretary—argued that building the shuttle would reaffirm America's superpower status and help restore confidence, at home and abroad, in America's technological genius and will to succeed. This was purely an issue of national prestige.[84]

The prestige factor belies a critical component. U.S. leaders supported the shuttle not on its merits but on the image it projected. In so doing, the space shuttle that emerged in the early 1970s was essentially a creature of compromise that consisted of three primary elements: a delta-winged orbiter spacecraft with a large crew compartment, a cargo bay 15 by 60 feet in size, and three main engines; two solid rocket boosters; and an external fuel tank housing the liquid hydrogen and oxidizer burned in the main engines. The orbiter and the two solid rocket boosters were reusable. The shuttle was designed to transport approximately 45,000 tons of cargo into low Earth orbit, 115 to 250 statute miles above the Earth. It could also accommodate a flight crew of up to 10 persons (although a crew of 7 would be more common) for a basic space mission of 7 days. During a return to Earth, the orbiter was designed so that it had a cross-range maneuvering capability of 1,265 statute miles to meet requirements for liftoff and landing at the same location after only one orbit.[85]

Many of those design modifications came directly from the Department of Defense; in return for DOD monetary and political support for the project, which might have not been approved otherwise, military astronauts would fly on classified missions in Earth orbit. Most of those missions were for the purpose of deploying reconnaissance satellites.

The national security implications of the space shuttle decision must not be underestimated. Caspar Weinberger was key to the movement of the decision through the White House, and he believed the shuttle had obvious military uses and profound implications for national security. "I thought we could get substantial return" with the program, he said in a 1977 interview, "both from the point of view of national defense, and from the point of view [of] scientific advancement which would have a direct beneficial effect."[86] He and others also impressed on the President the shuttle's potential for military missions. John Ehrlichman, Nixon's senior advisor for domestic affairs, even thought it might be useful to capture enemy satellites.[87] The Soviets, who built the *Buran* in the 1980s and flew it without a crew only one time, pursued a shuttle project as a counterbalance to the U.S. program solely because they were convinced that the U.S. shuttle was developed for military purposes. As Russian space watcher James Oberg suggested: "They had actually studied the shuttle plans and figured it was designed for an out-of-plane bombing run over high-value Soviet targets. Brezhnev believed that and in 1976 ordered $10 billion of expenditures. They had the *Buran* flying within ten years and discovered they couldn't do anything with it."[88]

After a decade of development, on April 12, 1981, *Columbia* took off for the first orbital test mission. It was successful, and President Reagan declared the system "operational" in 1982 after only its fourth flight. It would henceforth carry all U.S. Government payloads; military, scientific, and even commercial satellites could all be deployed from its payload bay.[89] To prepare for this, in 1979, Air Force Secretary Hans Mark created the Manned Spaceflight Engineer program to "develop expertise in manned spaceflight and apply it to Department of Defense space missions." Between 1979 and 1986, this organization trained 32 Navy and Air Force officers as military astronauts.[90]

Even so, the shuttle soon proved disappointing. By January 1986, there had been only 24 shuttle flights, although in the 1970s NASA had projected more flights than that each year. Critical analyses agreed that the shuttle had proven to be neither cheap nor reliable, both primary selling points, and that NASA should never have used those arguments in building a political consensus for the program.[91] All of these criticisms reached crescendo proportions following the loss of the *Challenger* during launch on January 28, 1986.[92] A result of this was the removal from the shuttle of all commercial and national security payloads and the reinvigoration of the expendable launch vehicle production lines. It became another instance of DOD seeking a military human mission that eventually went awry.

This quest for military astronauts did not end there. In the 1980s, DOD along with NASA began work on a single-stage-to-orbit (SSTO) vehicle for military purposes. If there is a holy grail of spaceflight, it is the desire for reusable SSTO technology—essentially a vehicle that can take off, fly into orbit, perform its mission, and return to Earth, landing like an airplane. This is an exceptionally difficult flight regime with a multitude of challenges relating to propulsion, materials, aerodynamics, and guidance and control. Fueled by the realization that the space shuttle could not deliver on its early expectations, DOD leaders pressed for the development of a hypersonic spaceplane. During the Reagan administration and its associated military buildup, Tony DuPont, head of DuPont Aerospace, offered an unsolicited proposal to the Defense Advanced Research Projects Agency (DARPA) to design a hypersonic vehicle powered by a hybrid integrated engine of scramjets and rockets. DARPA program manager Bob Williams liked the idea and funded it as a black program code-named COPPER CANYON between 1983 and 1985. The Reagan administration later unveiled it as the National Aero-Space Plane (NASP), designated the X–30. Reagan called it "a new Orient Express that could, by the end of the next decade, take off from Dulles Airport and accelerate up to twenty-five times the speed of sound, attaining low Earth orbit or flying to Tokyo within two hours."[93]

The NASP program initially proposed to build two research craft, at least one of which should achieve orbit by flying in a single stage through the atmosphere at speeds up to Mach 25. The X–30 would use a multicycle engine that shifted from jet to ramjet and to scramjet speeds as the vehicle ascended burning liquid hydrogen fuel with oxygen scooped and frozen from the atmosphere.[94] After billions of dollars were spent, NASP never progressed to flight stage. It finally died a merciful death, trapped as it was in bureaucratic politics and seemingly endless technological difficulty, in 1994.[95] Thus fell another military astronaut program.

Elements of DOD remain committed to this mission to the present. Throughout the 1990s, a succession of studies argued for the potential of military personnel in space. One 1992 study affirmed:

> It is absolutely essential for the well being of today's space forces as well as the future space forces of 2025, that DOD develop manned advanced technology space systems in lieu of or in addition to unmanned systems to effectively utilize military man's compelling and aggressive warfighting abilities to accomplish the critical wartime mission elements of space control and force application. National space policy, military space doctrine and common sense all dictate they should do so if space superiority during future, inevitable conflict with enemy space forces is the paramount objective. Deploying military man in space will provide that space superiority and he will finally become the "center of gravity" of the U.S. space program.[96]

Another analysis found 37 reasons why military personnel in space would be required in the future, ranging from problem-solving and decisionmaking to manipulation of sensors and other systems. It concluded that "a military space plane could play a key role in helping the United States Air Force transform itself from an air force into an aerospace force."[97] Yet another study found: "Our National Security Strategy must take full advantage of the full political, economic, and military power of this nation to be successful. That means soldiers, sailors and airmen able to operate in every region of the world critical to national security, whether it be on land, at sea, in the air, or in space. A strategy built on anything less is incomplete and shortsighted."[98] Of course, if *Aviation Week and Space Technology* is to be believed, DOD not only wished for a military human mission in space but also developed a spaceplane named Blackstar and began flying missions as early as 1990.[99]

It is obvious the decision made initially by Eisenhower to split the civil and military space programs and to assign the human mission to the civil side has been a bitter pill that remains difficult for DOD to swallow. It represents one instance among many in which a continuum between cooperation and competition has taken place in the interrelationships between the civil and military space programs. It is one of the many policy decisions made in the 1950s that may be overturned in the post–Cold War environment.

Conclusion

The fact that this survey of civil space history in relation to the national security arena has been oriented largely toward human spaceflight does not mean that other areas are insignificant in these interrelations—tracking and recovery, launch complexes and ranges, technology development, and a host of other issues come to mind—but the overwhelming amount of the funding spent on the civil space side has been for human spaceflight. Well over half of the NASA budget since the agency's creation has been expended on the human program, and therefore an emphasis on the part of the civil program appears appropriate. We have seen that there has been a long mating dance between the civil and military space programs over the years, and it appears that in the post–Cold War era, there may be a much closer relationship than was allowed earlier.

In terms of lessons learned, what might spacepower analysts take from this discussion? First, spacepower possesses a major civil space, soft-power component that has been critical in the conduct of foreign policy during the last 50 years. It was a positive development in the winning of the Cold War, and the soft power element of spaceflight must be considered in the context of any policy issue. Second, there is so much overlap between the technology of civil and military spaceflight that it is critical that these two realms be kept as separate as possible. Finally, human spaceflight has long been a province of the civil space program in the United States, but the military has always wanted to become a part of it. There may well come a time when this becomes a reality, but probably not until humans have made their homes in space.

As scientists and entrepreneurs spread into space, military personnel are likely to accompany them. Although the space frontier differs considerably from the American West, one aspect of the military role on the American frontier is worth remembering. For most of the time during the era of expansion, military personnel on the American frontier performed many tasks. They restrained lawless traders, pursued fugitives, ejected squatters, maintained order during peace negotiations, and guarded Indians who came to receive annuities. This was largely peaceful work, with the military catalyzing the processes of economic and social development.

If humans develop a base on the Moon or even an outpost on Mars, the military may perform these duties once more. Remembering the role of the U.S. Corps of Topographical Engineers and the U.S. Army Corps of

Engineers in opening the American West, military leaders may propose the creation of a U.S. Corps of Space Engineers. The role they could play would be analogous to military activities in Antarctica. The U.S. Navy oversees the American station at McMurdo Sound and, every winter, the U.S. Air Force conducts a resupply airdrop at the South Pole station. Similar arrangements could take place on the Moon. Military personnel could construct and maintain an isolated lunar outpost or a scientific station on the back side of the Moon. By providing support, military personnel would establish a presence in space and help secure national interests. This is a strikingly different perspective than what has been pursued militarily in space to date.

Notes

[1] Solid overviews of the history of space exploration include William E. Burrows, *This New Ocean: The Story of the First Space Age* (New York: Random House, 1998); Howard E. McCurdy, *Space and the American Imagination* (Washington, DC: Smithsonian Institution Press, 1997); and Roger D. Launius, *Frontiers of Space Exploration* (Westport, CT: Greenwood Press, 1998).

[2] Dwayne A. Day, "Invitation to Struggle: The History of Civilian-Military Relations in Space," in *Exploring the Unknown: Selected Documents in the History of the U.S. Civil Space Program*, vol. II, *External Relationships*, ed. John M. Logsdon, Dwayne A. Day, and Roger D. Launius (Washington, DC: NASA SP–4407, 1996), 233.

[3] No better example of dual-use technology may be found than launch vehicles; almost all of those in the American inventory began as ballistic missiles developed to deliver nuclear weapons. On the history of this subject, see Roger D. Launius and Dennis R. Jenkins, eds., *To Reach the High Frontier: A History of U.S. Launch Vehicles* (Lexington: University Press of Kentucky, 2002).

[4] R. Cargill Hall, "Origins of U.S. Space Policy: Eisenhower, Open Skies, and Freedom of Space," in *Exploring the Unknown: Selected Documents in the History of the U.S. Civil Space Program*, vol. I, *Organizing for Exploration*, ed. John M. Logsdon and Linda J. Lear (Washington, DC: NASA, 1995), 222.

[5] Vernon Van Dyke, *Pride and Power: The Rationale of the Space Program* (Urbana: University of Illinois Press, 1964).

[6] John P. Lovell, review of *Pride and Power: The Rationale of the Space Program*, in *Midwest Journal of Political Science* 9 (February 1965), 119.

[7] This is the fundamental thesis of Van Dyke, *Pride and Power*; Derek Wesley Elliott, "Finding an Appropriate Commitment: Space Policy Development under Eisenhower and Kennedy, 1954–1963," Ph.D. dissertation, George Washington University, 1992. It is also borne out in several essays contained in Roger D. Launius and Howard E. McCurdy, eds., *Spaceflight and the Myth of Presidential Leadership* (Urbana: University of Illinois Press, 1997), especially chapters 2, 3, 6, and 7.

[8] The best discussion of the evolution of space policy and the sorting of roles and missions for the various government entities remains John M. Logsdon, "The Evolution of U.S. Space Policy and Plans," in Logsdon and Lear, 377–393. See also Roger D. Launius, ed., *Organizing for the Use of Space: Historical Perspectives on a Persistent Issue*, vol. 18, AAS History Series (San Diego: Univelt, Inc., 1995); James R. Killian, Jr., *Sputnik, Scientists, and Eisenhower: A Memoir of the First Special Assistant to the President for Science and Technology* (Cambridge: MIT Press, 1977); George B. Kistiakowsky, *A Scientist in the White House* (Cambridge: Harvard University Press, 1976); T. Keith Glennan, *The Birth of NASA: The Diary of T. Keith Glennan*, ed. J.D. Hunley (Washington, DC: NASA SP–4105, 1993); and Robert L. Rosholt, *An Administrative History of NASA, 1958–1963* (Washington, DC: NASA SP–4101, 1966).

[9] On the grandiose visions of military personnel in space, see Wernher von Braun, "Crossing the Last Frontier," *Collier's*, March 22, 1952, 24–28, 72–73; Michael J. Neufeld, "'Space Superiority': Wernher von Braun's Campaign for a Nuclear-Armed Space Station, 1946–1956," *Space Policy* 22 (February 2006), 52–62; Curtis Peebles, *High Frontier: The U.S. Air Force and the Military Space Program* (Washington, DC: USAF History and Museums Program, 1997), 15–31; and Timothy D. Killebrew, "Military Man in Space: A History of Air Force Efforts to Find a Manned Space Mission," master's thesis, Air Command and Staff College, February 1987.

[10] On Sputnik, see these important works: Rip Bulkeley, *The Sputnik Crisis and Early United States Space Policy: A Critique of the Historiography of Space* (Bloomington: Indiana University Press, 1991); Robert A. Divine, *The Sputnik Challenge: Eisenhower's Response to the Soviet Satellite* (New York: Oxford University Press, 1993); and Paul Dickson, *Sputnik: The Shock of the Century* (New York: Walker and Company, 2001).

[11] On Apollo, see John M. Logsdon, *The Decision to Go to the Moon: Project Apollo and the National Interest* (Cambridge: MIT Press, 1970); Walter A. McDougall, . . . *The Heavens and the Earth: A Political History of the Space Age* (New York: Basic Books, 1985); Charles A. Murray and Catherine Bly Cox, *Apollo, the Race to the Moon* (New York: Simon and Schuster, 1989); and Andrew Chaikin, *A Man on the Moon: The Voyages of the Apollo Astronauts* (New York: Viking, 1994). Good introductions to the history of planetary exploration may be found in Ronald A. Schorn, *Planetary Astronomy: From Ancient Times to the Third Millennium* (College Station: Texas A&M University Press, 1998).

[12] On the International Space Station, see Roger D. Launius, *Space Stations: Base Camps to the Stars* (Washington, DC: Smithsonian Institution Press, 2003). On the space shuttle, see Dennis R. Jenkins, *Space Shuttle: The History of the National Space Transportation System, the First 100 Missions*, 3[d] ed. (Cape Canaveral, FL: Dennis R. Jenkins, 2001); T.A. Heppenheimer, *The Space Shuttle Decision: NASA's Search for a Reusable Space Vehicle* (Washington, DC: NASA SP–4221, 1999); T.A. Heppenheimer, *Development of the Space Shuttle, 1972–1981*, vol. 2, *History of the Space Shuttle* (Washington, DC: Smithsonian Institution Press, 2002); and David M. Harland, *The Story of the Space Shuttle* (Chichester, UK: Springer-Praxis, 2004).

[13] This is an expression of Frederick Jackson Turner's "Frontier Thesis" that guided inquiry into much of American history for a generation. It also continues to inform many popular images of the American West. Turner outlined the major features of the subject in *The Frontier in American History* (New York: Holt, Rinehart, and Winston, 1920), which included the seminal 1893 essay, "The Significance of the Frontier in American History."

[14] This frontier imagery was overtly mythic. Myths, however, are important to the maintenance of any society, for they are stories that symbolize an overarching ideology and moral consciousness. As James Oliver Robertson observes in his book *American Myth, American Reality* (New York: Hill and Wang, 1980), xv, "Myths are the patterns of behavior, or belief, and/or perception—which people have in common. Myths are not deliberately, or necessarily consciously, fictitious." Myth, therefore, is not so much a fable or falsehood, as it is a story, a kind of poetry, about events and situations that have great significance for the people involved. Myths are, in fact, essential truths for the members of a cultural group who hold them, enact them, or perceive them. They are sometimes expressed in narratives, but in literate societies like the United States, they are also apt to be embedded in ideologies. Robertson's book is one of many studies that focus on American myths—such as the myth of the chosen people, the myth of a God-given destiny, and the myth of a New World innocence or inherent virtue.

[15] This is the thesis of William Sims Bainbridge, *The Spaceflight Revolution: A Sociological Study* (New York: John Wiley and Sons, 1976). See also Willy Ley and Chesley Bonestell, *The Conquest of Space* (New York: Viking, 1949).

[16] George H. Gallup, *The Gallup Poll: Public Opinion, 1935–1971* (New York: Random House, 1972), 1:875, 1152.

[17] As an example of his exceptionally sophisticated spaceflight promoting, see Wernher von Braun, *The Mars Project* (Urbana: University of Illinois Press, 1953), based on a German-language series of articles appearing in the magazine *Weltraumfahrt* in 1952.

[18] "What Are We Waiting For?" *Collier's*, March 22, 1952, 23; Wernher von Braun with Cornelius Ryan, "Can We Get to Mars?" *Collier's*, April 30, 1954, 22–28; Randy L. Liebermann, "The *Collier's* and Disney Series," in Frederick I. Ordway III and Randy L. Liebermann, *Blueprint for Space* (Washington, DC: Smithsonian Institution Press, 1992), 141; and Ron Miller, "Days of Future Past," *Omni*, October 1986, 76–81.

[19] The dichotomy of visions has been one of the central components of the U.S. space program. Those who advocated a scientifically oriented program using nonpiloted probes and applications satellites for weather, communications, and a host of other useful activities were never able to capture the imagination of the American public the way the human spaceflight advocates did. For a modern critique of this dichotomy, see Alex Roland, "Barnstorming in Space: The Rise and Fall of the Romantic Era of Spaceflight, 1957–1986," in *Space Policy Reconsidered*, ed. Radford Byerly, Jr. (Boulder, CO: Westview Press, 1989), 33–52. That the human imperative is still consequential is demonstrated in William Sims Bainbridge's sociological study, *Goals in Space: American Values and the Future of Technology* (Albany: State University of New York Press, 1991).

[20] "What Are We Waiting For?" 23.

[21] Elaine Tyler May, *Homeward Bound: American Families in the Cold War Era* (New York: Basic Books, 1988), 93–94, 104–113.

[22] See Roger D. Launius, John M. Logsdon, and Robert W. Smith, eds., *Reconsidering Sputnik: Forty Years Since the Soviet Satellite* (Amsterdam, The Netherlands: Harwood Academic Publishers, 2000).

[23] Roger D. Launius, "Eisenhower, Sputnik, and the Creation of NASA: Technological Elites and the Public Policy Agenda," *Prologue: Quarterly of the National Archives and Records Administration* 28 (Summer 1996), 127–143; Roger D. Launius, "Space Program," in *Dictionary of American History: Supplement*, ed. Robert H. Ferrell and Joan Hoff (New York: Charles Scribner's Sons Reference Books, 1996), 2:221–223.

[24] See James A. Van Allen, *Origins of Magnetospheric Physics* (Washington, DC: Smithsonian Institution Press, 1983); and Matthew J. Von Benke, *The Politics of Space: A History of U.S.-Soviet/Russian Competition and Cooperation in Space* (Boulder, CO: Westview Press, 1997).

[25] "National Aeronautics and Space Act of 1958," Public Law 85–568, 72 Stat., 426, Record Group 255, National Archives and Records Administration, Washington, DC; and Alison Griffith, *The National Aeronautics and Space Act: A Study of the Development of Public Policy* (Washington, DC: PublicAffairs Press, 1962), 27–43.

[26] Roger D. Launius, *NASA: A History of the U.S. Civil Space Program* (Malabar, FL: Krieger Publishing Co., 1994), 29–41.

[27] The standard works on this subject are Asif A. Siddiqi, *Challenge to Apollo: The Soviet Union and the Space Race, 1945–1974* (Washington, DC: NASA SP-2000–4408, 2000); and James J. Harford, *Korolev: How One Man Masterminded the Soviet Drive to Beat America to the Moon* (New York: John Wiley and Sons, 1997).

[28] Dwight D. Eisenhower, "Are We Headed in the Wrong Direction?" *Saturday Evening Post*, August 11, 1962, 24.

[29] Dwight D. Eisenhower, "Why I Am a Republican," *Saturday Evening Post*, April 11, 1964, 19.

[30] In addition to the above books on Apollo, see Edgar M. Cortright, ed., *Apollo Expeditions to the Moon* (Washington, DC: NASA SP-350, 1975); W. Henry Lambright, *Powering Apollo: James E. Webb of NASA* (Baltimore: The Johns Hopkins University Press, 1995); and David West Reynolds, *Apollo: The Epic Journey to the Moon* (New York: Harcourt, 2002).

[31] These observations are based on calculations using the budget data included in the annual *Aeronautics and Space Report of the President, 2003 Activities* (Washington, DC: NASA Report, 2004), appendix E, which contains this information for each year since 1959; "National Aeronautics and Space Administration President's FY 2007 Budget Request," February 6, 2006, part I, NASA Historical Reference Collection, NASA History Division, NASA Headquarters, Washington, DC.

[32] Stephanie A. Roy, Elaine C. Gresham, and Carissa Bryce Christensen, "The Complex Fabric of Public Opinion on Space," IAF–99–P.3.05, presented at the International Astronautical Federation annual meeting, Amsterdam, The Netherlands, October 5, 1999.

[33] *The Gallup Poll: Public Opinion, 1935–1971*, part III: *1959–1971*, 1952, 2183–2184, 2209; *The New York Times*, December 3, 1967; *Newsweek* is quoted in *An Administrative History of NASA*, chap. II, 48, NASA Historical Reference Collection.

[34] This analysis is based on a set of Gallup, Harris, NBC/Associated Press, CBS/*New York Times*, and ABC/*USA Today* polls conducted throughout the 1960s; copies are available in the NASA Historical Reference Collection.

[35] Roger D. Launius, "Kennedy's Space Policy Reconsidered: A Post–Cold War Perspective," *Air Power History* 50 (Winter 2003), 16–29.

[36] "Treaty on the Non-Proliferation of Nuclear Weapons," March 5, 1970, available at <http://disarmament.un.org/TreatyStatus.nsf>; "Missile Technology Control Regime," 1987, available at <www.mtcr.info/english/index.html>; and "Wassenaar Arrangement on Export Controls for Conventional Arms and Dual-Use Goods and Technologies," available at <www.wassenaar.org/>.

[37] A journalistic muckraking account of this story may be found in Bill Gertz, *Betrayal: How the Clinton Administration Undermined American Security* (Washington, DC: Regnery Publishing, Inc., 1999), which includes a useful collection of important government facsimile documents.

[38] Linda Neuman Ezell, *NASA Historical Data Book*, vol. II: *Programs and Projects, 1958–1968* (Washington, DC: NASA SP–4012, 1988), 61–67; and Richard P. Hallion, "The Development of American Launch Vehicles Since 1945," in *Space Science Comes of Age: Perspectives in the History of the Space Sciences*, ed. Paul A. Hanle and Von Del Chamberlain (Washington, DC: Smithsonian Institution Press, 1981), 126–127.

[39] Wernher von Braun, "The Redstone, Jupiter, and Juno," in *The History of Rocket Technology*, ed. Eugene M. Emme (Detroit: Wayne State University Press, 1964), 107–121.

[40] Richard E. Martin, *The Atlas and Centaur "Steel Balloon" Tanks: A Legacy of Karel Bossart* (San Diego: General Dynamics Corp., 1989); Robert L. Perry, "The Atlas, Thor, Titan, and Minuteman," in Emme, 143–155; and John L. Sloop, *Liquid Hydrogen as a Propulsion Fuel, 1945–1959* (Washington, DC: NASA SP–4404, 1978), 173–177. See also Edmund Beard, *Developing the ICBM: A Study in Bureaucratic Politics* (New York: Columbia University Press, 1976); and Jacob Neufeld, *Ballistic Missiles in the United States Air Force, 1945–1960* (Washington, DC: Office of Air Force History, 1990).

[41] For able histories of the Atlas, see Dennis R. Jenkins, "Stage-and-a-Half: The Atlas Launch Vehicle," in Launius and Jenkins, eds., *To Reach the High Frontier*, 70–102; John Lonnquest, "The Face of Atlas: General Bernard Schriever and the Development of the Atlas Intercontinental Ballistic Missile, 1953–1960," Ph.D. dissertation, Duke University, 1996; and Davis Dyer, "Necessity is the Mother of Invention: Developing the ICBM, 1954–1958," *Business and Economic History* 22 (1993), 194–209. Although dated, a useful early essay is Robert L. Perry, "The Atlas, Thor, Titan, and Minuteman," in Emme, ed., *History of Rocket Technology*, 143–155.

[42] "Report of the Ad Hoc Mercury Panel," April 12, 1961, NASA Historical Reference Collection.

[43] James M. Grimwood and Ivan D. Ertal, "Project Gemini," *Southwestern Historical Quarterly* 81 (January 1968), 393–418; James M. Grimwood, Barton C. Hacker, and Peter J. Vorzimmer, *Project Gemini Technology and Operations* (Washington, DC: NASA SP–4002, 1969); and Robert N. Lindley, "Discussing Gemini: A 'Flight' Interview with Robert Lindley of McDonnell," *Flight International*, March 24, 1966, 488–489.

[44] Despite the very real need to move beyond the ICBM technologies of the 1950s and 1960s, credit must be given to the utilization of these to develop a nascent space launch capability when only the Soviet Union had one elsewhere in the world. For instance, Europe, without an experience building early ballistic missiles, lost 20 years in the spacefaring age. Only when it successfully began launching the Ariane boosters in 1979 did it enter the space age in any serious way.

[45] Richard P. Hallion and James O. Young, "Space Shuttle: Fulfillment of a Dream," Case VIII of *The Hypersonic Revolution: Case Studies in the History of Hypersonic Technology*, vol. 1, *From Max Valier to Project PRIME (1924–1967)* (Washington, DC: U.S. Air Force History and Museums Program, 1998),

957–962; Spiro T. Agnew, *The Post-Apollo Space Program: Directions for the Future* (Washington, DC: Space Task Group, September 1969), reprinted in Logsdon, *Exploring the Unknown*, vol. I, *Organizing for Exploration*, 270–274.

[46] This was a powerful argument when made to the Europeans in 1971 and 1972—thereby assuring space access on an American launcher—and prompted them to sign up to a significant involvement in shuttle development. Only when the United States reneged on its offers of partnership did the European nations create the European Space Agency and embark on a launch vehicle of their own design, Ariane. See Roger D. Launius, "NASA, the Space Shuttle, and the Quest for Primacy in Space in an Era of Increasing International Competition," in *L'Ambition Technologique: Naissance d'Ariane*, ed. Emmanuel Chadeau (Paris: Institut d'Histoire de l'Industrie, 1995), 35–61.

[47] Hans Mark, *The Space Station: A Personal Journey* (Durham, NC: Duke University Press, 1987), 61–65; Heppenheimer, *Space Shuttle Decision*, 275–280; and David M. Harland, *The Space Shuttle: Roles, Missions and Accomplishments* (Chichester, England: Praxis Publishing, Ltd., 1998), 411–412.

[48] Few individuals have yet discussed the competing priorities that the shuttle was asked to fulfill. It seems truer as time passes, however, that the "one-size-fits-all" approach to technological challenges that the shuttle was asked to solve was unfair to the launch vehicle, the people who made it fly, and the organization that built and launched it. This would not be the first time in American history when such an approach had been used. The Air Force had been forced in the 1960s to accept a combination fighter and bomber, the FB–111, against its recommendations. That airplane proved a disaster from start to finish. The individuals operating the space shuttle soldiered on as best they could to fulfill all expectations but the task was essentially impossible. See Michael F. Brown, *Flying Blind: The Politics of the U.S. Strategic Bomber Program* (Ithaca: Cornell University Press, 1992); and David S. Sorenson, *The Politics of Strategic Aircraft Modernization* (Westport, CT: Praeger, 1995).

[49] "NSDD–254," in *Exploring the Unknown: Selected Documents in the History of the U.S. Civil Space Program*, vol. IV, *Accessing Space*, ed. John M. Logsdon (Washington, DC: NASA SP–4407, 1999), 382–485.

[50] John M. Logsdon and Craig Reed, "Commercializing Space Transportation," in *Exploring the Unknown*, vol. IV, 405–422.

[51] "Commercial Space Launch Act Amendments of 1988," in *Exploring the Unknown*, vol. IV, 458–465.

[52] Isakowitz, Hopkins, and Hopkins, *International Reference Guide to Space Launch Systems*, 3[d] ed., passim.

[53] Office of the President, National Security Presidential Directive 4, "National Space Launch Strategy," July 10, 1991, available at <http://fas.org/spp/military/docops/national/nspd4.htm>; William B. Scott, "ALS Cost, Efficiency to Depend Heavily on Process Improvements," *Aviation Week and Space Technology*, October 23, 1989, 41.

[54] This problem is discussed in some detail in Roger D. Launius, "After Columbia: The Space Shuttle Program and the Crisis in Space Access," *Astropolitics* 2 (July–September 2004), 277–322; and John M. Logsdon, "'A Failure of National Leadership': Why No Replacement for the Space Shuttle?" in *Critical Issues in the History of Spaceflight*, ed. Steven J. Dick and Roger D. Launius (Washington, DC: NASA SP–2006–4702, 2006), 269–300.

[55] Project RAND, Douglas Aircraft Company's Engineering Division, *Preliminary Design of an Experimental World-Circling Spaceship* (SM–11827), May 2, 1946.

[56] The term was coined in Joseph S. Nye, *Bound to Lead: The Changing Nature of American Power* (New York: Basic Books, 1990). See also Joseph S. Nye, *Soft Power: The Means to Success in World Politics* (New York: PublicAffairs, 2004).

[57] Joseph S. Nye, "Propaganda Isn't the Way: Soft Power," *The International Herald Tribune*, January 10, 2003.

[58] "Russian 'Moon' Casts Big Shadow," *Chicago Daily News*, October 7, 1957. See also "Russia in Front," *Chicago Tribune*, October 6, 1957; and "The Good Side of a 'Bad' Moon," *Chicago Daily News*, October 8, 1957.

[59] Lyndon B. Johnson, *The Vantage Point: Perspectives of the Presidency, 1963–1969* (New York: Holt, Rinehart, and Winston, 1971), 272.

[60] George E. Reedy to Lyndon B. Johnson, October 17, 1957, Lyndon B. Johnson Presidential Library, Austin, TX.

[61] Gallup polls, October 1, 1957, August 1, 1958, December 1, 1959, December 1, 1960, May 1, 1961, August 1, 1962, February 1, 1963, June 1, 1963, May 1, 1964, June 1, 1965, July 1, 1969, and May 1, 1971.

[62] Caspar W. Weinberger to President Richard M. Nixon, via George Shultz, "Future of NASA," August 12, 1971, White House, Richard M. Nixon, President, 1968–1971 File, NASA Historical Reference Collection.

[63] Kenneth Osgood, *Total Cold War: Eisenhower's Secret Propaganda Battle at Home and Abroad* (Lawrence: University Press of Kansas, 2006), 353.

[64] Greg Easterbrook, "The Space Shuttle Must Be Stopped," *Time*, February 2, 2003, available at <www.mercola.com/2003/feb/8/space_shuttle.htm>.

[65] I made this argument in relation to the space shuttle in two articles: "After Columbia: The Space Shuttle Program and the Crisis in Space Access," *Astropolitics* 2 (July–September 2004), 277–322; and "Assessing the Legacy of the Space Shuttle," *Space Policy* 22 (November 2006), 226–234.

[66] Von Braun, "Crossing the Last Frontier," 24–29, 72–74; and Launius, *Space Stations*, 26–35.

[67] The Man-in-Space-Soonest program called for a four-phase capsule orbital process, which would first use instruments, to be followed by primates, then a pilot, with the final objective of landing humans on the Moon. See David N. Spires, *Beyond Horizons: A Half Century of Air Force Space Leadership* (Peterson Air Force Base, CO: Air Force Space Command, 1997), 75; and Loyd S. Swenson, Jr., James M. Grimwood, and Charles C. Alexander, *This New Ocean: A History of Project Mercury* (Washington, DC: NASA SP–5201, 1966), 33–97.

[68] Swenson, Grimwood, and Alexander, 73–74.

[69] Lieutenant General Donald L. Putt, USAF, Deputy Chief of Staff, Development, to Hugh L. Dryden, NACA Director, January 31, 1958, Folder 18674, NASA Historical Reference Collection.

[70] NACA to USAF Deputy Chief of Staff, Development, "Transmittal of Copies of Proposed Memorandum of Understanding between Air Force and NACA for Joint NACA-Air Force Project for a Recoverable Manned Satellite Test Vehicle," April 11, 1958, Folder 18674, NASA Historical Reference Collection.

[71] The breakdown for this budget was aircraft and missiles, $32 million; support, $11.5 million; construction, $2.5 million; and research and development, $87 million. See Memorandum for ARPA Director, "Air Force Man-in-Space Program," March 19, 1958, Folder 18674, NASA Historical Reference Collection.

[72] Maurice H. Stans, Director, Bureau of the Budget, Memorandum for the President, "Responsibility for 'Space' Programs," May 10, 1958; Maxime A. Faget, NACA, Memorandum for Dr. Hugh L. Dryden, June 5, 1958; Clotaire Wood, Headquarters, NACA, Memorandum for files, "Tableing [sic] of Proposed Memorandum of Understanding Between Air Force and NACA For a Joint Project For a Recoverable Manned Satellite Test Vehicle," May 20, 1958, with attached Memorandum, "Principles for the Conduct by the NACA and the Air Force of a Joint Project for a Recoverable Manned Satellite Vehicle," April 29, 1958; and Donald A. Quarles, Secretary of Defense, to Maurice H. Stans, Director, Bureau of the Budget, April 1, 1958, Folder 18674, all in NASA Historical Reference Collection.

[73] Hugh L. Dryden, Director, NACA, Memorandum for James R. Killian, Jr., Special Assistant to the President for Science and Technology, "Manned Satellite Program," July 19, 1958, Folder 18674, NASA Historical Reference Collection.

[74] David N. Spires and Rick W. Sturdevant, "' ... to the very limit of our ability ... ': Reflections on Forty Years of Civil-Military Partnership in Space Launch," in *To Reach the High Frontier: A History of U.S. Launch Vehicles*, ed. Launius and Jenkins, 475.

[75] Memorandum for Dr. Abe Silverstein, "Assignment of Responsibility for ABMA Participation in NASA Manned Satellite Project," November 12, 1958; Abe Silverstein to Lt. Gen. Roscoe C. Wilson, USAF, Deputy Chief of Staff, Development, November 20, 1958; and Hugh L. Dryden, Deputy Admin-

istrator, NASA, Memorandum for Dr. Eugene Emme for NASA Historical Files, "The 'signed' Agreement of April 11, 1958, on a Recoverable Manned Satellite Test Vehicle," September 8, 1965, Folder 18674, all in NASA Historical Reference Collection.

[76] Roy W. Johnson, Director, ARPA, Department of Defense, Memorandum for the Administrator, NASA, "Man-in-Space Program," September 3, 1958, Folder 18674, NASA Historical Reference Collection.

[77] Roy W. Johnson, Director, ARPA, DOD, Memorandum for the Administrator, NASA, "Man-in-Space Program," September 19, 1958, with attached Memorandum of Understanding, "Principles for the Conduct by NASA and ARPA of a Joint Program for a Manned Orbital Vehicle," September 19, 1958, Folder 18674, NASA Historical Reference Collection.

[78] Minutes of Meetings, Panel for Manned Space Flight, September 24, 30, October 1, 1958; NASA, "Preliminary Specifications for Manned Satellite Capsule," October 1958; and Paul E. Purser, Aeronautical Research Engineer, NASA, to Mr. R.R. Gilruth, NASA, "Procurement of Ballistic Missiles for Use as Boosters in NASA Research Leading to Manned Space Flight," October 8, 1958, with attached, "Letter of Intent to AOMC (ABMA), Draft of Technical Content," October 8, 1958, Folder 18674, all in NASA Historical Reference Collection.

[79] As the weight and complexity of Dynasoar grew, it quickly surpassed the capabilities of the Titan II and was switched to the Titan III. Just before the program was canceled, it looked like weight growth had outclassed even the Titan IIIC, and plans were being made to use Saturn IBs or other boosters.

[80] Roy F. Houchin III, "Air Force-Office of the Secretary of Defense Rivalry: The Pressure of Political Affairs in the Dyna-Soar (X–20) Program, 1957–1963," *Journal of the British Interplanetary Society* 50 (May 1997), 162–268; Matt Bacon, "The Dynasoar Extinction," *Space* 9 (May 1993), 18–21; Roy F. Houchin III, "Why the Air Force Proposed the Dyna-Soar X–20 Program," *Quest: The History of Spaceflight Magazine* 3, no. 4 (Winter 1994), 5–11; Terry Smith, "The Dyna-Soar X–20: A Historical Overview," *Quest: The History of Spaceflight Magazine* 3, no. 4 (Winter 1994), 13–18; Roy F. Houchin III, "Interagency Rivalry: NASA, the Air Force, and MOL," *Quest: The History of Spaceflight Magazine* 4, no. 4 (Winter 1995), 40–45; Donald Pealer, "Manned Orbiting Laboratory (MOL), Part 1," *Quest: The History of Spaceflight Magazine* 4, no. 3 (Fall 1995), 4–17; Donald Pealer, "Manned Orbiting Laboratory (MOL), Part 2," *Quest: The History of Spaceflight Magazine* 4, no. 4 (Winter 1995), 28–37; and Donald Pealer, "Manned Orbiting Laboratory (MOL), Part 3," *Quest: The History of Spaceflight Magazine* 5, no. 2 (1996), 16–23.

[81] Paul B. Stares, *The Militarization of Space: U.S. Policy, 1945–1984* (Ithaca: Cornell University Press, 1985), 242.

[82] This is not at all unlike that analyzed by longshoreman philosopher Eric Hoffer. See Eric Hoffer, *The True Believer: Thoughts on the Nature of Mass Movements* (New York: Harper and Row, 1951), 3–23, 137–155. See also Max Weber, "The Pure Types of Legitimate Authority," in *Max Weber on Charisma and Institution Building: Selected Papers*, ed. S.N. Eisenstadt (Chicago: University of Chicago Press, 1968), 46.

[83] George M. Low, NASA Deputy Administrator, Memorandum for the Record, "Meeting with the President on January 5, 1972," January 12, 1972, NASA Historical Reference Collection. The John Ehrlichman interview by John M. Logsdon, May 6, 1983, NASA Historical Reference Collection, emphasizes the political nature of the decision. This aspect of the issue was also brought home to Nixon by other factors such as letters and personal meetings. See Frank Kizis to Richard M. Nixon, March 12, 1971; Noble M. Melencamp, White House, to Frank Kizis, April 19, 1971, both in Record Group 51, Series 69.1, Box 51–78–31, National Archives and Records Administration, Washington, DC.

[84] Caspar W. Weinberger, Memorandum for the President, via George Shultz, "Future of NASA," August 12, 1971, White House, Richard M. Nixon, President, 1968–1971 File, NASA Historical Reference Collection.

[85] Alfred C. Draper, Melvin L. Buck, and William H. Goesch, "A Delta Shuttle Orbiter," *Astronautics and Aeronautics* 9 (January 1971), 26–35; Charles W. Mathews, "The Space Shuttle and Its Uses," *Aeronautical Journal* 76 (January 1972), 19–25; John M. Logsdon, "The Space Shuttle Program: A Policy Failure," *Science* 232 (May 30, 1986), 1099–1105; Scott Pace, "Engineering Design and Political

Choice: The Space Shuttle, 1969–1972," master's thesis, Massachusetts Institute of Technology, May 1982; and Harry A. Scott, "Space Shuttle: A Case Study in Design," *Astronautics and Aeronautics* 17 (June 1979), 54–58.

[86] Caspar W. Weinberger, interview by John M. Logsdon, August 23, 1977, NASA History Division Reference Collection.

[87] Jacob E. Smart, NASA Assistant Administrator for DOD and Interagency Affairs, to James C. Fletcher, NASA Administrator, "Security Implications in National Space Program," December 1, 1971, with attachments, James C. Fletcher Papers, Special Collections, Marriott Library, University of Utah, Salt Lake City; James C. Fletcher, NASA Administrator, to George M. Low, NASA Deputy Administrator, "Conversation with Al Haig," December 2, 1971, NASA History Division Reference Collection.

[88] James Oberg, "Toward a Theory of Space Power: Defining Principles for U.S. Space Policy," May 20, 2003, 5, copy of paper in possession of author.

[89] The standard work on the shuttle and its operational history is Jenkins, *Space Shuttle: The History of the National Space Transportation System, the First 100 Missions.*

[90] USAF Fact Sheet 86–107, "Manned Spaceflight Engineer Program," 1986; Michael Cassutt, "The Manned Spaceflight Engineer Program," *Spaceflight* (January 1989), 32.

[91] Roger D. Launius, "The Space Shuttle—Twenty-five Years On: What Does It Mean to Have Reusable Access to Space?" *Quest: The History of Spaceflight Magazine* 13, no. 2 (2006), 4–20.

[92] By far the best work on the *Challenger* accident is Diane Vaughan, *The* Challenger *Launch Decision: Risky Technology, Culture, and Deviance at NASA* (Chicago: University of Chicago Press, 1996).

[93] Ronald Reagan, State of the Union Address, February 4, 1986.

[94] Larry E. Schweikart, "Command Innovation: Lessons from the National Aerospace Plane Program," in *Innovation and the Development of Flight*, ed. Roger D. Launius (College Station: Texas A&M University Press, 1999), 299–322.

[95] Carl H. Builder, "The NASP as a Time Machine," RAND Internal Note, August 1989, copy in possession of author; Roger Handberg and Joan Johnson-Freese, "NASP as an American Orphan: Bureaucratic Politics and the Development of Hypersonic Flight," *Spaceflight* 33 (April 1991), 134–137; Larry E. Schweikart, "Hypersonic Hopes: Planning for NASP," *Air Power History* 41 (Spring 1994), 36–48; Larry E. Schweikart, "Managing a Revolutionary Technology, American Style: The National Aerospace Plane," *Essays in Business and Economic History* 12 (1994), 118–132; and Larry E. Schweikart, "Command Innovation: Lessons from the National Aerospace Plane Program," in Roger D. Launius, ed., *Innovation and the Development of Flight* (College Station: Texas A&M University Press, 1999), 299–323.

[96] Daniel L. Hansen, "Exploration of the Utility of Military Man in Space in the Year 2025," NASA report 1992STIN, 9318267H, March 1992.

[97] David M. Tobin, "Man's Place in Space-Plane Flight Operations: Cockpit, Cargo Bay, or Control Room?" *Airpower Journal* 13 (Fall 1999), 62.

[98] Joseph A. Carretto, Jr., "Military Man in Space: Essential to National Strategy," Executive Research Project, Industrial College of the Armed Forces, National Defense University, NDU–ICAF–95–S3, April 1995, 47.

[99] William B. Scott, "USAF's Top Secret Two-Stage-to-Orbit Manned 'Blackstar' System," *Aviation Week and Space Technology*, March 5, 2006, available at <www.aviationnow.com/avnow/news/channel_awst_story.jsp?id=news/030606p1.xml>.

Chapter 10

Commercial Space and Spacepower

Henry R. Hertzfeld

It is increasingly apparent that commercial opportunities for using space to make money by selling goods and services to governments and private customers are growing. Over the past 50 years, the United States has been the technological and commercial world leader in space. U.S. space policies, as reflected particularly in Presidential Directives but also in legislation and in regulations, reflect this leadership role. From the very first space policies in the Dwight D. Eisenhower administration to the present, policy documents assume that the United States is the world leader, attempt to ensure that role continues, and reserve the right to use the necessary means to protect space assets.

Until the 1980s, private companies in the United States were contractors and suppliers to the government space program and projects. They did not offer space services to the public. The one exception to this was in the important area of telecommunications. From the very beginning of the space age, U.S. private companies (in particular, AT&T) designed, built, and operated communications satellites and sold services to the public under strict government regulations and supervision.

Today, the landscape has changed. Companies in the United States are in direct competition with many foreign entities in space in almost all areas: launch vehicles, remote sensing satellites, telecommunications satellites of all kinds (voice, direct TV, fixed and mobile services), and navigation services. The technological capability to build and operate sophisticated space equipment has spread worldwide.

All evidence points to a continuation of this trend. Space has become a global enterprise with the number of nations and firms with space goods and services growing rapidly. And not only are more people involved in space but also the unique advantages of the space environment have contributed greatly to the growing trend toward globalization through its almost universal coverage of populated areas with communications and observation products and services.

In turn, an increase in globalization can stimulate the further growth of commercial space by making even larger markets with corresponding sales potentially available to companies. Globalization must be viewed as a summation of various components (political, business, and cultural). Space capabilities and technologies contribute differently to each component, and the extent of meaningful globalization must be analyzed by its components, not in the aggregate. This chapter will discuss the long-run trend toward globalization and how the growth of multinational companies and the global marketplace has influenced commercial space and spacepower.

Although no other nation spends as much on space as the United States, the ability of the U.S. Government to influence the rest of the world in space policy and in the use of space has greatly diminished over time. In some ways, space has become just another commodity. But government policy and security aspects of space do not treat commercial space as they treat automobiles, soap, or furniture. Because of the strategic value of space as well as the huge dependence of almost every industry on the space infrastructure, space commands special importance and has become a critical national resource.

This chapter will also review the process by which the U.S. Government has developed official policies toward space that have fueled the technological lead and put the United States at the forefront of space activity, while at the same time transferring some of the responsibility of this lead from purely government programs to the domestic commercial sector. However, other policies of the U.S. Government have had the opposite effect, encouraging foreign nations to develop similar and competitive space capabilities.

Questions without clear answers are the degree to which U.S. policy has sped up foreign space capabilities and what the effect has been on spacepower. Of course, not all foreign space programs can be attributed to U.S. policy actions. Because of the obvious advantage of using space for global monitoring, communications, and other activities, other nations naturally have had the desire and have developed independent space assets and capabilities.

Spacepower

Spacepower can be viewed from a commercial perspective in two ways. The first is economic: encouragement of commercial U.S. space ventures to be dominant in the world marketplace, either through creation of a monopoly or by sheer market dominance. The latter often makes competitors follow the leader's standards and practices, which in turn practically assures that others will adopt systems compatible with those of the market leader.[1] The second is by a show of strength: aggressively denying others access or interfering with the operations of foreign space assets.

This chapter will focus on policies of commercial market dominance. Therefore, spacepower will be discussed without the notion of military control or aggressive action to protect space assets or deny others the ability to operate in space. A truly competitive commercial world assumes that companies can operate on a level playing field and that the deciding factor is the ability to make a profit rather than the ability to take out a potential competitor by military action.[2]

Looking to the future growth of commercial space companies and the multinational aspects of commercial space raises an interesting question regarding spacepower. Specifically, will it be possible for commercial interests to supersede other national interests in space? The short answer is *no*. Besides the clear dual use of all space products, space law, as defined by current United Nations treaties on outer space, makes nations responsible for the actions of their citizens in outer space. To get to space and to do anything there, a company will need the formal approval of a parent nation. Since each nation may be both jointly and separately liable for certain types of damage from space objects, it will be difficult, if not impossible, for a company to operate in space without supervision. Therefore, unless the major legal tenets of space activity change, commercial interests will be subservient to national interests in space and will face major regulatory controls.[3]

Globalization and the Changing International Economic Environment

Globalization is the process of human interaction characterized by the ease of transcending national borders for variously defined ends.[4] There are many different aspects of globalization occurring at any given point in time. It is important to distinguish between geopolitical globalization, multinational economic globalization, and cultural/information networks that have become global.

Figure 10–1. Degrees of Globalization

Degrees of Globalization

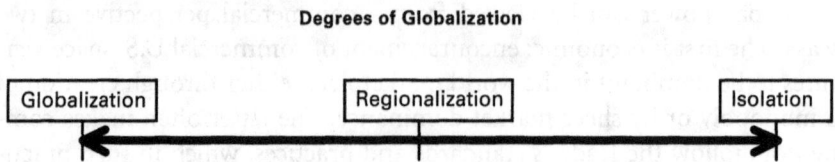

Figure 10–1 illustrates the range of possible degrees of globalization. As one moves to the left of the diagram, the degree of interaction among nations increases. At the other extreme, nations may choose to isolate themselves and raise barriers to global interactions. The concept of regionalization is intended to meet a middle ground where select groups of nations agree to form alliances. Since the overall concept of globalization is the combination of the different elements suggested above, it is instructive to look at the relative position on the continuum for each major element. In general, economic and cultural globalization today has moved toward the left of center, while geopolitical globalization is somewhere to the right of that.

Some of the most visible trends in today's world are the growth of multinational firms, the ease of financial transactions internationally, and the spread of ideas, culture, and entertainment through the advances in communication technologies. The availability and advantages of satellite communications have greatly contributed to these trends through both global coverage and the opening of the global communications services and markets to all nations.

Globalization is not a new phenomenon, nor is it inevitable.[5] Decreases in barriers to trade—most recently through the North American Free Trade Agreement and the World Trade Organization, but through other bilateral agreements in the past as well—and better coordination among nations characterized the decade of the 1990s. Similar eras of increased interaction among people have existed before the most recent times but have then been followed by wars, economic depressions, or other occurrences, which slowed or stopped the trend toward globalization. Even in the first few years of the 21st century, the changed policies and attitudes toward international travel and security because of the events of September 11 have, at least temporarily, slowed the rapid globalization pace established in the 1990s.[6]

Other influences may also slow economic globalization. As described by Rawi Abdelal and Adam Segal, the speed of globalization may become less rapid in the upcoming years for the following reasons: politicians are more nervous about letting capital goods and people move more freely across borders, energy is the object of intense resource nationalism, and bilateral agreements appear to be replacing multilateral agreements (particularly with the United States skeptical of "global rulemaking").[7]

As impressive as the economic and cultural spread of ideas and interactions has been during the past several decades, it has been balanced by the decided lack of geopolitical globalization. With the important exception of the European Union (a limited form of primarily economic globalization on a regional basis), nations have not changed their approach to territorial rights.[8] These rights are jealously guarded and are strong limits to true international geopolitical globalization.

Although there has been a trend toward multinational firms and a global economic regime, history has shown that there is no assurance that this trend will continue on a smooth path. Current economic globalization is dependent on nations moving toward a free market–based economy that also implies some form of democratic government. Economic globalization also depends on the establishment of a relatively uniform regulatory system that is predictable, fair, and enforceable.

Space is a global industry. Within limits established by the political system, companies compete for launch services internationally. Satellite manufacturing, once heavily dependent on U.S. companies, is now an industry with companies located around the world. Space services are also available internationally. However, because of the dual-use nature of many space activities, there are regulatory and legal limits on the degree of international trade that can occur in this industry.

There are many good economic reasons that explain why commercial space needs to be global in nature to survive in a competitive world. Primarily, it is the satellite capability to connect to ground stations anywhere in the world and to transmit data and information globally (or, if not to all nations, to a vast majority of the world's populated areas). To make a profit on an investment that has high technological risk and very high up-front demands, a large market is essential. The additional cost of adding a new ground station is small in comparison to the cost of the space system. Since satellites can have global coverage, having a global market becomes an attractive profit potential. It can be easily argued that many space services are "natural monopolies." That is, one large provider can have the ability to serve all customers much more inexpensively than can multiple providers.[9]

However, in economic government regulatory policy, a monopoly of any sort is counter to a free market competitive philosophy. It should be noted, though, that early U.S. policy encouraged a U.S. monopoly in international telecommunications, not for reasons of economic efficiency, but for U.S. control and security (see the discussion below on U.S. telecommunications policy).

Globalization can have both positive and negative effects on the growth of the space sector and on the development of specific space applications. On the positive side, privatization of space assets would be possible if markets were large enough to be profitable for some space activities. If this were to occur, governments would have to be willing to relinquish some control of space activities. Applications that involve very large international markets—such as launch services, remote sensing, distance learning, and telemedicine—would benefit.

Globalization also would mean rising per capita income among most nations (although at different rates of growth), which would create the potential for more markets for space (and other) goods and services. New and larger markets might open opportunities for the expansion of currently profitable consumer space-related services such as global positioning system (GPS) navigation equipment and telecommunications (information-based) services, and perhaps the use of space for entertainment services (such as real-time distribution of movies and new music delivery services).

On the negative side, globalization and economic growth are likely to stimulate a backlash among some in society who will push for a "simpler" life and are against using new technology. A cultural backlash can also be expected that, coupled with the spread of highly advanced communications and space technology, is likely to encourage countermeasures by advocates wanting to block or reduce the influence of alien cultures.

Security and defense issues will be of major governmental concern. Space applications will be used to monitor and control these activities, and this should be a growth sector for government programs using new satellites. However, this can easily lead to a decline in market-based commercial space applications as government demands and regulations supplant the development of private market opportunities.

In the financial community, commercial space activities would have to be shown to have a greater opportunity cost and return on investment (ROI) than other high-technology and high-risk investments. As with other "negative" aspects of globalization, the availability of sufficient private capital for space investments will depend more on opportunity costs and the expected ROI of specific projects than it will on globalization.

When dual-use technologies are involved, a lack of private capital will necessitate government subsidies.

Regionalization

The effects of regionalization are likely to be similar to those of globalization on space, although at somewhat lower levels of activity due to:

- less harmonization among nations in areas of regulation
- possibility of more regional conflicts
- lower per capita income growth
- less convergence of growth rates in general.

Nevertheless, satellite capabilities will be used for additional security concerns and for global monitoring. There is likely to be less private sector investment in space under this scenario than under the globalization scenario. However, regional markets may be large enough to support sizable space investments by the private sector. Other than the European Union, regional cooperation in space has not been a market or security issue to date.

Crisis/Independence

If nations increasingly choose to develop independent space systems, defense and other government uses of space will become more important with governments discouraging private investment in space because of the potential dangers of dual-use technologies in the hands of companies and other nations. Since each nation will attempt to develop its own space systems, the duplication and oversupply of both hardware and space products will act to discourage commercial space investments. Technological progress in areas such as space science and exploration would be hurt greatly by the divergence of funds to more immediate problems.

Finally, private investment in space will be even more challenged, but governments may opt to purchase space services directly from domestic commercial private firms. These firms may be precluded by regulation or contract from offering services to customers in the general marketplace.

Globalization and Spacepower

Globalization is not an inevitable outcome of current and past trends, but some very important aspects of globalization are on a steadily expanding path that is unlikely to be deterred. They include multinational business and financial connections and networks as well as cross-border information, cultural, and entertainment products and services. Space assets provide a key enabling infrastructure component of both of these developments.

The commercial space activities that are profitable today are those that serve these sectors by providing rapid worldwide communications. Whether it is navigation and timing services of the GPS satellites, or direct TV broadcasts, or very small aperture terminal links of the credit card companies, or electronic financial trading, the global economic system is now linked via satellites and space capabilities. If it were not for the existence of a large and well-funded global market for these services, the satellite systems serving them would likely not be profitable. What has developed over time is a circular dependence: technologies create new economic opportunities, and large markets create profitable infrastructure investments with subsequent multiplicative terrestrial businesses.

However, this evolution of satellite services (from the early space years when governments provided and controlled the telecommunications satellites) has created dilemmas. No longer can a nation such as the United States even rationally plan for control of the systems or capabilities. In time of conflict, it would be almost impossible to interrupt services because businesses and governments as customers depend on them. In fact, the government is one of the major users of commercial communications networks.

Another dilemma is that satellite signals do not cleanly begin and end at national borders. Some nations are increasingly incensed at their inability to censor or control economic and political messages received by their populations. Similarly, some cultures are attempting to resist the intrusions of Western values that are predominant in the business and entertainment sectors. This is creating political and regional isolationist sentiments that may someday result in attempts to interrupt certain satellite transmissions. Such attempts make the issue of spacepower integral to both the growth of globalization and the continued development of large world markets for satellite services that can create profits and new commercial space endeavors. The nation that leads in commercial space will have a larger share of economic growth and be able to dictate industry standards, an important tool for future economic dominance as well as for space security.

Thus, if globalization continues its rapid advance, then a nation's commercial spacepower is of greater importance; if globalization stalls, dedicated national security and military uses of space will increase, and a nation's ability to garner larger market shares for commercial services will be more limited.[10] Spacepower may then be determined more by military power than market power.

U.S. Government Approach to Commercial Space over Time

This brief review of U.S. Government space policy documents as they relate to commercial space activities clearly shows a changing attitude and increasing dependence on private space activities. U.S. Government space policy, however, is very complex and is not adequately or comprehensively reflected in any one document or even any one series of documents (such as Presidential Decision Directives [PDDs] on Space Policies). When viewed from a commercial space perspective, even analyzing only unclassified policies yields a set of guidelines that is sometimes inconsistent. At any given time, one can point to both documents in which the government provides incentives for commercial space to develop and mature and ones in which significant barriers to commercial space exist. Sometimes these incentives and barriers are erected purposefully and sometimes they are inadvertent, being unintended byproducts of other government priorities and initiatives Several categories of government policies will be described below. First, trends in PDDs that have direct implications for commercial space are analyzed. Second, PDDs and documents concerning the satellite communications sector are described. Third, major legislative changes that have had an impact on the development of commercial space and regulations imposed on commercial space endeavors over time are reviewed. Fourth, other government policies such as the deregulation of many industries and the decision of the Department of Defense (DOD) to encourage the consolidation of aerospace companies are discussed.

A summary of government policy toward commercial space produces a confused set of signals to the industry and to foreign governments and potential competitors. The reasons for the contradictions include:

- the important role of space in national security and a goal of reserving some space capabilities, whether commercially or government owned, for national purposes

- a rapidly changing industry that has not yet reached commercial maturity

- the use of space assets for international political purposes

- changes in government policy over time concerning competition and deregulation.

Finally, it should be noted that most other nations have developed space capabilities and space programs to encourage and subsidize economic growth through cutting-edge technological developments (as well as to create jobs).[11] The charters of most foreign space agencies specifically state this as one goal.[12] That provides a basis for an overt and active "industry policy" toward space. The United States has a government philosophy of not having an industry policy for any economic sector, therefore making it more difficult for the government to find a unified way of providing incentives to any industry, aerospace included.[13]

Presidential Space Documents and Decisions

Since 1960, there have been seven major Presidential documents on space policy. Changes over time to the policies have never been radical but have reflected changing technological, political, and economic conditions. The following discussion will broadly summarize the approach over time of the various administrations to commercial space and will analyze the significance of those changes to the U.S. economy and to how commercial space plays a role in spacepower.[14] It is clear from the very rudimentary count of words in these documents that the economic and commercial aspects of space only became important policy considerations in the 1980s (see figure 10–2).

Figure 10–2. Commercial Space in Presidential Space Policy

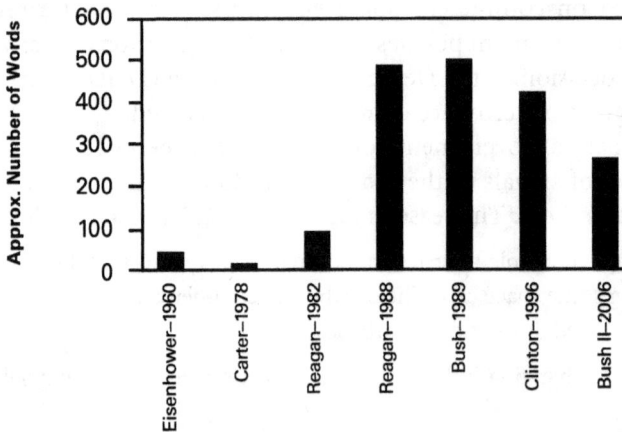

Space policy emerged from the Cold War as a security, political, and technological endeavor for the United States. Early space policies focused on ensuring the security of the United States through winning the technological race with the former Soviet Union. In addition, there were concerns and issues of nuclear proliferation and deterrence in those early space policies, reflecting the capabilities of launch vehicles to deliver weapons. The economic capabilities of the United States were mentioned in the Eisenhower Policy but more as a general recognition that the design and development of space equipment would stimulate the economy. That is, jobs would be created and possible spin-off products would enter the economy. The Eisenhower Policy also recognized the future potential economic aspects of two civilian applications of space technologies, communications and meteorology, but these technologies were not discussed in detail in this overall policy document.[15]

It is also interesting to note that the Eisenhower Policy called for international cooperation in civilian space exploration, but at the same time space was to "demonstrate an over-all U.S. superiority in outer space without necessarily requiring the United States supremacy in every phase of space activities."[16]

The beginnings of change were apparent in the 1978 National Space Policy of the Jimmy Carter administration that focused on remote sensing; it called for a study and report on private sector involvement and investment in civil remote sensing systems.[17]

The official encouragement of commercial space did not occur until the 1980s.[18] Several different domestic factors, as well as several international developments, were responsible. First was the beginning of the maturation of the Earth observation satellites and the growth of a private value-added industry selling specialized products based on Landsat imagery. Second was the successful partial commercialization of the upper stages of launch vehicles (the Payload Assist Modules). Third was the *Challenger* accident in 1986 that suddenly changed the launch scenario for commercial satellites (mostly telecommunications).[19]

On the international scene, the 1980s were marked by the success of the French Ariane launch vehicle and Spot remote sensing satellites. Both were designed to directly compete with U.S. systems and were marketed by private companies but were essentially vehicles funded through government sources. Other nations were also beginning to design and build competitive commercial space systems and satellites.

Therefore, on both the domestic and foreign fronts, commercial companies that had been solely government contractors for space equipment were branching into independent offerings of space components and systems. The industry was beginning to mature and, at the same time, the United States was entering an era of overall policy shifts toward economic deregulation of all industry. Although space would never be "deregulated," the philosophical shift meant more attention to commercial capabilities and opportunities along with the recognition that the government could be a customer for rather than a producer of some space goods and services.

The Ronald Reagan administration policies of 1982 and 1984 further extended the mandate for the government to both "obtain economic and scientific benefits through the exploitation of space, and expand United States private-sector investment and involvement in the civil space and space-related activities.[20] Collectively, these policies emphasized that the space systems were to be for national economic benefit and that the U.S. Government would provide a climate conducive to expanded private sector investment and involvement in civil space activities with due regard to public safety and national security. It also called for a regulatory and supervisory system.

It should be noted that all policies that encouraged private sector space activity and commercialization of space also contained caveats that required the consideration of national security. Thus, any commercial space venture had, and still has, investment risk that is subject to deliberately vague government rules and possible decisions on what might constitute a breach of national security.[21]

The George H.W. Bush administration expanded these commercial policies.[22] Collectively, they called for the active encouragement of commercial investments in space as well as for the promotion of commercial space activities. There were even directions in the policy of 1991 to study the possible disposition of missiles by converting them into commercial launchers. (This was subject to a number of security and economic caveats.) Also of significance was the mandate for the government not only to promote commercial remote sensing, but also to "not preclude" private sector remote sensing activities.

The Bill Clinton administration took further steps to encourage commercial space. In particular, remote sensing again was the focus of attention, with not only the previous security limits on the resolution of imagery that could be made public greatly relaxed, but also with specific policies on remote sensing that were to support and enhance U.S. global competitiveness in the international remote sensing market. Success in this type of commercial activity was viewed as contributing to our critical industrial base.[23]

Another Clinton policy directive called for the private sector to have a significant role in managing the development and operation of a new reusable space transportation system. The National Aeronautics and Space Administration (NASA) was directed to "actively involve the private sector."[24] Although this system (the X–33/VentureStar Project) was begun but never completed, it was one of the first major initiatives in space for a public/private partnership in the research and development (R&D) of a new launch system.

By the mid-1990s, the GPS military navigation satellites, which had a free and open signal, had stimulated a rapidly growing private sector market for ground receivers. A policy directive issued in 1996 clearly recognized that the private sector investment in U.S. GPS technologies and services was important for economic competitiveness, and the policy encouraged continued private activity in this area, subject to issues of national security.[25]

The George W. Bush administration issued a set of space policies dealing with specific issues (Earth observations, transportation, navigation, and the vision for exploration) as well as the final policy document that covers overall space policy.[26] The commitment to promoting and encouraging commercial activity is continued in all of these policies. However, in the overall policy document issued in August 2006, there is a noticeable decrease in references to commercial objectives and a noticeable increase in references to national security issues.

This should not be interpreted as a retreat from supporting commercial space endeavors. In fact, there are more companies involved in entrepreneurial space activities than ever before in the United States and the rest of the world. And the U.S. Government is actively promoting commercial ventures, both independently of and with government support, in programs such as NASA's commercial-off-the-shelf initiative. In addition, NASA is actively seeking foreign national and commercial partnerships and initiatives for future activities on the Moon.

But this new policy should also serve as a sobering warning that national security will supersede commercial issues, if necessary, adding a significant risk to commercial investments on one hand, and insuring that U.S. commercial interests in space will be backed by some form of government protective action if they are threatened.

In summary, overall space policy directives have slowly been transformed from a Cold War emphasis that marginalized the economic and commercial implications of space activities into a truly integrated policy that recognizes the maturity of many space applications, sophisticated industrial capabilities, the globalization of space technologies, and the importance of the space infrastructure to both civilian uses and security concerns. It is important to recognize that events in the past 6 years in the United States have led to a new space policy that continues to recognize and encourage commercial space, but with a greater emphasis on security and on the protection of both public and private U.S. space assets.

In the early years of space, the dominance of the United States in its technology permitted spacepower to be practically a given, rivaled only by the competition with the Soviet Union. Today, the reality is that the Nation is still the leader in space expenditures but no longer dominates or controls developments in many space applications. Spacepower, as it might be measured by dominance in economic or commercial space activity, is broadly spread around the globe. There are only limited ways the United States can use commercial space for maintaining elements of control over the industry. One is to have the largest market share in any sector, which encourages others who may want to compete to adopt compatible standards for interoperability. The other is to be the leader in developing new technology and establish dominant control over particular markets by protecting that technology. Both methods are risky, expensive, and do not necessarily guarantee success.

The only other way the United States can assert spacepower in the commercial sector is by using nonmarket (political, diplomatic, or military) actions to discourage or deny others access to commercial space. It is highly unlikely in today's world that such measures would be successful. Other nations have independent access to space and space assets. Many companies using space for commercial purposes are multinational enterprises, often with significant U.S. corporate investments and components. And the U.S. Government itself depends not only on U.S. commercial space goods and services but also on foreign systems.[27] Therefore, at this time, disrupting the fragile market and price system that is developing for space commercial assets would not be in the best interests of the United States.

Government Policy toward Telecommunications Satellites

Until the 1990s, most space policy topics were covered in overall policy statements.[28] Telecommunications was handled separately from the very beginning of the space era, mainly because in the 1950s and 1960s, its relevance to security and its obvious commercial potential were much further developed than other space applications. In addition, telecommunications was truly a public/private endeavor, mainly developed in the private sector by AT&T. As early as the mid-1950s, comparisons were made that showed the tremendous capacity increases that could be available through satellite telephone calls when compared to the capacity of the transatlantic cable at that time.[29]

The change in 1961 from the Republican Eisenhower administration to the Democratic John F. Kennedy administration also signaled a change in attitude toward the telecommunications satellite system. In the Eisenhower era, it was accepted that AT&T was the monopoly provider of long-distance telephone service, and having the company expand into satellite service was not disputed. In fact, there was a clear recognition that a U.S. monopoly in satellite communications would be advantageous from many perspectives, ranging from control over the world system (and also, therefore, increasing the military and economic power of the United States) to cost efficiencies from scale economies of operation.

The Kennedy administration altered this perspective and encouraged competition in the United States for privately funded satellite systems by awarding contracts for the development of new communications satellites by several firms. AT&T launched the Telstar system of two satellites in 1962, NASA awarded a competitive contract to RCA for the Relay satellites, also first launched in 1962, and Hughes received a sole-source NASA contract for the Syncom satellites, launched first in 1963.

As the need for a world satellite communications system developed, COMSAT was formed in 1962 as a U.S. public corporation with shares held by both the communications companies as well as the general public. It was not only the manager for the International Telecommunications Satellite Corporation (Intelsat), but also was its U.S. official representative. Intelsat was formed in 1964, and its first satellite, Early Bird, was launched the next year. As early as 1969, there was global coverage, with agreements in place for ground stations across the world.

In 1965, the Lyndon Johnson administration approved National Security Action Memorandum 338, which clearly stated the U.S. policy toward foreign communications capabilities.[30] The essence of this policy was to encourage a single global commercial communications satellite system. It stated that the United States should refrain from providing assistance to other countries that would significantly promote, stimulate, or encourage proliferation of communications satellite systems. It went on to say that the United States should not consider foreign requests for launch services in connections with communications satellites (except for those satellites that would be part of the international system).

The European (French-German) Symphonie satellite program begun in 1967 presents an interesting case study. This was the first European-built telecommunications satellite, and the Europeans requested a launch to geosynchronous orbit from NASA. The United States, as a matter of policy, would not guarantee them a launch opportunity for Symphonie as an *operational* satellite. (Eventually, the United States did launch the satellite in 1974 under the policy exception that the satellite was an *experimental* one.) This U.S. refusal to launch a foreign, and possibly competing, satellite was one of the main factors prompting the development in Europe of the Ariane launch vehicle so that Europe would have an independent capability to launch its own operational satellites.[31]

What this example illustrates is that a policy of spacepower (denying others access to space while attempting to create a U.S.-led monopoly) can backfire by providing incentives for others to be able to ignore U.S. policies by building and operating their own systems. As is well known, the Ariane launch system was optimized to capture the launch market for commercial telecommunications satellite launches to geosynchronous orbit. It became a huge tactical and market success, capturing over 60 percent of the commercial launch market by the 1990s and effectively eliminating any hope of U.S. "control" of the launch vehicle market, particularly for telecommunications satellites.[32]

Over time, with the trend in the United States toward deregulation, the telecommunications industry monopolies have disappeared. At the same time, many nations have built and launched domestic telecommunications satellites. COMSAT became a private company and has now disappeared after being sold to Lockheed-Martin. Intelsat (and Inmarsat) are now privately operated. Many firms around the world are able to build new telecommunications satellites, and the U.S. position in this industry has changed from a virtual monopoly to a large, but by no means dominant, competitor.

Other Government Regulatory Actions

Besides the official administration PDDs on space activities, there are numerous other social, technological, budget, political, and economic actions that are decided by all branches of the government—executive, legislative, and judicial. Some are related to space issues but are handled through other venues. Antitrust reviews, for example, done by the Department of Justice and the Federal Trade Commission, often have far-reaching space and spacepower implications when dealing with firms engaged in space activities. The list of direct and tangential actions with an impact on spacepower would span almost the entire spectrum of government activities, from securities regulations to decisions from the courts.

Examples

Below, some examples are listed.[33] The major issue for consideration in the context of spacepower, however, is that many actions taken by the government for very valid purposes that are unrelated to space may create conditions that negate the ability to carry out space policies as proscribed in PDDs and/or create incentives for other nations or the companies in other nations to more aggressively develop systems in direct competition with U.S. capabilities. Taken collectively, many of these actions may make any attempt at a U.S. policy that emphasizes economic spacepower very difficult, if not impossible, to carry out. And looking historically, many of these nonspace policies and actions may have created and sped up the development of robust space capabilities in other nations, which, in turn, has weakened U.S. economic leadership in space and diluted the Nation's power in space systems development as well as in the technology and use of space applications.[34]

Overall U.S. Government philosophy toward economic deregulation of industry. Deregulation, along with policies to avoid developing government enterprises, is oriented toward letting the market and price system allocate resources more efficiently than government fiat can do. This works well in a truly competitive industry with many producers and many consumers. Unfortunately, space is an industry characterized by only a few producers and with governments as the major purchasers. What has occurred is a shift in power and human resource capability from governments to large corporations. Whether this is advantageous to either the development of space commerce or to U.S. spacepower is a matter of empirical analysis and further research, neither of which has been done as yet.[35]

Overall government attempts to privatize and outsource functions. Examples such as the attempted privatization of remote sensing satellites, first in the late 1970s and again in the mid-1980s, were premature and not very successful. In fact, the suggestion that the satellite weather service be privatized resulted in Congress declaring that meteorology and weather systems were a "public good" and would not be privatized. Essentially, the private market for space goods and services has never developed as rapidly as was expected, and most of these proposals have not happened due mainly to a lack of a sizable nongovernment market as well as to the large up-front investments.

DOD incentives for mergers and combinations of firms since the 1990s. As discussed below, this has encouraged a more oligopolistic space industry in the United States. It also encouraged similar combinations abroad as the only way other nations could compete with U.S. companies. Lower-tier suppliers have been subsumed under larger companies, and the result has been a different type of competition than existed before these developments in the space sector. It has also created more powerful and capable foreign competition.

Examples from Space-related Decisions

Imposition of strict export controls on space systems and high-technology products. Both U.S. and foreign industries as well as foreign governments have complained bitterly about the strict enforcement of export control laws since the late 1990s. It is increasingly more difficult to share R&D information, to sell U.S. space goods and services abroad, and to cooperate with foreign nations, even on government projects. The hardest hit space industry has been satellite manufacturing in the United States, where foreign competitors have built and are selling equipment worldwide at the expense of a market that formerly was controlled and dominated by U.S. firms.

Sunset provisions on indemnification of space third-party liability. Although perhaps of a lesser economic disadvantage to the United States in providing competition in launch services, most foreign launch companies fully indemnify their domestic industry from the unlikely, but possibly very expensive, liability claims that could accrue if there were a major disaster from a space object destroying property or taking lives upon reentering the Earth's atmosphere. The United States requires private insurance and indemnifies firms (with a cap) on claims above what insurance would pay. That is a reasonable policy, but it has never been made permanent. Congress has consistently put a sunset provision into that authorizing legislation and therefore has increased the risk of investment for U.S. launch firms compared to our foreign competitors.

Decision in the 1970s to put all commercial payloads on the space shuttle and not fund R&D for expendable vehicles. The economic results of the *Challenger* disaster in 1986 clearly highlighted the potential problems with this policy. In particular, Arianespace, the French/European launch vehicle company, was developing a series of vehicles mainly designed for the commercial market in geosynchronous telecommunications satellites. As a result of the United States falling behind in R&D and manufacturing of expendable rockets and the change in policy toward commercial space shuttle launches after *Challenger*, Arianespace was able to capture up to 60 percent of the launch market. The United States needed over a decade and a major policy shift toward stimulating commercial launch developments before being able to regain some of the lost market share.

Decision not to authorize launches of foreign operational telecommunications satellites on U.S. launch vehicles. As with other restrictive policies, nations were given the incentive to develop independent capabilities. With the ensuing maturation of launch and satellite technologies, they were able to build very competitive and capable equipment without U.S. components or assistance.[36]

DOD decision to retain governance of GPS. Even though GPS was funded, designed, built, and operated by DOD, it had provided an unencrypted free signal for worldwide use as part of the program. Use of this signal has grown into a multibillion-dollar industry very quickly. Receivers are manufactured in many nations, and the system has become one of the important infrastructure services offered from space. It is important now to both the military and to civilian communications and timing systems. From the mid-1990s to today, it has been the only fully operating space navigation system. That is about to change as Europe, Russia, and possibly China develop their own systems. Nobody questions the integrity or value of the U.S. global positioning system, but partially because it is controlled by DOD without any inputs from other nations, there are incentives to invest billions of dollars abroad to duplicate the capability. From a military viewpoint, not giving up control of a critical technology is understandable, but from a practical and economic perspective, the United States likely could have maintained a monopoly position, or at least greatly stalled foreign developments, if the government had been able to compromise on this policy.

Delayed decision to allow release of higher resolution images from Earth observation satellites for civil and commercial purposes. By the early 1990s, when the restriction was lifted on releasing or permitting private U.S. companies to collect or sell imagery with a resolution of less than 10 meters, France had been selling such imagery on the open market, as had Russia. Again, nations with aggressive economic and industry space policies were able to capture market shares from U.S. companies hindered by policies designed for security, not commercial purposes.

The United States and the Changing International Space Environment

In the early days of space activity, the United States and the Soviet Union were alone in having a full range of space capabilities. National security, particularly with respect to fear of the use and/or spread of nuclear weapons, and Cold War–era jockeying for both economic and technological supremacy were the driving forces behind the space race.

Private sector initiatives and the commercialization of space were concepts and ideas far from being realized. Even telecommunications through satellites was in its infancy and, at least in the United States, involved private companies but only under careful economic regulatory supervision. Essentially, there was no commercial or economic issue of any great magnitude for the government to be concerned about. And where it might be possible, the United States had a virtual lock on competition.

Today, just about everything has turned around. There is no technological race with another superpower. Nuclear technology has spread across the world despite remaining under strict controls. Likewise, space capabilities ranging from launch vehicles to satellites are available to almost any nation with the money and inclination to purchase them. Space technical and manufacturing capability exists in just about every developed region of the world, and nations are not dependent on the United States. The world economy has become far more interconnected, and U.S. dependence on international trade in goods and services has grown from approximately 5 percent of the gross domestic product in the 1960s to about 20 percent.

The issue that confronts U.S. space policy in regard to economic and commercial spacepower is whether *any* policy that attempts to put the United States in a dominant economic role in space will be effective. The above discussion has amply illustrated that most such policies have backfired. They have encouraged other nations to invest in competitive systems so as to develop and maintain their own independent capabilities in space. Although worldwide competition in space infrastructure as well as space-related products and services may have many benefits, it does severely limit the amount of control any one nation might have on important dual-use technologies in space.

Economic competition does encourage the development and deployment of new products and services, but not all of them may be of domestic origin. However, some U.S. policies, such as those that have encouraged the merger of many companies involved in space and defense work into an oligopolistic framework, have led to an interesting new economic structure where competition is among a few giant firms rather than among many providers. It also has led to similar conglomerations of firms abroad. This type of competition may not yield the same advantages (particularly to consumers—including the government as a purchaser of services) that usually are attributed to true competitive industries.

In summary, for a variety of reasons, the United States cannot return to the space era and space policies of the 1960s. It can be and is a leader in space technology, but it is not the leader in all aspects of space. Spacepower through commercial prowess is likely to be shared among spacefaring nations. Policies aimed at isolation and at protection of commercial industries only encourage others to develop similar (and sometimes better) products. The only policy that can now be effective in developing a larger and more powerful economic competitive engine for space products is one that encourages R&D investments by space firms. The introduction of new and more advanced products will create a larger global market for the United States. A policy emphasizing offense rather than defense would be advantageous for stimulating spacepower through space commerce.

Conclusion

Economic and commercial spacepower is about market dominance and control. When the United States has a monopoly or near-monopoly in space goods or services, control is not a problem, and it can dictate (and has done so) to the rest of the world what it was willing to sell and provide. History has amply illustrated that this is a short-term phenomenon and that, given the value of space technologies to many sectors and to domestic security, nations with the ability and resources will develop their own independent capabilities.

When other nations have similar capabilities, control becomes a problem assuming, as is the case with space, that control is also a critical issue in security. Options for control through spacepower change and become more limited. Once lost, it is almost impossible to regain economic control; therefore, spacepower may revert to issues of bargaining and negotiating power and/or military might.

Exerting spacepower may be inconsistent with expanded commercial developments in space, raising investment risks and creating incentives for foreign competitors. At the same time, spacepower is highly correlated with increased dual-use government purchases of space services as well as with other security issues in space activities.

Economic investments are made on the basis of expected rates of return. Expanding potential market opportunities is one of the prime motivators for private investment. The government may be a large customer for commercial goods and services. The economic question is whether it is better for a firm to invest in space because there are expanding private markets resulting from growth in global opportunities or because of expected domestic government sales, primarily for dual-use and security services.

To the extent that the global market opportunity is denied by restrictive commercial policies, spacepower from a purely international economic competitive perspective is diminished. As encouraging as the U.S. commercial space policies are in Presidential documents over the past 20 years, they have been unintentionally undermined to a large extent by other policies. In the United States, security almost always trumps commerce.

The United States is still the largest investor in space in the world and the technological and commercial space leader in many areas. This leadership is being challenged. From an economic standpoint alone, it will become increasingly important for the United States to stimulate its industry to develop better and less expensive space products in order to maintain its competitive position. A strong commercial space industry can and will contribute to spacepower. It must be recognized that space is no longer the province of one or two strong nations and that other nations will continue to enter the market and continuously challenge this leadership.

Notes

[1] The advantage is twofold: it encourages purchases of technical components from the market leader, and it gives the market leader a military advantage in understanding the technological workings of others' systems.

[2] The police power to ensure a status quo (or improvement) is recognized as an important component of a level playing field. For this chapter, the purpose is to isolate economic and business arguments from military and security issues.

[3] Even international nongovernmental organizations, such as the European Space Agency, that have independently agreed to the principles of the United Nations (UN) Treaties on Outer Space cannot make claims for liability directly to a nonmember offending nation or to the UN. They are required to make such claims through one of their member nations that has ratified the treaties.

[4] This section is based on a working paper by Henry Hertzfeld and Michel Fouquin, "Socioeconomic Conditions and the Space Sector," Organisation for Economic Co-operation and Development, Working Paper SG/AU/SPA (2004) 3, May 12, 2004.

[5] See Stanley Fischer, "Globalization and Its Challenges," *American Economic Review Papers and Proceedings* 3, no. 2 (May 2003), 3.

[6] Some actions such as the tightening of visa requirements for entrance to the United States have had a definite effect on the number of foreign students in U.S. universities. These actions have also made it more difficult for professionals to attend conferences and workshops in the United States, both evidence of a slowing of at least some global communications links. Globalization is also closely tied to overall economic growth trends. The early 2000s were marked by a slowdown in growth that may have temporarily slowed globalization trends. The 9/11 events had a particularly strong influence on U.S. policies. It is unclear how much those policies affected other nations.

[7] Rawi Abdelal and Adam Segal, "Has Globalization Passed its Peak?" *Foreign Affairs* 86, no. 1 (January–February 2007), 103–114.

[8] Even in the European Union, nations have retained jurisdiction over many areas, including telecommunications policy. It is important to note the failure of a popular vote on establishing a European constitution.

[9] That does not guarantee that the prices charged to customers will necessarily be lower than if the industry were competitive (that is, if multiple providers had been offering services to the same customers). Economic theory tells us otherwise. Monopoly means higher prices and less quantity of-

fered on the market. Regulatory licensing, oversight, and enforcement can compensate for this. The trade-off in the case of space is one of avoiding duplication of expensive assets coupled with the spacepower inherent with a monopoly that is owned by a company within the United States and under the supervision of U.S. laws. Arguments that the space sector should be "competitive" and respond fully to market prices sound persuasive but fail to recognize the reality that space economic activity is, at best, the province of a handful of companies and is beholden to large purchases from governments—both factors clearly denying space enterprise from fitting any textbook definition of a price-competitive sector. Competition in the space sector has to be viewed as a goal, not a reality.

[10] This is because there will be a combination of more satellites serving only one nation or region, and there will also be restrictions on sales of services within particular nations and market areas.

[11] The former Soviet Union is the obvious exception to this. Its goals were very similar to those of the United States in the space and technological race of the 1960s through the 1980s, but because of the socialist nature of the government it did not seek commercial involvement during those years.

[12] See, for example, article VII of the European Space Agency Charter, SP–1271(E), March 2003.

[13] Not having an industry policy is, in itself, an industry policy. And in spite of that overall philosophy, the United States has provided many specific incentives and subsidies to the aerospace industry. For example, the Independent Research and Development funds that are part of many Department of Defense research and development contracts to commercial funds provide incentive for new commercial technological development. The Export-Import Bank provides loans to industry to encourage trade. Import restrictions on some products protect domestic industry. And the largest incentive is the sales to the U.S. Government of equipment and services.

[14] National Security Space Project, "Presidential Decisions: NSC Documents," ed. Stephanie Feyock and R. Cargill Hall (Washington, DC: George C. Marshall Institute, 2006). This volume (along with its supplement) is a collection of all of the unclassified and declassified Presidential Decisions on space. That document is the source of the information in this section.

[15] Telecommunications, meteorology, and remote sensing have all been subjects of separate policy documents over time.

[16] National Security Council (NSC) 5918/1, "Draft Statement of U.S. Policy on Outer Space," December 17, 1959.

[17] Presidential Decision Directive (PDD)/NSC–37, "National Space Policy," May 22, 1978, available at <http://fas.org/spp/military/docops/national/nsc-37.htm>.

[18] The exception was telecommunications satellites, which are discussed in separate policy documents.

[19] With an operational shuttle, the U.S. Government had adapted two related policies: one was to put all commercial U.S. payloads on the shuttle, and the second was to stop performing advanced research and development on expendable launch vehicles. After the *Challenger* accident, it was clear that the United States needed both capable expendable vehicles and the shuttle. The commercial launch sector was at this point mature enough to manufacture and sell launches of expendable vehicles to both the government and private customers. The 1984 Commercial Space Launch Act was significantly amended in 1988 to encourage government purchases of launch vehicles and licensing of U.S. vehicles for commercial satellite launches rather than having the government be the intermediary between the commercial firms and the vehicle manufacturers.

[20] National Security Decision Directive (NSDD)–42, "National Space Policy," July 4, 1982, available at <www.hq.nasa.gov/office/pao/History/nsdd-42.html>; NSDD–94, "Commercialization of Expendable Launch Vehicles," May 16, 1982, available at <www.fas.org/irp/offdocs/nsdd/nsdd-094.htm>; "Fact Sheet: National Space Strategy," August 16, 1984; and NSDD–254, "United States Space Launch Strategy," December 27, 1986, available at <www.fas.org/irp/offdocs/nsdd/nsdd-254.htm>.

[21] One could argue that any commercial venture in any industry might be subject to a similar constraint. However, given the dual-use nature of all space activities, along with the history of the space industry, this constraint is of a more direct and significant importance for most activities in space.

[22] NSDD–30 (National Security Presidential Directive [NSPD]–1), "National Space Policy," November 2, 1989, NSPD–4, "National Space Launch Strategy," July 10, 1991, available at <http://fas.

org/spp/military/docops/national/nspd4.htm>; NSPD–5, "Landsat Remote Sensing Strategy," February 13, 1992, available at <www.au.af.mil/au/awc/awcgate/nspd5.htm>; NSPD–6, "Space Exploration Initiative," March 13, 1992, available at <http://fas.org/spp/military/docops/national/nspd6.htm>.

[23] PDD/NSC–23, "Statement on Export of Satellite Imagery and Imaging Systems," March 10, 1994.

[24] PDD/National Science and Technology Council (NSTC)–4, "National Space Transportation Policy," August 5, 1994, available at <www.fas.org/spp/military/docops/national/launchst.htm>.

[25] PDD/NSTC–6, "U.S. Global Positioning System Policy," March 29, 1996, available at <www. fas.org/spp/military/docops/national/gps.htm>.

[26] George W. Bush, "U.S. Commercial Remote Sensing Policy," Section VI, "Foreign Access to U.S. Commercial Remote Sensing Space Capabilities," April 25, 2003, available at <http://ostp.gov/ html/Fact%20Sheet%20-%20Commercial%20Remote%20Sensing%20Policy%20-%20April%20 25%202003.pdf>; George W. Bush, "A Renewed Spirit of Discovery: The President's Vision for Space Exploration" (Washington, DC: The White House, January 2004), available at <http://ostp.gov/html/ renewed_spirit.pdf>; "Fact Sheet: U.S. Space-Based Positioning, Navigation, and Timing Policy," December 15, 2004, Background, §II; "Fact Sheet: U.S. Space Transportation Policy," January 6, 2005, available at <http://ostp.gov/html/Space_Transportation_Policy05.pdf>, U.S. National Space Policy, August 31, 2006.

[27] This is particularly important for the purchase of communications bandwidth as well as for Earth observation imagery. In addition, there are many scientific and meteorology satellites that provided data that are shared with many nations and are important for U.S. security as well.

[28] Today, remote sensing, navigation, transportation, and NASA's "vision" are all enumerated in separate policy documents. The administration's overall space policy addresses general issues and direction, as well as topics not dealt with in the separate policy documents.

[29] The brief summary in this paper is based on information in David J. Whalen, "Communications Satellites: Making the Global Village Possible," available at <www.hq.nasa.gov/office/pao/History/ satcomhistory.html>, and in Joseph Pelton, "The History of Satellite Communications," in *Exploring the Unknown*, ed. John M. Logsdon (Washington, DC: National Aeronautics and Space Administration, SP–4407, 1998). It is also interesting to note that the most profitable private use of satellites has changed and is now in the broadcast of direct-to-home television. Technology has changed and copper-wire cables have been superseded by fiber optic cables, which now carry the majority of voice communications, although they cannot serve point-to-multipoint transmissions as effectively as satellites. The U.S. Department of Defense, in addition to having its own communications satellites, also purchases a large amount of bandwidth from private satellite providers.

[30] Reproduced in Pelton, *Exploring the Unknown*, 91.

[31] M. Bigner and J. Vanderkerckhove, "The Ariane Programme," *Philosophical Transactions of the Royal Society of London* A312, no. 1519; "Technology in the 1990s: The Industrialization of Space" (July 26, 1984), 83–88, available at <http://links.jstor.org/sici?sici=00804614%2819840726%29312%3 A1519%3C83%3ATAP%5BD%3E2.0.CO%3B2-A>.

[32] See below for a brief discussion of the remote sensing industry and the navigation space sector. In both cases, subsequent to the telecommunications experience, Europe (led by France) developed, launched, and successfully operated a competitive remote sensing system (Spot) and is actively engaged in a competitive navigation system (Galileo).

[33] A full analysis of this issue is far too lengthy and complex for this chapter but would be a useful topic for further research.

[34] Given the overall maturity of parts of the space industry and the very obvious advantages of having space systems, foreign technological and economic development of competing systems is inevitable and advantageous in many cases. However, the argument given above relates to unilateral U.S. actions that have created unusually strong incentives for foreign development of competing systems and resulted in a competitive disadvantage for U.S. industry.

[35] A hint of the effects might be found in the telecommunications sector where COMSAT as the U.S. monopoly representative to Intelsat was supposed to do advanced telecommunications research and development (R&D). After COMSAT was formed, the government did not fund much new basic

research in that area. However, COMSAT, as a private company, had other research objectives, mainly developing new products rather than doing more fundamental R&D. NASA, with great political difficulty, finally did establish a new R&D program in telecommunications (the Advanced Communications Technology Satellite program) in the 1980s to attempt to catch up to other nations that had continued government funding in that area.

[36] See discussion of the French-German Symphonie satellite above.

Chapter 11

Merchant and Guardian Challenges in the Exercise of Spacepower

Scott Pace[1]

Over 20 years ago in a speech at Moscow State University, President Ronald Reagan noted the implications of space-based information technologies: "Linked by a network of satellites and fiber-optic cables, one individual with a desktop computer and a telephone commands resources unavailable to the largest governments just a few years ago. . . . Like a chrysalis, we're emerging from the economy of the Industrial Revolution."[2]

The linkages between space, information technologies, and the global economy have accelerated and become even more profound with the widespread use of global positioning system (GPS) technologies and remote sensing imagery and the deeper integration of satellites with terrestrial communications networks. Traveling toward the Earth from deep space, one encounters whole fleets of satellites in geosynchronous and polar orbits that feed and transfer information to their commercial, military, and scientific users. Even a few educational and hobbyist payloads are in orbit or hosted on other spacecraft.

Given the scope and diversity of these space systems, it is impossible to imagine the modern global economy—not to mention modern U.S. military forces—functioning without them. This dependency in turn has led to concerns about potential attacks against space systems. While media and academic debates focus on the prospect of weapons in space—in particular, the offensive application of force from space—in actuality, existing or even prospective military capabilities are nonexistent.[3] Instead, the United States has focused on improving space situational awareness, defensive counterspace (that is, protecting friendly space capabilities from

241

enemy attack or interference), and repairing military space programs that have encountered cost, schedule, and technical difficulties.

Spacepower has been a difficult concept to define even with a half-century of global experience with space flight and operations. Although the topic has been raised in professional military circles for decades, space-based forces lack widely accepted military doctrine, which is not the case for land, sea, and air forces. Part of the challenge is that space systems do not directly represent "hard" or traditional military capabilities. Rather, space systems enable these capabilities. Space systems tend to represent or imply other capabilities that may have great political significance (for example, the Soviet demonstration of its intercontinental ballistic missile [ICBM] capabilities with the launch of Sputnik and the U.S. demonstration of precision strike using GPS in the first Gulf War). These capabilities take time to comprehend and understand. Even purely civilian space activities, such as the Apollo missions to the Moon or the creation of the International Space Station, can be forms of spacepower. They shape and influence international perceptions of the United States, even though they have no direct relation to U.S. military capabilities. Finally, the ability to design, develop, and deploy space systems is also a form of economic power. Not only can U.S. entities create the hardware and integrate the systems, they also have the business management skills needed to raise funding in open markets across international boundaries.

The use of space today reflects the full range of national and international interests, and its use tomorrow likely will reflect those same interests. If humanity succeeds in expanding civilization beyond Earth, what will be the values and the national and international interests that shape the expansion? Spacepower is not the same as, and need not imply, space-based weapons (which do not exist). Nor can spacepower be considered a purely symbolic concept given the criticality of space to military and economic systems. As will be argued, spacepower will be shaped and defined by national security and commercial objectives, and more generally by the competing and cooperating interests of the public and private sectors.

What is Spacepower?

In an analogy to airpower and seapower, the term *spacepower* would seem to imply the employment of military forces operating in a distinct medium (the space environment) to achieve some national goal or military objective. A decade ago, U.S. Air Force doctrine defined *spacepower* as the "capability to exploit space forces to support national security strategy and achieve national security objectives."[4] It also defined *air and space power* as "the synergistic application of air, space, and information systems to project global strategic military power." These definitions were criticized as incomplete, as they did not capture important realities of existing and potential military space activities.[5]

First, there was the implied assumption that the identification of military space forces alone provides the necessary and sufficient conditions for understanding the strategic power of the Nation with respect to space. Yet the reality of modern space activity is that civil and commercial systems also play an important role in the Nation's space capabilities and affect their ability to achieve national security objectives. Partnerships between military, civil, and commercial communities are vital to the successful execution of national and military security strategies (for example, communications, environmental monitoring, and logistics). Thus, spacepower should be understood as more than military forces. As General Hap Arnold said of airpower: "Airpower is the total aviation activity—civilian and military, commercial and private, potential as well as existing."[6] The same thought can and should be applied to a complete definition of spacepower.

Second, the definitions implied that spacepower was focused on "global" and "strategic" concerns alone. This is understandable, as national security space capabilities (including military and intelligence uses) have historically been thought of as enabling strategic functions for nuclear operations and national-level intelligence collection, for example. This is, however, an overly narrow view that became outmoded by the first Gulf War. Through the 1990s, space capabilities were becoming increasingly visible and vital to military operations. They assisted in the execution of hostile actions but also played a role in peacekeeping and humanitarian relief. Consequently, space forces were recognized as more than a tool for achieving strategic global objectives, as was the case during the Cold War. They became an integral part of how U.S. forces operated across the spectrum.

Third, the definitions gave the impression of being taken at one point in time—that is, at the instant during which power is being projected in support of a national objective. Power can be thought of as the ability to not only employ forces but also to shape the battlespace before the initiation of conflict. As with other forms of national power, both absolute and relative capabilities are important: what are my forces capable of doing, and how do they compare with those of potential adversaries? Since spacepower is more than military forces alone, it should be understood as something that can evolve. The ability to shape the actions of others may be as significant as what can be accomplished unilaterally.[7]

As with any evolving military field, one can expect intense debates over doctrine. Like the emergence of airpower and seapower, spacepower is both similar to and different than other forms of military and national power. As the following examples illustrate, spacepower has many different facets depending on one's perspective and objectives. From the viewpoint of the tactical commander, spacepower represents capabilities that can help put "bombs on target." To the regional commander, spacepower represents capabilities that shape the entire battlespace, including the provision of logistical support and the use of joint and combined arms. The regional commander's view is broader than the lower level commander's view.[8] From the viewpoint of the President and Congress, the battlespace is only one of several areas of concern. Domestic political support, relations with allies and coalition partners, and economic conditions also must be considered. Spacepower, therefore, is connected to other forms of national power, including economic strength, scientific capabilities, and international leadership. National leaders may use military spacepower to achieve nonmilitary objectives or exploit nonmilitary capabilities to enhance military spacepower.

An assessment of spacepower should include all of the Nation's space capabilities, at all levels and timeframes, even in peacetime before conflict begins. In this regard, spacepower would be more properly defined as *the pursuit of national objectives through the medium of space and the use of space capabilities.*[9] Although broad and general, this definition focuses on national objectives, the use of space as a medium distinct from land, air, or sea, and the use of space-based capabilities. The effective exercise of spacepower may require, but is not limited to, the use of military forces.

More recent Air Force definitions of spacepower have become more inclusive:

> Space power. a. The capability to exploit space forces to support national security strategy and achieve national security objectives (Air Force Doctrine Document [AFDD] 1). b. The capability to exploit civil, commercial, intelligence, and national security space systems and associated infrastructure to support national security strategy and national objectives from peacetime through combat operations (AFDD 1–2). c. The total strength of a nation's capabilities to conduct and influence activities, to, in, through, and from space to achieve its objectives.[10]

The first definition is a traditional, military-focused one, while the second includes use of nonmilitary capabilities to achieve national security objectives. The third definition refers to the total strength of the Nation. However, there are no definitions that refer to using nonmilitary capabilities to shape the environment before conflicts occur or using military capabilities to advance nonmilitary national objectives. This chapter focuses on the nature and uses of spacepower at strategic and policy levels in both military and nonmilitary applications.

Schools of Thought in Space Advocacy

Pioneering space advocates, such as Wernher von Braun, readily adopted the idea that government can and should fund space work. In a series of articles for *Collier's* magazine in the 1950s, von Braun sketched out his vision for space development. First came orbiting satellites, followed by manned reusable vehicles, then a space station, bases on the Moon, and finally an expedition to Mars. The color drawings were vivid and realistic, and the magazine was inundated with inquiries on how one could become an astronaut. The "von Braun paradigm" of space development—represented by the step-by-step creation of reusable shuttles, space stations, lunar bases, and Mars expeditions—seemed so logical and direct that it continues to hold sway years later.[11] Over the past few decades, reports recommending future space activities have repeatedly endorsed these same basic elements, building progressively more complex capabilities on the basis of government-funded research.

Disappointment with the ending of the first lunar explorations and reduction in National Aeronautics and Space Administration (NASA) spending in the 1970s led space advocates to form educational and advocacy organizations, including the National Space Institute and the L5 Society. The latter was particularly interesting in that it did not advocate a variation of the von Braun paradigm but rather envisioned creating large settlements in free space, mining the Moon and asteroids for resources, and constructing solar-power satellites to beam energy back to Earth. In reaction in part to the "Limits to Growth" arguments, which predicted a looming disaster due to overpopulation, accelerated industrialization, malnutrition, dwindling resources, and a deteriorating environment, these advocates saw space as a means to adventure and a solution to environmental and natural resource problems on Earth.[12] American space advocates typically shared the view that human expansion into space was both desirable and inevitable. This new form of manifest destiny was consistent with U.S. history. The frontier always has been viewed as a utopian wilderness, ripe for satisfying various philosophical and emotional needs, while at the same time being subject to extensive military and economic government interventions to meet those needs.[13] Examples of government interventions on the frontier include land grants, support for education and transcontinental railways, and the use of the Army to protect settlers and traders.[14] In contrast to the westward expansion across North America between 1800 and 1890, however, much more substantial technical, economic, and political constraints exist that hinder space development. These constraints quite literally create higher barriers to entry. This has prompted some advocates to support greater government spending, while others have looked to private enterprise to "open the frontier."

In the 1980s, President Ronald Reagan called for a Strategic Defense Initiative to use space weapons to defend the Nation from ballistic missile attacks. Multiple groups formed educational organizations, such as High Frontier, to support space development as part of a stronger national defense. In a variation on the von Braun paradigm, advocates supported the creation of massive launch systems and a space infrastructure to support a global defense network. With this infrastructure in place, other space activities, such as mining the Moon or sending probes farther into the solar system, would become easier and more affordable.

A common thread running through the various "post-Apollo" visions was the need for a revolutionary effort, like Apollo, to meet some overarching goal. In some cases, the motivation was to solve an energy crisis; in others, it was to defeat a military threat. The L5 Society thought that space could be colonized by a large number of people who could create whole new societies and earn their way through exports of energy back to Earth. But even they saw the need for government involvement and leadership to start the process. While the details may vary, the fundamental rationale for a national-level space effort has remained unchanged. The Nation pursues space as a way to secure scientific knowledge, security, international cooperation, and other benefits to humanity.

Meanwhile, new commercial space capabilities grew independently of the government, and now commercial investment exceeds government spending (civil and military) on space.[15] Rather than a government-driven, revolutionary development, the growth of space commerce has been largely a market-driven, evolutionary one. Given the cost of access to space, it is not surprising that the primary "cargo" now being transported between Earth and space is massless photons carrying bits of data. But these bits are part of a larger global information infrastructure that has created a new "skin" for the planet. Some of this skin is buried under the sea and underground in cables; some of it is composed of microwave relays and cellular phone networks; and some of it is in orbit, consisting of communications, GPS, and remote sensing satellites. Some of these satellites are purely commercial, while others are government-owned but used by private companies for commercial applications. The term *dual-use* in space systems, therefore, encompasses both "civil-military" and "public-private" applications.

The growth of commercial space capabilities calls attention to the interplay between public and private interests in dual-use space technologies, which include launch services, communications, navigation, and remote sensing. These technologies have great potential to shape which national capabilities actually occur and whether American interests are advanced or harmed as they are adopted in global markets. In contrast to when the von Braun paradigm was created, the size and scope of commercial space activity are immense. Events such as SpaceShipOne's 2004 suborbital flight and Bigelow Aerospace's 2006 demonstration of an inflatable structure in space, and private financing of new launch vehicles, such as SpaceX's Falcon, indicate the increasing sophistication of space entrepreneurs. The combination of well-established industries and dynamic new entrants is creating opportunities for governments as well. The Defense Department hopes to use the Falcon launch vehicle for small payloads, and NASA hopes to buy commercial launch services to support the International Space Station after the administration retires the space shuttle in 2010. Public interest in space tourism was not created by government policy; private citizens have expressed a desire to travel to space and have spent millions of dollars of their own money for the privilege. This interest could some day evolve into a viable market that will attract entrepreneurs, who in turn may create capabilities that governments can use without having to pay for their development.

Single government projects by themselves may be vital, but they are not always interesting or indicative of future challenges. Many commercial activities rely on government policies and actions, but they are independent of government command or direct control. Markets, funding, and even technologies are almost completely international. Government spending, while still dominant in many space markets, is not as important or even as attractive as it once was. As a consequence, it is insufficient to focus only on government space programs and budgets. Space analysts and policymakers need to address the more subtle relations between government actions and private markets. New schools of thought are needed that recognize a greater role for the private sector in creating and sustaining capabilities relevant to the Nation's spacepower.

Two Cultures: Merchants and Guardians

The scope and size of public-private interactions in space have implications for space doctrine, advocacy, and policy. Some of these interactions arise from debates over the choice of mechanisms, markets, or governments for accomplishing some objective.[16] For example, to what extent should the government rely on commercial space services, such as communications satellites or expendable launch vehicles? To what extent should the government provide space-based navigation and environmental monitoring services, which have commercial applications? Other interactions concern the competitiveness of commercial capabilities and how their viability affects choices by foreign governments. For example, can the proliferation of ballistic missile technologies be discouraged by the availability of low-cost launch services? What restrictions should be applied to private remote sensing activities if a country objects to having its territory imaged? Finally, some interactions affect common needs, such as international security, global trade, and even the radio spectrum. Does the widespread availability of Earth remote sensing data enhance regional stability? What restrictions, if any, should apply to sales of launch services from nonmarket economies? How should the use of the radio spectrum by public safety and national security organizations be protected from commercial interests and vice versa?

Public policy choices, whether those of the U.S. Government, foreign governments, or the international community in general, are subject to many distinct influences. Perhaps the most pervasive influences, however, are the underlying assumptions the public and private sectors bring to these choices. These assumptions constitute what has been termed as two cultures, those of the *Guardians* and those of the *Merchants*.[17] The term *Guardians* comes from Plato's *The Republic*. It includes members of the political class who are responsible for governing and teaching. In space policy, one finds many examples of Guardians, good and bad, among career civil servants, military officers, political appointees, congressional staff, journalists, academics, and even the occasional corporate officer and professional politician. The term *Merchants* refers to the group of people whose culture encourages energy and risk-taking. Although examples are mostly found in business and to a lesser extent in international science, they sometimes are represented in government, the military, and academia.

Merchant behavior is found in peaceful competition; contracts and the ability to work with strangers are accepted as normal parts of commerce. People divided by language, ethnicity, and distance will come together in a marketplace, if nowhere else, to trade. Relationships need not be permanent, outside of family, but rather flexible and transitory as necessary to make mutually beneficial deals. This flexibility creates opportunities for social movement, the absorption of immigrants, and invention. The motto "city air is free air" arose in the Middle Ages. It recognized a society free from the restrictions imposed by nobility and the church.

The role of Guardians is to protect some larger goal or system, such as society, the government, or a political philosophy. As a consequence of their public functions, Guardians are expected to be loyal, obedient, and disciplined. To avoid corruption and treason, they are enjoined from engaging in trade. To ensure that political decisions are carried out, they must respect hierarchy and the decisions made by recognized authorities. These are not necessarily modern or Western concepts. The samurai of feudal Japan were forbidden to engage in trade, just as tradesmen were forbidden to own weapons. One of the main features of a functioning government is an effective monopoly on the exercise of force. This monopoly enables Guardians to carry out other state functions. They can impose and collect taxes, establish rules and regulations, and negotiate agreements with other states.

The roles of Guardians and Merchants are in tension, but intimately linked. For the "invisible hand" of Adam Smith's market economy to function, a predictable, supportive environment must exist to create wealth. The creation and maintenance of such an environment requires the use of government power as the hidden (or sometimes overt) fist to enable the rule of law. Ideally, the need for actual force is minimized when the consent of the governed is secured via a democratic process. Whether by diplomats or soldiers, it is government power that establishes justice and provides for the common defense. Even the staunchest advocates of limited government recognize the need for preventing cases of force (by protecting against criminal violence or military aggression) and fraud (through enforcement of contracts). Thus, the key characteristics of the West—democracy, a liberal, pluralistic civil society, and capitalism—are shaped by the competition and cooperation of Merchant and Guardian cultures.

While both Guardians and Merchants may be necessary to society, they can create serious problems when they either fail to do their duty or seek to take on the role of the other. In space policy, these problems arise when the government conducts space transportation and communications or other commercial-like activities. Similarly, conflicts occur when the government does not carry out its duties and inhibits industry. Failing to uphold regulations or respond to complaints of unfair competition from foreign governments is a good example. Conversely, Merchants should not be made responsible for Guardian functions. For space activities, these can mean the enforcement of export controls, the negotiation of international spectrum allocations, or even the conduct of crucial military functions (for example, missile warnings). This is not to say Merchants cannot be patriotic or reliable, but their functions require the public service traits of a Guardian culture.

It has been said that the environments of business and government are alike in all the unimportant ways. Civil servants and businesspeople may use the same telephones and office software, occupy similar offices and parking spaces, read the same newspapers, and even attend the same churches. But their daily work and worldviews are likely alien to each other. Businesspeople in foreign countries are likely to speak a common cultural language, just as civil servants and soldiers find common touchstones with their foreign counterparts. Conversations across these separate cultures can avoid mutual incomprehension if they first recognize that they possess distinct worldviews and personalities.

"Merchants and Guardians" in the 21st Century

In the 10 years since the original presentation of the "Merchants and Guardians" paper,[18] several dramatic events have occurred, notably the 2001 attacks on New York and Washington and the global war on terrorism, the 2003 loss of the space shuttle *Columbia*, and President Bush's 2004 speech on the "Vision for Space Exploration." Over the same period, conditions in the commercial space industry have evolved greatly. Space-based information systems have continued to grow, with direct TV, direct audio broadcasting, and ancillary terrestrial components to mobile satellite services (MSS) filling in for the collapse of overly optimistic MSS expectations. After emerging from bankruptcy, Iridium and Globalstar are today serving customers worldwide. A new generation of better financed entrepreneurs is developing suborbital and orbital launch vehicles and Soyuz-based tourist flights to the International Space Station. The provision of these services has become a familiar, if not routine, occurrence. The prospects of space tourism are being taken more seriously, and as a result, commercial space ventures are starting to progress beyond the movement of photons (information) and into the movement of actual mass, including people.

The most significant event for the civil space sector was the loss on reentry of *Columbia* on February 1, 2003. As in the case of the *Challenger* accident, the tragic loss of the crew and one-fourth of the Nation's shuttle fleet led to a deep reexamination of why the United States was risking human lives in space. In the aftermath of *Challenger*, President Reagan directed NASA to use the space shuttle only to launch those satellites that could not use commercial launch services. Human lives would not be risked to perform tasks that could be done just as effectively by unmanned rockets. This action also eliminated the shuttle as a source of government competition to commercial suppliers and helped to jump-start a viable commercial launch industry.

In the aftermath of the tragedy, the *Columbia* Accident Investigation Board (CAIB) criticized NASA not only for the technical failures leading to the accident, but also for a lack of national focus and rationale for risking human life. In its report, the CAIB observed that there had been a "lack, over the past three decades, of any national mandate providing NASA a compelling mission requiring human presence in space."[19] So while the *Challenger* accident resulted in a decision forbidding the risking of human life for certain purposes, the *Columbia* accident raised the question: for what purposes was human life worth risking? These questions sparked internal White House discussions during the fall of 2003, which were expanded to include NASA and other agencies.[20] The answer was provided in President Bush's January 14, 2004, announcement at NASA headquarters of a new "Vision for Space Exploration." With the completion of the International Space Station, the shuttle program would end in 2010, and a new generation of spacecraft would conduct a "sustained and affordable human and robotic program to explore the solar system and beyond."[21] If human lives were to be placed at risk, the potential gain would be commensurate and require explorations beyond low Earth orbit.

Congress later endorsed the objectives of the President's speech in the passage of the 2005 NASA Authorization. After a prolonged start-up phase in 2004, as NASA considered a range of technologies and options to fulfill the direction of the President and Congress, work accelerated with the arrival of Michael Griffin as the new NASA administrator in April 2005. He summarized the proposition of the "Vision for Space Exploration" in a speech before the National Space Club on February 9, 2006:

> We assume risk in human spaceflight because leadership in this endeavor is a strategic imperative for the United States. . . . Our Nation needed to decide whether the goals and benefits of human spaceflight were commensurate with the costs and risks of this enterprise, and that for this to be true, those goals must lie beyond the simple goals achievable in low-Earth orbit. . . . The Agency is directed to "establish a program to develop a

sustained human presence on the Moon, including a robust precursor program, to promote exploration, science, commerce, and United States preeminence in space, and as a stepping stone to future exploration of Mars and other destinations". . . . We will do these things in concert with other nations having similar interests and values. And, as we look forward to the events that will define this century and beyond, I have no doubt that the expansion of human presence into the solar system will be among the greatest of our achievements.[22]

During 2005, NASA defined its architecture for returning humans to the Moon. The agency designed a new generation of launch vehicles for taking humans and cargo to space, including a heavy-lift cargo launcher that would play a vital role in sending humans to Mars. In contrast to the von Braun paradigm, NASA's exploration plans build new capabilities gradually and incrementally to adapt to changing budget priorities. In essence, it is a "go-as-you-pay" philosophy. These plans also make more intentional use of commercial capabilities. The largest single example is the $500-million Commercial Orbital Transportation Services (COTS) program to help develop commercial sources of crew and cargo services for the International Space Station. In August 2006, NASA selected SpaceX and Rocketplane Kistler to develop and demonstrate their vehicles with partial NASA support. Under the Space Act Agreements, the work will be performed before a competitive award of service contracts. If successful, commercial suppliers could help support the International Space Station after NASA completes the shuttle assembly missions. They also could provide alternatives to the use of foreign launch systems. This would in turn free up the shuttle's planned follow-on systems, including the Crew Launch Vehicle (Aries) and Crew Exploration Vehicles (Orion), to support lunar operations.

The "Vision for Space Exploration" is an example of the use of spacepower to achieve national objectives. While the NASA effort is exclusively civil, the capabilities created have the potential to advance U.S. economic, foreign policy, and national security objectives. The process of creating new technologies and systems to operate routinely on the Moon will enable the Nation to venture farther into the solar system—exploring, using local resources, learning new skills, and making new discoveries. In the broadest sense, the "Vision for Space Exploration" is not about repeating Apollo. In the words of the President's science advisor, John Marburger, it seeks to "incorporate the Solar System in our economic sphere."[23] Thus, the civil space strategy chosen by the United States can be seen as an effort to advance national interests of a Guardian culture, while using the narrower interests of a Merchant culture. Commercial capabilities strengthen the Nation's space abilities; they also deepen the Nation's interest in securing and protecting any resulting economic benefits.

U.S. national space policy has routinely recognized three distinct sectors of space activity: national security (military, intelligence), commercial, and civil (including both scientific research and services, such as weather forecasting).[24] The functions performed by each can be organized along a spectrum, depending on whether they are driven by governments or markets. Satellite communications occupy one end of the spectrum and are largely driven by commercial interests, such as numbers of customers, revenue, and the deployment of new technologies. At the other end are force applications that include space-based weapons and ballistic missile defense systems. Although they may use commercially derived technologies, they are driven by political-military requirements. In the middle are civil government functions that involve public safety. These include weather monitoring and navigation. These positions are not static; they can change over time. For example, GPS was developed to meet military requirements, but civil and commercial entities developed many useful applications of the technology. Space launch capabilities are considered to underlie all space activities and are thus a primary concern for all sectors.

Government and commercial interests in space technologies, systems, and services can intersect. They can be categorized in three segments. First, there are those that only the government would require due to their associated high costs or specialized nature. Examples include space-qualified fission-power reactors and space-based observatories. Interactions are at government direction, mainly through contracts and grants. Second, there are segments dominated by the private sector due to the size of global markets and diffusion of underlying technologies. Examples of this segment include information technologies and biotechnologies. Governments are important for a variety of purposes but do not exercise control. Interactions can be more commercial-like, particularly where the government is another customer or partner. Third, there are gray areas, namely launch services, navigation, and remote sensing. The government is crucial, but not dominant. In these cases, the government may play the role of the research and development patron, anchor customer, service provider, and regulator. It is in these gray areas where the Merchant and Guardian cultures are more likely to clash because of evolving and changing roles. Such clashes can be expected to continue as human activity expands beyond low Earth orbit.

In its major outlines, U.S. space policy has remained remarkably stable since the end of the Cold War. The 2006 National Space Policy of the Bush administration can be seen as a continuation of the 1996 National Space Policy of the Bill Clinton administration, which in turn continued many of the themes of the 1989 National Space Policy of the George H.W. Bush administration. Much of the media commentary after the release of the 2006 policy focused not so much on substance as on presentation and tonal differences, particularly with respect to U.S. national security interests. Foreign governments expressed concern with the new policy, which prompted State Department Under Secretary Robert Joseph to state:

> At its most basic level, U.S. space policy has not changed significantly from the beginning of our ventures into space. Consistent with past policies, the United States does not monopolize space; we do not deny access to space for peaceful purposes by other nations. Rather, we explore and use space for the benefit of the entire world. This remains a central principle of our policy. What the new policy reflects, however, are increased actions to ensure the long-term security of our space assets in light of new threats and as a result of our increased use of space.[25]

In addition to stressing increased U.S. reliance on space assets and clarifying what the new policy did not mean, Joseph tried to bring attention to items that were novel: "The new policy also gives prominence to several goals only touched upon in previous policy documents, including: strengthening the space science and technology base, developing space professionals, and strengthening U.S. industrial competitiveness, especially through use of U.S. commercial space capabilities."

Not surprisingly, these are areas of great common interest for the public and private sectors and areas of friction between the Merchant and Guardian cultures. In addition, the 2006 policy included the need to assure "reliable access to and use of radio frequency spectrum and orbital assignments," which is a logical corollary to ensuring access to the space assets themselves. One cannot run wires to satellites; therefore, spectrum access and protection are of crucial importance, perhaps second only to the launch itself.

A comparison of the 1999 discussion of "Merchant and Guardian" policy conflicts with those seen today reveals many recurring issues. Spectrum management and the burden of export controls remain important, while concerns about competition from nonmarket economies seem to have abated—perhaps as a side effect of continuing export control limitations. However, there is increased interest in space tourism and related regulations, particularly with the 2004 flight of SpaceShipOne and the 2006 coverage of space tourist Anousheh Ansari. The prospect of commercial involvement in lunar operations, in addition to commercial supply of the International Space Station, has led to renewed discussions of private property rights on the Moon and other celestial bodies (to be discussed below).

In recent years, the national security space sector has not experienced developments as outwardly dramatic as those occurring in the commercial and civil space sectors, which have included everything from major accidents and Presidential initiatives to mass media interest. However, the implications of these developments to national security space are just as important, if not more so, for the Nation's spacepower. The past decade has seen a growing concern with the ability of the Defense Department to develop and deploy space systems on time and on budget. Difficulties with major missile warning, communications, and imagery programs, just to name a few, have been widely reported in the press, although specific details are usually highly classified. Even relatively mature programs, such as GPS, have faced difficulties keeping to modernization schedules due to changing requirements, contractor difficulties, and gaps in system engineering expertise. So severe are these difficulties that the U.S. Air Force is reportedly considering "hiring outside engineers or consultants to oversee systems integration of its next-generation navigational satellites."[26]

In fact, most of the new initiatives in the 2006 National Space Policy address four areas now considered to be serious problems for the U.S. Government: developing a high-quality cadre of space professionals, improving development and procurement systems for space systems, enhancing interagency cooperation, and strengthening the space science, technology, and industrial base.[27] Thus, while international media coverage painted the United States as taking a more aggressive military posture in space, the substance of the policy reflected problems in military acquisition programs that in turn stem from deficiencies in government management and contractor capabilities. It is not so much a question of which military capabilities the United States *wants* to deploy in space, but rather which capabilities it *can* employ, and whether they are commensurate with the threats and critical dependencies faced by the United States. Rather than the deployment of space-based weapons, as was contemplated during the Cold War, the immediate concerns of the military space sector are more basic. Can the military deliver space-derived services to deployed forces? Can it improve space situational awareness? And can the military get acquisition programs under control?

The organizational challenges for U.S. military spacepower are formidable and too extensive to be treated in this chapter. However, as with all other parts of the national security community, the attacks of September 11 and the conflicts in Afghanistan and Iraq have affected U.S. spacepower in three important areas: capabilities, objectives, and relations with allies and partners.

First, space capabilities have been and will continue to be crucial to almost all types of military operations, in all regions, and at all levels of conflict. That said, fiscal and technological limitations make it impossible to create space capabilities ideally suited to all conflicts in all regions, and choices must be made in what to buy and field. This in turn requires choosing among different U.S. military strategy objectives and the consequent force infrastructure to implement that strategy. Prosecuting a conventional conflict against one or more states, up to and including a peer competitor,[28] is very different than fighting nonstate actors, rebuilding failed states, and carrying out operations other than war. Uncertainties over strategy objectives create tensions between funding development and operations, between competing technologies, and between which armed services, contractors, and parts of the industrial base should receive resources and attention. It would be easier if the United States could afford two different but interoperable force structures. However, it cannot, and space systems are caught in the debate over objectives.

Second, unrelated to the September 11 attacks, the U.S. defense industrial base has experienced a dramatic consolidation since the end of the Cold War. On one hand, U.S. defense spending is very large—by some estimates almost half of global total spending.[29] On the other, like all U.S. industries, defense and space firms have been affected by globalization. New international competitors, increased competition for talent, and concern over market access have become issues. The size and sophistication of U.S. military capabilities, in particular the use of space systems, has made it difficult for all but a few countries (such as the United Kingdom, Australia, and North Atlantic Treaty Organization members) to operate easily with U.S. forces. The problems of the U.S. space industrial base cannot be solved by going outside the United States, even if the country wanted to.

Comparable sources for the capabilities that the United States needs simply do not exist.

Third, given the divergent but overlapping interests of Merchant and Guardian cultures engaged in space activity, uncertainty over national security objectives, and challenges to the creation of military space capabilities, it is increasingly important that the United States find partners to help shape the global environment before conflict occurs. Potential partners include public and private actors, international civil agencies, and foreign militaries. Shaping the environment means creating mutually beneficial relationships to reduce unintentional as well as intentional threats to crucial space dependencies. Examples include international protection of the space spectrum from interference, effective international enforcement of missile proliferation controls, promotion of common protocols to enhance interoperability of space-based communications, remote sensing and navigation services, and rules for international trade in space-related goods and services. While these steps may benefit foreign countries and companies, they would be even more beneficial to the United States given the country's reliance on space for economic stability and security.

One of the newer and perhaps more difficult areas of conflict between Merchants and Guardians will be that of protecting commercial space infrastructure. As the U.S. military and economy rely more heavily on space, it is natural to worry about potential threats to the infrastructure, just as one might worry about critical ground-based infrastructure. Yet what can or should be done to protect those assets? Should they be hardened or made redundant? Should they carry sensors to warn of attack? Should the protected entity pay for the protection, or should the U.S. Government provide the enhanced security as a public good and cover the costs with tax money? What about internationally financed space infrastructure, which is practically everything commercial in orbit? It is easy to imagine the commercial sector resisting what it would perceive as new regulatory burdens or an "unfunded mandate." Likewise, it is easy to imagine the Defense Department's reluctance to absorb new costs when existing programs face difficulties. Yet the result for failing to protect these assets may be increased vulnerability of the United States and a threat to its ability to exercise spacepower.

To summarize, events over the past several years have accelerated and intensified trends observed in the 1990s. They have shaped public and private sector interactions in space. As a result, leading challenges to the Merchant and Guardian relationship now include:

■ globalization and the characteristics of a "Flat World." This means that technology, capital, and talent move ever more freely and can create competitors to government programs.[30] This is true even in the space world, with American tourists flying on Russian rockets, with small satellites being built from Surrey to Bangalore, and with European-Chinese collaborations to build constellations of navigation-satellite systems.

■ increased government dependence on commercial space capabilities. This has created new concerns, in addition to traditional government resistance to the loss of control over independent commercial space markets.

■ a recognizable loss of government "intellectual property" necessary to develop, oversee, and manage complex space systems. NASA is somewhat better positioned than the Air Force due to the talent of its field-center personnel. But NASA's workforce is getting older, and the agency has limited ability to hire. For Apollo, NASA was able to import skilled systems engineers from the Air Force's ICBM programs. That, however, is not an option today. NASA is trying to rebuild its internal systems engineering skills, and the Defense Department is proposing to create a new cadre of technical "space professionals."

■ a competitive environment and limited resources. Today, execution is the paramount policy issue. So to whom does spacepower flow? More than likely, it will be to those who can deliver capabilities necessary to meet threats or exploit opportunities— whether they are military, economic, scientific, or political.

The Guardians within the U.S. space community are facing great difficulties, but the Merchants also are vulnerable. Weakness in security can be destabilizing because it invites opportunistic attacks and changes the deterrence calculations of adversaries. Weakness in commerce can cause commercial losses as well as longer term damage, especially if weak Guardians allow market distortions to persist because they fail to enforce international trade rules, spectrum regulations, intellectual property protections, and even export controls. In short, globalization is creating greater interdependency between the public and private sectors, not less.

Space Exploration and Spacepower

In spite of uncertainties and challenges in the national security sector, the Nation's interest in pursuing military spacepower is unquestioned. Similarly, the demands of a competitive global economy underscore the national interest in maintaining space-based information systems—most of which are dual use in nature (such as GPS, remote sensing, and communications). Separate from the military and commercial needs are the scientific ones. Although science and exploration are not required to ensure spacepower, the pursuit of knowledge can be seen as a discretionary activity that great nations undertake to help define their society, enhance their international prestige, and create new technologies to benefit people worldwide. What, then, is the enduring role of science and exploration in the spacepower of the Nation?

The Cold War and competition with the Soviet Union for technological preeminence drove the Apollo, Gemini, and Mercury programs. Despite the desires of space advocates for the robust industrialization and settlement of space, the United States had not made their aspirations a compelling national interest. Even though the military and commercial sectors benefit enormously from space, it is not impossible to imagine a nation retreating from human spaceflight once it achieved the capability. That was not the case for the former Soviet Union. Even during the most extreme economic turmoil following the fall of communism, Russia did not abandon human spaceflight. In fact, it strived to maintain its program through every possible means. The U.S. "Vision for Space Exploration" is neither Apollo redux nor a commercial venture, and debates among space advocates continue over its purpose and meaning. It is therefore instructive to understand differing perceptions of the rationale for U.S. space exploration plans.

Only tiny minorities of those engaged in space-related policy debates oppose government-funded space activities. Those who do are more concerned with particular uses and technologies, namely nuclear power, space-based weapons, and ballistic missile defenses. In fact, apathy and taking space capabilities for granted are arguably greater problems than direct opposition. At the risk of oversimplification, if not caricature, at least five different schools of thought have evolved from discussions about the priorities of human exploration of the Moon, Mars, and beyond, and how the Nation should carry out the program.

Baseline

The first school is that NASA itself is simply responding to the 2004 direction of President Bush and the 2005 NASA Authorization Act. The

United States is fulfilling its commitments to its partners under the International Space Station agreements, ending the space shuttle program in 2010 once NASA completes assembling the space station, building a new generation of launch vehicles to ferry crew and cargo to space after the shuttle retires, establishing an outpost on the Moon, and laying the foundations for human expeditions to Mars—all while maintaining a diverse program of scientific research. Given limited budgets, the program is a "go-as-you-pay" effort, and programmatic priorities follow the policy priorities defined by the President and Congress. Given those same limited resources, NASA is open to international cooperation and commercial partnerships in all areas—with the exception of core launch and communications/navigation capabilities that are so strategic as to require avoiding foreign dependency.

Technology First

The second school argues that the United States does not have the technology to return to the Moon and travel to Mars, at least in a way that will be sustainable and affordable. Thus, the Nation should make the funding and development of new technologies the first priority and not commit to a specific architecture until several years from now. Arguably, NASA tried this approach for about a year after President Bush's speech, generating many interesting ideas and concepts. But the lack of tangible momentum was unsatisfactory to the White House and Congress. Upon confirmation in 2005, the new NASA administrator initiated a 90-day Exploration Systems Architecture Study precisely to help define a specific architecture for implementing human missions to the Moon. Funds were shifted from technology development to pay for new launch vehicles that were based on shuttle components and workforce skills.

Science First

This school argues that supporting peer-reviewed science should be the highest priority of NASA and that by implication, exploration efforts are little more than government-funded "tourism." Peer review is seen as providing the most objective assurance of quality; consequently, civil space activities not subject to peer review are seen, almost by definition, as less worthy. More practically, supporters of this school will say they are not intrinsically opposed to exploration because it may generate new opportunities for scientific research. However, they do not believe that funds should be shifted from science missions to pay for exploration. To fund the development of a new launch vehicle while maintaining the shuttle and space station programs, however, NASA chose to slow the rate of growth of science spending to 1 percent over the next several years. In previous budgets, the science community had planned for increases of up to 5 percent for a few years and then 2.4 percent per year as NASA's top line grew with inflation. This slower rate of growth required deferring several planned missions to keep international partner commitments on the space station. The resulting unhappiness with this decision was understandable, but it also reflected a fundamental difference in policy priorities for government funding.

Commercial First

This school is an example of Merchant culture. It argues that the government is so incapable of or grossly inefficient in the creation of space capabilities, especially compared with the private sector, that it should take an entirely different approach to human spaceflight. Instead of development contracts with government oversight, NASA should offer contracts for services, prizes, and other "pay-on-delivery" mechanisms to excite entrepreneurs. The rationale is that this will attract more private capital, create more diverse solutions, and offer a better chance of success than a government "all-eggs-in-one-basket" approach. NASA is seeking to test this argument in part through the COTS program but is hedging its bets (post-shuttle) by having multiple backups for space station supply (use of the Crew Launch Vehicle, Russian launchers). Advocates of this school have argued that the very act of having backups shows NASA is insufficiently committed to commercial sources and therefore is deterring investments that would otherwise occur. Given the policy priorities of the President and Congress, however, it is hard to see how NASA could do otherwise than to hedge its bets. Again, this school reflects a fundamental difference in policy objectives for exploration—in this case, the highest good is growing commercial capabilities rather than doing science.

Regional Interests

The fifth school is a form of the old adage, "All politics is local." The primary concern lies with where the government spends its money. States with NASA field centers and major contracts can be expected to support programs that build on existing capabilities. This is not necessarily a bad thing, as minimizing new developments can help control costs. On the other hand, it can cause political resistance, especially if NASA tries to move work from one center to take advantage of workforce skills and efficiencies at another. Therefore, debates over program priorities will be less about policy or products and more about process and the impact on the workforce. As with the "science first" and "commercial first" schools, giving priority to regional interests can result in misdirecting resources. It places parochial interests above national interests and national spacepower.

These differing forms of advocacy for space exploration can obviously affect how NASA pursues international and commercial partnerships. While technological, regional, and scientific advocates can be expected to be lukewarm to government-to-government international cooperation in exploration, the reality of limited budgets and need for such cooperation would suggest that these types of advocates would not be opposed. Even so, the Merchant culture of commercial advocates can be expected to be skeptical of contributions from other governments on a nonmarket basis. For them, it is the process by which space capabilities are acquired, not the product, that matters. In other words, government competition should be opposed. This is another area of Merchant and Guardian conflict. It would be worthwhile for NASA to explain, multiple times if need be, what it sees as a proper role of government in space exploration. Examples could include being a patron of science and other activities, being a reliable customer of commercially available goods and services, and being a fair and transparent regulator to ensure national security and public safety.

Given the competing views, even among space exploration advocates, what does this say about the sustainability of an exploration enterprise that requires several decades? Again at the risk of caricature, advocates of long-term, civil space exploration tend to fall into different camps based on their underlying values. The traditional von Braun paradigm represents a Guardian approach. It sees space exploration as a government activity that adds indirectly to the spacepower of the Nation via new technologies, dual-use capabilities, and increased international influence. There are established government and private-sector interest groups that promote funding for technologies, systems, and partnerships with near-term benefits, especially scientific ones.

Astronomer and author Carl Sagan was an advocate of robotic exploration of the solar system and the search for extraterrestrial intelligence. He also was an advocate of human spaceflight for one fundamental reason:

> every surviving civilization is obliged to become spacefaring—
> not because of exploratory or romantic zeal, but for the most
> practical reason imaginable: staying alive. . . . The more of us

beyond the Earth, the greater the diversity of worlds we inhabit . . . then the safer the human species will be.[31]

While initially skeptical of the scientific value of human spaceflight, Sagan became an advocate for noncommercial and nonmilitary reasons. The use of robots to obtain scientific knowledge was well and good, but humanity itself had a transcendent value, and human spaceflight could contribute to its survival. This Sagan paradigm is very much a Guardian approach, but one that does not yet have an established base in or outside of government, as the potential benefits are beyond the planning horizons of governments, not to mention industry.

Gerard O'Neill was a physicist and author who became an advocate of space colonies, not necessarily on the Moon or Mars, but in free space. He proposed using space resources, via mining the Moon and asteroids, to construct large space habitats and solar-powered satellites to beam energy back to Earth.[32] Space development, rather than space exploration, was the focus. It was to be carried out by private companies and quasi-government corporations. In addition to the practical benefits of tapping space resources and energy, the O'Neill paradigm envisioned opportunities in the image of the American frontier. The images of self-sustaining human space settlements appeal to both Merchant and Guardian cultures and with plausible, nearer term steps. Beyond just survival, the O'Neill image offered a way to advance American (or Western, to be more general) values beyond Earth. Unfortunately, the economics of the O'Neill scenario are not realizable with current space capabilities. Even so, the attraction of this encompassing paradigm is as powerful today among space advocates as the one advocated by von Braun.

The point of reviewing the varying visions of space exploration and development is to observe that each represents decades-long efforts. They are adaptable and could persist even in the face of temporary political or fiscal setbacks. Like the "Vision for Space Exploration," they represent directions and purposes to which many different types of space activity could make contributions.

The space capabilities implied by successful space settlements, particularly those in which the United States is a leader, also represent a gigantic increase in the Nation's spacepower. Unfortunately, it is not clear that such capabilities are realizable, although many advocates believe they are. Two important questions are: can humans "live off the land" in space and function independently of Earth for long periods, and are there economically useful activities in space that can sustain human communities there?

If the answer to both questions is *yes*, then the long-term future in space includes human space settlements. If the answer to both is *no*, then space remains a place that one might visit briefly for science or tourism, much like going to Mount Everest or other remote locations. If the answer is that one can, in part, live off the land or at least be reliably supplied, then one can imagine space as akin to Antarctica—a place for science, tourism, and habitation by government employees and contractors. Finally, if one cannot live off the land, but the tasks to be performed are economically attractive, then one can imagine habitats like the North Sea oil platforms. These locations may be privately owned and operated, but they cannot really be called settlements (see table 11–1).

Table 11–1. Viability of Space Settlement

	Can live off land/be supplied	Cannot live off land
Nothing commerically useful	Antarctica	Mount Everest
Commercially sustainable	Settlements	North Sea oil platform

These outcomes do not preclude other motivations, such as protection of Earth from hazardous asteroids or the protection of U.S. and allied space infrastructure from hostile attacks. The point is, we do not know which of these outcomes represents our long-term future. Advocates and skeptics may believe one outcome or another is most likely, but no one actually knows. Determining the future of humans in space would be a watershed event not only for spacepower, but also for the United States and humanity. Just as space science can be organized around great questions (How did the solar system form? Is there life elsewhere in the universe?), so might human spaceflight be organized to answer similarly great questions. One of the purposes of human spaceflight is to explore the unknown and see what humans are capable of doing, where they are capable of going, and what communities they can sustain. Taking risks to get that knowledge would seem to be a worthwhile activity for nations that are technically sophisticated and wealthy enough to do so.

Policy Challenges for the Second Space Age

The period from the launch of Sputnik to the last Apollo mission can be considered the first space age—driven by Cold War competition across civil and military sectors. It is unclear when the second space age might begin; some say it started with the launch of the space shuttle, and others say it will start with the end of shuttle flights in 2010. More commercial and international involvement, as well as deep cooperation and conflict across public and private sectors, will characterize the second space age and the role of Merchant and Guardian cultures.

With stable national space policies, many old debates have long remained settled. Save for historians, it is difficult to recall the intense debates over military versus civilian leadership in human spaceflight in the 1960s or the U.S. Government's resistance to commercial space innovations in the 1980s. New debates over spacepower in the second space age will reflect both the growing strength of the Merchants and the worrying weaknesses of the Guardians. As discussed earlier, government space programs are increasingly facing difficulties in delivering capabilities on time and on budget. Limited fiscal resources and concerns over lack of management skills have stoked interest in outsourcing and privatizing government space functions (for example, launch communications, remote sensing, and navigation). Whether it makes sense to change responsibilities for some or any of these functions will make for much debate.

The civil space sector, notably NASA, also sees potential advantages in relying more on the private sector for launch services and other operational capabilities. At the same time, the private sector is looking to open new markets, particularly in the area of space tourism. These markets are not directly of interest to the government, but the dual-use capabilities they could support are. The ongoing issue for the civil space sector likely will be what kinds of mutual interest there might be in human space exploration for the commercial, scientific, international, and perhaps the national security communities. Exploration can be hard to justify on commercial, military, or even purely scientific grounds (one will not find "exploration" among the top priorities of the decadal surveys done by the National Academy of Sciences), but the conduct of exploration can create opportunities for commercial, scientific, and even military interests. Identifying and acting on those mutual interests will be an ongoing part of the second space age as the United States establishes a lunar outpost and prepares for Mars.

The priority for NASA when it returns to the Moon for the first time in decades will be to do so successfully, safely, and affordably. In moving beyond the space shuttle and low Earth orbit operations, NASA is effectively learning to fly again. Just as Gemini was a necessary forerunner to Apollo, so too is the Moon a necessary precursor to Mars. Not only technologies but also organizational and management skills need to be demonstrated. The International Space Station was, and is, a massive educational experience in the assembly and operation of a multinational space facility, and the establishment of a lunar outpost will be as well. This effort will be different from the space station, however. Both international and commercial partners will be involved.

Commercial involvement in a return to the Moon has been the subject of much speculation, but little is definitive.[33] Proposals have been made for extracting platinum metals to use in commercial fuel cells as part of a global hydrogen economy, mining of helium-3 for fusion reactors, and the construction of solar-power beaming stations on the lunar surface or in free space using lunar materials. Other proposals see commercial firms separating oxygen from lunar rocks and providing support services to government facilities on the Moon, or even offering tourism and entertainment activities. Some of these endeavors may make commercial sense, but it is possible that none will.

In the near term, expectations are that the U.S. Government will want to ensure that necessary research and technology development occurs to support a lunar outpost, that a robust space transportation network is created (which may or may not be government-owned in the long term), that accurate maps and surveys of the Moon exist (we have better maps of Mars today than we do of the Moon), and that reliable communications and navigation services are available at the Moon. In short, the government should ensure that basic services are present to enable scientific and commercial opportunities, but it will not be a governmental responsibility to do everything possible on the Moon. It simply will not have the resources. As a policy matter, the most difficult area for Merchant and Guardian cultures likely will not be how to provide any particular good or service, but what legal rights private parties have on and, most crucially, on the way to the Moon. This is not an area in which the United States can or should act unilaterally. It affects what values are recognized beyond the Earth, and therefore the type and character of spacepower available to the United States.

Space Property Rights

Current international law recognizes the continued ownership of objects placed in space by governments or private entities. Similarly, resources removed from outer space (such as lunar samples from the Apollo missions) can be and are subject to ownership. Other sorts of rights in space, such as to intellectual property and spectrum, are also recognized. Article II of the 1967 Outer Space Treaty, however, specifically bars national appropriation of the Moon or other celestial bodies by claims of sovereignty or other means. It also says that states shall be responsible for the activities of persons under their jurisdiction or control. Thus, the central issue is the ability to confer and recognize real property rights on land, including in situ resources found on the Moon and other celestial bodies.

In common law, a sovereign is generally required to recognize private property claims. Thus, the Outer Space Treaty, by barring claims of sovereignty, is usually thought to bar private property claims. Many legal scholars in the International Institute of Space Law and other organizations support that view. Other scholars, however, make a distinction between sovereignty and property and point to civil law that recognizes property rights independent of sovereignty.[34] It has also been argued that while article II of the treaty prohibits territorial sovereignty, it does not prohibit private appropriation. The provision of the Outer Space Treaty requiring state parties to be responsible for the activities of persons under their jurisdiction or control leaves the door open to agreements or processes that allow them to recognize and confer property rights, even under common law.

Current international space treaties are built on the assumption that all matters can and should trace back to states. This is in contrast to admiralty law and the growing field of commercial arbitration in which the interests and responsibilities of owners, not necessarily the state, were the legal foundation. It can be argued that the Outer Space Treaty was not the final word on real property rights in space even within the international space law community, as drafters of the 1979 Moon Treaty felt it necessary to be more explicit on this point. The treaty states:

> Article 11. (1) The moon and its natural resources are the common heritage of mankind. (2) The moon is not subject to national appropriation by any claim of sovereignty, by means of use or occupation, or by any other means. (3) *Neither the surface nor the subsurface of the moon . . . shall become property of any State, international intergovernmental or nongovernmental organization, national organization or nongovernmental entity or of any natural person* [emphasis added]. The placement of personnel, space vehicles, equipment, facilities, stations . . . shall not create a right of ownership over the surface or subsurface of the moon or any areas thereof. The foregoing provisions are without prejudice to the international regime referred to in Paragraph 5 of this Article . . . (5) State parties to this Agreement hereby undertake to establish an international regime . . . to govern the

exploitation of the natural resources of the moon as such exploitation is about to become feasible . . . (7) The main purposes of the international regime to be established shall include: a) The orderly and safe development of the natural resources of the moon, b) the rational management of those resources, c) the expansion of opportunities in the use of those resources, d) an equitable sharing by all State parties in the benefits derived from those resources, whereby the interests and needs of the developing countries, as well as the efforts of those countries, which have contributed either directly or indirectly to the exploration of the moon shall be given special consideration.[35]

Article 11 was the most controversial aspect of the Moon Treaty when it was introduced. The Outer Space Treaty had already excluded claims of national appropriation, and this provision is repeated in article 11, part 2. Article 11 goes further, however, in part 3 to exclude property claims of any sort, and if any benefits are derived, they are presumably to be shared in accordance with the "common heritage" provision of article 11, part 1. Even the exercise of effective control of a region, as in placing a permanent base, would not support a claim of ownership by any entity. There is no mention of any limitations that would be placed on a regime controlling nonterrestrial resources or what mechanisms would be considered to resolve disputes. One might argue that article 11 prejudges the design of an international regime for the orderly and safe development of the Moon in that a system of internationally recognized property rights could, in fact, be the more rational way to manage those resources, expand opportunities for their use, and equitably share the benefits therein derived.

Furthermore, privacy and the right of persons to be secure in their dwellings are not rights supported by the Moon Treaty. Article 15 reads:

Article 15(1). All space vehicles, equipment, facilities, stations and installations on the moon shall be open to other State parties. Such State parties shall give reasonable advance notice of a projected visit, in order that appropriate consultations may be held and that maximum precautions may be taken to assure safety and to avoid interference with normal operations in the facility to be visited.[36]

No limits are placed on the reach of article 15, and the right to inspect space-based facilities would presumably extend to individual quarters and personal effects and papers. If state parties owned all facilities on the Moon and all persons on the Moon were state employees, an inspection regime, based on reciprocity, would seem to be a simple requirement. If some facilities are privately owned and their occupants are private citizens (which the Moon Treaty does not forbid), then a broad inspection require-ment like article 15 would necessarily supersede those privacy rights enjoyed in the United States and other democracies. Thus, the Moon and other celestial bodies would be regions where inhabitants enjoyed fewer liberties than in the United States or other nations on Earth.

The 1979 Moon Treaty may not appear very relevant since the United States and almost all other spacefaring nations did not sign it and none has ratified it.[37] However, the view that real property rights are forbidden by international law is widely prevalent. This in turn creates uncertainty in the minds of potential private sector partners and is inconsistent with the goals enunciated by the President and Congress in supporting the "Vision for Space Exploration." At minimum, real property rights in space are legally ambiguous and the United States need not accept flat statements that the Outer Space Treaty per se forbids such rights.

There is a wide variety of options for the establishment of a system of real property rights in space. These could include negotiation of a new international treaty to replace the Moon Treaty, extend existing interna-tional structures (such as the World Trade Organization), and use interna-tional arbitration mechanisms (for example, the London Court of International Arbitration). Alternatively, other regimes, such as the Inter-national Seabed Authority, could be modified to enable more predictable exploitation without recognizing private property rights. Or they could create a claims registry that would leave definition of a recognition regime to future specific cases. These options intentionally exclude more extreme positions, such as rejection of the Outer Space Treaty, or the unilateral assertion that the United States recognizes private property claims. Such actions would not engender international acceptance and the predictability required for such claims to be effective.

Conclusion

Spacepower encompasses all aspects of national power: military, eco-nomic, political, and even cultural as represented by the values that shape the Nation's space activities. The differing outlooks of Merchant and Guardian cultures are central aspects of today's space policy debates and can be expected to continue no matter what the human future in space turns out to be. The commercial space sector is continuing to grow and diversify. While it is easy to overestimate the potential of space commerce, weaknesses in the management and technical skills of the national security and civil space sectors are arguably a greater concern for the Nation's spacepower than the rate of growth of private space enterprise. In short, Guardian weaknesses are a more serious problem than Merchant strengths, as there is no substitute for Guardian responsibilities assuring national security and public safety.

In the national security sector, the key challenges will be to strengthen the ability to implement and execute major space acquisition programs and partner with commercial interests to shape the international environment to the advantage of the United States and its allies. In the civil space sector, the key challenges will be to implement the "Vision for Space Exploration" in an affordable manner and create partnerships with commercial and international interests to ensure the long-term sustainability of human exploration beyond low Earth orbit. The capabilities created by the successful establishment of a lunar outpost and human missions to Mars will add greatly to the Nation's spacepower.

There are many uncertainties with meeting these challenges because they require government agencies to work across traditional lines, partner with organizations having very different worldviews, and integrate policy, acquisition, and operational functions more thoroughly. Highly complex systems tend to create internal stovepipes that control the amount of information with which decisionmakers have to deal. For space systems, this can lead to disconnects between the acquisition and operational communities, and national policy objectives. Keeping these communities in sync with evolving world conditions is a major and daunting challenge for U.S. agencies and the entire executive branch.

Human and robotic exploration of space is a decades-long effort that has no clear end, but there are vastly different potential outcomes for humans' long-term future in space. Humans could live permanently in thriving communities beyond Earth or embark on limited to relatively brief expeditions and not establish a permanent presence. If it is assumed that humans are not permanently limited to the Earth and that the future exercise of spacepower includes humans living and working in space, then the questions become: who will make these expeditions, and what values will they hold? If they are Americans, then it is to be hoped that there will be room for Merchant as well as Guardian cultures on the Moon, Mars, and beyond.

Legal issues will become increasingly more important as the "Vision for Space Exploration" proceeds and humans attempt to expand farther and more permanently into space. In exercising spacepower, the United States should seek to ensure that its citizens have at least as many rights and protections in space, including the right to own property, as they do on Earth. Whether such rights would be as complete as those in the United States would be the subject of negotiation and debate. Simply put, however, the Moon and other celestial bodies should not be a place of fewer liberties than those enjoyed on Earth.

Recognizing conflicts between Merchants and Guardians is only a first step. The pursuit of spacepower should serve to increase national power, whether measured in economic, military, or political terms, as a way to advance American values and interests. This does not mean the pursuit of an isolationist or unilateral approach by the U.S. Government or the United States as a whole. The reality is that the United States must be engaged in shaping the international environment, and the Nation needs partners and friends to succeed. The task is to craft partnerships and strategies with Merchants and Guardians worldwide as human activities of all kinds expand into space.

Notes

[1] I am grateful for the comments I received and the lively discussions I participated in at workshops and seminars hosted by the National Defense University. I am also grateful for comments I received from colleagues who could not attend these sessions in person. The chapter also draws on prior works, in particular:

Scott Pace, "Merchants and Guardians," in *Merchants and Guardians: Balancing U.S. Interests in Global Space Commerce*, ed. John M. Logsdon and Russell J. Acker (Washington, DC: Space Policy Institute, George Washington University, May 1999)

Scott Pace, "Merchants and Guardians in the New Millennium," in *Space Policy in the Twenty-first Century*, ed. W. Henry Lambright (Baltimore: The Johns Hopkins University Press, 2003)

Dana J. Johnson, Scott Pace, and C. Bryan Gabbard, *Space: Emerging Options for National Power*, MR–517 (Santa Monica, CA: RAND, 1998).

NASA identification is for biographical purposes only.

[2] Ronald Reagan, "Speech at Moscow State University—May 31, 1988," in *The American Reader*, ed. Diane Ravitch (New York: HarperCollins, 1990), 364–365.

[3] Simon Worden, "Forget about space dominance: U.S. interests should start focusing on space competence," *Bulletin of the Atomic Scientists* (March–April 2006), 21–23.

[4] *Air Force Basic Doctrine*, Air Force Doctrine Document 1 (Washington, DC: U.S. Air Force Headquarters, September 1997).

[5] Much of this discussion is drawn from Dana J. Johnson, Scott Pace, and C. Bryan Gabbard, *Space: Emerging Options for National Power*, MR–517 (Santa Monica, CA: RAND, 1998), chapter 2.

[6] General Henry H. Arnold, USAF, *Global Mission* (New York: Harper and Brothers, 1949), 290–291.

[7] Having low-cost access to space is useful in its own right and can be an additional deterrent to the entry of potential competitors. Similarly, the provision of free, high-quality navigation signals from global positioning systems makes it more difficult to raise commercial funds for competing systems. States may, of course, choose to build such capabilities for their own reasons, but they will bear the costs more directly.

[8] Unfortunately, the exercise of spacepower by field commanders would require a more technical and detailed analysis of specific space capabilities than we have room for in this chapter.

[9] Johnson, Pace, and Gabbard.

[10] Air Force Doctrine Document 2–2, *Space Operations* (Maxwell AFB, AL: Air Force Doctrine Center, November 27, 2001), 54.

[11] I am indebted to Dwayne Day for the term *von Braun paradigm*.

[12] Donella H. Meadows, Dennis L. Meadows, Jørgen Randers, and William W. Behrens III, *Limits to Growth* (New York: Universe Books, 1972). See <www.nss.org/settlement/L5news/index.html> for a brief history of the L5 Society.

[13] Interestingly, this view of space did not find much support outside Anglophone cultures. Most international advocates of space development saw large-scale human activities in space as useful in building cooperation among existing societies, not in building new ones.

[14] During the Civil War, President Lincoln signed several key legislative initiatives for the American frontier such as the 1862 Homestead Act, the Morrill Land-Grant Colleges Act, and the Pacific Railway Acts of 1862 and 1864.

[15] The Space Foundation, *The Space Report: The Guide to Global Space Activity* (Colorado Springs: The Space Foundation, 2006).

[16] For a deeper treatment of choice, see Charles Wolf, Jr., *Markets or Governments: Choosing between Imperfect Alternatives* (Cambridge: MIT Press, 1988).

[17] I am indebted to Jim Bennett for first using these terms together. This discussion is drawn from my 1999 paper of the same title.

[18] Scott Pace, "Merchants and Guardians," in *Merchants and Guardians: Balancing U.S. Interests in Global Space Commerce*, ed. John M. Logsdon and Russell J. Acker (Washington, DC: Space Policy Institute, George Washington University, May 1999).

[19] *Columbia Accident Investigation Board Report*, vol. 1 (Washington, DC: NASA and U.S. Government Printing Office, August 2003), 209, available at <http://caib.nasa.gov/>.

[20] John M. Logsdon, "A Failure of National Leadership," in *Critical Issues in the History of Spaceflight* (Washington, DC: NASA, 2006), 270.

[21] See <www.whitehouse.gov/infocus/space/vision.html>.

[22] Michael Griffin, remarks to the National Space Club, Washington, DC, February 9, 2005.

[23] John Marburger, keynote address, 44th Robert H. Goddard Memorial Symposium, Greenbelt, MD, March 15, 2006.

[24] Office of Science and Technology Policy, Executive Office of the President, *U.S. National Space Policy* (Washington, DC: The White House, August 31, 2006).

[25] Robert G. Joseph, remarks on the President's National Space Policy at The George C. Marshall Institute, Washington, DC, December 13, 2006.

[26] Andy Pasztor, "Air Force May Hire Outsiders to Oversee Projects," *The Wall Street Journal*, December 28, 2006, 3.

[27] John Logsdon, "Missing the Point?" *Space News*, November 6, 2006.

[28] A peer competitor is a state capable of fielding multiple types and robust numbers of both emerging and current weapons, then developing a concept of operations to realize the full potential of this mix. Its goal is to capture a vital interest of the United States and then defeat the military response.

[29] Petter Stålenheim, Damien Fruchart, Wuyi Omitoogun, and Catalina Perdomo, "Military Expenditure," in *SIPRI Yearbook 2006: Armaments, Disarmament and International Security* (New York: Oxford University Press on behalf of Stockholm International Peace Research Institute, June 2006).

[30] Thomas Friedman, *The World is Flat* (New York: Farrar, Straus and Giroux, 2005).

[31] Carl Sagan, *Pale Blue Dot: A Vision of the Human Future in Space* (New York: Random House, 1994), 371.

[32] Gerard K. O'Neill, *The High Frontier* (Princeton: Space Studies Institute Press, 1989).

[33] Rick Tumlinson and Erin Medlicott, eds., *Return to the Moon* (Ontario, Canada: Collectors Guide Publishing Inc., Apogee Books, November 2005).

[34] Wayne N. White, "Real Property Rights in Outer Space," in *Proceedings of the 40th Colloquium on the Law of Outer Space*, American Institute of Aeronautics and Astronautics on behalf of the International Institute of Space Law (1998), 370.

[35] *Agreement Governing the Activities of States on the Moon and Other Celestial Bodies*, United Nations Office for Outer Space Affairs (1979), available at <www.unoosa.org/oosa/SpaceLaw/moon.html>.

[36] Ibid.

[37] Ibid.

Part IV: The Future of Spacepower

Emerging Domestic Structures: Organizing the Presidency for Spacepower

John M. Logsdon

> *Organizational arrangements are not neutral. Organization is one way of expressing national commitment, influencing program direction, and ordering priorities.*
> —Harold Seidman[1]

This chapter addresses a single, rather straightforward question: Is there a best organizational structure or approach at the Presidential level if the United States wants to maximize the contributions of its civilian, military, intelligence, and commercial space capabilities to the pursuit of its national goals and purposes?

Developing a sound and comprehensive theory of spacepower is a necessary but insufficient condition for ensuring the full contribution of space capabilities and activities to furthering national interests. To be meaningful, such a theory must be used as a foundation for a spacepower strategy, and it may be that such a strategy cannot be successfully implemented unless that implementation is managed, or at least carefully overseen, by some sort of organizational structure at the national level. There are too many separate interests and centrifugal forces at work in the U.S. space sector to expect an automatic coherence of space actions in pursuit of national objectives; there needs to be some means of coordinating the behavior of various separate space actors to be consistent with national purposes. As Harold Seidman comments:

A President is not self-sufficient. The Congress can perform its constitutional functions without the executive establishment and the bureaucracy. A President cannot.

It is the agency heads, not the President, who have the men, money, material, and legal powers. . . . To work his will . . . the President must have at his disposal the trade goods controlled by the agencies and be able to enlist the support of their constituencies.

An alliance—which is what the executive branch really is—is by definition a confederation of sovereigns joined together in pursuit of some common goal. . . . Individual purposes and goals are subordinated only to the extent necessary to hold the alliance intact.[2]

The capabilities that form the basis of U.S. spacepower are controlled, not by the President, but by executive branch agencies such as the Department of Defense and its constituent elements, the National Aeronautics and Space Administration (NASA), the National Oceanic and Atmospheric Administration (NOAA), and the National Reconnaissance Office (NRO). The Department of State relates space capabilities to U.S. foreign policy objectives and oversees the implementation of the International Traffic in Arms Regulations, which influence space technology exports. The Departments of Commerce and Transportation and the Federal Communications Commission also play important regulatory roles vis-à-vis the U.S. commercial space sector. That sector increasingly is developing with private capital and is operating capabilities that are an essential part of U.S. spacepower. Each of these space actors, and subelements within them (for example, NASA's Science Mission Directorate), has its own set of relationships with supportive nongovernmental constituencies. Bringing these separate organizations together in pursuit of common goals is a challenging task.

A President has limited power to pursue national interests as he defines them in the face of this distribution of power with the executive branch. The President can set priorities through policy directives and budget decisions and can appoint people who share his values and perspectives to head the executive agencies, but almost inevitably those individuals find their loyalties divided between White House priorities and their own agency's interests, which only occasionally are the same.

In addition, congressional oversight and funding responsibilities with respect to executive branch space activities are diffused over many committees and subcommittees. They reflect the decentralized organization of the executive branch, and the dispersion of power among congressional committees makes a coherent congressional perspective on any particular space issue, much less a comprehensive approach to U.S. spacepower, almost impossible to achieve. Relationships between executive agencies and Congress may pull agency leaders in directions inconsistent with the President's priorities. Congress and the White House are separate institutions sharing power, and the President must convince Congress to agree with his priorities for U.S. spacepower capabilities if those capabilities are to be maximized. Congress cannot substitute for the President in this regard.

There are also many nongovernmental interests trying to influence the direction taken by one or the other element of the government's space agencies. Each actor in the space industry, labor unions, representatives of state and regional governments, universities, and science and engineering associations, among others, attempts to align the government's space activities with its particular interests.

The U.S. approach to spacepower must also be formulated in a global context, with an increasing number of other spacefaring countries pursuing policies that mix competitive and cooperative elements. The post–Cold War period during which the United States was the unchallenged space superpower is rapidly becoming only a memory, and the United States has to craft an approach to advancing its interests, both in space and through the use of space capabilities, with high sensitivity to its overall relationships with other spacefaring countries and to their differing approaches to the use of their own spacepower.

If there is to be a national strategy for space informed by a comprehensive theory of spacepower, it must come from the center of government: "The bureaucracy is no more equipped to manufacture grand designs for Government programs than carpenters, electricians, and plumbers are to be architects. But if an architect attempted to build a house, the results might well be disastrous."[3] The White House must act as the "architect" for a U.S. space strategy and must persuade the various centers of spacepower within and outside the Federal Government that it is in their mutual interest to work together in turning that strategy into action. How best to achieve Presidential control over executive branch agencies is a classic problem of government organization, and it is basically no different in the space sector than in other areas of government activity.

Recent Organizational Proposals

Recognizing these realities, the Commission to Assess United States National Security Space Management and Organization (the Space Commission) put forth a proposal in January 2001 for dealing with space issues at the White House level. The Space Commission noted that "the United States has a vital national interest in space. . . . [Space] deserves the attention of the national leadership, from the President on down." The commission recognized that "only the President can impress upon the members of the Cabinet . . . the priority to be placed on the success of the national space program." The commission added, "The National Security Council can assist the President with measures to monitor the progress of the national space program toward defined goals."[4]

The Space Commission made detailed recommendations on how best to organize for space within the White House structure, noting that "the present interagency process is inadequate to address the number, range, and complexity of today's space issues, which are expected to increase over time. A standing interagency coordination process is needed." The commission proposed that a Senior Interagency Group (SIG) for Space be established within the National Security Council (NSC) structure. In order to develop the SIG (Space) agenda and to provide coordination at the working level, the Space Commission recognized the need for "dedicated staff support . . . with experience across the four space sectors."[5]

The role of SIG (Space) would be to oversee the activities of the various executive branch space agencies to:

- leverage the collective investments in the commercial, civil, defense, and intelligence sectors to advance U.S. capabilities in each

- advance initiatives in domestic and international fora that preserve and enhance U.S. use of and access to space

- reduce existing impediments to the use of space for national security purposes.

To achieve these objectives, the SIG "would oversee the implementation of national space policy" and "focus on the most critical national security space issues, including those that span the civil and commercial sectors."[6]

The Space Commission also observed that "the President might find it useful to have access to high-level advice in developing a long-term strategy for sustaining the nation's role as the leading space-faring nation." Thus, the commission recommended the creation of a "Presidential Space Advisory Group" that would be "unconstrained in scope and provide recommendations that enable the nation to capitalize on its investment in people, technology, infrastructure and capabilities in all space sectors." Such an independent group could also "identify new technical opportunities that could advance U.S. interests in space."[7]

From the perspective of maximizing and making best use of U.S. spacepower, these organizational recommendations seem to have been particularly well conceived. But when the administration of George W. Bush came to the White House and the chairman of the Space Commission, Donald Rumsfeld, became Secretary of Defense, they were not implemented, and many of the problems pointed out by the Space Commission persisted or even worsened. In 2008, a congressionally mandated "Independent Assessment Panel on the Organization and Management of National Security Space"—more frequently known as the Allard Commission, after its congressional sponsor, Senator Gordon Allard (R–CO), or the Young Committee, after the panel's chair, A. Thomas Young—reached similar conclusions to those of the Space Commission. The group recommended that "the President should establish and lead the execution of a National Space Strategy" and that "to implement the strategy, the President should reestablish the National Space Council, chaired by the National Security Adviser, with the authority to assign roles and responsibilities, and to adjudicate disputes over requirements and resources."[8]

The Executive Office structure for space policy as it existed at the start of the administration of President Barack Obama was thus rather different from that recommended by either the Space Commission or the Allard Commission. And those recommendations with respect to structures at the White House level were only one part of both groups' recommendations for reorganizing the management of national security space. This chapter will conclude with a discussion of whether there is merit in reconsidering these recommendations, if the precepts of a spacepower theory are to be put into practice. But first it would be useful to see if there are lessons that can be learned from a brief review of White House organization for space over the last half-century.

Alternative Organization Approaches: A Historical Perspective

There *has* been some form of White House (including the Executive Office of the President) structure for managing U.S. space efforts since the Eisenhower administration, which was faced with the issue of how to organize the U.S. space effort in response to the October 1957 Soviet launch of Sputnik. A brief review of the various ways in which different Presidents organized their management of U.S. space matters can provide a rather comprehensive catalogue of possible organizational alternatives or elements that might be employed by future Presidents.

Eisenhower Administration

In the aftermath of the first two Soviet satellite launches, President Dwight D. Eisenhower appointed the President of the Massachusetts Institute of Technology, James Killian, as his advisor on science and technology and gave Killian the responsibility for suggesting an organizational approach for space. In December 1957, Killian recognized that the Department of Defense was "committed to a space program and is in the process of setting one up," but that there was a "broad area of non-military basic research relating to space." He noted that there were several alternatives for the conduct of this nonmilitary space research, including having it managed through the Department of Defense or through an existing or new civilian agency. Whatever approach the President chose, suggested Killian, "there should be some mechanism . . . which gives coherence to the broad program."[9] From the very beginnings of the U.S. space program, the need for a central coordinating mechanism was thus recognized.

Eisenhower at first did not see the need for a new, separate space agency; his initial inclination was to keep all U.S. space activities within the Department of Defense. But he soon became persuaded that space science and exploration should be under civilian control. That decision spread U.S. Government space capabilities between two agencies, the Department of Defense and a new National Aeronautics and Space Administration. By assigning control over the initial U.S. reconnaissance satellite program Corona to a separate mechanism outside of both the Department of Defense and the Central Intelligence Agency in February 1958, Eisenhower also laid the foundation for a separate intelligence space organization. As he sent his proposals for a civilian space agency to Congress in April 1958, Eisenhower did not include a mechanism for coordinating the national space effort.

However, as Congress debated the administration's proposal, both the House of Representatives and the Senate came to the view that some such mechanism was necessary. The House suggested an Aeronautics and Space Advisory Committee that would be comprised of individuals outside the government and would meet only four times a year. This position was also favored by Killian. The Senate, under Majority Leader Lyndon B. Johnson, favored a high-level policy board along the lines of the NSC to exercise centralized policymaking authority for a coordinated national space program and to ensure that questions of broad national strategy were considered in formulating that program. The Senate position prevailed, and the 1958 Space Act established a nine-person National Aeronautics and Space Council in the Executive Office of the President. The council would be chaired by the President and would include as members the Secretaries of State and Defense, the administrator of NASA, the chairman of the Atomic Energy Commission, one other senior government official, and three private citizens.[10]

Although he had agreed to establish the council at Johnson's urging, Eisenhower did not fully implement the intent of Congress. Rather, he added a few people to the NSC staff to deal with space matters and handled space policy issues through the National Security Council process, adding the NASA administrator to those in attendance when space issues were to be discussed and declaring such an occasion a meeting of the Space Council. By 1960, Eisenhower had concluded that the idea that there could be a comprehensive, integrated U.S. space program was incorrect, and thus called for a revision of the 1958 Space Act that would eliminate "those provisions which reflect the concept of a single program embracing military as well as non-military space activities," since "in actual practice, a single civil-military program does not exist and in fact is unattainable." Given this conclusion, Eisenhower judged that he did not need a separate council for space matters and proposed that it be abolished.

Both NASA and the House of Representatives supported Eisenhower's proposal, but it was blocked in the Senate by Lyndon Johnson, who observed that there would be a Presidential election in a few months and that "the next President could well have different views as to organization and function of the military and civilian space programs." By the time he made this comment on August 31, 1960, Johnson knew that John F. Kennedy and not he was the Democratic nominee for the Presidency, but he still believed in the strategic importance of space and the need to deal with space issues at the national level.[11]

A broad 21-page statement of national space policy was developed during the Eisenhower administration and issued inside the government (but not made public) as a National Aeronautics and Space Council document in January 1960. The statement noted that "although the full potentialities and significance remain largely to be explored, it is already clear that there are important scientific, civil, military, and political implications for the national security."[12] This was to be the last Presidentially approved statement on national space policy for 18 years.

Kennedy Administration

As he prepared to enter the White House after his 1960 election, John F. Kennedy was advised that there was a need for policy coordination between the civilian and military space programs and that a revitalized National Aeronautics and Space Council, with fewer members (none from outside the government) and with the Vice President rather than the President as its chair, might be a useful means of achieving such coordination with respect to "high priority policy issues."[13] Kennedy accepted this advice and submitted the legislation needed to amend the 1958 Space Act to create a National Aeronautics and Space Council along these lines.

An opportunity to use the council mechanism arose early in the new administration. In the wake of the April 12, 1961, launch of the first human, Soviet cosmonaut Yuri Gagarin, into space, President Kennedy asked his Vice President, Lyndon Johnson, "as Chairman of the Space Council to be in charge of making an overall survey of where we stand in space."[14] At this point, the Space Council had only one staff person, a former congressional staff member named Edward Welsh. Together, he and Johnson organized hurried consultations involving NASA, the Department of Defense, the Atomic Energy Commission, NASA official Wernher von Braun, Air Force General Bernard Schriever, several businessmen, and senior members of the Senate. Then NASA and Department of Defense staff (without Welsh's involvement) prepared a lengthy memorandum titled "Recommendations for Our National Space Program: Changes, Policies, and Goals." This memorandum was sent to the Vice President on May 8. Johnson endorsed it and forwarded it to the President on the same day. The memorandum called for an across-the-board acceleration of the U.S. space effort and increased integration of the civilian and military space programs, which Dwight Eisenhower a few months earlier said was impossible. It also recommended setting a manned lunar landing as a national goal.[15]

The Space Council acquired a small staff of its own in 1961–1962 and was active on other space issues, in particular on how best to organize the government for the development and operation of communications satellites. The Space Council principals met a number of times as a body during the Kennedy administration. However, the council never again was the primary source of space policy advice to the President, who relied on those with whom he had a personal relationship, such as his science advisor Jerome Weisner and his staff, and on NASA Administrator James Webb for counsel on space matters. (Webb was never happy to find the Space Council and its staff between himself and the President.) Attempts by the Space Council to develop a comprehensive statement on national space policy were not successful, and there is no indication that the council staff was able to exert any influence on defense and national security space issues.

Johnson Administration

Lyndon Johnson once remarked that he had spent much more time on space matters as Vice President than he did as President. This is not surprising, given that issues such as the war in Southeast Asia and the demands of his Great Society programs were high-priority issues during his time in the White House. Vice President Hubert Humphrey, who became chairman of the Space Council in 1965, had shown little interest in space matters as a member of the Senate, and there is no indication that the council was particularly active between 1964 and 1968. Edward Welsh stayed on as executive secretary, but the White House depended more on James Webb, its science advisory apparatus, and budget director Charles Schultze for space policy advice. Vice President Humphrey did try to use the Space Council mechanism to stimulate discussions on how better to use the space program as an instrument of foreign policy, but with little apparent impact. By the end of the Johnson administration, the Space Council was basically a moribund structure. Welsh stayed on as executive secretary until Johnson left office in January 1969.

Nixon Administration

As he assumed office in January 1969, President Richard M. Nixon was advised that, with the first landing on the Moon in the near future, there was a need for a comprehensive review of the national space program. Nixon asked his Vice President, Spiro Agnew, to head up a Space Task Group to carry out such a review. The review did not use the formal mechanism of the National Aeronautics and Space Council, which in 1969 was without a dedicated staff, to carry out this review. Staff support for the Space Task Group came instead from the White House Office of Science and Technology.

In June 1969, toward the end of the Space Task Group review, Apollo 8 astronaut William Anders was appointed executive secretary of the Space Council, with a mandate to revitalize the organization. Over the next 3½ years, Anders and his small staff were active participants in the White House discussions on the content of the post-Apollo space program, on a new approach to international cooperation in space, and on whether to approve development of the space shuttle. They had little apparent involvement with the military or national security space programs. But the Space Council never met at the principals level, and its staff was only one of several sources of space policy advice within the Executive Office. The Science Advisor and his Office of Science and Technology and what in 1970 became the Office of Management and Budget had more weight in most White House policy debates.

As he began his second term in January 1973, Richard Nixon announced that he was abolishing the National Aeronautics and Space Council (and the Office of Science and Technology). His message to Congress announcing this action said that:

> basic policy issues in the United States space effort have been resolved, and the necessary interagency relationships have been established. I have therefore concluded, with the Vice President's concurrence, that the Council can be discontinued. Needed policy coordination can now be achieved through the resources of the executive departments and agencies, such as the National Aeronautics and Space Administration, augmented by some of the former Council staff.[16]

Ford Administration

During most of the administration of President Gerald R. Ford, there was no Executive Office unit with specific responsibilities for space policy. General science and technology advice was provided by the director of the National Science Foundation, who was also designated as the President's science advisor. In 1976, Congress passed a bill reestablishing a White House Office of Science and Technology Policy (OSTP) to provide advice to the President on the full range of science and technology policy issues, including space. Defining space as a science and technology policy issue, rather than as an issue of broad national policy, had the effect of limiting the influence of OSTP on non–research and development space matters.

Carter Administration

Space policy remained the responsibility of OSTP during the 4 years that Jimmy Carter was President. Given the broad purview of OSTP responsibilities and its small staff, only one or two staff members worked on space issues. With OSTP leadership, for the first time since the end of the Eisenhower administration, a broad statement of national space policy was developed. The senior OSTP staff member with space responsibilities was dual-hatted as a National Security Council staff member, establishing a pattern of close cooperation on space matters between the two organizations that has persisted for most of the time since. This arrangement also allowed this staff person access to highly classified programs and intelligence information. As the Carter administration began talks on space arms control with the Soviet Union in 1978, OSTP was very much involved.

Reagan Administration

For the first 18 months of Ronald Reagan's Presidency, OSTP remained the lead White House organization for space policy; its staff managed the development of the first Reagan statement on national space policy, which was issued on July 4, 1982. That policy stated that:

> Normal interagency coordinating mechanisms will be employed to the maximum extent possible to implement the policies enunciated in this directive. To provide a forum to all Federal agencies for their policy views, to review and advise on proposed changes to national space policy, and to provide for orderly and rapid referral of space policy issues to the President for decision as necessary, a Senior Interagency Group (SIG) on Space shall be established. The SIG (Space) will be chaired by the Assistant to the President for National Security Affairs and will include the Deputy or Under Secretary of State, Deputy or Under Secretary of Defense, Deputy or Under Secretary of Commerce, Director of Central Intelligence, Chairman of the Joint Chiefs of Staff, Director of the Arms Control and Disarmament Agency, and the Administrator of the National Aeronautics and Space Administration.[17]

The National Security Council, using the SIG (Space) mechanism, held the White House lead for space policy for the remainder of the Reagan administration and issued a number of space policy statements with associated public "fact sheets."[18] There was usually only one NSC staff member with specific space responsibility who worked closely with one or two colleagues from OSTP.

George H.W. Bush Administration

The Democratic leadership in Congress was not happy with the shift of space policy jurisdiction to the NSC. This meant that space decisions would be made in the secretive style characteristic of NSC operations and that Congress could not force the NSC director, who was also assistant to the President for national security affairs, to testify at congressional hearings, since he was not a Senate-approved Presidential nominee. There were several attempts in the 1980s to reestablish a separate space council through legislation; doing so would mean that the Senate had to approve the nomination of an individual to be Space Council executive secretary and could compel that individual to testify before Congress. The White House opposed such a congressional initiative until 1988, when the measure was incorporated in the NASA fiscal year 1989 authorization bill. In its revised form, the Space Council executive secretary was not a Presidential nominee requiring Senate confirmation. That bill was signed by the President.

A new National Space Council came into being on February 1, 1989; it was chaired by Vice President J. Danforth Quayle. The law establishing the council was silent on membership but did provide for up to six council staff members in addition to an executive secretary.

For the next 4 years, the Space Council staff played an extremely activist role in attempting to revitalize what it judged to be a stagnant civilian space program. The staff was the primary mover behind what became known as the Space Exploration Initiative, announced by President Bush on July 20, 1989. This initiative called for a return to the Moon and then human journeys to Mars. In December 1989, the council assembled a blue ribbon commission for a 2-day meeting to comment on what was perceived as NASA's disappointing response to that initiative, and then convened a synthesis group to examine alternative approaches to human space exploration. In 1990, the council staff initiated another high-level examination of the civilian space program, chaired by Lockheed Martin executive Norm Augustine; this review took place over several months and went into great depth. In 1991, council staff convinced the Vice President and the President that NASA administrator Richard Truly should be replaced and played a key role in selecting his successor, Daniel Goldin. After the collapse of the Soviet Union, the council took the lead in outreach to the new Russian government with respect to both commercial and government-to-government space cooperation. In mid-1992, the National Space Council finally established a 12-person Vice President's Space Policy Advisory Board that had been called for in the legislation establishing the council. The board was composed of nongovernmental members with long experience in the various sectors of U.S. space activity, and it issued three reports on space issues during the second half of 1992.

There is no evidence that the council staff played an equally activist role with respect to the national security space program, and its interventions into the day-by-day management of NASA's efforts were strongly resented by senior NASA officials. The Vice President convened occasional meetings of senior executive branch officials involved in space matters, and there were several statements of national space policy issued under the council's auspices, but the National Space Council was primarily a staff-intensive activity rather than a forum for top-level policy discussions. Given the council's central role in space policy, neither OSTP nor NSC played a major role with respect to space policy during the Bush administration.

Clinton Administration

One of Bill Clinton's campaign promises was to reduce the size of the institutional Presidency by 25 percent. As part of this effort, the National Space Council and the Vice President's Space Policy Advisory Board were abolished soon after Clinton took office in January 1993. Jurisdiction over civil space policy matters was assigned to OSTP as part of the portfolio of its associate director for technology, with national security space being assigned to the associate OSTP director for national security and international affairs. For most of the 8 years of the Clinton administration, there were two or three OSTP staff members with specific space policy responsibilities, and for the most part they limited their activities to the civilian space sector. The administration also established a National Science and Technology Council as the inside-the-government mechanism for policy review. That council had several standing committees in various areas of science and technology, but none for space. President Clinton in 1993 established the President's Council of Advisors on Science and Technology as a source of external advice on science and technology; space policy was not among the topics that came before that body during the Clinton administration.

There were a number of space policy statements generated through an interagency process coordinated by OSTP, with a new statement of national space policy issued in September 1996. Vice President Al Gore and his staff also paid particular attention to space issues and had a major role in the decision to invite Russia to join the space station program and in several other space initiatives. Staff cooperation between OSTP and NSC continued. The National Security Council lead for space matters was its director for space, who reported to the NSC senior director for defense policy and arms control and who worked closely with the OSTP staff on space issues.

George W. Bush Administration

At the outset of his administration, President Bush created a number of policy coordinating committees (PCCs) that were to be the main day-to-day fora for interagency coordination of national security policy, rather than establishing separate senior interagency groups for high-priority issues. The PCCs were to provide policy analysis for consideration by more senior committees of the NSC system, such as the Deputies Committee, the Principals Committee, and the NSC itself, and to ensure timely responses to decisions made by the President.[19] Space policy was not originally a focus of one of the PCCs, but a Space Policy Coordinating Committee, chaired by the National Security Council, was soon established and in June 2002 was assigned the responsibility for carrying out a comprehensive review of national space policy.

Members of the Space Policy Coordinating Committee are mid-level political appointees (for example, assistant secretaries) of the executive agencies dealing with space matters. Staff support is provided by the NSC Director for Space, the Assistant Director for Space and Aeronautics of the White House OSTP, and a senior OSTP analyst. These three individuals are thus the only people (except for Office of Management and Budget staff) with a primary responsibility for space policy in the Executive Office structure.

A National Defense University review of the work of the PCCs suggests that "PCC planning is focused more on advance planning at the political and strategic level. . . . An effective interagency process reduces the complexity of the policy decisions and focuses the planning on mission success." The review added: "Collaboration is central to a PCC's success, but teamwork and unity is [sic] vulnerable to political risks, bureaucratic equities, and personal relationships. . . . Policy disagreements and turf battles are inevitable because of divergent political philosophies, different departmental objectives and priorities, disagreements about the dynamics or implications of developing situations, or because departments are seeking to evolve or formulate new roles and missions." In addition, "hard problems do not lend themselves to easy solutions, and frequently there are genuine differences between departments over the best ways, means, and objectives for dealing with a national security problem. . . . As one former NSC staff member observed, the easiest outcome to produce in the interagency process is to *prevent* policy from being made." For the PCC process to work, "the wide range of issues, the different policy perspectives of various departments, the nature of bureaucratic politics, contests over turf and responsibilities, disagreements over which department has the lead, and the clash of personalities and egos all place a premium on ensuring that the equities of all involved agencies are considered, and on building an informal policy consensus amongst the players."[20] This recent description of the relationship between the President's policymaking apparatus and various executive agencies is strikingly similar to the more general observations made by Harold Seidman 38 years ago.

These general observations also appear to reflect the recent experience in the space policy sector. Reportedly, interagency disagreements slowed the progress of the space policy review ordered in June 2002 and required multiple drafts of a national space policy statement before it could be sent to the President for approval in August 2006. In the space sector, "an informal policy consensus" seemingly proved very elusive, and the distribution of power between the Executive Office and the disagreeing agencies made it almost impossible to force agreement from the White House.

Lessons Learned

One clear observation that follows from the above review is that many approaches to organizing White House space policy management have been tried in the last half-century. Thus, any structure that might emerge in the future is likely to resemble a prior structure or include elements of prior structures that had previously been tried.

A second observation is that a separate White House space policy organization, such as a space council, has not been successful in demonstrating its superiority as an organizational approach. Although the National Aeronautics and Space Council existed from 1958 to 1973, it never became the major, much less the sole, means for developing a national approach to what would now be called spacepower. With only a few exceptions, other Executive Office organizations, particularly the Office of Science and Technology Policy and the National Security Council, not to mention the White House budget office, and the heads of the executive branch space agencies were not willing to defer to the council as the primary forum for developing space policy options for the President. Reestablishing the National Space Council in 1989 was an initiative forced on a reluctant White House by Congress. In its 4 years of operation, an activist council staff managed to alienate most executive agencies. Its major policy proposal, the Space Exploration Initiative, was stillborn; the council did not prove an effective mechanism for rallying broad support for a Presidential space initiative or for convincing the NASA leadership that the initiative was the proper course of action to follow. One possible reason for the space council's lack of influence is that it has been headed during most of its history by a Vice President who was not a close ally of the President, who had no strong Washington political base of his own, and thus could not call on either the President's or his own power to back up the guidance provided by the council and its staff. In addition, by operating outside of the National Security Council structure, the space council found it very difficult to exert influence on national security space issues.

On the positive side, the National Space Council between 1989 and 1992 did commission two high-level external reviews of space issues and did create a well-qualified external Space Policy Advisory Board that was able to produce three insightful reports in a short period of time, demonstrating that there could be value in such an advisory body. As a Presidential appointee, the executive secretary of the National Space Council could serve as a spokesman for the White House on space policy matters. But the Space Council mechanism did not demonstrate sufficient value to be maintained in existence as the administration changed in 1993.

Giving the Office of Science and Technology Policy and the National Science and Technology Council the lead responsibility in space policy, as was the case during the Clinton administration, is likely to have biased the policy debate toward treating space as a research and development issue. Approaching space issues from this perspective is not likely to fully capture all dimensions of a spacepower approach to national space policy. The reality is that the OSTP and NSC staffs have worked closely together, whichever parent organization has lead responsibility, but at the more senior levels of decisionmaking, OSTP leaders come from different backgrounds than their NSC counterparts, and as space issues have worked their way up the OSTP chain of command they were viewed differently than if they had been considered issues of broad national security policy.

A persistent problem for White House control over the totality of the Nation's space effort has been the diffuse structure and strongly entrenched position of the various elements of the national security space sector. It has been extremely difficult for the Executive Office staff to penetrate and then influence the inner workings of that sector. The 2001 recommendations of the Space Commission and the 2008 recommendations of the Allard Commission were intended to provide a more integrated national security space sector, more amenable to central management within the Department of Defense (and by implication, the White House).

It seems that only the National Security Council within the White House structure brings to bear the requisite perspectives and institutional position to have a reasonable chance to be effective in advancing U.S. spacepower and linking it to U.S. scientific, economic, and national security interests. As the most recent statement of national space policy notes:

In this new century, those who effectively utilize space will enjoy added prosperity and security and will hold a substantial advantage over those who do not. Freedom of action in space is as important to the United States as air power and sea power. In order to increase knowledge, discovery, economic prosperity, and to enhance the national security, the United States must have robust, effective, and efficient space capabilities.[21]

Is the Present Structure Working?

Saying that in principle the National Security Council is the appropriate venue for managing U.S. space activities in ways most likely to maximize the contributions of spacepower to broad national objectives does not mean that in practice it now has either the mandate or the organizational capabilities to carry out that role. As noted earlier, in January 2001, the Space Commission concluded that "the present interagency process is inadequate to address the number, range, and complexity of today's space issues, which are expected to increase over time." Would an objective review of the management of national space policy since the Space Commission submitted its report reach a similar conclusion today? It seems as if the answer is "yes," given how close the conclusions and recommendations of the 2008 Allard Commission were to those of the 2001 Space Commission.

There were a number of changes in the White House and interagency management of the U.S. space program during the Presidency of George W. Bush. As has already been discussed, in 2001 the lead in space policy at the Presidential level was switched from OSTP to the NSC, and an NSC official chaired the Space Policy Coordinating Committee. The NSC staff (working with the OSTP) drafted the initial versions of the five new space policy statements that were issued between 2002 and 2006, which in a bureaucratic context provide an important point of leverage. However, space matters have been dealt with at a relatively junior level within the NSC structure, including the membership of the PCC, and there is still only one NSC staff person with primary responsibility for space matters.

The August 2006 national space policy identifies key areas for top-level attention:

- developing space professionals
- improving space system development and procurement
- strengthening and maintaining the U.S. space-related science, technology, and industrial base

■ increasing and strengthening interagency partnerships.

Indeed, innovative interagency mechanisms in specific areas of space activity have recently emerged as complements to the central management of space policy and programs. These include (dating from 1994) the Integrated Program Office for the troubled National Polar Orbiting Environmental Satellite System and, since 2004, a National Space-based Positioning, Navigation, and Timing (PNT) Executive Committee chaired by Deputy Secretaries of Defense and Transportation, supported by a dedicated staff, and with an external Space-based PNT Advisory Board. These two structures are intended to provide a national perspective in their areas of focus; they operate under the guidance provided by White House space policy statements.

In addition, since 1997, NASA and the national security space community have jointly worked through a Partnership Council to discuss issues of mutual interest. Current members of the Partnership Council include NASA, U.S. Strategic Command, the Air Force Space Command, Defense Research and Engineering, the Office of the Undersecretary of the Air Force for Space, the NRO, and the Central Intelligence Agency. The council meets at least twice a year at the principals level. This mechanism, operating at the interagency level, could be a particularly useful tool if it were linked to a broad national perspective on the development and use of spacepower.

Even so, significant problems in the integration of U.S. space efforts across the four sectors of activity remain. A "Committee on U.S. Space Leadership" in March 2009 noted that "there are serious and systemic problems which portend a broad erosion of U.S. leadership and advantage in space." The committee called for establishing a "White House focal point and mechanism" for establishing strategic direction and priorities, for providing management oversight, and for coordinating decisions and actions across departments and agencies.[22]

Modest Proposals for Change

Two of the various recent recommendations seem to have continuing merit for the Obama administration:

■ Creating within the National Security Council context (perhaps with OSTP involvement as well) some sort of standing interagency body for space involving more senior officials than has been the case for the Space Policy Coordinating Committee. This would provide for the White House a continuing focus on the condition of the Nation's spacepower capabilities and on their use to achieve various national objectives. Such a body would need to go beyond the traditional National Security Council focus to reflect the interests and perspectives of the civilian and commercial space sectors.

■ Providing this body with adequate staff support with experience in all space sectors. A separate small space office could be created with one senior director for space and two or three other staff members, with one or two coming from outside the national security community. Rather than depend on only OSTP staff for support, this would mean that the NSC staff would have all the capabilities needed to manage the development of space policies and oversee their implementation.

In essence, what could be done is creating a mini-Space Council, but within the overall National Security Council structure rather than separate from it. The National Security Council historically has had good links to U.S. foreign policy and international interests. However, it has more limited experience in dealing with science and technology and commercial issues. Creating a National Security Council staff element with officials experienced in such issues could provide a comprehensive perspective on spacepower issues for the Senior Interagency Group for Space and ultimately for the President.

The benefits of creating a Presidential Space Advisory Group are not as clear. There is limited precedent for the NSC staffing a standing external advisory committee, which would have to be the case if the NSC became the central focal point for national space issues. (One important exception to this statement is the President's Foreign Intelligence Advisory Board.) Given the sensitivity of most issues that are considered in the NSC context, there might be issues of adequate clearances and confidentiality of such a group's deliberations; and an advisory committee operating under the guidelines of the Federal Advisory Committee Act is somewhat at odds with the character of National Security Council activities. The Vice President's Space Policy Advisory Board was active for only 6 months in 1992 at the end of the first Bush administration, so it is difficult to assess its value to space policymaking. On the other hand, that board did produce four useful reports in its brief existence, suggesting that there could be value in an external advisory group operating under rules that allowed access to classified information and confidential advice to the Executive Office and the President.

Most fundamental, however, is convincing the President that the Space Commission was correct in its 2001 assessment that "the United States has a vital national interest in space. . . . [Space] deserves the attention of the national leadership, from the President on down." Providing a structure for effective Presidential space leadership will have limited impact if that leadership itself is missing. To enable full value from the Nation's spacepower, "sustained leadership must emerge, as it did early in the first [space] age, to guide and direct transformation of U.S. space efforts toward realizing their potential to serve the national interest."[23]

During his Presidential campaign, Barack Obama issued a lengthy statement of his views on space that seemed to reflect such a perspective. In addition, he called for reestablishing a National Space Council, reporting to him as President. Such a council, he suggested, would "oversee and coordinate civilian, military, commercial, and national security space activities." It would "solicit public participation, engage the international community, and work toward a 21st-century vision of space."[24] As this essay is written, the Obama administration is still considering how best to organize itself for space policy. But there are strong indications that President Obama recognizes the important contributions that space leadership can make to advancing U.S. interests. That realization is more important than whatever organizational scheme is ultimately adopted, but its translation into policy and actions can certainly be facilitated by an effective White House structure for space.

Notes

[1] Harold Seidman, *Politics, Position, and Power: The Dynamics of Federal Organization* (New York: Oxford University Press, 1970).

[2] Ibid., 73–74.

[3] Ibid., 76.

[4] Report of the Commission to Assess United States National Security Space Management and Organization, January 11, 2001, 82–83.

[5] Ibid., 84–85.

[6] Ibid., 84.

[7] Ibid., 83–84.

[8] Institute for Defense Analyses, *Leadership, Management and Organization for National Security Space*, July 2008, ES–4.

[9] John M. Logsdon et al., eds., *Exploring the Unknown: Selected Documents in the History of the U.S. Civil Space Program*, vol. I, *Organizing for Exploration* (Washington, DC: NASA Special Publication 4407, 1995), 629–630.

[10] See John M. Logsdon, *The Decision to Go to the Moon: Project Apollo and the National Interest* (Cambridge: MIT Press, 1970), 23–24, for an account of these organizational steps.

[11] Ibid., 27.

[12] The statement can be found in Logsdon, *Exploring the Unknown*, 362–373. The quoted material is from page 362.

[13] Ibid., 415.

[14] Ibid., 424.

[15] Ibid. See 439–452 for a copy of the memorandum.

[16] White House, Reorganization Plan 1, January 26, 1973, available at <www.washingtonwatch-dog.org/documents/usc/ttl5/app/0167/0167/index.html>.

[17] Logsdon, *Exploring the Unknown*, 593.

[18] However, the SIG (Space) mechanism was bypassed as the question of whether to approve development of a space station was considered by President Reagan in favor of a Cabinet Council on Commerce.

[19] The White House, National Security Policy Directive 1, "Organization of the National Security Council System," February 13, 2001, available at <www.fas.org/irp/offdocs/nspd/nspd-1.htm>.

[20] Alan G. Whittaker, Frederick C. Smith, and Elizabeth McKune, *The National Security Policy Process: The National Security Council and Interagency System* (Washington, DC: Industrial College of the Armed Forces, National Defense University, August 2005), 25–26.

[21] The text of the fact sheet summarizing the unclassified version of the policy is available at <www.ostp.gov/html/US%20National%20Space%20Policy.pdf>.

[22] Committee on U.S. Space Leadership, Memorandum for the President, "America's Leadership in Space," March 10, 2009.

[23] Joseph Fuller, Jr., "It's Time for a New Space Age," *Aviation Week and Space Technology* 166, no. 2 (January 8, 2007), 7.

[24] Barack Obama, "Advancing the Frontiers of Space Exploration," August 17, 2008.

Chapter 13

Space Law and the Advancement of Spacepower

Peter L. Hays

Space law has and should continue to play an essential role in the evolution of spacepower. Testing the principle of "freedom of space" and helping establish the legality of satellite overflight were primary objectives of National Security Council Directive 5520, the first U.S. space policy, approved by President Dwight D. Eisenhower in May 1955;[1] during the 1960s, the superpowers and other emerging spacefaring states negotiated a far-reaching and forward-thinking Outer Space Treaty (OST);[2] and today, a variety of transparency and confidence-building measures (TCBMs) for space are being discussed and debated in a number of fora.[3] Law can be perhaps the single most important means of providing structure and predictability to humanity's interactions with the cosmos. Justice, reason, and law are nowhere more needed than in the boundless, anarchic, and self-help environment of the final frontier. The topics that space law is designed to address, the precedents from which it is drawn, and the pathways ahead that it illuminates will be critical determinants of the future development of spacepower.

Although there is some substance to arguments that the OST only precludes those military activities that were of little interest to the superpowers and does not bring much clarity or direction to many of the most important potential space activities, the treaty nonetheless provides a solid and comprehensive foundation upon which to build additional legal structures needed to advance spacepower. Spacefaring actors can most effectively improve on this foundation through a number of actions including further developing and refining the OST regime, adapting the most useful parts of analogous regimes such as the Law of the Sea and Seabed Authority mechanisms, and rejecting standards that stifle innovation, inadequately address threats to humanity's survival, or do not provide opportunities for rewards commensurate with risks undertaken. In the three sections below, this chapter explores other specific ways improvements in space law may contribute to furthering the quest for sustainable space security, enabling more direct creation of wealth in and from space, and ultimately improving the odds for humanity's survival by helping to protect the Earth and space environments. Without clearer and better developed space law, humanity may squander opportunities and investments, making it more difficult for spacepower to enable these and other critical contributions to our future.

While desires for better refined space law to advance spacepower may be clear, progress toward developing and implementing improvements is not likely to be fast or easy. Terrestrial law evolved fairly steadily and has operated over millennia. Space law, by contrast, is a relatively novel concept that rapidly emerged within a few years of the opening of the space age and thereafter greatly slowed. The objectives of space law must include not just aspirational goals such as structuring competition between humans and helping define and refine fundamental interactions between humanity and the cosmos but also more mundane issues such as property rights and commercial interests. It is likely there will be growing pressure for space law to provide greater predictability and structure in many areas despite the fact that it can be very difficult to establish foundational legal elements for the cosmic realm such as evidence, causality, attribution, and precedence. Moreover, any movement toward improving space law is likely to be slowed by discouraging attributes associated with spacepower that include very long timelines and prospects for only potential or intangible benefits. These factors can erode acceptance of and support for improving space law at both the personal and political levels, but they also point to the need for an incremental approach and reinforce the long-term value of law in providing stability and predictability.

Other impediments to further developing space law are exacerbated by a lack of acceptance in some quarters that sustained, cooperative efforts are often the best and sometimes the only way in which humanity can address our most pressing survival challenges. Cosmic threats to humanity's survival exist and include the depletion of resources and fouling of our only current habitat, threats in the space environment such as large objects that could strike Earth and cause cataclysmic damage, and the eventual exhaustion and destruction of the Sun. The message is clear: environmental degradation and space phenomena can threaten our existence, but humanity can improve our odds for survival *if* we can cooperate in grasping and exploiting survival opportunities. Law can provide one of the most effective ways to structure and use these opportunities. Sustained dialogue of the type this volume seeks to foster can help raise awareness, generate support for better space law, and ultimately nurture the spacepower needed to improve our odds for survival.

The Quest for Sustainable Security

In examining space law, spacepower, and humanity's quest for sustainable security, it is prudent for spacefaring actors to transcend traditional categories and approaches by considering resources in novel, broad, and multidimensional ways. This chapter attempts to employ the spirit of this unrestrained approach but is not suggesting that everything discussed would necessarily turn out to be useful or implementable in the real world. In addition, it is often not practical or even possible to examine space law developments in discrete ways by delineating between legal, technical, and policy considerations or between terrestrial and space security concerns. Over the long run, however, an expansive approach will undoubtedly reveal and help create the most opportunities to advance space law and spacepower in the most significant and lasting ways. Nonetheless, when beginning the journey, small, incremental steps are the most pragmatic way to develop and implement more effective space law, and the process should first focus on improving and refining the foundation provided by the OST regime.

Most spacefaring actors understand the merits and overall value of the OST regime; they are much more interested in building upon this foundation than in creating a new structure. As the most important first steps toward further developing space law, the international community needs to find better ways to achieve more universal adherence to the regime's foundational norms and embed all important spacefaring actors more completely within the regime. Beginning work to include major non-state actors in more explicit ways could prove to be a difficult undertaking that would require substantial expansion of the regime and probably should be approached incrementally. Fortunately, the security dimensions of the regime have opened windows of opportunity and important precedents have been set by expanding participation in the United Nations Committee on the Peaceful Uses of Outer Space and the World Radio Conferences of the International Telecommunications Union (ITU) to include nonstate actors as observers or associate members. Some form of two-tiered participation structure within the OST regime might be appropriate for a number of years and it may prove impractical to include nonstate actors in a formal treaty, but steps toward expanded participation should begin now, both to capture the growing spacepower of nonstate actors and to harness their energy in helping achieve more universal adherence to the regime. Perhaps most importantly, these initial steps should help promote a sense of stewardship for space among more actors and increase attention on those parties that fail to join or comply with these norms. Of course, these first steps alone would be insufficient to make large improvements or assure compliance with the regime, yet they might be among the most easily undertaken and significant ways to advance space law in the near term. Other specific areas within the OST regime that should be better developed, perhaps through creation of a standing body with implementation responsibilities, include the article VI obligations for signatories to authorize and exercise continuing supervision over space activities and the article IX responsibilities for signatories to undertake or request appropriate international consultations before proceeding with any activity or experiment that would cause potentially harmful interference.

One key way the United States could help better define OST implementation obligations and demonstrate leadership in fostering cooperative spacepower would be to share space situational awareness (SSA) data globally in more effective ways through the Commercial and Foreign Entities (CFE) program or some other approach. Congress has extended the CFE Pilot Program through September 2010 and, following the February 2009 collision between the Iridium and Cosmos satellites, there is more worldwide attention focused on space debris and spaceflight safety as well as considerable motivation for the United States to improve the program by providing SSA data to more users in more timely and consistent ways. A most useful specific goal for the CFE program would be development of a U.S. Government–operated data center for ephemeris, propagation data, and premaneuver notifications for all active satellites; consideration should also be given to the utility and modalities of creating or transitioning such a data center to international auspices.[4] Users would voluntarily contribute data to the center, perhaps through a Global Positioning System (GPS) transponder on each satellite, and the data would be constantly updated, freely available, and readily accessible so that it could be used by satellite operators to plan for and avoid conjunctions.[5] Difficult legal, technical, and policy issues that inhibit progress on sharing SSA data include bureaucratic inertia, liability, and proprietary concerns; nonuniform data formatting standards and incompatibility between propagators and other cataloguing tools; and security concerns over exclusion of certain satellites from any public data. Some of these legal concerns could be addressed by working toward better cradle-to-grave tracking of all catalogued objects to help establish the launching state and liability; using opaque processes to exclude proprietary information from public databases to the maximum extent feasible; and indemnifying program operators, even if they provide faulty data that results in a collision, so long as they operate in good faith, exercise reasonable care, and follow established procedures.

History suggests there is a very important role for militaries both in setting the stage for the emergence of international legal regimes and in enforcing the norms of those regimes once they are in place. Development of any TCBMs for space, such as rules of the road or codes of conduct, should draw closely from the development and operation of such measures in other domains such as sea or air. The international community should consider the most appropriate means of separating military activities from civil and commercial activities in the building of these measures because advocating a single standard for how all space activities ought to be regulated or controlled is inappropriately ambitious and not likely to be helpful. The U.S. Department of Defense requires safe and responsible operations by warships and military aircraft but they are not legally required to follow all the same rules as commercial traffic and sometimes operate within specially protected zones that separate them from other traffic. Full and open dialogue about these ideas and others will help develop space rules that draw from years of experience in operating in these other domains and make the most sense for the unique operational characteristics of space. Other concerns surround the implications of various organizational structures and rules of engagement for potential military operations in space. Should such forces operate under national or only international authority, who should decide when certain activities constitute a threat, and how should such forces be authorized to engage threats, especially if such engagements might create other threats or potentially cause harm to humans or space systems? Clearly, these and a number of other questions are very difficult to address and require careful international vetting well before actual operation of such forces in space. Finally, consider the historic role of the Royal and U.S. Navies in fighting piracy, promoting free trade, and enforcing global norms against slave trading. Should there be analogous roles in space for the U.S. military and other military forces today and in the future? What would be the space component of the Proliferation Security Initiative and how might the United States and others encourage like-minded actors to cooperate on such an initiative? Attempts to create legal regimes or enforcement norms that do not specifically include and build upon military capabilities are likely to be divorced from pragmatic realities and ultimately be frustrating efforts.[6]

Seemingly new U.S. focus and direction on space TCBMs initially was provided by a statement that appeared on the Obama administration White House Web site on January 20, 2009: "Ensure Freedom of Space: The Obama-Biden administration will restore American leadership on space issues, seeking a worldwide ban on weapons that interfere with military and commercial satellites."[7] The language about seeking a worldwide ban on space weapons was similar to position papers issued during the Obama-Biden campaign but much less detailed and nuanced; it drew considerable attention and some criticism.[8] By May 2009, the "Space" part of the Defense Issues section on the White House Web site had been changed to read:

> Space: The full spectrum of U.S. military capabilities depends on our space systems. To maintain our technological edge and protect assets in this domain, we will continue to invest in next-generation capabilities such as operationally responsive space and global positioning systems. We will cooperate with our allies and the private sector to identify and protect against intentional and unintentional threats to U.S. and allied space capabilities.

Ongoing space policy reviews including a congressionally directed Space Posture Review and Presidential Study Directives on National Space Policy are likely to encourage policies that are more supportive of pursuing TCBMs as well as greater reliance on commercial and international partners.[9] Consideration is also being given to the best ways to reconcile any new approaches with the 2006 U.S. National Space Policy language about opposing "development of new legal regimes or other restrictions that seek to prohibit or limit U.S. access to or use of space" while encouraging "international cooperation with foreign nations and/or consortia on space activities that are of mutual benefit."[10] Spacepower actors can expect to continue making progress in developing effective, sustainable, and cooperative approaches to space security by building on the ongoing thoughtful dialogue between all major space actors in several venues that emphasizes a number of mainly incremental, pragmatic, technical, and bottom-up steps. Prime examples of this approach include the February 2008 adoption by the United Nations General Assembly of the Inter-Agency Debris Coordination Committee (IADC) voluntary guidelines for mitigating space debris and the December 2008 release from the Council of the European Union of a draft Code of Conduct for outer space activities.[11]

Beyond the OST, efforts to craft comprehensive, formal, top-down space arms control or regulation continue to face the same significant problems that have overwhelmed attempts to develop such mechanisms in the past. The most serious of these problems include disagreements over the proper forum, scope, and object for negotiations; basic definitional issues about what is a "space weapon" and how they might be categorized as offensive or defensive and stabilizing or destabilizing; and daunting concerns about whether adequate monitoring and verification mechanisms can be found for any comprehensive and formalized TCBMs. These problems relate to a number of thorny specific issues such as whether the negotiations should be primarily among only major spacefaring actors or more multilateral, what satellites and other terrestrial systems should be covered, and whether the object should be control of space weapons or TCBMs for space; the types of TCBMs that might be most useful (for example, rules of the road or keep-out zones) and how these approaches might be reconciled with the existing space law regime; and verification problems such as how to address the latent or residual antisatellite (ASAT) capabilities possessed by many dual-use and military systems or how to deal with the significant military potential of even a small number of covert ASAT systems.

New space system technologies, continuing growth of the commercial space sector, and new verification and monitoring methods interact with these existing problems in complex ways. Some of the changes would seem to favor TCBMs, such as better radars and optical systems for improved SSA, attribution, and verification capabilities; technologies for better space system diagnostics; and the stabilizing potential of redundant and distributed space architectures that create many nodes by employing larger numbers of smaller and less expensive satellites. Many other trends, however, would seem to make space arms control and regulation even more difficult. For example, micro- or nanosatellites might be used as virtually undetectable active ASATs or passive space mines; proliferation of space technology has radically increased the number of significant space actors to include a number of nonstate actors that have developed or are developing sophisticated dual-use technologies such as autonomous rendezvous and docking capabilities; satellite communications technology can easily be used to jam rather than communicate; and growth in the commercial space sector raises issues such as how quasi-military systems could be protected or negated and the unclear security implications of global markets for dual-use space capabilities and products.

There is disagreement about the relative utility of top-down versus bottom-up approaches to developing space TCBMs and formal arms control but, following creation of the OST regime, the United States and many other major spacefaring actors have tended to favor bottom-up approaches, a point strongly emphasized by U.S. Ambassador Donald Mahley in February 2008: "Since the 1970s, five consecutive U.S. administrations have concluded it is impossible to achieve an effectively verifiable and militarily meaningful space arms control agreement."[12] Yet this assessment may be somewhat myopic since strategists need to consider not only the well-known difficulties with top-down approaches but also the potential opportunity costs of inaction and to recognize when they may need to trade some loss of sovereignty and flexibility for stability and restraints on others. Since the United States has not tested a kinetic energy ASAT since September 1985 and has no program to develop such capabilities, would it have been better to foreclose this option in order to purse a global ban on testing kinetic energy ASATs, and would such an effort have produced a restraining effect on Chinese development and testing of ASAT capabilities? This may have been a lost opportunity to pursue legal approaches but is a complex, multidimensional, and interdependent issue shaped by a variety of other factors such as inabilities to distinguish between ballistic missile defense and ASAT technologies, reluctance to limit technical options after the end of the Cold War, emergence of new and less easily deterred threats, and the demise of the Anti-Ballistic Missile Treaty.

Moreover, the Chinese, in particular, apparently disagree with pursuing only bottom-up approaches and, in ways that seem both shrewd and hypocritical, are currently developing significant counterspace capabilities while simultaneously advancing various top-down proposals in support of prevention of an arms race in outer space initiatives and moving ahead with the joint Chinese-Russian draft treaty on Prevention of Placement of Weapons in Outer Space (PPWT) introduced at the Conference on Disarmament in February 2008. If the Chinese are attempting to pursue a two-track approach to space arms control, they need to present that argument to the international community much more explicitly. The current draft PPWT goes to considerable lengths in attempting to define space, space objects, weapons in space, placement in space, and the use or threat of force, but there are still very considerable definitional issues with respect to how specific capabilities would be classified. An even more significant problem relates to all the terrestrial capabilities that are able to eliminate, damage, or disrupt the normal function of objects in outer space, such as the Chinese direct ascent ASAT. One must question the utility of a proposed agreement that does not address the significant security implications of current space system support for network enabled terrestrial warfare, does not deal with dual-use space capabilities, seems to be focused on a class of weapons that does not exist or at least is not deployed in space, is silent about all the terrestrial capabilities that are able to produce weapons effects in space, and would not even ban development and testing of space weapons, only their use.[13] Given these weaknesses in the PPWT, it seems plausible that it is designed as much to continue political pressure on the United States and derail U.S. missile defense efforts as it is to promote sustainable space security.

Since Sino-American relations in general and space relations in particular are likely to play a dominant role in shaping the quest for spacepower and sustainable security during this century, other proposed Sino-American cooperative space ventures or TCBMs are worthy of further consideration, including inviting a taikonaut to fly on one of the remaining space shuttle missions and making specific, repeated, and public invitations for the Chinese to join the International Space Station program and other major cooperative international space efforts. The United States and China could also work toward developing nonoffensive defenses of the type advocated by Philip Baines.[14] Kevin Pollpeter explains how China and the United States could cooperate in promoting the safety of human spaceflight and "coordinate space science missions to derive scientific benefits and to share costs. Coordinating space science missions with separately developed, but complementary space assets, removes the chance of sensitive technology transfer and allows the two countries to combine their resources to achieve the same effects as jointly developed missions."[15] Michael Pillsbury outlined six other areas where U.S. experts could profitably exchange views with Chinese specialists in a dialogue about space weapons issues: "reducing Chinese misperceptions of U.S. Space Policy, increasing Chinese transparency on space weapons, probing Chinese interest in verifiable agreements, multilateral versus bilateral approaches, economic consequences of use of space weapons, and reconsideration of U.S. high-tech exports to China."[16] Finally, Bruce MacDonald's report for the Council on Foreign Relations, "China, Space Weapons, and U.S. Security," offers a number of noteworthy additional specific recommendations for both the United States and China. For the United States, MacDonald recommends assessing the impact of different U.S. and Chinese offensive space postures and policies through intensified analysis and "crisis games" in addition to wargames; evaluating the desirability of a "no first use" pledge for offensive counterspace weapons that have irreversible effects;

pursuing selected offensive capabilities meeting important criteria—including effectiveness, reversible effects, and survivability—in a deterrence context to be able to negate adversary space capabilities on a temporary and reversible basis; refraining from further direct ascent ASAT tests and demonstrations as long as China does, unless there is a substantial risk to human health and safety from uncontrolled space object reentry; and entering negotiations on a kinetic energy ASAT testing ban. MacDonald's recommendations for China include providing more transparency into its military space programs; refraining from further direct ascent ASAT tests as long as the United States does; establishing a senior national security coordinating body, equivalent to a Chinese National Security Council; strengthening its leadership's foreign policy understanding by increasing the international affairs training of senior officer candidates and establishing an international security affairs office within the People's Liberation Army; providing a clear and credible policy and doctrinal context for its 2007 ASAT test and counterspace programs more generally, and addressing foreign concerns over China's ASAT test; and offering to engage in dialogue with the United States on mutual space concerns and become actively involved in discussions on establishing international space codes of conduct and confidence-building measures.[17]

Harvesting Energy and Creating Wealth in and from Space

Spacefaring actors should again consider revising and further developing the OST regime as a key first step when seeking better ways to harvest energy and create wealth in and from space. Expanding participation in the OST as recommended above would also be helpful, but other steps such as reducing liability concerns and clarifying legal issues with respect to harvesting energy and generating wealth are likely to be more effective in furthering commercial development of space. Of course, as with security, a range of objectives and values are in tension and require considerable effort to change or keep properly balanced. The OST has been extremely successful thus far with respect to its primary objective of precluding replication of the colonial exploitation that plagued much of Earth's history. The international community should now consider whether the dangers posed by potential cosmic land grabs continue to warrant OST interpretations that may be stifling development of spacepower, and, if these values are found to have become imbalanced, how impediments might best be reduced. Spacefaring actors should again use an expansive approach to consider how perceived OST restrictions and the commercial space sector have evolved and might be further advanced in a variety of ways including reinterpreting the OST regime itself, becoming more intentional about developing spacepower, creating space-based solar power capabilities, and improving export controls.

While the OST has thus far been unambiguous and successful in foreclosing sovereignty claims and the ills of colonization, it has been less clear and effective with respect to de facto property rights and other liability and commercialization issues. OST language, negotiating history, and subsequent practice do not preclude some level of commercial activity in space and on celestial bodies, but various articles of the OST support different interpretations about the potential scope of and limitations on this activity. The treaty most clearly allows those commercial activities that would be performed to support exploration or scientific efforts. It is far more problematic with respect to commercial space activity that would result in private gain or not somehow equitably distribute gains among all states. Even if it were found that commercial activities would not "appropriate" space resources, however that might be defined, it would be difficult to reconcile such activity with the spirit of the OST regime, especially since the regime provides no guidance on how private or unequal gains might be distributed. In addition to clarifying potential property rights and wealth distribution mechanisms, consideration should be given to reevaluating liability standards. The OST and 1972 Liability Convention establish two distinct liability structures: launching states are absolutely liable to pay compensation for any damages caused by space objects on Earth or to aircraft in flight but are only liable for damages caused in space by space objects if found to be negligent. A challenge for the international community is how best to evolve the existing space law regime based on either absolute liability or fault/negligence, depending upon the location of the incident, into a structure that might provide enough clarity to help establish liability for damages in space and perhaps provide better incentives for commercial development.[18]

Additional interpretation issues stem from the fact that OST is embedded within a larger body of international law and that broad regime is evolving, sometimes in ambiguous and contradictory ways. Elements within this large regime are of unclear and unequal weight: the Moon Agreement with its Common Heritage of Mankind (CHM) approach to communal property rights and equally shared rewards undoubtedly has some effect in advancing the CHM principle in both formal and customary international law. At the level of formal international law, however, the Moon Treaty falls well short of the OST due to its lack of parties, especially among major spacefaring states, particularly in contrast to the OST, a treaty that has been ratified by some 94 states and in force for over 40 years.

Most fundamentally, however, the current lack of clarity within space law about property rights and commercial interests is the result of both space law and space technology being underdeveloped and immature. Of course, there is also a "chicken-and-egg" factor at work since actors are discouraged from undertaking the test cases needed to develop and mature the regime because of the immaturity of the regime and their unwillingness to develop and employ improved technologies and processes as guinea pigs in whatever legal processes would be used to resolve property rights and reward structures. The most effective way to move past this significant hurdle would be to create more clear mechanisms for establishing property rights and processes by which all actors, especially commercial actors, could receive rewards commensurate with the risks they undertake. In addition, any comprehensive reevaluation of space property rights and liability concerns should also consider how these factors are addressed in analogous regimes such as the Seabed Authority in the Law of the Sea Treaty. Unfortunately, however, there are also several problems with attempting to draw from these precedents. First, several of the analogous regimes like the Law of the Sea build from CMH premises in several ways and it is not clear this approach is entirely applicable or helpful when attempting to sort through how the OST should apply to issues like property rights and reward structures. Second, while these analogous regimes are undoubtedly better developed than the OST and have a significant potential role in providing precedents, today they are still somewhat underdeveloped and immature with respect to their application in difficult areas such as property rights and reward structures, again limiting the current utility of attempting to draw from these precedents.

Provisions of the OST regime are probably the most important factors in shaping commercial space activity, but they are clearly not the only noteworthy legal and policy factors at work influencing developments within this sector. Legacy legal and policy structures developed during the Cold War were probably adequate for the amount of commercial space activity during that period, but it is far from clear they will be sufficient to address the significant and sustained increase in such activity since that time. In the 1960s, the United States was the first to begin developing space services such as communications, remote sensing, and launch capabilities but did so within the government sector. This approach began to change in the 1980s, first with the November 1984 Presidential Determination to allow some commercial communication services to compete with Intelsat and continuing with subsequent policies designed to foster development of a commercial space sector. By the late 1990s, commercial space activity worldwide had outpaced government activity, and although government space investments remain very important, they are likely to become increasingly overshadowed by commercial activity. It would be helpful if governments, and the U.S. Government in particular, could more explicitly develop and consistently implement legal structures and long-term policies that would better define and delineate between those space activities that ought to be pursued by the private and public sectors as well as more intentionally and consistently develop the desired degree of international cooperation in pursuing these objectives.

Other clear commercial and economic distinctions with the Cold War era have even more significant implications for the future of spacepower: whereas the Soviet Union was only a military superpower, China is a major U.S. trading partner and an economic superpower that recently passed Germany to became the world's third largest economy, is poised to pass Japan soon, and is on a path to become larger than the U.S. economy, perhaps within only about 10 years. Because of its economic muscle, China can afford to devote commensurately more resources to its military capabilities and will play a more significant role in structuring the global economic system. For example, China holds an estimated $1.4 trillion in foreign assets (mainly U.S. treasury notes), an amount that gives it great leverage in the structure of the system.[19]

The United States and other major spacefaring actors lack, but undoubtedly need, much more open and comprehensive visions for how to develop spacepower. This study is one attempt to foster more dialogue about these issues, but the process should continue, become more intentional and formalized, and be supported by an enduring organizational structure that includes the most important stakeholders in the future of spacepower. Legal structures should be a foundational part of creating and implementing the vision to develop spacepower, but a broader approach should be:

> focused on opening space as a medium for the full spectrum of human activity and commercial enterprise, and those actions which government can take to promote and enable it, through surveys, infrastructure development, pre-competitive technology, and encouraging incentive structures (prizes, anchor-customer contracts, and property/exclusivity rights), regulatory regimes (port authorities, spacecraft licensing,

public-private partnerships) and supporting services (open interface standards, RDT&E [research, development, test, and evaluation] facilities, rescue, etc.).[20]

In addition, consideration should be given to using other innovative mechanisms and nontraditional routes to space development, including a much wider range of Federal Government organizations and the growing number of state spaceport authorities and other organizations developing needed infrastructure. Finally, the United States should make comprehensive and careful exploration of the potential of space-based solar power its leading pathfinder in creating a vision for developing spacepower. Working toward harvesting this unlimited power source in economically viable ways will require development of appropriate supporting legal structures, particularly with respect to indemnification and potential public-private partnerships.

Global licensing and export controls for space technology have often been developed and implemented in inconsistent and counterproductive ways. It is understandable that many states view space technology as a key strategic resource and are very concerned about developing, protecting, and preventing the proliferation of this technology, but the international community, and the United States in particular, needs to find better legal mechanisms to balance and advance objectives in this area. Many current problems with U.S. export controls began after Hughes and Loral worked with insurance companies to analyze Chinese launch failures in January 1995 and February 1996. A congressional review completed in 1998 (Cox Report) determined these analyses violated the International Traffic in Arms Regulations (ITAR) by communicating technical information to the Chinese. The 1999 National Defense Authorization Act transferred export controls for all satellites and related items from the Commerce Department to the Munitions List administered by the State Department.[21] The stringent Munitions List controls contributed to a severe downturn in U.S. satellite exports.[22] To avoid these restrictions, foreign satellite manufacturers, beginning in 2002 with Alcatel Space (now Thales) and followed by European Aeronautic Defense and Space, Surrey Satellite Company, and others replaced all U.S.-built components on their satellites to make them "ITAR-free."[23]

There are two key reasons why the United States should move away from the priorities in its current space export control regime. First, an overly broad approach that tries to guard too many things dilutes monitoring resources and actually results in less protection for "crown jewels" than does a focused approach, and second, a more open approach is more likely to foster innovation, spur development of sectors of comparative advantage, and improve efficiency and overall economic growth. Congress and the Obama administration should make it a priority to reevaluate current U.S. export controls and adjust laws and policies accordingly. Excellent starting points are the recently released recommendations for rebalancing overall U.S. export control priorities in the congressionally mandated National Academies of Science study.[24] In addition, the United States should implement key recommendations from the Center for Strategic and International Studies study on the space industrial base such as removing from the Munitions List commercial communications satellite systems, dedicated subsystems, and components specifically designed for commercial use.[25]

Environmental Sustainability and Survival

Work toward developing space law to advance spacepower and improve environmental sustainability and humanity's odds for survival faces a number of daunting challenges, including a high "giggle factor," long timelines that can be beyond our political and personal awareness, and potential returns that are uncertain and intangible. While difficult, work in this area is absolutely critical since it may hold the key to humanity's survival, and it must be pursued with all the resources, consistency, and seriousness it deserves. The quest to improve space law to support environmental and survival objectives should focus on three areas: space debris, environmental monitoring, and planetary defense.

Human space activity produces many orbital objects; when these objects no longer serve a useful function, they are classified as space debris. Over time, human activity has generated an increasing amount of debris; the number of catalogued debris objects has gone from about 8,000 to over 18,000 during the past 20 years.[26] The most serious cause of debris is deliberate hypervelocity impacts between large objects at high orbital altitudes such as the Chinese direct ascent kinetic energy ASAT weapon test of January 2007, which now accounts for more than 25 percent of all catalogued objects in low Earth orbit (LEO).[27] If current trends continue, there is growing risk that space, and LEO in particular, will become increasingly unusable. Fortunately, there is also growing awareness and earnestness across the international community in addressing this threat. Overall goals for spacefaring actors with respect to space debris include minimizing its creation while mitigating and remediating its effects—space law can play an important role in all these areas. Key approaches to minimizing creation of debris are commercial best practices and evolving regimes such as the

IADC voluntary guidelines adopted by the United Nations General Assembly in February 2008. Spacefaring actors also need to consider mechanisms to transition these voluntary guidelines into more binding standards and ways to impose specific costs such as sanctions or fines on actors that negligently or deliberately create long-lived debris. Fines could be applied toward efforts to further develop and educate spacefaring actors about the debris mitigation regime as well as to create and implement remediation techniques. An additional potential source of funding for mitigation and remediation would be establishing auctions for the radio frequency spectrum controlled by the ITU that would be analogous to the spectrum auctions conducted at the national level by organizations like the Federal Communications Commission. Finally, it must be emphasized that techniques for remediating debris using lasers or other methods are likely to have significant potential as ASAT weapons, and careful international consideration should be given to how and by whom such systems are operated.

Space provides a unique location to monitor and potentially remediate Earth's climate. It is the only location from which simultaneous in situ observations of Earth's climate activity can be conducted, and such observations are essential to developing a long-term understanding of potential changes in our biosphere. Because so much is riding on our understanding of the global climate and our potential responses to perceived changes, it is particularly important to apply apolitical standards in getting the science right and controlling for known space effects such as solar cycles when making these observations. If fears about global warming are correct and the global community wishes to take active measures to remediate these effects, space also provides a unique location to operate remediation options such as orbital solar shades.

It is also imperative that the United States and all spacefaring actors think more creatively about using spacepower to transcend traditional and emerging threats to our survival. Parts of space law can help to illuminate paths toward and develop incentives for creating a better future. Space, perhaps more than any other medium, is inherently linked to humanity's future and survival. We need to link these ideas and better articulate ways spacepower can light a path toward genuinely cooperative approaches for protecting the Earth and space environments from cataclysmic events such as large objects that may collide with Earth or gamma ray bursts that may have the potential to render huge swaths of space uninhabitable. Better knowledge about known threats such as near Earth objects (NEOs) is being acquired but more urgency is needed. All predicted near approaches and possible NEO impacts such as that of the asteroid Apophis, predicted for April 13, 2029, ought to be seen as opportunities since they provide critical real-world tests for our ability to be proactive in developing effective precision tracking and NEO mitigation capabilities. In the near term, it is most important for national and international organizations to be specifically charged with and resourced to develop better understanding of NEO threats and mitigation techniques that can be effectively applied against likely impacts. Ultimately, however, we cannot know of or effectively plan for all potential threats to Earth but should pursue a multidimensional approach to develop capabilities to improve our odds for survival and one day perhaps become a multiplanetary species.

There will be inevitable missteps, setbacks, and unintended consequences as we refine space law to improve our quest for sustainable space security, generate wealth in and from space, and protect the Earth and space environments. The inexorable laws of physics and of human interaction indicate that we will create the best opportunities for success in improving space law by beginning long-term, patient work now rather than crash programs later. This patient approach will allow the best prospects for space law to provide a solid foundation for the peaceful advancement of spacepower.

Notes

[1] The best and most comprehensive analysis of the complex maneuvering by the superpowers at the opening of the space age remains Walter A. McDougall's Pulitzer Prize–winning . . . *the Heavens and the Earth: A Political History of the Space Age* (New York: Basic Books, 1985). National Security Council Directive 5520 is reprinted in John M. Logsdon, ed. *Exploring the Unknown: Selected Documents in the History of the U.S. Civil Space Program*, vol. I, *Organizing for Exploration* (Washington, DC: NASA History Office, 1995), 308–313. McDougall in *Heavens and Earth* and R. Cargill Hall's introductory essay, "Origins of U.S. Space Policy: Eisenhower, Open Skies, and Freedom of Space," in *Exploring the Unknown* masterfully develop the context and purposes of the directive. Hall uses the term *stalking horse* to describe the purpose of the IGY satellite in relation to the WS–117L (America's first reconnaissance satellite program). *Peaceful purposes* for space activity are often referenced and cited but never authoritatively defined.

[2] Treaty on Principles Governing the Activities of States in the Exploration and Use of Outer Space, including the Moon and Other Celestial Bodies (General Assembly resolution 2222 [XXI], annex), adopted December 19, 1966, opened for signature January 27, 1967, and entered into force October 10, 1967.

[3] The term *transparency* apparently connotes espionage when translated into Chinese and since the Chinese are a key party that spacefaring actors wish to engage, consideration should be given to finding an alternative term, perhaps *clarity of intensions.*

[4] For an outstanding and detailed analysis of the benefits and challenges associated with creation of an international data center, see Lee-Volker Cox, "Avoiding Collisions in Space: Is It Time for an International Space Integration Center?" research paper, U.S. Army War College, March 30, 2007, available at <www.dtic.mil/cgi-bin/GetTRDoc?AD=ADA469676&Location=U2&doc=GetTRDoc.pdf>.

⁵ Space situational awareness (SSA) issues are framed by specialized concepts and jargon. *Conjunctions* are close approaches, or potential collisions, between objects in orbit. *Propagators* are complex modeling tools used to predict the future location of orbital objects. Satellite operators currently use a number of different propagators and have different standards for evaluating and potentially maneuvering away from conjunctions. Maneuvering requires fuel and shortens the operational life of satellites. Orbital paths are described by a set of variables known as ephemeris data; two-line element sets are the most commonly used ephemeris data. Much of this data is contained in the form of a satellite catalog. The United States maintains a public catalog at <www.space-track.org>. Other entities maintain their own catalogs. Orbital paths constantly are perturbed by a number a factors including Earth's inconsistent gravity gradient, solar activity, and the gravitational pull of other orbital objects. Perturbations cause propagation of orbital paths to become increasingly inaccurate over time; beyond approximately 4 days into the future, predictions about the location of orbital objects can be significantly inaccurate. For more about SSA concepts, see Brian Weeden, "The Numbers Game," *The Space Review*, July 13, 2009, available at <www.thespacereview.com/article/1417/1>. For discussion about ways to share SSA data and other space security ideas fostered by meetings between the Department of Defense Executive Agent for Space and the Chief Executive Officers of commercial satellite operators, see David McGlade, "Commentary: Preserving the Orbital Environment," *Space News*, February 19, 2007, 27.

⁶ On the role of militaries in enforcing legal norms and analogies between the law of the sea and space law, see R. Joseph DeSutter, "Space Control, Diplomacy, and Strategic Integration," *Space and Defense* 1, no. 1 (Fall 2006), 29–51.

⁷ The statement appeared on the Defense Agenda section of the White House Web site, available at <www.whitehouse.gov>.

⁸ See in particular, the *Space News* editorial for February 2, 2009, "Banning Space Weapons—and Reality."

⁹ Section 913 of the Fiscal Year 2009 National Defense Authorization Act (P.L. 110–417) directs the Secretary of Defense and Director of National Intelligence to submit a Space Posture Review to Congress by December 1, 2009. In addition, the Obama administration has ongoing Presidential Study Directives that are examining the need for changes to current National Space Policy; see Amy Klamper, "White House Orders Sweeping U.S. Space Policy Review," *Space News*, July 15, 2009.

¹⁰ The unclassified version of current National Space Policy was posted on the Office of Science and Technology Policy Web site on October 14, 2006.

¹¹ United Nations General Assembly Resolution 62/217, "International Cooperation in the Peaceful Uses of Outer Space," February 1, 2008, and Council of the European Union, "Council Conclusions and Draft Code of Conduct for Outer Space Activity," December 3, 2008.

¹² Ambassador Donald A. Mahley, remarks at the State of Space Security Workshop, Space Policy Institute, George Washington University, Washington, DC, February 1, 2008.

¹³ Fact sheet, "Preventing the Placement of Weapons in Outer Space: A Backgrounder on the Draft Treaty by Russia and China," ReachingCriticalWill.org, available at <www.reachingcriticalwill.org/legal/paros/wgroup/PAROS-PPWT-factsheet.pdf>. For an outstanding analysis of trigger events for space weaponization and why space-basing is not necessarily the most important consideration, see Barry D. Watts, *The Military Use of Space: A Diagnostic Assessment* (Washington, DC: Center for Strategic and Budgetary Assessments, February 2001), 97–106. Watts argues:

> There are at least two paths by which orbital space might become a battle-ground for human conflict. One consists of dramatic, hard-to-miss trigger events such as the use of nuclear weapons to attack orbital assets. The other class involves more gradual changes such as a series of small, seemingly innocuous steps over a period of years that would, only in hindsight, be recognized as having crossed the boundary from force enhancement to force application. For reasons stemming from the railroad analogy . . . the slippery slope of halting, incremental steps toward force application may be the most likely path of the two.

Watts discusses high-altitude nuclear detonations, failure of nuclear deterrence, and threats to use nuclear ballistic missiles during a crisis as the most likely of the dramatic trigger events.

[14] Philip J. Baines, "The Prospects for 'Non-Offensive' Defenses in Space," in *New Challenges in Missile Proliferation, Missile Defense, and Space Security,* ed. James Clay Moltz (Monterey: Center for Nonproliferation Studies Occasional Paper no. 12, Monterey Institute of International Studies, July 2003), 31–48.

[15] Kevin Pollpeter, *Building for the Future: China's Progress in Space Technology during the 10th 5-year Plan and the U.S. Response* (Carlisle, PA: Strategic Studies Institute, U.S. Army War College, 2008), 48–50.

[16] Michael P. Pillsbury, "An Assessment of China's Anti-Satellite and Space Warfare Programs, Policies, and Doctrines," report prepared for the U.S.-China Economic and Security Review Commission, January 19, 2007, 48.

[17] Bruce W. MacDonald, *China, Space Weapons, and U.S. Security* (New York: Council on Foreign Relations, September 2008), 34–38.

[18] Although article VII of the Outer Space Treaty discusses liability, that article was further implemented in the Convention on International Liability for Damage Caused by Space Objects, commonly referred to as the Liability Convention. Under the Liability Convention, article II, a launching state is absolutely liable to pay compensation for damage caused by its space object on the surface of the Earth or to aircraft in flight. However, under articles III and IV, in the event of damage being caused other than on the surface of the Earth by a space object, the launching state is liable only if the damage is due to its fault or the fault of persons for whom it is responsible (that is, commercial companies) under a negligence standard. Convention on International Liability for Damage Caused by Space Objects (resolution 2777 [XXVI] annex), adopted November 29, 1971, opened for signature March 29, 1972, and entered into force September 1, 1972.

[19] James Fallows, "The $1.4 Trillion Question," *The Atlantic* (January–February 2008).

[20] Peter Garretson, "Elements of a 21st-century Space Policy," *The Space Review,* August 3, 2009, available at <www.thespacereview.com/article/1433/1>.

[21] The January 1995 failure was a Long March 2E rocket carrying Hughes-built Apstar 2 spacecraft, and the February 1996 failure was a Long March 3B rocket carrying Space Systems/Loral-built Intelsat 708 spacecraft. Representative Christopher Cox (R–CA) led a 6-month long House Select Committee investigation that produced the "U.S. National Security and Military/Commercial Concerns with the People's Republic of China" report released on May 25, 1999 (available at <www.house.gov/coxreport>). In January 2002, Loral agreed to pay the U.S. Government $20 million to settle the charges of the illegal technology transfer and in March 2003, Boeing agreed to pay $32 million for the role of Hughes (which Boeing acquired in 2000). Requirements for transferring controls back to the State Department are in Sections 1513 and 1516 of the Fiscal Year 1999 National Defense Authorization Act. Related items are defined as "satellite fuel, ground support equipment, test equipment, payload adapter or interface hardware, replacement parts, and non-embedded solid propellant orbit transfer engines."

[22] Satellite builders claim that their exports dropped 59 percent in 2000 and that since March 1999 their share of the global market declined sharply (from 75 percent to 45 percent). Evelyn Iritani and Peter Pae, "U.S. Satellite Industry Reeling Under New Export Controls," *The Los Angeles Times,* December 11, 2000, 1. According to *Space News,* 2000 marked the first time that U.S. firms were awarded fewer contracts for geostationary communications satellites than their European competitors (the Europeans were ahead 15 to 13). Peter B. de Selding and Sam Silverstein, "Europe Bests U.S. in Satellite Contracts in 2000," *Space News,* January 15, 2001, 1, 20.

[23] Peter B. de Selding, "European Satellite Component Maker Says it is Dropping U.S. Components Because of ITAR," *Space News Business Report,* June 13, 2005; and Douglas Barrie and Michael A. Taverna, "Specious Relationship," *Aviation Week & Space Technology,* July 17, 2006, 93–96.

[24] National Research Council, *Beyond "Fortress America:" National Security Controls on Science and Technology in a Globalized World* (Washington, DC: National Academies Press, 2009). With the new administration and Congress as well as former Congresswoman Ellen Tauscher confirmed in the key

position of Under Secretary of State for Arms Control and International Security, conditions for changing the space export control law are the most favorable they have been for the last decade.

[25] *Briefing of the Working Group on the Health of the U.S. Space Industrial Base and the Impact of Export Controls* (Washington: Center for Strategic and International Studies, February 2008).

[26] Comprehensive and current information about orbital debris is provided by NASA and the European Space Agency at <www.orbitaldebris.jsc.nasa.gov> and <www.esa.int/esaMI/Space_Debris/index.html>.

[27] "Fengyun 1–C Debris: Two Years Later," *Orbital Debris Quarterly News* 13, no. 1 (January 2009), 2. As a result of the January 11, 2007, Chinese ASAT test, the U.S. Space Surveillance Network has catalogued 2,378 pieces of debris with diameters greater than 5 centimeters, is tracking 400 additional debris objects that are not yet catalogued, and estimates the test created more that 150,000 pieces of debris larger than 1 square centimeter. Unfortunately, less than 2 percent of this debris has reentered the atmosphere so far and it is estimated that many pieces will remain in orbit for decades and some for more than a century. By contrast, destruction of the inoperative USA–193 satellite on February 21, 2008, occurred at a much lower altitude and did not produce long-lived debris; the last piece of catalogued debris from this intercept reentered on October 9, 2008. On the engagement of USA–193 see, in particular, James Oberg, "OPERATION BURNT FROST: Five Myths about the Satellite Smashup," NBC News Analysis, February 27, 2008, and James E. Oberg, "Down in Flames: Media 'Space Experts' Flub the Shoot-Down Story," *The New Atlantis*, no. 24 (Spring 2009), 120–129.

Chapter 14

Future Strategy and Professional Development: A Roadmap

Simon P. Worden

> *Once upon a time there was a dear little chicken named Chicken Little.*
> *One morning as she was scratching in her garden, a pebble fell off the roof*
> *and hit her on the head. "Oh, dear me!" she cried, "The sky is falling. I must*
> *go and tell the King," and away she ran down the road.*

The fable of Chicken Little has many versions. In some, she is saved by the King or another altruistic entity. In most, she and her colleagues are eaten by the evil Foxy Loxy. In my fable, however, the sky is not falling on Chicken Little—but that the sky is receding at an ever increasing pace.

In the 1980s and 1990s, space capabilities, and in particular their security-related aspects, were all the rage. In the 1980s, the United States was mounting a major missile defense program based largely on space capabilities. The Strategic Defense Initiative promised to lead to the end of the Cold War, and many experts believe it did. Our civil space program was beginning to fly the space shuttle, a reusable space transportation system that was heralded as ushering in a new era of space access and expansion. In the 1990s, commercial space programs such as the global space communications system Iridium were touted as the first step toward explosive growth for commercial space endeavors. Perhaps most significant was the apparent realization of the central role that space would play in national security. The bipartisan 1999 Commission to Assess National Security Space Management and Organization (the Rumsfeld Commission, named after its chairman, Donald Rumsfeld) resulted in huge growth in national security space spending and sweeping reorganization and centralization of national security space endeavors.[1]

Alas, none of the ambitious prospects for space appear to have been met. Our missile defense systems have little to do with space capabilities; indeed, the entire program has effectively been transferred to the U.S. Army's ground-oriented management. The space shuttle has not met its promise and is being phased out in favor of the older Apollo approach. Most communications systems now rely on global fiber connections and not commercial space capabilities. And practically all of the Rumsfeld Commission's space recommendations have been abandoned.

Of growing concern is what is going on outside the United States. Several states have expressed alarm over an alleged U.S. space weapons program. While these nations, particularly China and Russia, know that little is going on in this area, they have enjoyed stirring up international outrage for their own purposes. While this may seem harmless enough in the short term, it could itself be an impetus or perhaps an excuse for others to mount a counterspace effort of their own. In the past, such challenges to U.S. space utilization might have seemed laughable, but that is not so today.

Many nations are mounting impressive programs in space technology and utilization. Key to these efforts has been the development of so-called microsatellites and low-cost means of getting them into space. The pioneer in this technology has been Surrey Satellite Technology, Ltd. (SSTL) at the University of Surrey.[2] Part of SSTL's success has been its programs to assist other nations develop small (100-kilogram-class) space systems. Over a dozen nations have benefited from SSTL collaborations. Today, for less than $20 million, just about any nation can build and launch a satellite capable of significant security-related functions such as 1-meter-class imagery.

While the rest of the world aggressively develops these low-cost systems, the United States is increasingly mired in cost overruns and failed space systems. Practically every major U.S. security-related system is grossly overrun and significantly behind schedule. Moreover, with some exceptions (mostly driven by congressional insistence), the U.S. security community has shown little interest in small, fast-paced space systems.

Part of the U.S. malaise stems from rather uninspired leadership in military space system development and operation. Most military space discussions begin with something along the lines of "support to the war fighter." This attitude has led to the perspective that space capabilities, and correspondingly military space leaders, are secondary to "warfighters." The U.S. Air Force highlights its combat pilots, not its space engineers. This is not the type of environment that will attract aggressive, creative leaders.[3]

The first premise of this chapter is that the primary value of space capabilities is not their support to warfighters; rather, it is that they are the primary means for war prevention through the forging of collaborative international security arrangements.

Interestingly, SSTL has developed an impressive prototype for future use of space systems for security purposes: cooperative international space security measures based on small satellites. The SSTL-inspired and -led Disaster Monitoring Constellation consists of five microsatellites built and launched by Algeria, China, Nigeria, Turkey, and the United Kingdom.[4] Each satellite obtains wide-area 36-meter imagery with planned improvements to 4-meter resolution. The member states get frequent revisit imagery suitable for detecting and managing responses to natural disasters such as floods and earthquakes. Key for the purposes of this discussion is the postulate that such systems represent a broader meaning of security and a new means to link diverse states in a common security endeavor. The United States would do well to learn from this success and find ways to involve itself in and lead such future cooperative ventures.

One such possibility for cooperative international leverage is the new U.S. "Vision for Space Exploration." As with the Apollo program of the 1960s, the new space exploration initiative, involving the goal of permanent international settlements on other worlds, has considerable security-related possibilities.

Significantly, space capabilities such as precision positioning, navigation, and timing through such systems as the global positioning system (GPS) have become true global utilities. Protecting and expanding these capabilities, which are critical elements in global economic lynchpins such as transportation and communication, are in the global interest. A new security regime based on shared global utilities, including long-term goals such as space exploration and settlement, offers the United States a new opportunity to lead international security regimes. Aggressive U.S. development of technology—for example, distributed small space systems such as microsatellites—is key.

The Problem

Foreign Progress

The United States prides itself on its space leadership, particularly in the security use of space. Indeed, it regards space as critical to its overall national security stature. The National Space Policy reiterates this importance when it states, "United States national security is critically dependent upon space capabilities, and this dependence will grow."[5]

The United States also recognizes that its space stature is being challenged by many nations. The Rumsfeld Commission noted:

> The relative dependence of the U.S. on space makes its space systems potentially attractive targets. Many foreign nations and non-state entities are pursuing space-related activities. Those hostile to the U.S. possess, or can acquire on the global market, the means to deny, disrupt or destroy U.S. space systems by attacking satellites in space, communications links to and from the ground or ground stations that command the satellites and process their data. Therefore, the U.S. must develop and maintain intelligence collection capabilities and an analysis approach that will enable it to better understand the intentions and motivations as well as the capabilities of potentially hostile states and entities.[6]

This concern is translated in many minds, particularly those of national security space professionals, as a direct military challenge. However it does not appear that direct threats are the only, or perhaps even the most severe, ones.

Many nations are developing significant dual-use capabilities that meet both security and other, often commercial and scientific, purposes. Other nations frequently have a broader view of security than just military concerns, to include economic and environmental aspects. Particularly within Europe, perspectives about military space are both uncertain and rapidly changing. In the multipolar world that emerged after the Cold War, security issues that were originally military driven have become more complicated. As European roles in the world grow, particularly peacekeeping roles outside the continent, the need for space system support in such areas as communications and navigation also grows.

The emerging technology of small, low-cost space systems (microsatellites) is changing the dynamic. Microsatellites are 100- to 200-kilogram systems that cost approximately $5 million to $20 million to construct. Coupled with low-cost space launch, generally provided as a piggyback payload on a larger booster, the entire mission cost is $10 million to $30 million—an order of magnitude less costly than conventional space missions. Using new off-the-shelf technology, these microsatellites can perform many of the security-related functions that formerly required large, expensive systems. For example, several nations are now producing microsatellites with 1-meter imagery resolution and significant signals intelligence functions. SSTL, a world leader in developing this capability, has led a global revolution in using the new, more affordable technology not only in Europe but also around the world. While microsatellites probably will not totally supplant large space systems, they can certainly perform many functions currently done by such large systems and could work in concert with them to provide extended capabilities—particularly in the context of shared international constellations such as the Disaster Monitoring Constellation.

The trend toward smaller, more affordable space capabilities has enabled European nations and others to produce significant security capabilities within individual nations' space budgets. Examples of this approach are embodied in the German Synthetic Aperture Radar (SAR)–Lupe imaging satellite system and others now under development.[7] The proliferation of this new national capability offers a new set of opportunities for use of space systems in security modes.

The U.S. challenge in space is more than a strictly military one. The use of smaller, lower cost systems for a series of dual-use purposes is the real challenge. Meeting it will require a change in both the mindset of our security professionals as well as in technological direction—toward small, affordable dual-use systems with direct applicability to economic and environmental security as well as collective security.

Nowhere is the trend toward small, internationally available capabilities more noticeable than in high resolution imaging and synthetic aperture radar systems. Most new efforts (see figure 14–1) are non-U.S. and/or wholly commercial endeavors. The U.S. national security community clearly no longer has a monopoly or even a lead role in this important area.

U.S. Failures

The U.S. security community's recent track record compares unfavorably to the impressive work being done internationally. The American focus on large, complicated systems may have been well founded in the Cold War, but in light of the rest of the world's success in smaller, more affordable space systems, the wisdom of maintaining this direction is dubious. More to the point, the United States is increasingly unable to even field these large systems.

Figure 14–1. Timetable: High Resolution and Synthetic Aperture Radar Satellites

Satellite or Mission/Sensor	Agency or company country	Resolution min/max in m	Swath min/max in km	# of bands/ SAR band	2004	2005	2006	2007	2008	2009	2010	Remarks
Very High resolution												
IC IKONOS-2	Space Imaging US	0.8 3.2	11	1 4								
IC IKONOS-BlockII	Space Imaging US	0.4 1	15 4	1 4								
IC EROS-A1	ImageSat ISRAEL	1.8	13.5	pan								
IC EROS-B1-3	ImageSat ISRAEL	0.72 8	10 4	1 3								3 Satellites
IC Quickbird-2	DigitalGlobe/US	0.6 2.5	16 5	1 4								New/Mod
IC OrbView-3	Orbimage US	1 4	8	1 4								New/NewII
IC ROCSat-2	NSPO Taiwan	2 8	24	1 4								Stereo
I Theos	GISTDA Thailand	2 15	22 90	1 4								Stereo
IC CartoSat-1	IsRO. ANTRIX IND	2 5	30 60	pan								Stereo
IC CartoSat-2	ISRO. ANTRIX IND	1	12	pan								
IC KOMPSAT-2	KARI Korea	1 4	15	1 4								
IC Resurs-DK1	Spaceproject FSA/RUS	1/2.5	28 3	1/3								2 Satellites
Synthetic Aperture Radar (SAR)												
IP Radarsat-1	CSA.RSI/CAN	8/100	45/500	C								
IP ALOS-PalSAR	NASDA/JAP	7/100	70/350	L Q								4 Satellites
IC Radarsat-2	RSI/CAN	3/100	10/300	C Q								
I SAOCOM 1A B	CONAE Argentina	10	100	L								2 Satellites
I RISAT	ISRO/IND	3/50	10/240	C								

9th ISU International Symposium, Dec 2004

Source: Chart extracted from "High Resolution Earth Observation Imaging Satellites in the Next Decade: European Perspectives" by G. Schreier, Head of Business Development, DLR German Remote Sensing Data Centre, Germany, presented at the 2004 ISU Symposium, "Civil, Commercial, and Security Space: What Will Drive the Next Decade?" November 30–December 3, 2004, Strasbourg, France.

In the 1970s, the U.S. Air Force launched the world's first comprehensive missile warning program, the Defense Support Program. These satellites carry infrared sensors that see the heat of a missile launch. In the 1980s, the United States began developing a follow-on system, now named the Space-based Infra-red System (SBIRS), which was intended to replace the Defense Support Program missile warning satellites with more capable and sensitive sensors. It was also intended to support comprehensive missile defenses. The first SBIRS satellites were to be launched in the early 1990s. Today, after at least a $20 billion expenditure, we are years away from a working system.[8] Moreover, SBIRS is no longer capable of supporting comprehensive missile defenses, and the system is by no means the exception. Other major programs, such as next-generation weather satellites (the National Polar-orbiting Operational Environmental Satellite System [NPOESS]), are seriously behind schedule and considerably overrun.[9]

Congress is increasingly critical of the U.S. national security community and has insisted that it pay more attention to small, low-cost "responsive" space systems. The responsive feature is the ability to respond to crises inside an adversary's act-react cycle as well as being a more effective response to direct military threats. The ability to quickly replace a lost space capability might prove a much better deterrent to foreign space military challenges than various forms of active space control, particularly when most potential adversaries have little reliance on space capabilities themselves.

Congress has now mandated an Operationally Responsive Space program. Its rationale is impeccable. Consider the statement by Terry Everett (R–AL), chairman of the House Strategic Forces Subcommittee:

> We must also embrace innovative ways to advance our strategic enterprise. One innovative approach to getting key space capabilities into the hands of our military forces is Operationally Responsive Space (O-R-S). O-R-S is an effort to develop smaller, less expensive satellites that can launch on short notice to meet the immediate needs of the warfighter.
>
> In this year's [2006] defense bill, Congress created a joint O-R-S program office, bringing together: Science and technology; Acquisition; Operations; and Warfighter support. With this effort, I see a stronger national security space portfolio where O-R-S systems complement large traditional space programs.
>
> For this Office to be successful it must retain a strong joint core, bringing together leaders and participants from across the Services, Agencies, research labs, and industry. It must also create an environment that expects and rewards innovation.
>
> I said earlier that the strain of rising costs and affordability will continue to put pressure on our space and defense programs. At the same time, technologies are evolving at much higher rates than our current ten-plus year acquisition timelines. Therefore, I see two key thrusts to O-R-S: First, it is a means to get simple, low cost solutions rapidly on-orbit to meet the dynamic needs of our combatant commanders; Secondly, it provides more frequent opportunities to prove-out innovative concepts and technologies at a lower cost, while strengthening our industrial base and technical workforce. I've said low-cost twice. I can't emphasize this enough; we must control the costs of our space programs.[10]

The national security space community's internal problems stem largely from a variety of "red herring" excuses for the community's shortcomings. As detailed in a paper by Randall Correll and this author, many excuses have been given, from masking symptoms for causes such as citing immature technologies and lack of good requirements definition, claiming insufficient system engineering expertise, poor cost analysis, shifting incumbent contractors, and others. The paper places the blames squarely on poor, often technically unqualified, leadership.[11]

Our bad national security space posture stems from two major difficulties. First, we have not developed a coherent strategy, and second, we have developed neither a cadre of qualified experts to lead it nor the necessary space capabilities to support it. What follows is a prescription for remedying this, starting with a coherent strategy.[12]

Coherent Security Space Strategy

Progress in information technologies has completely reshaped the way humans communicate. The globalization of the economy and culture and the growing importance of worldwide information (such as the Internet) and human (such as al Qaeda) networks have changed relationships between not only people but also states from an exclusive to an inclusive paradigm. In this new era, it is often in the interest of all parties to cooperate with rather than oppose each other. This does not imply that competition has disappeared, but it has changed in nature, being more strongly related to confidence-building and "win-win" strategies.

This new paradigm fits well with space capabilities that are inherently global in nature. Investments are often too costly for a single nation to make. The new developments in space capabilities may enable new security regimes. These possibilities generally come under the heading of soft power. The new options involve shaping the global environment to maximize collective security. They also entail changes in space policy on the part of various nations. Several approaches are possible in this direction.

The world has entered an era of *global utilities*: capabilities, generally in the information collection and distribution regimes, that enable the emerging global economy, culture, and society. First among them is the Internet, followed closely by global positioning, navigation, and timing systems such as GPS and the European Galileo. Note that the GPS conceived in the 1980s remains exclusive to the U.S. Government, whereas Galileo is more collaborative, including major players outside of the European Union such as India and China.

Other global utilities include global communications grids and global situation awareness such as imaging. New possibilities in this area include identification and tracking of moving objects such as aircraft. Many of these utilities grew out of military needs, but they have become the glue that holds the global economy and culture together. Almost all global utilities depend in some part on space capabilities. Even the Internet uses space systems for many of its long-range communications connections and precision timing. The breakdown of even one satellite can have devastating consequences to the global economy. In 1998, a failure of a single communications satellite carrying remote pager signals plunged much of North America into an unexpected business "holiday."[13]

The first and possibly most potent element of soft power is inclusion in global utility services. Inclusion of a nation, group of nations, or even private concerns in the development of a global utility such as Galileo is a potent inducement for a desired behavior. Europe's experience with China and its inclusion in Galileo is a positive demonstration of this potential. Once connected by the utility, the parties have a strong mutual interest in protecting and advancing it. This provides a lever to bind and influence diverse interests. Finally, the possibility of being denied access to one or more global utilities in response to aggression by a state can be a compelling dissuasion from embarking on a hostile tack. Without global information support mechanisms, a nation would find its economy swiftly devastated.

A related concept to global utilities is the rising importance of a global information connectivity or infosphere. The rise of a global information marketplace, largely originating in the Internet, is apparent. Although some of the explosive growth of the 1990s has slowed, the Internet is still the fastest growing impetus to global commerce. Equally important is its role as a marketplace of ideas—a two-edged sword, as the Internet has become a medium through which modern terrorist groups recruit members and plan acts. Yet the global infosphere could also mean the end of narrow, fundamentalist ideologies. Modern terrorists do best recruiting among disillusioned and often isolated young individuals. These same individuals might have been recruited and organized through the Internet, but that same medium can and will also expose them to broader and more inclusive philosophies.

A second element of future soft power is to connect the world into a global infosphere. Again, confidence building is a key driver. Space capabilities are integral to this linkage to build cohesion and shared values as space communications segments are the only way to reach much of the developing world. Indeed, India's interest in space began as a way to link remote regions and foster development and education across the entire society. India's success in forming a coherent and rapidly developing nation out of diverse peoples and traditions can be partly attributed to building this space-based connectivity.[14]

With the emergence of low-cost space capabilities such as those developed by SSTL, numerous nations can now afford space developments. However, one or even a handful of low Earth orbit satellites provides limited capability, whereas constellations of small satellites can provide significant capability. If a group of nations pools their efforts, each one providing a single satellite, all can benefit from a new space capability. The Disaster Monitoring Constellation discussed earlier is a prototype of such a multinational system. This cooperation represents a third approach to soft power—a means whereby smaller nations can pool capabilities to provide significant new space options. In the process of building the capability, the member nations also build technology interdependence and open new economic opportunities in other spheres.

The concept of collective security is a longstanding one. During the Cold War, both competing blocs established collective security arrangements where an attack on one party would be met with a response from all. This was particularly effective for the North Atlantic Treaty Organization (NATO); its collective defense arrangements kept the peace in Europe for almost half a century. Only with the end of the Cold War did conflict again break out on the European continent. Yet even with the disturbances in the former Yugoslavia, NATO's collective response has proven effective. Part of the key to collective security is in the pooling of defense resources, but even more important are the perception aspects of collective security arrangements. A potential aggressor must face the prospect of united defense against him. The psychological and societal impact of standing alone against united opposition is a significant factor in preventing war and aggression. A similar concept is especially applicable to global space security.

Perhaps the most interesting aspect of cooperative international space development is its symbolic value as a pathfinder for other agendas. During the Cold War, space cooperation in the 1975 Apollo-Soyuz test project became a symbolic first in an attempt to lead to broader cooperation in arms control and other security and economic issues. The symbolic role of civil space cooperation truly blossomed in the International Space Station. Despite the political difficulties of building and maintaining such a complex space effort, its symbolic value to both governments and people has carried it through. It has been particularly valuable as a means whereby the United States and Russia have been able to divert technical expertise (particularly within Russia immediately after the end of the Cold War) from missile proliferation endeavors. In a similar vein, a European Community European Space Program is viewed by many as the path to broader European unity. Recently, the United States and India have used civil space cooperation as a step in building closer ties for united action against terrorism. With the major new U.S. push for human exploration of the Moon and Mars, cooperative programs in these areas could similarly prove to be effective vanguards for other agendas.

This approach is not without its problems. Space technology is inherently dual-use, with advances in space providing new military possibilities. Moreover, space technology is often the impetus of and source for new economic products and markets, particularly in the important aerospace field. These considerations are particularly central to U.S. policy. A nation has the choice of ignoring other nations' space exploration interests, dominating mankind's expansion into the solar system, or cooperatively leading the world into the solar system. The United States has chosen the third option. Working to establish consensus on space exploration among numerous global partners could slow progress. However, an open space exploration architecture such as that advocated by Randall Correll and Nicolas Peter would allow nations to proceed at their own pace without sacrificing future opportunities for collaboration.[15]

Space is an important component of global economic development. Space-reliant global utilities such as global positioning, communications, and situation awareness are critical to modern economic development. Communications connectivity is particularly important to remote regions. With new K_a band connectivity, high-speed Internet is available and affordable worldwide. Direct broadcast radio provided by such commercial concerns can bring education and information to even the most disadvantaged peoples. By offering these critical capabilities worldwide, a nation or group of nations will take a major step in providing the means for rapid economic development as well as building global cohesiveness. No element of soft power is more significant than the information-enabling aspect and its associated free exchange of information and ideas.

Space information connectivity may be the key element in combating terrorism, which thrives in regions with little outside information and few economic opportunities. Global information connectivity is a powerful tool for combating both problems. The country of Jordan is a primary example of the power of a successful information strategy and its effect on terrorist activities. In the mid 1990s, Jordan embarked on an aggressive, private sector–oriented information and Internet connectivity campaign.[16] Although still in progress, this campaign is succeeding in connecting schools, businesses, and publics nationwide. It is significant that terrorist attacks against U.S. targets in Jordan were met with wide public outrage there and strong support for Jordan's Western-oriented government.

The first significant philosophical result of deep-space exploration in the 1960s was the view of the entire Earth as a small, interconnected entity. This global awareness continues today with new technology such as the Internet bringing the global perspective to each individual through such tools as Google Earth.[17] Geospatial data is now accessible not only to top-level decisionmakers but also to media and the general public. Every citizen with Internet capability can now access and assess what is happening locally as well as globally. This global perspective will have a huge impact on governments and their decisionmaking. From it will emerge new influences on national policies: a new form of soft power. The National Aeronautics and Space Administration's collaboration with Google to include the Moon and Mars in the products of Google Earth is an example of how governments can work with private sector entities to further the new global perspective.[18] These efforts should pay off not only in expanding space exploration but also in enhancing U.S. soft power influence.

Over and above space exploration and space science, systems such as the international Disaster Monitoring Constellation and European Global Monitoring for Environment and Security are at the forefront of a different definition of security. The security aspects of collaborative efforts offer new opportunities to build soft power influence. By promoting a new strategy where space and associated global utilities function as the primary elements of our security posture rather than as support to warfighters, we could once again attract the best and brightest to space fields.

Developing Leaders and Supporting Systems

A major problem discussed by Correll and Worden is the lack of competent leadership for our national security space programs.[19] There are a number of interconnected issues. First is the intensive requirements process, which has resulted in a cadre of "space professionals" whose expertise is in procurement rather than technical competence. This in turn has produced an aerospace industry dominated by those versed not in technological prowess but in meeting procurement regulations. Often, these corporate leaders are recently retired military leaders. The solution to this problem is to insist on technological competence as a prerequisite for leadership.

Even a change of leadership toward technical excellence will accomplish little if the mindset of technical leaders is one of maintaining the status quo. In today's dynamic new industries such as information technology and biotechnology, growing attention has been paid to what is called *disruptive technologies*.[20] By paying slavish attention to customers—in the case of the national security space community, warfighters—many technologically oriented industries fail to recognize that a new technology that may not interest current customers could offer a way to develop a new, much larger client base. The new disruptive technologies for security space possibilities are small, responsive, information-oriented space systems. The new customers are practitioners of soft power information operations designed for war prevention and not warfighting. As with industries confronted with disruptive technologies, a separate organization that is chartered specifically to ignore current customers is needed. The space community does not have such an organization but desperately needs a disruptive technology development arm.

A major problem is the aging of the aerospace workforce. With an average employee age of near 50 (as compared to an average age of under 30 during the Apollo era), the U.S. aerospace industry is in crisis. Moreover, there is significant evidence that neither industry nor government is able to replace the retiring infrastructure with comparable talent.[21] This problem stems from a perception that aerospace technologies are yesterday's excitement, with much greater future potential in new areas such as bio- and nanotechnology. Moreover, with security space programs in the doldrums and little chance for advancement based on technical prowess, these programs and associated industries are unlikely to attract the top people. For the general aerospace industry, the new "Vision for Space Exploration," with its goal of settling the solar system, could provide a much-needed and exciting new perspective. A similar impetus would exist for security space endeavors with a new strategic purpose. However, to be convincing and sustainable, this new direction must be accompanied by a revised organizational structure. These three basic recommendations are expanded upon below.

Technological Prowess

Our problems begin with the requirements process mentality. The current acquisition approach grew out of Defense Secretary Robert McNamara's Planning, Programming, and Budgeting System of the 1960s. Since then, the defense community has built an enormous construct to develop requirements and budget for achieving them. Every time a new system fiasco occurs, a new review process and bureaucratic overlay are added. One such overlay occurred during the 1990s when the Office of the Joint Chiefs of Staff implemented a whole new process, the Joint Requirements Oversight Council. Carefully considering what a new system is supposed to do and what capabilities it must have, in itself, is advisable. However, the current process does not seem to do that. Most of the people staffing these requirements process offices have little technical, acquisition, or management experience. Few have the breadth of background and perspective to understand what is really needed and how it will be used. But each office can and does have the power to halt the process. Usually, a program is held up until every office is satisfied that its special interest item is included. Few have any idea of the feasibility of adding their demands, let alone the cost of doing so. There is supposed to be a process to accurately assess the cost of the requirements and capabilities, but it is bankrupt. With leadership and workforce so short on technical expertise or engineering experience, the government repeatedly deludes itself into believing that a requirements-laden system can be built on time and on budget. This tendency to swell the scope and budget of programs is inherent in the military-industrial complex even in the best of circumstances, but experienced and competent management is usually able to deliver in the end.

The response to recent space acquisition problems of the lead Service for space, the U.S. Air Force, has been to emphasize the acquisition process. Primary focus has been on repeated bouts of acquisition reform, back-to-basics campaigns, and other methods. In 2006, this translated to large cuts in technical engineering specialties among Air Force officers with increases in system engineering and acquisition expertise without relevant space technical experience.[22] Nowhere is the problem worse than in the Air Force space programs.

The lack of technological competence in security space leadership is simple to fix. The first step is to demand that all leaders in military and security space programs begin with a certified technical grounding. While the U.S. Air Force and other Services and organizations continuously emphasize developing and certifying a space cadre,[23] the actual educational programs and requirements do not include rigorous engineering and scientific content; rather, they emphasize space doctrine and acquisition skills. This soft skill mix contrasts unfavorably with the rigorous technical requirements for officers either entering or maintaining certification in the U.S. Navy's submarine corps.[24] To remedy these shortcomings, individuals entering space career areas, particularly in military officer or civilian management levels, should be required to have technical degrees. Specific qualification courses and certification should subsequently emphasize technical skills over management-oriented expertise. It is more important that all space professionals be versed in orbital dynamics mathematics than being able to recite the elements of total quality management.

A related problem is that top-quality civilian academic credentials matter. While it is true that people with degrees from a local college sometimes perform as well or better than someone with a degree from a prestigious technical school, this is the exception rather than the rule. Thus, security space organizations should make special efforts to recruit graduates of the highest rated civilian institutions. Moreover, graduate degrees from these institutions should be honored and sought. Finally, courses taught and certified by such institutions are much more likely to be more rigorous than internally organized "Space 101" courses developed and taught by the military Services and commands.

Perhaps most important is for senior civilian leaders and Congress to demand technical backgrounds and extensive space experience for those placed in space command or senior leadership positions. Until recently, most flag-level leaders in Air Force space organizations had little or no actual space background. Often, these leaders were aircraft pilots sent to a space billet for career broadening. Consider that the Air Combat Command has never had nonpilots in its senior positions, while the Air Force Space Command has had few (and at times no) senior leaders with space backgrounds. Congress can ensure this is remedied by insisting that senior officers and other appointed officials are not accepted unless they have demonstrable and extensive space technical credentials and backgrounds.

Disruptive Technology Development

While it is important to have a new strategic construct such as the one outlined in this chapter (namely, that space capabilities are a primary means of preventing wars versus fighting them), such ideas do little good if the hardware and systems do not support this approach. It is unlikely that traditional acquisition organizations, such as the Air Force Space and Missile Center, will pursue systems to support these new missions. The type of capabilities needed for information and global utilities–oriented collaboration probably will not be acquired by an organization attending to requirements levied by a Service fixated on space only as support to warfighters. However, even these existing organizations recognize that current structures focused on acquisition are not well suited to developing new types of capabilities.[25]

What is needed are development organizations chartered to identify new possibilities and develop these to the point of capability demonstration. The Department of Defense has such an organization: the Defense Advanced Research Projects Agency (DARPA), which has a specific mandate to develop new technological capabilities to meet potential long-range security needs. In 2002, in specific response to the Rumsfeld Commission recommendations, DARPA greatly increased its focus on space capabilities, particularly on fast-paced launch systems in its Falcon program.[26] In a similar vein, the short-lived DOD Office of Force Transformation (OFT) pushed the development of responsive, low-cost satellites—those systems capable of being launched during a crisis, not so much to fight a war as to provide a means of preventing a war. For example, a responsive space surveillance system might be launched by the United States or another nation to guarantee an agreement between two potentially hostile neighbors. Just such a move could have helped defuse the crisis between nuclear-armed India and Pakistan in 2002. Each nation accused the other of preparing for an attack. A space-based means of verifying that no such attack was in the works and launched by a neutral third party could have served much the same way as space systems functioned as national technical means of treaty verification during the Cold War. Such systems allowed agreements to be developed and verified as a way to keep the peace, not fight a war.

Unfortunately, neither DARPA nor OFT had a charter or resources to carry the new capabilities beyond technical proof-of-concept. Converting these potential new capabilities into reality requires a development organization specially chartered for this purpose. In addition to lacking such an organization, DARPA also suffered much criticism for trying to develop new information technologies for conducting the global war on terrorism and has largely stopped pursuing such directions.[27] This lack can only be remedied with a new organization separate from traditional channels particularly chartered and funded to develop war prevention systems.

A New National Security Organization

While some personnel policies and even a new development organization are possible, none of this will be meaningful without a supportive home for such activities. The Rumsfeld Commission recommendations were quickly undone.[28] The commission recommended establishing a single national security space program including intelligence (the National Reconnaissance Office [NRO]) and DOD, mostly Air Force programs. A single leader was appointed to oversee both offices. However, no fundamental changes were made to any roles and missions. Consequently, traditional vested interests, particularly within the Intelligence Community, lobbied successfully to return to having the NRO completely separate from DOD programs. Similarly, within DOD, where the Rumsfeld Commission had advocated moving toward a new "space force," progress has been reversed, with the longstanding U.S. Space Command disestablished and its functions integrated into the U.S. Strategic Command (USSTRAT-COM), which was formerly focused solely on nuclear warfighting and strategic deterrence. The U.S. Air Force, once thought to be on the path toward becoming a "space and air" force, is now firmly in the "air" column. To show how far the ball has been dropped, the Air Force is now seeking to transition many formerly space functions into a new category called "near space," whose primary technology would be balloons and airships.[29]

In order for real progress to be made in either developing true professionals or novel technologies, a completely new organization devoted to a new mission is needed. This organization should have a specific charter to work the use of space, information, and collaborative international efforts as a crisis mitigation, war prevention focus. It is useful to note that USSTRAT-COM, which now incorporates most DOD space responsibilities, does include many of the necessary elements, including war prevention deterrence functions, information operations, space activities, command and control, and intelligence, surveillance, and reconnaissance functions. It may be easiest to expand USSTRATCOM's functions to include budget and direct operational control in much the same manner as Special Operations Forces are managed by the U.S. Special Operations Command. In this way, personnel, research, development, and acquisition would be run by leaders with a new focus. If this is done, however, it is essential that senior civilian leadership in DOD also exercise direct oversight.

If this new space and war prevention direction and management approach bears fruit, these moves could expand—unlike the Rumsfeld Commission's approach—to create a new arm of U.S. security assurance including separate budgets, military service, and civilian leadership. But it is essential that basic warfighting responsibilities be removed from the new organization's functions. Otherwise, backsliding into business as usual, as occurred with the good start in 2001 on developing a coherent space approach, will swiftly negate even the best intentions of our leaders.

Conclusion

The United States faces many security challenges. One of the most significant is the growing global use of space capabilities—not just for security but also for a broader range of economic, environmental, and political goals. We are not developing the necessary technological tools—

particularly low-cost, smaller, and fast-development-time space systems. We are losing technically competent leadership, resulting in unaffordable systems. And we do not have a compelling rationale for our large space expenditures. These problems can be remedied in two ways.

First, there exists a convincing security case for space systems. Space capabilities form an increasingly vital role as global utilities, which serve as the glue that enables a truly interconnected worldwide economy. By working hard to use new, lower cost space capabilities as a crisis management and war prevention device rather than as an adjunct to warfighting, space systems and the organizations and people who develop and support them can bring a new perspective to the public on space.

Second, armed with a persuasive rationale, we need to focus on a technically competent and intellectually responsive leadership cadre. We need to insist on having our space capabilities in the hands of the best and the brightest people. In addition to getting technically sophisticated staff, we need a DARPA-like development organization to create the affordable space tools to support the new direction. Finally, we need a new strategic organization—possibly growing out of the existing U.S. Strategic Command—to manage all aspects, especially budgeting and technology development. This organization needs to be completely separate from traditional national intelligence and warfighting military functions.

With these political recommendations (which, admittedly, will be difficult to implement), space can realize its full potential as the lynchpin for 21st-century global security.

Notes

[1] *Report of the Commission to Assess United States National Security Space Management and Organization*, Pursuant to Public Law 106–65, January 11, 2001, available at <www.defenselink.mil/pubs/space20010111.html>. This report is often referred to as the *Space Commission Report* or *Rumsfeld Report*.

[2] The University of Surrey and its Surrey Space Centre have chartered Surrey Satellite Technology, Ltd. (SSTL). SSTL's products and approach can be reviewed on its Web site at <www.sstl.co.uk/>. The history of small and micro satellites is available through the SSTL Web site at <http://centaur.sstl.co.uk/SSHP/>.

[3] The Department of Defense has long had a policy of disproportionately reducing its science and technology military expertise. The 2001 National Academy of Sciences' Review of the U.S. Department of Defense Air, Space, and Supporting Information Systems Science and Technology Program (available at <www.nap.edu/openbook/030907/6080/html/38.html>) raises an alarm about the quality and retention of qualified technical personnel. The Air Force reportedly has recently slashed its science and engineering officer billets as part of its "force shaping" flight plan. Even the Air Force Association warns against cutbacks, stating in its 2007 Statement of Policy (as approved at the AFA National Convention, September 24, 2006) that "the Air Force cannot afford cutbacks here if it hopes to retain air dominance in the future."

[4] The Disaster Monitoring Constellation is the creation of SSTL. It is now run by a spin-off consortium, DMC International Imaging, collocated with SSTL. Details of the systems and program are available at <www.dmcii.com/index.html>.

[5] President George W. Bush signed a new National Space Policy on August 31, 2006. On October 10, 2006, the White House Office of Science and Technology Policy released an unclassified summary, available at <www.ostp.gov/html/US%20National%20Space%20Policy.pdf>.

[6] *Report of the Commission to Assess United States National Security Space Management and Organization* (Washington, DC: Commission to Assess United States National Security Space Management and Organization, January 11, 2001).

[7] The manufacturer of SAR Lupe, OHB Systems of Bremen, Germany, has provided considerable information on the system including an extensive brochure, available at <www.ohbsystem.de/Security/sarlupe.html>.

[8] Much of the background on the space-based infra-red system (SBIRS) problems can be found in General Accounting Office (GAO) report GAO–04–48, "Defense Acquisitions: Despite Restructuring, SBIRS High Program Remains at Risk of Cost and Schedule Overruns," released on October 31, 2003. An additional "Nunn-McCurdy Overrun" breach occurred in 2005. The original contract consisted of two high Earth orbit satellite sensors and two to three geosynchronous orbit (GEO) sensors (and satellites) with an option to buy a total of five GEOs. In December 2005, following the third SBIRS Nunn-McCurdy violation, the government decided to compete GEO four and five, with an option to buy GEO three contingent on the performance of the first two. Additionally, the government started a potential SBIRS High replacement program in late 2006. See <www.spacewar.com/reports/USAF_Seeks_SBIRS_Alternatives_999.html>.

[9] NPOESS is also suffering bad overruns of at least 10 percent. Almost all major security space programs are similar, according to Government Accountability Office (GAO) report GAO–05–891T, "Space Acquisitions: Stronger Development Practices and Investment Planning Needed to Address Continuing Problems," statement of Robert E. Levin, Director, Acquisition and Sourcing Management, before the Strategic Forces Subcommittee of the Committee on Armed Services, U.S. House of Representatives, July 12, 2005, available at <www.gao.gov/htext/d05891t.html>.

[10] "Space: The Strategic Enabler," remarks by the Honorable Terry Everett, Chairman, Strategic Forces Subcommittee, at the Strategic Space and Defense Conference, Omaha, Nebraska, October 11, 2006.

[11] Randall R. Correll and Simon P. Worden, "The Demise of U.S. Spacepower: Not with a Bang but a Whimper," *Astropolitics* 3, no. 3 (Winter 2005).

[12] This discussion is based on an unpublished manuscript, "Soft Power and Space Capabilities" by Simon P. Worden and Major Patrick Chatard-Moulin of the French Air Force prepared in 2005–2006. *Soft power* is defined as power based on intangible or indirect influences such as culture, values, and ideology; see <www.wordspy.com/words/softpower.asp>.

[13] The May 1998 failure of the PanAmSat Galaxy 4 satellites stopped over 90 percent of electronic pagers in North America from operating. See BBC News, "Satellite Failure Silences Beepers," May 20, 1998.

[14] The India Space Research Organization has as its primary purpose national and eventual international educational and information connectivity. See, for example, a presentation by P.S. Roy from the UN-affiliated Centre for Space Science and Technology Education in Asia and the Pacific at the 15th UN/International Astronautical Federation Workshop on Space Education and Capacity Building for Sustainable Development, Kitakyushu, Japan, October 14–15, 2005.

[15] Randall R. Correll and Nicolas Peter, "Odyssey: Principles for Enduring Space Exploration," *Space Policy* 21, no. 4 (November 2005), 251–258.

[16] The nation of Jordan embarked in the late 1990s on an ambitious program to provide the population with good Internet and communications connectivity, particularly in schools. The European firm Alcatel played a key role. See a 2003 press release from that company for details of this success at <www.home.alcatel.com/vpr/archive.nsf/DateKey/09012003uk>.

[17] NASA and Google are partnering on a variety of new approaches to bring space data to the general public as well as a variety of new users. See NASA press release 06–371, "NASA and Google to Bring Space Exploration Down to Earth," December 18, 2006, available at <www.nasa.gov/home/hqnews/2006/dec/HQ_06371_Ames_Google.html>.

[18] See <http://earth.google.com>.

[19] Randall R. Correll and Simon P. Worden, "Leadership for New U.S. Strategic Directions," *Space Policy* 21, no. 1 (February 2005), 21–27.

[20] Disruptive technologies were identified in the late 1990s as a key to long-term industrial success. The seminal work is by Clayton M. Christensen, *The Innovator's Dilemma* (Cambridge: Harvard Business School Press, 1997).

[21] Commission on the Future of the U.S. Aerospace Industry, *Final Report of the Commission on the Future of the U.S. Aerospace Industry,* November 18, 2002, 4–4, available at <www.ita.doc.gov/td/aerospace/aerospacecommission/AeroCommissionFinalReport.pdf>. The commission was established by Congress and the President. It specifically identified that the fact that the average U.S. aerospace worker was over the age of 50 is a threat to national security and that aerospace fields are no longer high in the new generation's career aspirations.

[22] A report delivered in 2006 by the director of systems acquisition of the Air Force Space and Missile Systems Center summarized space experience of major space acquisition leaders. The following table is extracted from that report.

Total	Grade	Average acquisition experience (in years)	Average space experience (in years)
155	Captain	3.3	2.8
55	Major	0.5	1
34	Lieutenant colonel	3.3	1.8
22	Colonel	15	7.5

[23] The Air Force Space Command frequently identifies its shortcomings in developing space professionals and starts new programs. See, for example, a 2004 initiative on developing a space "cadre." Little technical rigor is apparent in the resulting programs. See <www.af.mil/news/story.asp?storyID=123008740>.

[24] The U.S. Navy requires substantial basic undergraduate education in engineering, mathematics, and physics to enter the submarine corps. In addition, the Navy provides graduate-level education before Sailors enter the submarine service; see <www.navy.com/careers/officer/submarine/>. The U.S. Air Force has no such technical requirements for entering the space field. It is hard to imagine how space operations are less "technical" than submarine operations, but the Air Force apparently thinks so.

[25] The establishment of a new Space Development and Test Wing by the Air Force Space Command suggests that some within the Air Force recognize the need for a new, different type of organization to develop new space capabilities. See <www.af.mil/news/story.asp?storyID=123024576>.

[26] The Defense Advanced Research Projects Agency's Falcon program is discussed at <www.darpa.mil/tto/programs/falcon.htm>: "The Falcon program objectives are to develop and demonstrate hypersonic technologies that will enable prompt global reach missions. This capability is envisioned to entail a reusable Hypersonic Cruise Vehicle (HCV) capable of delivering 12,000 pounds of payload a distance of 9,000 nautical miles from CONUS in less than two hours."

[27] According to Wikipedia:

> The Information Awareness Office (IAO) was established by the Defense Advanced Research Projects Agency (DARPA), the research and development agency of the United States Department of Defense, in January 2002 to bring together several DARPA projects focused on applying information technology to counter transnational threats to national security. The IAO mission was to "imagine, develop, apply, integrate, demonstrate and transition information technologies, components and prototype, closed-loop, information systems that will counter asymmetric threats by

achieving total information awareness." Following public criticism that the development and deployment of these technologies could potentially lead to a mass surveillance system, the IAO was defunded by Congress in 2003, although several of the projects run under IAO have continued under different funding.
See <http://en.wikipedia.org/wiki/Information_Awareness_Office>.

[28] Simon P. Worden, "High Anxiety," *Bulletin of the Atomic Scientists* 62, no. 2 (March–April 2006), 21–23.

[29] Hampton Stevens, "Near Space," *Air Force Magazine* 88, no. 7 (July 2005), available at <www.afa.org/magazine/July2005/0705near.asp>.

About the Contributors

Editors

Colonel Charles D. Lutes, USAF, is the Director for Nonproliferation on the National Security Council Staff, a White House position he has held for Presidents George W. Bush and Barack H. Obama. From 2004 to 2008, he was a Senior Military Fellow in the Institute for National Strategic Studies (INSS) at the National Defense University (NDU), where he served as a member of the Future Strategic Concepts Program and was the Principal Investigator for the Spacepower Theory Project. Prior to joining INSS, Colonel Lutes served as chief of the Weapons of Mass Destruction (WMD) division under the J–5 Deputy Director for the War on Terror. He also served in J–5 as chief of the Strategic Plans Branch. He holds degrees in engineering from Duke University and the Air Force Institute of Technology and was a National Security Fellow at the John F. Kennedy School of Government at Harvard. He is also an ABD doctoral candidate in The George Washington University's Executive Leadership Program. Colonel Lutes has logged over 3,000 hours piloting C–5s and KC–135s and has commanded an operational support squadron. His major awards include the Defense Superior Service Medal, the Defense Meritorious Service Medal, the Meritorious Service Medal with two oak leaf clusters, and the Aerial Achievement Medal with oak leaf cluster.

Peter L. Hays is a Senior Scientist for the Science Applications International Corporation supporting the Plans and Programs Division of the National Security Space Office (NSSO), a position he assumed upon retirement from a 25-year career as an Air Force officer. A subject matter expert for national security space policy issues, he led NSSO support for the 2005 Space Posture Review, 2005 Quadrennial Defense Review, 2006 Space Situational Awareness Strategy and Roadmap, National Security Space Strategy, and Air Force White Paper for Space Leaders. In addition, Dr. Hays is Chief of Staff for the National Defense University Spacepower Theory Study. He holds a Ph.D. in International Relations from the Fletcher School of Law and Diplomacy and a Master of Arts degree in Defense and Strategic Studies from the University of Southern California, and is a 1979 Honor Graduate of the USAF Academy. Dr. Hays's publications include *United States Military Space: Into the 21st Century* (USAF Institute for National Strategic Studies, 2002), *Spacepower for a New Millennium* (McGraw-Hill, 2000), *Countering the Proliferation and*

Use of Weapons of Mass Destruction (McGraw-Hill, 1998), and *American Defense Policy* (The Johns Hopkins University Press, 1997).

Vincent A. Manzo is a Research Assistant in the Future Strategic Concepts division of the INSS at NDU. He is a graduate of the Paul H. Nitze School of Advanced International Studies at The Johns Hopkins University. He is the author of *An Examination of the Pentagon's Prompt Global Strike Program: Rationale, Implementation, and Risks* (Center for Defense Information, 2008).

Lisa M. Yambrick is a Writer and Editor at NDU Press. In that capacity, she both edits *Joint Force Quarterly* and is the book review editor for the journal; edits *PRISM*, a journal produced by NDU Press for the Center for Complex Operations; and is the primary editor for books produced by NDU Press. Previously, Ms. Yambrick was an intelligence analyst and editor at the Defense Intelligence Agency and served in the U.S. Army. She holds a Master of Arts degree in Russian/Soviet history from Villanova University.

M. Elaine Bunn is an INSS Senior Fellow, where she is Director of the Future Strategic Concepts Program. Before joining INSS in 2000, she was a Senior Executive in the Office of the Secretary of Defense, where she worked for 20 years in international security policy. She served as Principal Director of Nuclear Forces and Missile Defense Policy from 1993 to 1998. During that time, she was executive director of the 1994 Nuclear Posture Review. She was a visiting fellow at the RAND Corporation from 1998 to 2000. Bunn was seconded from INSS to the Office of the Secretary of Defense to help frame issues for both the 2001 and the 2009 Nuclear Posture Reviews. She served on the Defense Science Board summer study on strategic strike in 2003, as well as with an expert working group of the Commission on Strategic Posture in 2008–2009. A 1988 graduate of the National War College, Ms. Bunn received a Master of Arts in International Security from the Johns Hopkins School of Advanced International Studies and a Bachelor of Arts from the University of Georgia, and was a Fulbright scholar at l'Université de Neuchâtel, Switzerland. Her publications include a number of articles and book chapters on strategic planning, nuclear policy, missile defense, preemption, and deterrence.

Contributing Authors

Henry F. Cooper, Jr., is Chairman of the Board of High Frontier. Ambassador Cooper's long and distinguished career includes service as the first civilian Director of the Strategic Defense Initiative Organization, Chief Negotiator at the Geneva Defense and Space Talks, Assistant Director of the Arms Control and Disarmament Agency, and Deputy Assistant Secretary of the Air Force. He is also Chairman of Applied Research Associates, Senior Associate of the National Institute for Public Policy, and Visiting Fellow at The Heritage Foundation. Author of over 100 technical and policy publications, Ambassador Cooper holds Bachelor of Science and Master of Science degrees from Clemson University and a Ph.D. from New York University, all in mechanical engineering.

Everett C. Dolman is Professor of Comparative Military Studies at the School of Advanced Air and Space Studies at the Air University. Dr. Dolman is also co-founder and managing editor of *Astropolitics: The International Journal of Space Power and Policy.* His published works include *Pure Strategy: Power and Principle in the Information Age* (Frank Cass, 2005), *The Warrior State: How Military Organization Structures Politics* (Palgrave, 2005), and *Astropolitik: Classical Geopolitics in the Space Age* (Frank Cass, 2002). He has written several book chapters as well as articles for the *Journal of Strategic Studies, Comparative Strategy, Journal of Small Wars and Insurgencies, Soviet and Post-Soviet Review, Citizenship Studies, Politics and Society,* and the *Journal of Political and Military Sociology.* Dr. Dolman received his Ph.D. in political science from the University of Pennsylvania.

Martin E.B. France is a Professor at the United States Air Force Academy and Head of the Department of Astronautics. His professional experience includes research and development assignments with the Air Force Research Lab working on high-energy laser systems, as the Air Force Engineer and Scientist Exchange Officer to France, and as a Program Manager at the Defense Advanced Research Projects Agency. Colonel France also served as a staff officer at Air Force Space Command, the Air Staff, and on the Joint Chiefs of Staff. Colonel France, a graduate of the United States Air Force Academy, earned a Master of Science degree in aeronautics and astronautics from Stanford University and a Ph.D. in engineering science and mechanics from Virginia Polytechnic Institute and State University.

Colin S. Gray is Professor of International Politics and Strategic Studies at the University of Reading and is a Senior Fellow at the National Institute for Public Policy. Dr. Gray has taught at the Universities of Lancaster, York, and British Columbia. He served as Executive Secretary of the Strategic Studies Commission at the Canadian Institute of International Affairs, and as Assistant Director of the International Institute for Strategic Studies. Dr. Gray became Director of National Security Studies at the Hudson Institute in 1976. From 1982 until 1987, he served on the President's General Advisory Committee on Arms Control and Disarmament. Dr. Gray is the author of several journal articles and books dealing with security issues.

Henry R. Hertzfeld is Research Professor of Space Policy and International Affairs in the Space Policy Institute and the Center for International Science and Technology Policy at The George Washington University's Elliott School of International Affairs. He is an expert on the economic, legal, and policy issues of space and advanced technological development. Dr. Hertzfeld has served as a Senior Economist and Policy Analyst at NASA and the National Science Foundation and has been a consultant to many U.S. and international organizations. Dr. Hertzfeld holds a Bachelor of Arts degree from the University of Pennsylvania, a Master of Arts degree from Washington University, and a Ph.D. in Economics from Temple University.

Theresa Hitchens is Director of the United Nations Institute for Disarmament Research. Her previous positions include Director of the Center for Defense Information, where she led the Space Security Project, and Director of Research at the British American Security Information Council, a think tank based in Washington and London. Her long career in journalism, focusing on military, defense industry, and NATO affairs, has included serving as editor of *Defense News*. The author of *Future Security in Space: Charting a Cooperative Course* (Center for Defense Information, 2004), she continues to write on space and nuclear arms control issues for a number of publications.

Michael Katz-Hyman was a Research Associate at the Henry L. Stimson Center on the Space Security and South Asia Projects from 2004 until 2007. He holds a Bachelor of Science degree in physics with a minor in technology and policy from Carnegie Mellon University.

Michael Krepon is co-founder of the Henry L. Stimson Center and the Diplomat Scholar at the University of Virginia. He is the author or editor of 13 books, including *Better Safe than Sorry: The Ironies of Living with the Bomb* (Stanford University Press, 2009), *Space Assurance or Space Dominance: The Case Against Weaponizing Space* (Henry L. Stimson Center, 2003), *Open Skies: Arms Control and Cooperative Security* (St. Martin's Press, 1992), and *Commercial Observation Satellites and International Security* (Palgrave Macmillan, 1990).

Benjamin S. Lambeth is a senior staff member at RAND, where he also directed the International Security and Defense Policy Program in 1989–1990. A specialist in Russian defense policy, airpower, tactical fighter operations, and force development, Dr. Lambeth has worked for the U.S. Central Intelligence Agency, the Center for Strategic and International Studies, and the Institute for Defense Analyses. He is also an experienced pilot who was the first U.S. citizen to fly the Soviet MiG–29 fighter. He serves on the editorial board of the *Journal of Slavic Military Studies* and is a member of the Council on Foreign Relations.

Roger D. Launius is Chair of the Division of Space History at the Smithsonian Institution. Prior to that, he was the Chief Historian of NASA. Dr. Launius has lectured widely on historical subjects to military, scholarly, and general audiences. He has also served on the faculties of several colleges and universities. He has written and edited books on aerospace, religious, and political history and has received numerous awards for his work. Dr. Launius received a Ph.D. in history from Louisiana State University.

John M. Logsdon is Director of the Space Policy Institute and Professor of International Affairs at The George Washington University's Elliott School of International Affairs. Previously, he was also Director of the School's Center for International Science and Technology Policy. Dr. Logsdon is the author of *The Decision to Go to the Moon: The Apollo Project and the National Interest* (MIT Press, 1970) and is general editor of the eight-volume series *Exploring the Unknown: Selected Documents in the History of the U.S. Civil Space Program* (NASA History Office, 1995). He has written numerous articles and reports on space policy and history and is on the editorial board of the journal *Astropolitics*. He holds a Bachelor of Science degree in physics from Xavier University and a Ph.D. in political science from New York University.

Michael E. O'Hanlon is a Senior Fellow in Foreign Policy Studies at the Brookings Institution, where he specializes in U.S. defense strategy, the use of military force, homeland security, and American foreign policy. He is a visiting lecturer at Princeton University and a member of the International Institute for Strategic Studies and the Council on Foreign Relations. Dr. O'Hanlon's latest book is *Defense Strategy for the Post-Saddam Era* (Brookings, 2005). He also recently completed *The Future of Arms Control* (Brookings, 2005), co-authored with Michael Levi, as well as *Neither Star Wars nor Sanctuary: Constraining the Military Uses of Space* (Brookings, 2004). He received Bachelor's and Master's degrees in the physical sciences and a Ph.D. in public and international affairs, all from Princeton University.

Scott Pace is the Associate Administrator for Program Analysis and Evaluation at NASA. Previously, he served as the Deputy Chief of Staff to the NASA Administrator and the Chief Technologist for Space Communications in the Office of Space Operations. Dr. Pace served in the White House Office of Science and Technology Policy as the Assistant Director for Space and Aeronautics and in the Department of Commerce as the Deputy Director and Acting Director of Space Commerce, where he coordinated international space policy issues. Dr. Pace received his Master of Science degree in aeronautics and astronautics from the Massachusetts Institute of Technology and his Ph.D. in policy analysis from the RAND Graduate School.

Robert L. Pfaltzgraff, Jr., is the Shelby Cullom Davis Professor of International Security Studies in The Fletcher School at Tufts University. He is also founder and President of the Institute for Foreign Policy Analysis, an independent, nonpartisan research organization. He has advised key U.S. Government officials on military strategy, defense modernization, the future of the Atlantic Alliance, proliferation and counterproliferation issues, and arms control policy. He has lectured widely at government, industry, and academic forums in the United States and overseas. He currently serves on the International Security Advisory Board at the U.S. Department of State and is a member of the board's WMD Terrorism Task Force.

Jerry Jon Sellers is an international research and development liaison officer in London, where he writes and consults on space mission analysis and design. He has over 13 years' experience at various astronautics assignments including the NASA Johnson Space Center, where he worked in Space Shuttle Mission Control, and the U.S. Air Force Academy, where he served on the faculty of the Department of Astronautics. He was a distinguished graduate from the U.S. Air Force Academy and has earned Master of Science degrees in physical science from the University of Houston and in aeronautics and astronautics from Stanford University, and a Ph.D. in satellite engineering from the University of Surrey.

John B. Sheldon is Professor of Comparative Military Studies at the School of Advanced Air and Space Studies, Air University. A former diplomat, Dr. Sheldon is the founding co-editor of the journal *Astropolitics* and has lectured and taught military space issues at the Royal United Services Institute for Defence Studies and the Higher Command and Staff Course at the Joint Services Command and Staff College. Dr. Sheldon has published in the *RUSI Journal, Airpower Journal,* and *Space News.*

Colonel M.V. Smith, USAF, is Director of the Air Force Space and Cyber Center at Air University. He served in the Pentagon's National Security Space Office as the Chief of the Future Concepts shop, which explores, develops, advocates, and links future concepts, capabilities, and promising technologies to advance the art of space faring across the security sector. Colonel Smith was the director of the Space-based Solar Power Study, and he served as a Visiting Military Fellow at National Defense University. He has served in various space and missile positions and as an instructor at the USAF Weapons School.

Harold R. Winton is Professor of Military History and Theory in the School of Advanced Air and Space Studies (SAASS) at Air University. Prior to assuming that post as one of the four founding faculty members of SAASS in 1990, he was a Professor of Military Art and Science and deputy director at the School of Advanced Military Studies, where he was a founding faculty member. Dr. Winton retired from Active Duty in the U.S. Army in 1989. He is a graduate of the United States Military Academy and received a Master of Arts and a Ph.D. in history from Stanford University. He is the author of *Corps Commanders of the Bulge: Six American Generals and Victory in the Ardennes* (University Press of Kansas, 2007) and *To Change an Army: General Sir John Burnett-Stuart and British Military Reform, 1927–1938* (University Press of Kansas, 1988), and is co-editor of *The Challenge of Change: Military Institutions and New Realities, 1918–1941* (University of Nebraska Press, 2000).

Simon P. Worden is Director of the NASA Ames Research Center. Prior to becoming Director, Dr. Worden was a Research Professor of Astronomy, Optical Sciences, and Planetary Sciences at the University of Arizona, where his primary research direction was the development of large space optics for national security and scientific purposes and near-Earth asteroids. Dr. Worden retired from the U.S. Air Force as a brigadier general in 2004 after 29 years of Active service. During his career, he commanded the 50th Space Wing, which is responsible for more than 60 Department of Defense satellites. He then served as Deputy Director for Requirements at Headquarters Air Force Space Command, as well as the Deputy Director for Command and Control with the Office of the Deputy Chief of Staff for Air and Space Operations at Air Force Headquarters. Dr. Worden received a Bachelor of Science degree from the University of Michigan and a Ph.D. in astronomy from the University of Arizona. He has authored or co-authored more than 150 scientific technical papers in astrophysics, space sciences, and strategic studies.

www.ingramcontent.com/pod-product-compliance
Lightning Source LLC
Chambersburg PA
CBHW070545270326
41926CB00013B/2211